W9-AYA-174

THE NATIONAL ASSOCIATION FOR LAW PLACEMENT

THE OFFICIAL GUIDE TO LEGAL SPECIALTIES

AN INSIDER'S GUIDE TO EVERY MAJOR PRACTICE AREA

Requests for permission to make copies of any part of the work should be mailed to: The BarBri Group, Attn: Permissions Department, 111 West Jackon Boulevard, 7th Floor, Chicago, IL 60604. Phone: 1-800-782-1272, Fax: 1-312-360-1842

Printed in the United States of America.

Cover Design: Pivot Design, Inc. (Chicago, IL)
Interior Design: Desktop Miracles (Stowe, VT)

For a complete listing of products and services visit www.gilbertlaw.com, or contact us at: The BarBri Group, 111 West Jackson Boulevard, 7ᵀᴴ Floor, Chicago, IL 60604. Phone: 1-800-782-1272, Fax: 1-312-360-1842.

Table of Contents

Acknowledgments

This book was created with the help of many wonderful legal professionals who graciously agreed be interviewed for *The Official Guide to Legal Specialties*. These delightful people cheerfully answered my calls, voice mails, and e-mails and made time in their busy schedules to share information and advice. When their schedules were too hectic to talk to me at the office, they set aside precious personal weekend and evening time to help with the book project. In addition, they were kind enough to refer me to attorney friends and colleagues who they believed would be able to make significant contributions to the book. Their willingness to share their network of contacts helped me land even more great interviews.

The attorneys featured in this book received no remuneration other than the knowledge that the expertise they shared with us would be immeasurably helpful to the career planning efforts of countless law students, pre-law students, and lawyers. For their generosity, their good nature and wit, and their concern for students entering the profession, I am profoundly grateful.

It was a joy to work on this project in conjunction with the staff of the National Association for Law Placement (NALP). NALP publishes a booklet called *Guide to Law Specialties*, which is based on an earlier booklet of the same name from the Law Placement Association of Cleveland. Lisa Shanholtzer Quirk, NALP's Director of Program Services, was instrumental in developing *The Official Guide*, and has worked on this enormous enterprise since its inception. She provided outstanding editorial support as well as encouragement. The project would not have been possible without Lisa's hard work, care, and concern. In addition, Paula Patton, Executive Director, deserves special thanks for her willingness to give me the opportunity to develop the voice and format for the *Official Guide* and for trusting me to make that vision a reality.

A number of people deserve special thanks for their continued assistance in writing *The Official Guide to Legal Specialties*. I am extraordinarily grateful for their willingness to share their knowledge of the legal marketplace, their experience in law practice, their extensive legal network and their knowledge of the substantive law involved in various practice areas. I am even more grateful for their confidence in the project and the encouragement they provided along the way:

> Susan Gainen, Director of Career Services, University of Minnesota Law School
>
> Jeanne Kraft, Assistant Dean of Career Services, Chicago-Kent College of Law, Illinois Institute of Technology
>
> Sue Schechter, Assistant Dean of Law Career & Alumni Services, Golden Gate University School of Law
>
> Ann Rainhart, Legal Personnel and Recruitment Manager, Chapman and Cutler
>
> Julie Fenton, Senior Staff Attorney, U.S. Court of Appeals, Seventh Circuit
>
> Stuart Chanen, Assistant U.S. Attorney, Northern District of Illinois
>
> John Young, Director of Print and On-line Communications, Chicago-Kent College of Law, Illinois Institute of Technology
>
> Marty Malin, Professor, Chicago-Kent College of Law, Illinois Institute of Technology
>
> Stuart Deutsch, Dean, Rutgers University School of Law

I also received assistance from many generous career services and legal recruiting professionals who are members of NALP. They are remarkably talented and knowledgeable, and their belief that this book would be an important resource for students inspired them to share their knowledge and their contacts. They include:

> Sarah Klaver Staup, Professional Personnel Specialist, Dykema Gossett, PLLC
>
> Mark Weber, Assistant Dean for Career Services, University of Illinois College of Law
>
> Joyce Elliott, former Director of Career Services, University of Illinois College of Law
>
> Judith Saunders, former NALP President and Principal of JS Consulting, Chicago
>
> Gail Peshel, Assistant Dean of Career Services, Valparaiso University School of Law

Bonnie Hurry, Legal Staff and Recruiting Administrator, Davis Polk
& Wardwell

Holly Hand, Director of Attorney Recruiting and Development,
Miller & Chevalier, Chartered

Most importantly, I want to thank my husband, Hugh. As a practicing lawyer who enjoys his work, he truly believes in the mission of *The Official Guide*; his unwavering enthusiasm for the project and confidence in me proved to be great motivators. He read and reread each chapter of the book, providing detailed suggestions and invaluable insights. He provided less sophisticated assistance as well; he cheerfully played endless games of tennis ball with our two noisy sheepdogs, with the objective of exhausting them so that I could conduct the next day's phone interviews in relative silence. Best of all, he made me laugh—often, and usually very hard!—through the inevitable joys and challenges of developing all 30 chapters.

Introduction

Finding the Right Legal Specialty for You

You may be one of those lucky people who has known you wanted to go to law school ever since you and little your brother watched Perry Mason reruns on late night cable. (And to think your parents worried you were wasting your life watching TV!) You may even be one of those fortunate folks who knows exactly what kind of law you want to practice. Inspired by your undergraduate courses in computer engineering and the daily headlines concerning Microsoft, you've decided you want to pursue intellectual property law. Or your mom, a doctor, has inspired you to pursue a career representing physicians accused of malpractice as an insurance defense litigator.

Maybe you're already practicing law and you have an inkling that there's another area of law practice that would suit you better. Say, like me, you were a star in your undergraduate speech classes and you were certain that working as a trial lawyer would be the right career for you. But as you head to the litigation firm every morning, you're possessed by a sinking feeling that another day of document production and depositions awaits you. You believe that there's got to be a legal career that would better fit you—and undoubtedly you're right! There's a huge range of legal careers in varied work environments. This book will help you discover, for example, that a career in estate planning can provide a work environment that focuses on collaboration rather than confrontation, the perfect area to use counseling and interpersonal skills. And estate planning may be an area you never would have considered exploring while in law school.

Whether you're thinking about law school and exploring many different practice areas or convinced that a particular practice area is for you, or you're already practicing law and hoping to find a better fit, this book is for you! We went straight to the experts. We talked to over 120 practitioners in 30 different practice areas. Some work in law firms, others in government agencies, still others in corporations and public interest organizations. They all have one thing in common—they enjoy their work. They look forward to getting up in the morning. As you read this book, you'll hear from attorneys who are passionate about practicing law. And you'll find out what makes their work not just exciting, but personally rewarding.

Why and How We Developed This Book

There are many books that talk about *how* to look for a legal job. (One of the best is *Guerrilla Tactics for Getting the Legal Job of Your Dreams* by Kimm Walton, J.D., also published by Harcourt). But law students and law school career services professionals, and law graduates have, until now, been able to find little information about the wide array of *legal career options*. That's why the National Association for Law Placement (NALP), a non-profit educational organization that serves law schools, legal employers, law students and graduates, developed *The Official Guide to Legal Specialties*, which focuses on 30 areas of law practice.

In my years as an assistant dean of career services at a Chicago law school, I worked with hundreds of law students and alumni. Finding a job is one thing, but finding a truly *satisfying* job, in which there is a good fit between the student or graduate and the employer, is another.

Whether they are looking for a summer job during law school, an attorney position post graduation, or to make a job change once they are practicing, students and graduates need information that will help them find the right *fit*, and this book is designed to provide that information.

Law school career services professionals at law schools across the country encouraged NALP to build upon an earlier booklet on legal specialties. With the help of NALP members, we distributed surveys to practitioners in a wide range of practice areas planning to assemble the information in an easy to read manual. As the project grew in scope, and as we made efforts to increase our diverse representation of practice areas, geographic locations, and academic background, race, gender and sexual orientation of the attorneys, we conducted scores of telephone and face-to-face interviews. We spent more than two years gathering the information that we knew students and alumni needed most—and the result is *The Official Guide to Legal Specialties.* This book wouldn't exist without the very generous attorneys who shared their valuable time, their passion for practice, their advice to students and their war stories with us. Their expertise is the heart of this book.

How Each Practice Specialty Chapter is Organized

Each of the 30 chapters in this book explores a major legal specialty. Bear in mind that while we've featured major practice specialties, legal specialty areas are not static—they're constantly changing. Specialty areas and their growth, viability, and development are profoundly affected by changes in the law as well as economic and societal changes. Telecommunications law and antitrust law, for example, are areas of law that are in flux as courts make decisions and as technology changes. A daily look at *The Wall Street Journal* will help you keep up to date on developments in these and other areas of law.

Each chapter begins with a brief overview of the area of law, such as "What is Real Estate Law?" These summaries aren't intended to be a law school course in real estate law or family law or municipal finance law, much less a hornbook or a legal treatise; rather, they are intended to give you a snapshot of the issues attorneys face in varied practice areas and a context in which to understand the information and advice the attorneys share.

To help students and graduates learn about the skills, law school classes, and law school experiences that would best prepare them for various practice areas, we asked every attorney we interviewed the same series of questions about their particular practice sector as well as questions about their advice for law students or attorneys hoping to enter their practice specialty. We asked:

- Where do attorneys in your practice specialty work?
- Who are your clients and what types of cases or issues do you work on?
- What daily activities are involved in your practice?

- What do you find rewarding about your field of practice?
- How do people generally enter the field in which you practice?
- What path did you take to practice in this specialty area?
- What skills are most important to this practice specialty?
- What classes and law school experiences (such as internships, club memberships, summer work experience, etc.) do you recommend to students?

How to Make the Most of this Book

Begin by reading through the chapters that interest you at first glance. Maybe you've always thought of being a public interest lawyer—start with the public interest chapter. But because there are public interest attorneys in a variety of legal specialties, take a look at other chapters in which we've included public interest lawyers, such as the environmental law chapter or the immigration law chapter. The parenthetical cross references that we've included in many chapters will lead you to related areas of law. For example, in the insurance law chapter we refer you to chapters covering tort law and environmental law. In some chapters, attorney comments or text will encourage you to explore other chapters. In the introduction to the intellectual property law chapter, we explain that intellectual property crosses over into numerous practice areas, such as international law and corporate law.

Follow up by skimming through chapters about specialities that you aren't sure you have an interest in. Pay particular interest to the skills required by each practice area. This is the key to finding a practice area that's a good fit for you. When I was in law school, it never crossed my mind to explore non-litigation careers. I never learned about specialty areas that would make the most of my counseling and relationship-building skills. I never even remotely considered a career in estate planning, but, after interviewing the attorneys in the estate planning chapter I learned it would be a very good match for my skills and interests. Further reading reveals that family lawyers and solo practitioners are also attorneys who lean heavily on their counseling skills.

Make use of your law school's career services office. Law school career services offices are staffed by professionals who are experienced at working with both law students and alumni. Make an appointment to discuss your skills and your interests. Making an appointment in advance of your visit will allow the career services professionals to pull together materials that will be especially helpful to you. Ask the staff member you meet with where you can find additional material on the areas of law in which you're interested.

Using this book as a starting point, conduct your own informational interviews with people in the areas of law in which you're interested! You can even use the questions we used when we interviewed attorneys. Add your own questions, too. What do you want to know about? You could ask, "How does the state's attorney in Dade County, Florida hire entry level attorneys?" or "What does the job market look like for real estate attorneys in San Francisco?" Talk to five or six attorneys in each of the practice areas in which you're interested. Where do you find these attorneys, you ask? Most law schools have a formal (computerized or notebook bound) or informal (by personal referral through the career services or alumni office) network through which you can meet graduates of your school who have volunteered to talk with students and alumni about their work. You may also want to explore your undergraduate school's alumni advisor network—there are undoubtedly attorneys in the network who would love to hear from someone who attended the same undergraduate school. This is one of the very best (and most underutilized) resources for gathering information about practice specialties.

Conducting your own informational interviews can help you prepare to market yourself in future job interviews. When you finally get that long-awaited interview, you'll be able to say, "After talking to a number of attorneys that practice bankruptcy law, I understand that bankruptcy attorneys need to have exceptional negotiation skills. I've worked hard during law school to sharpen my negotiation skills by . . . . ." Informational interviewing can also help you prepare to ask sophisticated questions in job interviews—questions that set you apart from other candidates. "Does your civil litigation department handle appeals, or are they handled by a separate department?" "Do summer associates interested in banking practice work with the banking department of the firm during the summer, or do they rotate through several corporate practice departments?" "From my informational interviews, I understand that e-commerce is a growing area of practice in general practice firms. In your firm, are these issues handled by intellectual property attorneys or corporate attorneys?" Questions that show your knowledge about practice specialties demonstrate that you're very seriously interested in a practice area, and your willingness to do informational interviews shows that you won't be afraid to develop relationships with the firm's or organization's clients, and demonstrate that—someday in the future—you'll be the type of lawyer who focuses on developing new clients.

Use the "recommended law school experiences" section of the book to help you maximize your job search credentials. No matter how good the economy, there's a great deal of competition for the best jobs, not just at large law firms, but in public interest organizations and government agencies as well. Your law school's career services office can help you assess the level of competition and employer expectations for a wide range of jobs in various practice areas and for different geographic locations. Most employers believe that grades are important, but grades are by no means the only factor by which employers evaluate prospective attorneys. In the "law school experiences" section at the end of each chapter, you'll find numerous practical suggestions for ways to distinguish yourself while in law school. Attorneys from different practice areas offer myriad suggestions based on their own experiences. These range from participating in Law Review or Moot Court to working in a community law clinic to participating in bar association activities to writing and publishing an article.

Look to your own law school experiences for hints as to which chapters of *The Official Guide* to read and re-read and which practice areas to explore. Starting with your first semester of law school, your classes will introduce you to areas of substantive law with related careers you may have never before considered exploring. Your work experience while in law school, whether as a volunteer, intern, clerk, summer associate, or in a legal clinic, will help you find out what law practice is like on a day to day basis. It will also allow you to work closely with practicing attorneys who can tell you what they enjoy about law practice. Law school activities, including clubs and student memberships in bar associations, will help you meet other students interested in particular areas of law as well as practitioners who speak at club events.

Talk to your professors. Professors can also be a wonderful resource for information about practice specialties. When I worked as a career services dean, we called certain professors "junior career services directors" because they were so wonderful about answering student questions about careers in labor law or environmental law or appellate practice. Professors are also a wonderful source of contacts for informational interviews and can often put you in touch with recent graduates who would be willing to share their own career planning experiences.

Remember that you don't have to be certain about your practice direction when you enter law school. Keep an open mind. Many of the practitioners we interviewed confided that it was serendipity, more than any other factor, that lead them to the legal specialty that gives them so much satisfaction.

Important Things We Learned from our Attorney Interviews

Practice specialty areas tend to overlap. As we mentioned earlier, it's impossible to draw clean lines across different practice areas. Some areas of law are closely related, such as securities law, municipal finance, and banking law. Be sure to read any of the chapters that are related to the practice areas in which you're interested.

If you have your heart set on working in the public interest, non-profit, or government sector, you'll find opportunities in nearly every practice specialty area. Over 30 public interest and government attorneys are profiled throughout the chapters of this book. So if you're interested in public interest or government work, read through most of the chapters to learn about the many interesting ways you can use your legal skills in public service.

Though every practice specialty requires its own set of skills, practitioners in virtually every specialty value essential lawyering skills: excellent legal analysis, well-developed problem solving skills, and clear and persuasive writing. The lawyers we talked to told us that above all things, their organizations are looking for lawyers who are smart, who use good judgment, who can think on their feet, and who are effective at developing working relationships.

Most practitioners agree that a judicial externship or judicial clerkship is one of the best credentials you can offer employers and likely to be one of the most meaningful and enjoyable parts of your law school or post-graduation experience. Without exception, the attorneys we talked to who had worked as judicial law clerks remembered the experience with fondness and said that their experience working closely with a judge had been extraordinarily helpful in preparing them for law practice.

Students with strong academic credentials can apply for judicial clerkships in their second year of law school. Students who are selected for a judicial clerkship generally work for a judge for one to two years after graduation from law school. Many law schools have a faculty committee that advises students regarding clerkship opportunities and assists students in preparing the applications they must submit to judges. Many law schools have judicial externship programs, through which qualified students have the opportunity to earn credit working for a judge and his or her clerks while in law school. Successful judicial externships can help you in your quest to land a judicial clerkship following graduation. Your law school's career services office can tell you more about judicial clerkships and externships and the application process.

The lawyers we interviewed spoke openly about their passion for their practice. What a joy it is to talk to professionals that find great satisfaction in their work! They told us, at length, about how much they like the daily rhythms of their work, how much they enjoy the intellectual challenge of their work, and how much pride they take in their relationships with their clients. As you read each chapter, take note of the many factors that result in the attorneys' genuine satisfaction as practitioners. The lawyers we interviewed made it clear that when they interview prospective attorneys, they look for people who share their passion for their practice specialty and their particular type of work. They told us that even when interviewing first and second year students for summer or part-time positions, they seek students who have carefully thought about their career plans and who demonstrate a sincere interest in their organization and in their practice specialty.

Many of the lawyers in today's legal marketplace are on the move. Twenty years ago, lawyers who worked in firms tended to begin at the firms after graduation and stay to become partners and eventually retire from the firm. This has changed dramatically. Many of the lawyers we interviewed have worked in a number of different firms or environments. Law firms, government agencies and corporations often hire "laterals"—attorneys with a significant amount of practice experience. In fact, a number of the attorneys we interviewed for this book changed positions between the time we interviewed them and the time the book went to publication. **You should find this reassuring. Though your first legal job may not be a perfect match, like many lawyers, you may find you make better matches as you advance in your career!**

Admiralty
and Maritime Law

What are Admiralty and Maritime Law?

Admiralty law or maritime law (the terms are used interchangeably) refers to the law that covers navigation and shipping. U.S. admiralty law dates back to colonial times. The colonies, dependent on navigation and shipping for survival, established admiralty courts similar to those that existed in Britain. Article III, Section 2 of the U.S. Constitution and the Judiciary Act of 1789 gave the federal district courts jurisdiction over admiralty issues.

Admiralty law covers an extraordinarily wide range of issues including commercial use of bodies of water; transport and shipping via oceans, rivers, and lakes; accidents, including the injury of seamen, cargo, and vessels; issues concerning docks, piers, and wharves; and recreational boating. Historically, many admiralty law cases involved goods damaged in shipping. Admiralty law has changed with changes in society. Now, goods are packed in containers for safekeeping during shipping. As the economy has become global, the American merchant fleet has been reduced. Developments in technology have resulted in increasingly sophisticated navigation systems that result in fewer accidents.

A ship flying the American flag is subject to the admiralty laws of the United States. Debate has recently erupted concerning cruise ships that serve American customers but are registered in other countries. These ships are not subject to American admiralty law even when in American ports and waters. There is increased concern that such ships may be trying to evade the jurisdiction of American courts, particularly with regard to environmental issues.

Admiralty law is a highly specialized area of law that is separate from, though similar to, civil law. The jurisdiction of the federal courts in admiralty cases was expanded by the Jones Act of 1936, which allows merchant seamen injured on American vessels to bring claims under federal jurisdiction. Many of the issues relevant to admiralty today are the same issues arising in civil litigation—environmental litigation, personal injury litigation, insurance coverage, and subrogation issues.

Life as an Admiralty Lawyer

Where do admiralty lawyers work?

There are a number of places one can practice admiralty law. Many admiralty lawyers work in private law firms; some mid-size and large firms have departments that specialize in admiralty law, and there are also some smaller, "boutique" firms that specialize in admiralty law. Other admiralty lawyers work as in-house lawyers for corporations such as oil companies, shipping and transport companies, cruise lines, and boat or ship manufacturing companies. Admiralty lawyers may also work for the government, whether for the United States Navy Office of the General Counsel, the Coast Guard, the Department of Justice, or other government agencies.

Who are their clients and what types of cases do they work on?

David (Dave) Martinez Gonden is an admiralty lawyer at Derby, Cook, Quinby & Tweedt LLP in San Francisco, California. Dave describes his practice as a civil litigation practice with a maritime orientation. About a third of his cases involve merchant seamen injured on American-flagged vessels. Dave generally represents the vessel owners, who are often defendants in the lawsuits brought by the seamen. The vessels involved might be container carriers, tugboats, barges, or yachts. The issues litigated include whether or not the vessel owner was negligent in some way that led to the injury and whether or not the vessel was seaworthy. Injured seamen are entitled to what is called "maintenance and cure." This means that they are entitled to a daily stipend (maintenance) and medical expenses (cure) while recuperating from an injury. Dave reports that the balance of his cases involve cargo damage and insurance issues, plus marine environmental and other types of litigation.

"The maritime industry is the biggest industry you've never heard of," claims Arthur (Art) Mead, in-house attorney for Crowley Maritime Corporation in Oakland, California. Crowley is a private company on the Forbes Private 500 list. Art's transactional practice relates to the "amazing engineering feats" undertaken by Crowley—from transporting oil to moving oil rigs to moving oil refineries via vessels. Crowley has container ships that carry cargo on the East Coast, including ships that are used to ship Ford automobiles to South America. On the West Coast, Crowley has barges and tugs. The company engages in salvage (rescue) and emergency response efforts, as well. When the Exxon Valdez was involved in an accident in Alaska, six Crowley tugs pulled the Valdez off of the Alaskan reef. "The work of the company requires careful insurance planning, risk planning, and development of contracts," says Art.

Lt. Rachel Canty and Lt. Mark Skolnicki of the United States Coast Guard, Washington, D.C., explain that their client is the Coast Guard itself. Rachel interprets current laws, regulations, and government policies as they relate to the Coast Guard, particularly in the areas involving migrant interdiction (situations in which noncitizens are illegally smuggled into the U.S. via ships) and fisheries law (this includes the harvesting of fish and seafood). Mark, too, interprets laws and regulations, particularly with regard to the documentation of vessels. He advises the National Vessel Documentation Center, other Coast Guard attorneys, and members of the public. "I receive three to five calls a week from citizens wanting to know about various Coast Guard regulations," he explains. After TWA Flight 800 crashed off the coast of New York in 1996, he provided the Coast Guard with advice regarding the site. Currently, he says, he is "*the* attorney reviewing and negotiating an annex [addition] to an environmental protocol [provision] of the Antarctic Treaty."

What daily activities are involved in admiralty law practice?

Art Mead explains that his practice at Crowley Maritime Corporation is transactional. He drafts, reviews, and negotiates agreements for the transport of oil and the movement of cargo. He also spends time counseling Crowley business executives concerning maritime law and commercial law issues. Most of his time is spent in-house, but he occasionally travels to London, since the insurance industry creates a substantial connection between the London insurance market and U.S. maritime interests and attorneys.

Dave Gonden says that his daily work in maritime-related litigation is similar to the work of any litigation attorney. He answers complaints, drafts pleadings, drafts and responds to written discovery, takes depositions, interviews witnesses, argues motions, and prepares for trial.

Rachel Canty and Mark Skolnicki report that they spend time researching and writing memos, letters, and reports and counseling their fellow Coast Guard members about immediate crises and long-term concerns. Rachel recalls one crisis situation in which "the Coast Guard interdicted a People's Republic of China flag vessel smuggling illegal immigrants into the U.S. Practical and political considerations made the case especially difficult. The discussions between U.S. agencies became pretty heated. One night things came to a head—so I spent at least three hours on the phone (on my couch, with my dog next to me, and my husband bringing me food) discussing the limits of Coast Guard authority with the legal adviser to the National Security Council, the General Counsel of the Department of Transportation [the Coast Guard is part of the Department of Transportation], the Chief Counsel of the Coast Guard, and two other Coast Guard lawyers. It was a pretty impressive experience, especially since I had been at that assignment for less than six months at the time."

What do admiralty lawyers find rewarding about their practice?

The lawyers we talked to said that one of the rewards of practicing maritime law is working with a special group of people. "It's the admiralty practice itself that makes the work so rewarding," says Dave Gonden. "The lawyers in the maritime bar are great lawyers and mentors. Within the bar, there's a remarkable level of trust, respect, and professionalism." Dave also finds each merchant seaman he meets through his practice to have some interesting story to tell. "All of the seamen are characters. Some of them have been working at sea for 30 years. Others have worked around the world. I *never* have an uninteresting case!"

The lawyers we interviewed also mentioned the rewards of working in a field in which they have a keen interest. Before law school Art Mead worked in the shipping industry. "I worked as a commercial ship's officer for a shipping company," he says. "I enjoy keeping up with the developments in the maritime field. I read articles and journals, attend meetings of the Maritime Law Association of the United States, and go to continuing education seminars—all on the subject of maritime law. I have a real interest in the subject matter." Dave Gonden talks enthusiastically about the practice. "Admiralty law has it all," he says. "This area of law has fascinating historical roots, great intellectual aspects, a federal practice, and a group of dedicated practitioners."

Rachel Canty and Mark Skolnicki enjoy the chance to have an impact on important national issues. Rachel explains, "The most rewarding aspect is that real action is taken on your advice, and sometimes (though not often) I change the minds of the government decision-makers. To some extent I make sure the Coast Guard can continue successfully its duty of law enforcement on the water." Mark adds, "I feel proud to be a part of this great organization. I feel like I am contributing to the mission of the Coast Guard. Semper Paratus (always ready—our motto)!"

The Training and Skills Important to Admiralty Law

How do people enter the field of admiralty law?

Some attorneys, like Art Mead, decide to practice admiralty law because of specialized work experience in the maritime industry. Art grew up in New York and attended college at the State University of New York Maritime College. The University is not a military school, but rather offers specialized education for those who want to work in the marine transportation industry. Art worked for four years in the operations department of a shipping company before attending law school. "I really wanted to get into this area of law," he says. "After law school I pounded the pavement in San Francisco looking for a maritime law job. My job at Crowley Maritime was advertised, but they were looking for someone with a couple of years of law practice experience. I applied; my practical experience in the industry made up for my lack of legal experience."

Mark Skolnicki earned an undergraduate degree in finance before serving as an engineering officer for the U.S. Navy. While an officer he became interested in environmental law. When deciding what career path to pursue, he conducted a LEXIS-NEXIS search to target prospective employers. He chose the search terms: Maritime & Environmental & International. "The Coast Guard was listed as a 'law firm' on my LEXIS cite list," he recalls. He called the toll free number they listed, went through the application process, and found the opportunity to pursue all three interests. He adds that students interested in working as lawyers for the Coast Guard can talk to their local Coast Guard recruiter for further information.

Though she didn't have maritime work experience, Rachel Canty earned an LL.M. in Ocean and Coastal Law. "I was always a beach bum and loved the water," she says. "I've always been interested in water-related topics in a hope that I would get to spend more time in, on, or near the water (which is how I ended up in landlocked Washington, D.C.)," Rachel muses. Rachel was also interested in international issues. "I honestly never thought of joining the military—but when I learned what type of issues the Coast Guard was involved in, it was what I was looking for." Rachel adds that her LL.M. degree "has definitely helped—though it's definitely not essential."

Other attorneys enter the practice because of an employer's needs or a mentor's influence. "My seagoing experience was limited to sailing in San Francisco Bay," says Dave Gonden. While in law school, Dave worked for a law firm as a summer associate. Though he didn't do maritime work that summer, he was supervised by an partner who practiced in the maritime group. He developed a good rapport with that partner, and when Dave joined that firm as an associate, the partner assigned him to the maritime group. Dave greatly enjoyed the practice, and later joined his current firm.

What skills are most important to admiralty lawyers?

❖ Whether drafting briefs, contracts, or opinion letters, admiralty and maritime lawyers need to have **strong writing skills**. Says Dave Gonden, "You've got to be able to write well, to write persuasively, to analyze issues effectively." **Good communication skills** are critical, as well, he says. "You have to be able to tell your client what you think. You have to give the good news with the bad."

❖ **A keen interest in the area of admiralty and maritime law** is important. Art Mead says that when he's hiring, he looks to see a commitment to the industry and a commitment to the practice area. "I consider whether candidates show a tenacity about serving clients in this industry and whether they are up to date on this area of the law." Most of all, he adds, "I like to see people who roll up their sleeves and work hard."

❖ Admiralty lawyers often get to challenge their **investigation skills.** Dave Gonden explains that when seamen or cargo are damaged in an accident, you have to be able to search out the facts. "You have to know the right questions to ask in a deposition. You have to be able to evaluate the credibility of witnesses." Mark Skolnicki adds that some of the best investigation is done through listening carefully to and asking the right questions of the client. "The challenge," he says, "is helping the client to focus the issue."

❖ **Good relationship-building skills** are helpful to these lawyers who work so closely with their clients. Dave Gonden explains that the small, tightly knit admiralty bar has a reputation for handling cases efficiently and with great professionalism. He advises students to build relationships that will last for the duration of their career.

❖ The **flexibility to work with a wide range of issues** is helpful to admiralty law attorneys, as they handle a broad range of legal issues. "Flexibility is the key," says Rachel Canty. "One day is chaos and you have the legal adviser to the National Security Council on the phone exploring what the Coast Guard thinks the limit of its authority is and the next you're writing an appeal decision for a mariner whose license was suspended for having a positive drug test." She adds, "You just have to learn to roll with the punches."

What classes and law school experiences do admiralty lawyers recommend?

❖ Take **a general survey course in admiralty and maritime law**. Law schools with programs specializing in admiralty and maritime law may offer more advanced courses and seminars in the area. Dave Gonden notes that he never took a maritime law course in law school, but a survey course would have been helpful.

❖ **A wide range of law school classes** is important. Civil procedure, corporations, federal courts, remedies, environmental law, negotiations, international law, and secured transactions can be helpful because of the expansive nature of the practice. If you are considering a litigation position, trial advocacy and moot court are helpful. "Take courses in a variety of areas—you never know what you will need," advises Rachel Canty.

❖ **Practical work experience in the field** can help you decide whether this is the right area of practice for you. Consider working as a summer associate for a firm that has an admiralty or maritime practice group or working as an intern for a governmental agency.

❖ **Work as a judicial law clerk.** A judicial externship during law school or a judicial clerkship after law school adds a great deal to your resume. Says Dave Gonden, "An externship or clerkship helps you hone your research skills and sharpen your writing skills. You have the chance to listen to attorneys argue in front of the judge, and the opportunity to observe the judge's interpretation of the arguments. This is especially helpful if you plan to litigate."

❖ **Write a law review or law journal article** on a case or issue related to admiralty law. Art Mead says that publishing a law review article helped give him credibility in his job search. A published article distinguishes your resume from those of your peers and shows an employer that you can follow through on large scale project. It also makes an excellent writing sample.

ADMIRALTY AND MARITIME ATTORNEYS
INTERVIEWED FOR THIS SECTION

Rachel Canty
> U.S. Coast Guard
> Washington, D.C.
> UNDERGRADUATE: Emory University
> LAW SCHOOL: University of Florida Levin College of Law

David Martinez Gonden
> Derby, Cook, Quinby & Tweedt LLP
> San Francisco, California
> UNDERGRADUATE: University of California at Berkeley
> LAW SCHOOL: Golden Gate University School of Law

Arthur Mead
> Crowley Maritime Corporation
> Oakland, California
> UNDERGRADUATE: State University of New York Maritime College
> LAW SCHOOL: Golden Gate University School of Law

Mark Skolnicki
> U.S. Coast Guard
> Washington, D.C.
> UNDERGRADUATE: University of Notre Dame
> LAW SCHOOL: Duquesne University School of Law

Antitrust Law

What is Antitrust Law?

With their potential for multimillion dollar damage awards as well as their potential for restructuring entire industries (such as the telecommunications or petro-chemical industries), antitrust cases are complex high-stakes cases that often make front page news. Antitrust law was responsible for the breakup of the Standard Oil Company into numerous competitors as well as the split of AT&T from the Bell Operating Companies (*e.g.*, Ameritech and Pacific Bell). Similarly, antitrust law was behind the U.S. government's actions against IBM in the 1970s and against Microsoft in the 1990s. Each of these complex cases had the potential, and often the result, of causing fundamental change in basic industries in the United States.

In many of the leading antitrust cases, the courts will state that the purpose of the antitrust laws is to protect competition, not competitors. Price reductions caused by competition in the marketplace, even if they result in economic loss to one or more competitors, are not necessarily a bad or illegal result. However, the antitrust laws prohibit price reductions that are designed to drive competitors out of business. In 1999, the Justice Department filed a suit against American Airlines, alleging that the airline engaged in predatory pricing—slashing prices and increasing the number of flights offered in order to drive out low-cost competitors from a common hub in Dallas-Ft. Worth. At a news conference following the filing of the suit, Attorney General Janet

Reno asserted that the government was acting to protect consumers. "It's the public who loses out when major airlines succeed in driving out low-cost competitors," she said. The airline responded that it was simply engaging in healthy competition and doing nothing illegal or improper.

The antitrust laws are intended to prevent the development of business monopolies and to preserve and encourage competition. Two provisions—the Sherman Antitrust Act and the Clayton Act—form the basis of our antitrust laws. The Sherman Act prevents any unreasonable anticompetitive conduct, such as interference with competitive pricing and distribution or attempts to monopolize a market. The Clayton Act prohibits price discrimination, exclusive contracts, mergers, and interlocking directorates which substantially lessen competition or tend to create a monopoly.

Anticompetitive Conduct

Actions for anticompetitive conduct can be brought by a private party or by a government agency, such as the U.S. Department of Justice (DOJ) or the Federal Trade Commission (FTC). Some types of anticompetitive conduct, such as a conspiracy to fix prices in a market, can result in criminal action against a company or an individual.

A wide range of acts can constitute anticompetitive conduct. For example, an agreement by two companies to refuse to sell certain products to a third company can be actionable. As another example, a group of small toy manufacturers accused large toy retailers of requiring that they be given priority access to items in hot demand; otherwise the small manufacturers would be excluded from prime shelf space in the stores. Similar allegations have been made in the food and beverage industry against large food product manufacturers who have allegedly tried to preserve prime shelf space for all of their products by threatening to limit the supply of their most popular products.

Another type of anticompetitive conduct that results in litigation is selling products below cost in order to obtain market share and drive a competitor out of business. For example, domestic companies will accuse off-shore manufacturers of "dumping," or selling products in the U.S. market at prices lower than in their home market in order to gain market share. Such allegations have been made with regard to consumer electronics products, such as televisions, that are manufactured outside the country, as well as commodity items such as steel.

Other types of anticompetitive conduct include "tie-ins," in which a manufacturer requires purchase of additional items in order to receive needed quantities of highly desired items. For example, a medical device maker may restrict purchases of a special catheter or a popular surgical device unless a hospital also agrees to purchase numerous commodity disposable items, such as surgical masks and latex gloves, from the same source. Manufacturers of semiconductors have been accused of withholding access to the latest and fastest version of a microprocessor chip for a computer unless the computer manufacturer also buys other related items such as printed circuit boards from the same source.

The Sherman Act also applies to efforts to monopolize a market or illegally use monopoly power in a market. The outcome of such litigation often hinges upon the definition of the market. The Department of Justice brought its antitrust action against Microsoft Corporation not on the premise that Microsoft had allegedly attained monopoly power with its Windows operating system, but rather that the company had illegally abused that monopoly power by requiring computer makers to use Microsoft's Internet Explorer browser instead of the rival Netscape Communicator browser. Software developers were allegedly denied access to the most current version of Windows unless they agreed not to write software programs for products of Microsoft's rivals.

Mergers and Acquisitions

The antitrust laws also govern mergers and acquisitions of companies through the Clayton Act, which restricts combinations that may lessen competition in a market. Some restrictions are placed on vertical integrations that involve mergers between suppliers and customers in a particular industry. For example, a vertical merger would be a combination of an oil drilling company, an oil refining company, and a retail distributor of gasoline. Horizontal mergers involve combinations at the same distribution level, such as a merger between competing brands of soft drinks or cigarettes. Anticompetitive concerns in mergers are often overcome by divesting (selling off) portions of the acquired company in either the vertical or horizontal chain of acquisition. In each case the court must evaluate the effect of the merger on competition in the relevant market.

Mergers and acquisitions are also subject to review and actions by government agencies. At the federal level, the Department of Justice and the Federal Trade Commission both review merger activity. The sheer size of the merger doesn't necessarily determine whether the government will object to the merger. For example, the merger between Daimler-Benz and Chrysler was approved despite the fact that they make up a significant segment of the automotive industry. In contrast, the government objected to a proposed merger between Office Depot and Staples as resulting in too much concentration in the office supply products industry. Other mergers, such as those between Exxon and Mobil, obtain government approval by the divestiture of certain portions of the operations of one company.

Life as an Antitrust Lawyer

Where do antitrust lawyers work?

Antitrust lawyers work in both law firms and in government. Those who work in law firms generally work in mid-size to large law firms that have departments specializing in antitrust issues. Those lawyers who work for the government may work for either state offices (such as the state's attorney general's office) or federal agencies such as the Department of Justice or the Federal Trade Commission.

Many antitrust lawyers start their careers at one of the government agencies such as the DOJ or the FTC. By learning the systems of operation of those agencies and the standards applied to review of merger activity, those lawyers are well-equipped to later advise companies that need to pass their activities through review by the agencies.

Regardless of whether they start in government service or in private practice, most antitrust lawyers have a keen interest in economics and the interplay between economic theory and law. Antitrust litigation requires detailed analysis of the relevant market, including factors such as whether substitutes are available for the product or services of the alleged monopolist. Economic experts also review data to determine the effects of actions on prices and market share and the influence of other factors, such as scarcity, advertising, and technological superiority.

Who are their clients and what types of cases do they work on?

In an antitrust practice, attorneys generally represent businesses. Explains Donald (Don) Schmidt, of Carlton Fields in Tampa, Florida, "My clients are, for the most part, businesses of all sizes, and they operate in all segments of the economy. Especially on the counseling side of the practice, they range from local mom-and-pop enterprises to multinational conglomerates. They may be headquartered anywhere in the country. What they have in common is the need for antitrust representation in Florida." Don's focus is antitrust litigation and counseling. "Common threads to most of my cases are that they are in federal court, involve litigating with and against sophisticated counsel and business personnel, and entail a great deal of time devoted to legal strategy and factual development. They usually involve lengthy discovery [*see* the Civil Litigation chapter], expert testimony, and a myriad of pre-trial issues and skirmishes. Especially in federal court, the litigation of antitrust cases lasts several years."

Ronald (Ron) Tenpas also specializes in antitrust law at Carlton Fields in Tampa. Most of Ron's clients are large institutions who are involved in antitrust litigation or who come to Ron for advice on how to avoid litigation in the first place. "Many of my clients are manufacturers, utilities, financial entities, and similar organizations that have regional or national operations. They want compliance counseling (to ensure that they're complying with federal antitrust laws) to keep them out of trouble and litigation services when they face a claim."

Toby Singer specializes in antitrust health care issues at Jones, Day, Reavis & Pogue in Washington, D.C. "My clients are hospitals, health care providers, and, more recently, HMOs and health insurance companies that provide health insurance financing services. They are located nationwide, from San Francisco to Atlanta, in both large and small cities." Toby reports that most of her work involves transactions. "My work involves complex transactions between competing hospitals which merge, and this is why they need antitrust lawyers." Toby describes a typical merger as a situation in which two non-profit hospitals [Toby notes that 80% of hospitals are non-profit] merge. "If they desire to merge and they are in the same market,

there will be an antitrust investigation by the U.S. government and sometimes by state government." Toby handles matters related to the filing of
the merger intention with the government and the government's investigation of the merger.

Geraldine (Gerry) Alexis is an antitrust attorney at Sidley & Austin in
Chicago. Her clients are corporations involved in antitrust litigation or
mergers and acquisitions. "I represent corporations that are sued in an
antitrust case or want to sue in an antitrust case. I also work with corporations that want to get clearance from the government on the antitrust
aspects of a merger or acquisition." Gerry explains that she works on a
wide range of antitrust issues. "In a merger, the issue may be whether the
merger or acquisition has an anticompetitive effect. Issues in other types of
antitrust cases include whether a party is acting in a monopolistic way or
whether two competitors have agreed to fix prices or done something to
dampen competition."

Anthony Swisher, an associate at Akin, Gump, Strauss, Hauer & Feld in
Washington, D.C., works on antitrust issues related to mergers and acquisitions. "Our firm's antitrust practice is part of the D.C. office's litigation
section. The litigation section of the firm is large, with over 70 attorneys
in D.C. alone. About seven of us specialize in antitrust issues. About 75%
of our antitrust lawyers focus on mergers, while the other 25% concentrate
on antitrust litigation, of which there are essentially two varieties," says
Anthony. "The first type of litigation is instigated by the FTC or the
antitrust division of the Department of Justice. The second type of
antitrust litigation is instigated by a private party, such as a company or a
group of consumers alleging anticompetitive practices or monopoliza-
tion." The firm's antitrust clients, Anthony says, range from "large Fortune 500 companies to small businesses, sole proprietors, and everything
in between."

Anthony explains, "My practice is unusual within the overall litigation
section in that about 95% of my work is merger-related. I work with clients
when they are involved in some type of transaction. The transaction is generally some type of merger or acquisition—the client may be selling off a
piece of the company or acquiring a company or a piece of a company, or
the client may be merging with another company. My role is to guide the
company through the complex range of government antitrust regulations
involved in putting together the deal. We get involved early in the transaction. The government agencies look carefully at the proposed transaction.

The agencies' overarching question is, 'Is this transaction likely to have an adverse effect on competition?'"

What daily activities are involved in antitrust practice?

Don Schmidt and Ron Tenpas report that their antitrust litigation and client counseling activities vary from day to day. Explains Don, "Every day I am working with complex issues of law and fact." Adds Ron, "There's no typical day in this practice area. Activity varies with the ebb and flow of litigation." Don says that most of his time is spent at his desk "developing analyses and strategy and dealing by telephone and via correspondence with clients, co-counsel and opposing counsel, witnesses, and experts, along with consulting with other firm attorneys and paralegals involved in the matter." Don notes that days spent behind his desk are only half the story. "This seemingly sedentary life is dramatically punctuated by aggressive deposition schedules, which often involve travel. In addition, although they do not do so often, when antitrust cases go to trial the rest of your life gets put on hold—the trials are intricate, lengthy, and multifarious."

Ron Tenpas is more specific. "There are periods when I am almost never at my desk because I am taking or defending depositions, meeting with the client to develop strategy, interviewing witnesses, or meeting with experts. At other periods I am involved intensely in writing and research, for example, preparing motions to dismiss or for summary judgment or appellate papers. And, of course, there are days that involve some of each. In addition, the practice often includes a fair amount of business counseling, advising clients about the antitrust risks associated with the various business practices and trying to develop ways of minimizing the risk while still helping the business people accomplish their objectives."

Ron says that he works closely with his litigation clients, and that the amount of contact he has with them depends on the stage of the litigation. "Early on in any antitrust litigation case, there is a great deal of contact with clients—often the general counsel and senior business personnel—in order to learn the history of the dispute and the nature of the business market within which the dispute arises. You learn how products are made, how they are marketed, who the competitors are, who the customers are, and how businesses compete to get those customers. This is done through witness interviews, site visits, discussions with industry experts, and review of key documents. In short, the challenge is often to become a 'mini-expert' on an industry through a short and intensive crash education."

The lawyers work to develop legal strategies for the case. Ron notes that legal research provides a foundation for legal theories. "There is likely to be a fair amount of legal research in the beginning of a case, as we see what courts have said about business practices that are similar, or identical, to the practices that are being subject to challenge. These activities then produce an overall strategy, again often as the result of extensive meetings with the counsel and business personnel of the client, in which decisions are made on what themes we will want to push in the litigation, what evidence we will need to support those themes, and how and where we will get the evidence."

Ron explains that the cases then move into the discovery phase. "At this point we are involved in frequent depositions of the key witnesses. We take depositions and defend them. We review documents and testimony in order to 'know the case.' The discovery will usually include working with numerous experts—economists, industry and trade group experts, and others— who can give testimony about how the challenged practices will affect competition." Finally, says Ron, if the case doesn't settle, "there is the intensive preparation for trial. This work is more 'office-focused,' as you spend time learning the record even more fully, drafting and replying to summary judgment motions, preparing exhibits, and trying the case."

Toby Singer reports that her activities vary depending on whether she's in the office or on the road. "I have two kinds of days—in the office days and on the road days. When in the office I am at my desk, on the phone with clients and government lawyers. I'm also reviewing documents and putting together written advice to clients. When I'm on the road, I am meeting with clients and advising them." Toby's work also depends upon which stage the merger or acquisition is in. "When two hospitals plan to merge, I meet with the clients (hospital administrators and hospital board members) in the city where the hospitals are located." These mergers require that the parties file a merger intention document with the government, which Toby helps her clients prepare. "Within 30 days of filing the merger intention, the government must let my client and me know if they are going to investigate the merger." If the government decides not to investigate, Toby says that the corporate lawyers in her firm complete the merger transaction with the client.

"If the government investigates the merger," explains Toby, "it sends a document request asking for certain information relevant to the merger that will assist the government in deciding whether an antitrust violation will result from the merger. I pull a team of lawyers together to meet with the client and obtain and produce documents relevant to the government's request. I prepare a defense of the merger by interviewing witnesses, preparing briefing papers, etc., to try to persuade the government lawyers to let the deal go through." Toby says that the investigation is an ongoing process. "I am on the phone and am corresponding with the government lawyers on a regular basis, even daily, to provide this information and to attempt to persuade them that there is no antitrust impediment to the deal." Once all the documents and evidence are submitted to the government, the government has 20 days to let Toby know whether the client can go ahead with the deal. "If the government chooses to challenge the deal, a lawsuit is filed in federal court and the case becomes a litigation matter." At this stage Toby brings in a team of litigation attorneys from her firm.

Though Gerry Alexis does some litigation, she says that her current practice primarily involves mergers and acquisitions. "My practice includes litigation, but it is primarily deal-making," she says. "Due to the economy, there are numerous mergers and acquisitions going on, and that side of my practice has simply swallowed me up as of late," she says. "I constantly use my litigation skills and experience, however. For example, when I present arguments to the government, I offer a lot of well organized facts. I use my persuasive skills to explain why the merger should go through. I let the government know that if the merger doesn't go through, we're ready and able to litigate."

Gerry says that a good part of her time is spent in conference calls in which she is talking to her clients, other lawyers, other parties to the deal, or to government officials (usually those with the antitrust division of the DOJ or the FTC). "Many of the meetings with the government are informal," she explains. "In such a meeting I might bring in an economist or an executive from my client company to explain some aspect of the proposed deal to the government." Gerry notes that she frequently works with economists. "Economics and antitrust law have come closer and closer together over the years. When you're developing an argument that a merger or acquisition isn't anticompetitive, it has to make sense under economic theory. I consult regularly with economists who write papers supporting my client's position. I also work with economists to determine what data we need to collect to persuade the government that the merger isn't anticompetitive."

Anthony Swisher says that his mergers and acquisitions work requires that he work closely with his client's chief financial officer or general counsel. "The first step in moving forward in a merger or acquisition involves putting together what is called a 'Hart-Scott-Rodino filing,' which is named after the three legislators who drafted the Hart-Scott-Rodino Antitrust Improvements Act of 1976. The filing requires detailed information about the proposed transaction. Federal agencies review the filing to determine whether there are anticompetitive aspects to the transaction. The agencies have 30 days to review the filing and can come back to me with questions or concerns about the transaction. Any questions the agencies raise are handled on an informal basis. We sometimes talk on the phone or in person, and sometimes go in and make a presentation to the agencies.

"At the end of the 30-day waiting period, the agencies do one of two things. In the large majority of cases, the agencies approve the transaction and allow it to go ahead and close. In some situations, however, the agencies issue what is called a 'second request' in which they initiate a full-blown investigation concerning the proposed transaction. In this case, the agencies send out a lengthy document (frequently 20 pages or more) involving numerous document requests, interrogatories, and deposition requests. It often takes several months to put together all the documents and other information required for a second request. Through this arduous process, the agencies are trying to determine whether there are any anticompetitive aspects involved in the transaction, and my role is to explain why the transaction doesn't pose anticompetitive problems. After we comply with the second request, the agencies determine whether to seek an injunction preventing the transaction from closing or determine that the client can go ahead and close the transaction."

Anthony's antitrust work requires a great dealt of client counseling. "I'm frequently on the phone with clients. There are days that I'm on the phone from the moment I arrive at the office to the moment I leave. I field numerous client questions. Clients may be thinking about getting involved in a transaction and want to talk about the antitrust implications of the deal. If we're in the process of preparing a Hart-Scott filing, or in the process of complying with a second request, I'm often on the phone with the client gathering the information that we need and learning as much as I can about the industry."

Anthony occasionally travels to his client's company headquarters to gather information for an investigation or to pull together documents for a second request. "Sometimes it's helpful to visit the client and interview them on-site in order to gather the information we need to provide to the agencies," he explains. Anthony also spends a fair amount of time reviewing documents and researching the regulations and statutes related to a particular transaction.

A significant amount of writing is involved in Anthony's practice. "I do less writing than I would do in a traditional litigation practice. Most of the writing I do involves drafting memos to clients. I also write what are called 'white papers,' which are lengthy legal arguments similar to a legal brief that are submitted to agencies such as the Federal Trade Commission and the Department of Justice. A white paper is essentially an advocacy piece setting forth the facts involved in a proposed transaction and explaining why the transaction doesn't pose anticompetitive problems. White papers are always tailored to the issues an agency has raised in their dialogue after they've reviewed the Hart-Scott filing. Most transactions don't require the submission of a white paper, but some do."

What do antitrust lawyers find rewarding about their practice?

The antitrust lawyers we talked to enjoy the role they play in helping their clients solve difficult problems. Explains Don Schmidt, "I like having the opportunity to think through competing strategies and potential solutions to problems. These are tough issues and a lot is at stake. Meeting this kind of challenge head-on is what puts the spark in this practice." Toby Singer likes the challenge of helping her clients work through tough issues. "This work is rewarding when there are difficult issues with regard to a merger and I am able to work them out to the benefit of my client. Antitrust lawyers can generally make a deal go through more easily," explains Toby. "I also like helping the client out of a hole they may have dug for themselves, getting them out of the predicament with a minimum of damage."

Adds Anthony Swisher, "There's nothing like feeling you've gotten an excellent result for your client. Clients come to you with make or break deals, and they are relying on you to shepherd them through the antitrust review process. It's a good feeling to know that you've had a part in making the deal close."

"I like putting together arguments, and I like winning them," says Gerry Alexis. "In litigation it takes a long time to get to the point where you go to trial and win. But the deals I'm involved in typically have a fairly short time frame from start to finish. It may take two to three months to put the facts together, put the arguments together, and then argue before the government. It's a fantastic feeling when a government official calls you up to tell you that the government is going to clear your deal."

Anthony Swisher, too, enjoys the fact that the deals on which he works generally have short time lines. "Litigation matters can go on for years, but the antitrust issues I work on generally last only a few months, or, if a second request is involved, may last up to a year. This shorter time line means that there's a lot of variety in the cases that I work on, which makes the practice especially interesting."

Antitrust lawyers also enjoy the relationships they develop with clients and other professionals. "Client counseling is particularly rewarding. I help the client set up structures and contracts that reduce the risk of litigation," says Gerry Alexis. Gerry particularly likes working with the new attorneys at the firm. "When you staff a deal, you staff it pretty leanly. There may be one partner and one associate assigned to a case. This gives me the opportunity to work closely with associates who have recently graduated from law school. I enjoy training these young lawyers," she says.

"One of the things I enjoy most about working as an antitrust attorney is working with bright and talented business people and counsel," confides Don Schmidt. "I've had the benefit of working with first-rate people. The camaraderie in the antitrust department—and in my firm—has been an important factor in my choosing and remaining in this practice."

Anthony Swisher says that he works with a remarkable group of partners at Akin Gump. "The people I work with are tremendous," he reports. "As an associate, I do over 85% of my work with two partners for whom I have nothing but the highest regard. Working with great people makes all the difference in the world in the level of satisfaction you have in law practice."

Antitrust work offers an especially interesting challenge to those interested in business issues. "The best part of my job," says Ron Tenpas, "is that each case gives you the chance to become a 'mini-expert' in a new field so that you are always learning. With one case you may be finding out how electric power plants work, in the next how pesticides are made, and in the next how insurance is priced and marketed. It makes for interesting work for anybody who is just generally curious about the way the world works, especially if they are curious about the way the world of commerce works."

Anthony Swisher agrees. "I really enjoy learning about the different industries in which my clients work. The diversity is truly amazing. I've worked on deals involving oil and gas, automobile retailing, trash hauling, grocery stores, telecommunications, and health care," he explains with enthusiasm.

In addition, Anthony says he enjoys the intellectual challenges offered by antitrust practice. "In law school, I found that constitutional law and antitrust law were the most intellectually stimulating courses I took. The practice of antitrust law is, in many ways, similar to the practice of constitutional law, in that the practice is based on a bare bones statute and has been developed by case law. It's simply a fascinating area of practice."

The Training and Skills Important to Antitrust Law

How do people enter the field of antitrust law?

Some attorneys enter antitrust practice directly out of law school. Those attorneys generally work as summer associates at law firms with antitrust departments. Others work for the government—often for the DOJ or the FTC or a state attorney general's office—after graduating from law school or after leaving judicial clerkships.

Antitrust lawyers may first develop an interest in the area in law school, either through their class work or through a summer associate or law clerking experience. "My summer clerkships convinced me that I wanted a 'big firm' type practice. My antitrust course in law school showed me that I enjoyed working with the substantive field of law and had some facility for doing so," says Don Schmidt. As a litigator, it's not surprising that Don says that he has "no trouble getting fired up for the heat of the contest."

Ron Tenpas says that he became an antitrust litigator because he was generally interested in litigation and then joined a firm that does a great deal of antitrust litigation. "My interest in litigation emerged due to three years of clerking—for a federal district court, the U.S. Supreme Court, and an international arbitration court located in The Hague. I combine my antitrust work with more general litigation practice that ranges from state court trial work to federal appellate work. I find the range satisfying and challenging."

Anthony Swisher fell under the spell of antitrust law as an undergraduate. "I was an economics major. I had a professor who taught a tremendously popular undergraduate class in antitrust law. I thoroughly enjoyed the class. The professor, a Ph.D. economist, was dynamic, and I emerged from the class hooked on antitrust law." When Anthony worked at Akin Gump as a summer associate while in law school, the head of the litigation practice group knew that he was interested in antitrust. "He was great about funneling antitrust work my way," Anthony recalls. It didn't take Anthony long to begin to develop a practice in the antitrust mergers and acquisitions area. "When I had been an associate at the firm for less than one month, a client called one of our antitrust partners with a question. I was asked to research the answer, and the partner sent me a copy of the letter he sent to the client. 'I have asked one of our antitrust people to take a look at the issue,' the letter said. It was pretty exciting to be regarded as an 'antitrust person' just one month into my legal career," says Anthony. "Over time, more and more work has come my way. I've gradually developed a niche in the antitrust area."

Anthony says that he's thankful he trusted his instincts when he chose a law firm as a summer associate and eventually as an associate. "I had a total gut feeling that this firm was the place for me. Now when I interview law students seeking summer associate positions, I tell them, 'Trust your gut.' Sometimes on paper, other firms may look like their antitrust practices are larger or better known. But when you meet the people who work in a department, that tells you so much more than a brochure. When I interviewed at this firm, I was very comfortable. I'm so thankful I trusted my instincts."

Toby Singer worked for the FTC before joining a law firm where she specializes in health care antitrust law. "When I was a second year student in law school, I worked as a part-time law clerk for a law firm. The partner I was assigned to was formerly with the FTC; he specialized in antitrust work. I enjoyed working with him and I liked the antitrust practice. The partner suggested that I apply for a summer internship position with the FTC. I applied, worked for the summer, and was hired upon graduation from law school. I remained at the FTC for 11 years. After five years of work at the FTC, I became part of the FTC's Health Care Antitrust Section, where I developed an expertise in health care antitrust work." Toby joined her current law firm in 1989.

Gerry Alexis had a long-standing interest in business and economics. She earned her law degree at Northwestern University School of Law the same year that she completed a Master of Management at Northwestern's Kellogg School of Management. Gerry clerked for a district court judge for a year after graduating from law school. Following the path of many antitrust attorneys, she then worked for the Department of Justice during some of her early years in practice.

What skills are most important to antitrust lawyers?

❖ Antitrust lawyers need exceptional **writing skills**. "In this area of law, it's important to write well," says Gerry Alexis. "You have to communicate clearly. You have to express your legal analysis in words that are clear to both your client and to the government. My practice requires submitting 'white papers' to the government. A white paper is like a brief in which you argue your side of the case. It must be both well written and persuasive." Don Schmidt is equally emphatic about the importance of strong writing skills to the antitrust lawyer. "There is no substitute for down-in-the-trenches legal research and writing to hone your analytical skills," he says. "Legal writing forces the practitioner to focus on the real crux of a multifaceted issue in order to present it most cogently."

❖ Antitrust lawyers must be skilled at **legal analysis**. "The ability to undertake detailed legal analysis and to convey that analysis persuasively both on paper and orally is a must," says Don Schmidt. Adds Gerry Alexis, "You have to be able to develop your arguments effectively. You must be able to think through the ramifications of one argument versus another. And you have to make sure that your analysis takes into account both law and economics." Says Anthony Swisher, "Antitrust practice requires strong analytical skills. You're looking at some complex regulations and a large body of case law and analyzing the facts in relation to those authorities."

❖ **Good judgment** is important for all lawyers, but particularly important for antitrust lawyers, because of the high-stakes nature of the practice and the economic consequences of the decisions made in this area. Explains Toby Singer, "Good judgment is the most important skill in this work, and I place that first over legal skills. Good judgment is acquired by experience, and by observing other people's mistakes. It is essential to work with more experienced lawyers—they essentially teach you how to use good judgment."

❖ Antitrust lawyers must have excellent **interpersonal skills**. "You do a lot of client counseling in this area," says Gerry Alexis. "Your clients must feel comfortable working with you." Gerry adds that antitrust lawyers need to work effectively in a team. "Teamwork—working closely with your clients and with other lawyers—is essential." Says Anthony Swisher, "Having good people skills is imperative. My practice requires that I spend a great deal of time gathering information from comptrollers, in-house attorneys, chief financial officers, and others who work for my clients. You have to be good at making these people feel at ease so that you can gather the information you need." Ron Tenpas says that as an antitrust litigator, his interpersonal skills allow him to work effectively with witnesses. "You have to have a knack for making witnesses feel comfortable in giving you the truth."

❖ Antitrust lawyers must be **attentive to detail**. "Attention to detail is imperative," says Anthony Swisher. "Any detail you miss comes back to haunt you. When you gather facts from a client, you must get the details. You must understand the nuances of the information you gather and know which details may have an impact on the issue at hand. If you miss information or gloss over it, the ramifications can be severe," he explains. "One of our partners has a great line. He says, 'He who represents facts to the government in haste repents at leisure.' It's a great line because it's absolutely true!"

❖ The antitrust lawyers we talked to mentioned the importance of **creativity**. "Antitrust practice requires the creative application of the simply-worded statutes to complex fact patterns," says Don Schmidt. "You have to be creative in gathering facts," says Gerry Alexis. "You can usually get the facts you need from your client. But getting facts from third-party witnesses can be hard. When you don't have subpoena power, you have to exercise creativity in order to get the facts you need."

What classes and law school experiences do antitrust lawyers recommend?

❖ Take an **antitrust class** in law school. "An antitrust class is key," says Anthony Swisher. "Antitrust is an area of law that is case driven. My law school antitrust professor required us to memorize the facts and holdings of 50 leading antitrust cases. At the time I couldn't understand why he made us do this. But in my first week of practice, the professor's reasoning was abundantly clear. At every meeting of our firm's antitrust lawyers, the attorneys threw around terms such as, 'We have a Pueblo issue here.' Because I memorized those case holdings, I knew what the attorneys were talking about." Classes that provide insight into business, such as **corporations**, are also helpful.

❖ **A well rounded legal education emphasizing critical thinking** is important. "The most valuable classes are those that are taught by good, demanding teachers who focus on the policies behind various legal rules and therefore teach you to develop careful analytical skills in thinking through why various arguments do, or do not, make sense. This overall ability to engage in 'critical thinking' is much more important than any particular substantive expertise," advises Ron Tenpas.

❖ **Undergraduate or graduate courses in business and economics** can be helpful. "You do need some background in economics," says Gerry Alexis, who earned a joint law and business degree. Explains Ron Tenpas, "Antitrust lawyers are benefited by some exposure to microeconomic theory, whether through an antitrust course, a law and economics course, substantial undergraduate work or graduate work, or the like."

❖ Working as a **federal judicial law clerk** can be helpful in preparing for a career in antitrust law. "A clerkship allows you to see things from the perspective of the bench," says Gerry Alexis, who clerked for a district court judge following graduation from law school. "You learn what impresses judges and what bothers them. You also add to your knowledge of civil procedure. You actually work with the judge to decide procedural questions and write opinions for the judge on procedural issues. A judicial clerkship is like a post-graduate course on federal procedure."

❖ **Gain practical experience as a summer associate or law clerk** at a law firm that has an antitrust practice. "A high-quality summer clerkship is an excellent foundation for practice," says Don Schmidt. Summer associate positions are generally available to second year students who interview during the fall of the second year of law school for positions available between their second and third year of law school. Smaller law firms often hire students to work part-time during the school year.

❖ **Work experience in the business world** can help you prepare to be an antitrust lawyer. "Some real-world business experience is invaluable," says Don Schmidt. Ron Tenpas agrees, noting, "Business experience, especially in corporate strategic planning, marketing, or finance can be very useful."

❖ **Sharpen your writing skills** through participating in your school's law review or law journal or participating in a writing competition. "Participating in law review is a way that you can demonstrate to prospective employers that you have excellent writing experience," says Gerry Alexis. "Law review hones writing and editing abilities," adds Anthony Swisher.

❖ Experiences such as **moot court** that develop oral advocacy skills are helpful. "The oral presentations I make to government agencies are similar to appellate advocacy," says Anthony Swisher. "In appellate advocacy, your goal is to answer the judges' questions and go where the judges want you to go. Presentations to the FTC or the Department of Justice are similar. The goal is to prepare to address the agency's concerns and answer the agency's questions. You have to anticipate where the agency 'wants to go.' To prepare for such presentations, you need to know facts about your client's industry as well as the facts surrounding the proposed transaction. You need to make the agency representatives feel that you are responding to their questions and concerns, and, at the same time, you need to be persuasive in your answers."

❖ **Participation in bar association activities** allows you to meet antitrust lawyers and learn about their practice. Student bar association memberships are reasonably priced, and student members are welcome to attend most bar association activities. "I recommend getting involved in the state or national bar associations. They often have sections or committees that focus on antitrust," says Ron Tenpas. Advises Don Schmidt, "Bar association activities are an excellent way to develop contacts in this field." Those contacts can be invaluable in the job search.

ANTITRUST ATTORNEYS INTERVIEWED FOR THIS SECTION

Geraldine Alexis
Sidley & Austin
Chicago, Illinois
UNDERGRADUATE: University of Rochester
LAW SCHOOL: Northwestern University School of Law

Donald Schmidt
Carlton Fields
Tampa, Florida
UNDERGRADUATE: University of Notre Dame
LAW SCHOOL: University of Notre Dame Law School

Toby Singer
Jones, Day, Reavis & Pogue
Washington, D.C.
UNDERGRADUATE: Wesleyan University
LAW SCHOOL: Georgetown University Law Center

Anthony Swisher
Akin, Gump, Strauss, Hauer & Feld, L.L.P.
Washington, D.C.
UNDERGRADUATE: University of Virginia
LAW SCHOOL: George Washington University Law School

Ronald Tenpas
Carlton Fields
Tampa, Florida
UNDERGRADUATE: Michigan State University
LAW SCHOOL: University of Virginia School of Law

Editor's note: Ronald Tenpas is no longer employed at Carlton Fields. After leaving Carlton Fields, Mr. Tenpas became an Assistant U.S. Attorney. He is currently employed in the U.S. Attorney's Office for the District of Maryland.

Appellate Practice

What is Appellate Practice?

In an appeal, a higher court—an appellate or supreme court—reviews the decision of a lower court—generally a trial court or an administrative agency. Lawyers specializing in appellate practice handle the process of appealing a final judgment. This may happen in a civil or criminal case after a trial before a judge or jury, or after dismissal of a case upon disposition of a motion (such as a motion for summary judgment, in which a party has argued that there is no genuine issue of material fact in a case and that he or she is entitled to prevail as a matter of law). An appeal is typically brought before an intermediate court of appeals and, if necessary, to a supreme court.

Both the state and federal courts have avenues of appeal for civil and criminal cases. Most states have an intermediate, or appellate, court that hears cases from lower courts in the same geographic district within the state. Appeals from the appellate courts are brought before a higher level court, typically called a supreme court. Appeals from decisions of federal district courts are brought in the court of appeals that has jurisdiction over the federal districts in one or more states. For example, appeals from federal courts in California proceed to the Ninth Circuit Court of Appeals, while appeals from the federal courts in Washington, D.C. proceed to the D.C. Court of Appeals.

A party generally has an appeal as a matter of legal right after a case has proceeded to conclusion at the trial court level and all avenues of review within that court have been exhausted. A criminal defendant who has exhausted appeals at the state trial court level is entitled to seek a review of his or her case through a request to a federal district court called a writ of habeas corpus. In the writ, the defendant claims that he or she is wrongfully imprisoned because he or she has been denied rights, such as due process, under the U.S. Constitution. In civil actions a plaintiff whose case is dismissed by grant of a motion to dismiss or a motion for summary judgment would proceed to an appeal after entry of a judgment.

Not all issues can be appealed as a matter of right. For many issues the appellate court needs to be convinced that there is a compelling reason to take the issue for consideration on appeal. Some issues or decisions of the trial court are within the discretion of the judge and thus are subject to appeal for the judge's abuse of discretion. The appellate courts thus have standards of review, or different tests that are applied to determine whether the trial court erred in its decision. Few issues are considered de novo (completely new) at the appellate level. Rather, decisions of the trial court may be reversed only if, for example, legal error occurred.

In other words, cases are not retried by appellate courts. A manufacturer that loses a product liability trial, and is required to pay $800 million in punitive damages for their negligence, is not permitted a second trial of the case on appeal. Instead, the defendant must establish on appeal that no reasonable jury could have come to such a conclusion. A plaintiff that loses an antitrust case may argue that the jury instructions explaining the law to the jurors were erroneous, and thus appeal. However, the plaintiff must have properly objected to those instructions at trial and must demonstrate that the error was not insignificant (legally referred to as "harmless" error).

The appellate lawyer must carefully review the lower court record to determine the grounds on which the decision can be appealed, and she must draft detailed written briefs that set forth her party's position on appeal. In criminal cases lawyers may review the record to determine whether the evidence should have been excluded as a result of improper search and seizure or whether the jury was representative of the community. Seldom will the appellate court consider issues such as the credibility of witnesses, which is left for the trial court and jury to determine. Appellate attorneys may also present oral arguments in front of the appellate court or supreme court.

In a majority of cases, an appellate or supreme court affirms lower court decisions. However, the higher courts have a number of options on appeal—they can vacate (throw out) lower court decisions; reverse the decisions, deciding for the other party; or reverse or affirm some issues on appeal and remand (send back) other issues to the lower court.

For more information on the trial process in general, *see* the Criminal Law, Civil Litigation, and Tort Law chapters.

Life as an Appellate Lawyer

Where do appellate lawyers work?

Attorneys specializing in appellate work are generally employed by law firms or by state or federal government organizations. Large and mid-size law firms with trial practices often have departments dedicated to appellate work. Small firms that handle trial work, such as plaintiffs' personal injury law firms or criminal defense firms, may have attorneys who work on appeals, or they may turn for assistance to an outside practitioner who specializes in appeals.

Government attorneys often work on criminal appeals, working for state appellate defenders' offices (which handle appeals for cases handled by public defenders), federal appellate defenders' offices, or U.S. Attorneys' offices. Appellate lawyers also work as staff attorneys for federal appeals judges. In addition, federal and state commissions sometimes employ attorneys to work on appellate matters.

Who are their clients and what types of cases do they work on?

Law firm attorneys who work in appellate practice have the opportunity to work with a wide range of clients. Charles Hinkle is an attorney at Stoel Rives LLP, of Portland, Oregon. "Stoel Rives is the largest firm in Oregon, and we have offices in Seattle, Boise, and Salt Lake City, so we practice in a wide variety of fields," he explains. "Our appellate practice is similarly varied: products liability, securities fraud, breach of contract, libel, election law, construction and design, environmental law, public records, even an occasional domestic relations matter. We also do a significant amount of appellate work in public interest fields; recently I argued a case in the Oregon Supreme Court attempting to stop the first execution in Oregon since the state reinstated the death penalty in 1984. Most of our clients are institutional, although we have a large estate planning practice that serves individual clients." He adds, "Our clients include public utilities, retailers, high tech companies, manufacturers, newspapers, colleges, brokerage houses, hospitals, and municipal corporations."

Theodora (Teddie) Gaitas works as an Assistant State Public Defender for the Minnesota State Public Defender's Office in Minneapolis, Minnesota. Teddie's office handles the appeals for criminal defendants in the state. "My clients are all indigent criminal defendants. They must be indigent to qualify for the assistance of a public defender. Most of my clients have already been convicted of state crimes, ranging from first degree murder to driving under the influence of alcohol. They are appealing to the Minnesota Court of Appeals and the Minnesota Supreme Court. In Minnesota, every convicted defendant is automatically, by statute, entitled to appeal their case," explains Teddie.

David Blair-Loy and Richard M. (Rick) Greenberg, who work for the Office of the Appellate Defender in New York City, also handle criminal appeals. The Office of the Appellate Defender is a not-for-profit public interest organization with 16 attorneys—five supervising attorneys and 11 staff attorneys. Besides working with staff attorneys, two of the supervising attorneys work with pro bono volunteers from law firms in New York.

"My clients are low-income criminal defendants who are appealing their convictions. Most of my clients are incarcerated, unless they have been paroled. Our office handles appeals of anything from a single mugging to buy-and-bust drug cases to multiple homicides," says David. Adds Rick, "Our office represents only indigent defendants, and we are appointed as their appellate counsel. All of our clients are people who have been convicted in state court of serious felonies. A large percentage of our cases are homicides, but we also handle matters such as rape, robbery, burglary, and occasionally kidnaping. Most of our clients are incarcerated, because they have been convicted of serious crimes. They are in state prisons throughout the state of New York."

Lawyers who work as staff attorneys for federal appellate courts assist judges with appellate matters. Julie Fenton is the Senior Staff Attorney for the U.S. Court of Appeals for the Seventh Circuit in Chicago, Illinois. "My clients are the judges of the Seventh Circuit Court of Appeals. We have 11 active judges and several senior judges. I supervise 20 staff attorneys who assist the judges with research and the drafting of proposed orders." Julie and the staff attorneys work on the large number of cases on appeal to the Seventh Circuit. The cases include direct criminal appeals, habeas corpus petitions, and prisoner civil rights cases, as well as employment discrimination, Social Security, bankruptcy, and immigration cases.

What daily activities are involved in appellate practice?

Large firm lawyer Charles Hinkle succinctly describes the role of the appellate lawyer in a law firm practice. "The job of the appellate lawyer is to make sense of what went on in the trial, and to give it structure and coherence, and to show why the facts fit the legal theories that you want to present on appeal. It is rare that I spend any time with a client when I am involved in the appellate aspect of the case. The record has already been made in the court or agency below, and the client has had the opportunity to say whatever she had to say. Thus most of my time is spent at my desk, reviewing the transcripts and exhibits, and placing the facts in the context of the law." Legal research is an important part of the job. "I used to spend more time in the library than I do now, but with legal research resources available on the desktop computer, there is less need to hit the books," he explains.

Appellate defenders spend their time "reading the record, researching issues, and writing briefs," says David Blair-Loy. Rick Greenberg provides a more in-depth description of the daily activities of an appellate practitioner. "In a nutshell," he says, "when we are assigned a case, we get the entire record from the lower courts—the trial transcript, the indictment—all the papers involved. Our job is to read and analyze all of that information and try to determine the most promising issues to use to obtain relief upon appeal. We are working generally for a reversal or a sentence reduction. The case documents can be literally thousands of pages long. We read, digest, and analyze everything that happened in the case, list potential appellate issues, research those issues, then narrow down the list based upon the research to focus on strategic issues for the appeal. We then write a brief containing all of the facts of the case and explaining why the particular issues we've focused on are grounds for reversal. The prosecutors then file a response and we write a reply to that response. Finally we proceed to oral arguments. Sometimes a case might require additional investigation, for example in light of newly discovered evidence.

"I think our office is somewhat unique in that we always double-team our cases," Rick adds. "We have a staff attorney and a supervising attorney working together for every case so that there is another set of eyes to spot potential appellate issues."

"A good part of my day is spent working on my appeals," says Teddie Gaitas. "I have to look at a case and see the issues, see how it's appealable. My cases are all in different stages of appeal. We have our own caseload—we handle the appeal from the beginning, when you file a notice of appeal, to the end. You stay with the client all the way through the process. You have the chance to get really familiar with the case. You start by reviewing the court transcript and doing a 'digest' in which you chart out each page of the transcript. Sometimes the transcripts are up to 6000 pages long. Digesting the transcript helps you think about what legal issues exist." Teddie explains that the next stage of the appeals process involves legal research. "I do lots of brainstorming and legal research. I figure out what legal issues to raise to the court. Then I write the brief. I generally write about two briefs per month. If the argument is weak, the brief may be as short as 10 pages, but most are in the range of 20 to 30 pages."

Teddie determines whether the appeals she works on merit oral arguments. "It's discretionary—our call—whether we want to argue the case in front of the appellate judges of the Court of Appeals (oral arguments are not discretionary for the Minnesota Supreme Court)." She says the court generally issues opinions three months after the oral argument or the date on which it considers the appeal. "When the opinion is issued, I notify the client right away." If clients lose the appeal, they can petition the Minnesota Supreme Court. "The Minnesota Supreme Court is generally looking at novel cases, in which there's a new and distinct legal issue to be addressed. I carefully explain this to my clients. But most of my clients who lose their appeals decide they want to petition the Supreme Court. They tell me, 'I need something to hope and wait for again, something to look forward to,' even if they don't succeed."

Both Teddie and David Blair-Loy report that they spend a significant amount of their time communicating with their clients. "Most of my communication with my clients is by letter," says David. Teddie agrees. But she reports that once she is assigned a new case, she tries to meet with the client in person. "I write a letter introducing myself and explaining the appellate process. Then I drive out to the prison to meet with them. I am very straightforward with my clients. I tell them about the appellate process, how lengthy it is, and their probable chances of success." Rick Greenberg adds, "Because some of the prisons are great distances from our office, we are not always able to meet with our clients face to face. We encourage face to face meetings whenever they are possible, but sometimes that's just not feasible. If we cannot meet our client in person, we are diligent about corresponding with them, and we accept collect calls from prisons throughout the state. We work hard to involve our clients as much as possible in the process and in the decisions."

As a senior staff attorney for the Seventh Circuit Court of Appeals, Julie Fenton's days are spent in person to person meetings with the judges and with staff attorneys she supervises. "When my two-and-a-half year old asks what I do at work, I tell her, 'I talk to people.' And that's an apt description of what I do. I meet with the judges to make sure their legal staffing needs are satisfied and that their research needs are met. I supervise, train, and hire new staff attorneys for the appellate court. I do my own research and writing on the substantive legal issues faced by the court. I also write policy proposals for the judges concerning the administrative aspects of our office's operations."

What do appellate lawyers find rewarding about their practice?

Both David Blair-Loy and Teddie Gaitas report that they find a special reward in working with their indigent clients. "Winning an appeal is certainly satisfying. But apart from winning," says David, "I find it rewarding to treat my clients with respect and dignity, and I receive the same in return from them, because most of them have rarely been treated that way. I am glad I can do so, if only for a short time, during my representation of them." Teddie adds, "I always wanted to do public defense. I enjoy being a defender of the Constitution; I enjoy being the underdog. My clients may have committed horrendous acts, but I get a chance to know them and to see beyond those acts. They have generally lived in poverty. They have little formal education. It's easy for me to look beyond the criminal act and look beyond the facts to the legal issues. I feel sympathy and empathy toward my clients."

Rick Greenberg agrees that client representation brings the greatest reward. "Really it's all about the clients," he comments. "Indigent clients in particular need to know that they are receiving the highest quality representation even though they're not paying for it. We try to give clients the same level of representation that they would pay for. I really enjoy developing the relationship with the client, reaching that level of understanding and trust. In reality you're going to lose 80-90% of your cases. The reward is not necessarily in winning, but in representing the client to the best of your ability, providing the highest quality counsel, leaving no stone unturned as far as your investigation and research and avenues for appeal."

Other lawyers find their reward in the effect their appellate arguments have on the law. Charles Hinkle explains that he finds it satisfying to write briefs and prepare oral arguments "with the aim of influencing the future direction of the law." He adds, "The question of whether initiative petitioners have a constitutional right to gather signatures on private property has been the subject of litigation in Oregon for more than 10 years, and the Oregon Supreme Court has yet to issue a definitive opinion as to whether such a right exists, or the scope of it if it does exist. We are in the middle of that issue, and our cases in the appellate courts will determine how that law develops. It is very satisfying to be able to research constitutional and political history and to write a brief that will influence the court as it considers these cases."

Charles also enjoys the challenge of working on appellate issues that arise in the context of real emergencies. "Such an appeal can arise in a death penalty case, when we have just a few days to try to prevent the execution from being carried out, or a prior restraint case, when we are attempting to get the appellate court to act immediately to overturn an unconstitutional order. In these situations the pressure is intense, and there is never enough time to be as thorough as one would like to be in researching the issues and crafting the arguments. Such cases are exciting and exhausting."

"I love my job," says Julie Fenton. "I look forward to going to work in the morning." Julie's job as senior staff attorney for the Seventh Circuit Court of Appeals allows her to pursue her academic interest in the law as well as her interest in mentoring young lawyers. "For me, this job is the perfect combination of appellate legal work—which is the core of what I like about the law—and teaching and managing. I love mentoring, and I have a mentoring job. I work with staff attorneys—most of them recent law school graduates—who are outstanding lawyers. It's an unbelievable privilege to be allowed to be part of how the judges decide cases—to learn how they think and talk through the issues. I have the inclination to be a permanent student. My work with the judges means that I'm a student of some of the greatest legal lights in the country." Julie adds that she enjoys keeping up with legal opinions as they're issued daily by the court, and she encourages her staff attorneys to do the same. "I also encourage my staff members to go to any oral arguments they would like to hear. It's exciting to see the judges in action," she says.

The Training and Skills Important to Appellate Practice

How do people enter the field of appellate practice?

Most law firms that hire appellate lawyers look for law school graduates who have clerked for judges upon graduation from law school. Judicial clerkships allow recent graduates to see firsthand how appellate judges approach legal issues. Once hired by a law firm, former clerks can put their knowledge to work preparing appeals for the firm's clients.

Rick Greenberg reports that he entered an appellate defender office directly out of law school. He adds, however, that if students attempt to take this path, "Whatever office they work for ought to have extensive training and the attorney should work under close supervision by someone with more experience. The key is to select the appropriate issues for the appeal, and someone without that experience might miss very significant issues."

There's a great deal of competition for appellate defender jobs. "People in this field like their jobs," says Teddie Gaitas. "No one leaves their job. There are few positions open. Get as much experience as you can before you apply. Work as a law clerk for an appeals judge after law school. I worked for an appellate judge for six months before finding this job." Adds David Blair-Loy, "Demonstrate a commitment to public interest law in general, and criminal defense in particular." Working for public interest organizations during law school can make it clear to a prospective employer that you're serious about doing public interest work.

Staff attorney positions for federal judges can be highly competitive, as well. "Appellate courts are very selective when hiring staff attorneys," explains Julie Fenton. "We tend to look for the same credentials that large law firms look for—rank in the top 10% of the law school class, law review, moot court, and extremely strong writing skills." Each federal circuit is structured differently. Some staff attorneys have two year terms; others are hired on a permanent basis. Julie strongly recommends that students interested in federal judicial clerkships also consider applying for staff attorney positions.

What skills are most important to appellate lawyers?

❖ The lawyers we talked to emphasized the importance of outstanding **writing skills**. "You need a clear, rigorous, systematic way of thinking and writing," says David Blair-Loy. "Clear writing is of primary importance," agrees Teddie Gaitas. Adds Rick Greenberg, "Appellate lawyers have to be able to craft their arguments in writing, as opposed to cross-examining a witness, so writing and analytical skills are very important. At the same time, there are also oral arguments in appellate practice, so oral advocacy skills are also important."

❖ The other attorneys we spoke with agree that **oral advocacy skills** are important. "You need the instincts of an advocate," says David Blair-Loy. Charles Hinkle attended seminary before going to law school. "Oral advocacy and writing skills are equally important for appellate practice. Public speaking experience of all kinds is helpful. I am a minister in the United Church of Christ and have had a lot of experience speaking from the pulpit, as well as in speaking to civic groups of all kinds on constitutional and civil liberties issues," he explains. Teddie Gaitas confides, "I like the thrill of oral argument; I like the tension. Oral arguments are one of the most enjoyable things I do."

❖ Excellent **legal research skills** are critical in appellate practice. "All of my research is in the area of criminal law, and it's fascinating," says Teddie Gaitas. Charles Hinkle is equally enthusiastic about legal research. "I enjoy legal research and writing. After 25 years in practice, I still like going to the library and reading the cases," he says. Julie Fenton's experience with staff attorneys, judicial law clerks, and law students (she was previously an assistant dean at a Chicago law school) allows her to offer this advice: "Students who genuinely enjoy researching and writing tend to enjoy appellate practice and find it exciting. Working as a staff attorney allows you to continue to be a student of the law."

❖ **Interpersonal communication skills** are important to those specializing in appellate practice. "As a staff attorney," says Julie Fenton, "you need to have poise. You have to field the judges' questions and make recommendations to them." Julie adds that in her job as a supervising staff attorney, her interpersonal skills are critical. "I lead a team charged with an important task—getting work for the judges accomplished. As a supervisor I find that leadership and team-building skills help me motivate staff members to work together effectively."

❖ Those working in appellate practice need the **ability to act as an advocate.** Explains David Blair-Loy, "This means you need to learn to think like an advocate, not a law student or a judge." Adds Julie Fenton, "You have to have a certain amount of assertiveness and self-confidence in dealing with the appellate judges. They don't like shrinking violets."

❖ Attorneys working in the public interest sector mention the **ability to empathize with the client.** "You have to be comfortable working with your clients," says Teddie Gaitas. "You have to have a certain comfort level talking to people who may have been convicted of terribly violent crimes." She adds, "This work also requires patience in working with clients. Many clients are completely unfamiliar with the system. It's easy to explain things in legal terms, but not everyone understands legal terms. Your clients are very dependent on you. Sometimes a client seems overly persistent, wanting too much contact, making too many calls, asking too many questions. You have to remember that this is because the client isn't familiar with the appellate process. You have to demystify the process for them."

What classes and law school experiences do appellate lawyers recommend?

❖ The appellate lawyers we talked to recommend taking law school classes that will sharpen your writing skills, such as **advanced legal writing classes and seminar classes.** Julie Fenton, who hires staff attorneys for the Seventh Circuit Court of Appeals (and who is familiar with the requirements for hiring judicial law clerks), recommends civil procedure and advanced civil procedure, federal courts, criminal law and criminal procedure, employment discrimination, and constitutional law. David Blair-Loy says that any class that "hones your ability to read, think, research, write, and argue as an advocate" can be helpful. Rick Greenberg agrees, commenting, "Not all writing is going to be the same—writing a brief is going to be different than writing a law review article or writing you might do in a clerkship—but any writing and analytical experience will be helpful." Adds Charles Hinkle, "Students interested in appellate practice should never turn away from the opportunity to research and write a paper or brief on some legal issue."

❖ Participating in your school's **law review** provides an excellent chance to sharpen your research, writing, and editing skills. If your grades aren't high enough to secure a position on your school's law review, find out whether your school has a writing competition through which you can "write onto" the law review. If you become part of your school's law review, make every effort to publish an article. If you are not on your school's law review, consider writing an article to submit to your school's **other law journals or a writing competition**. A published article makes an excellent writing sample for interviews with legal employers.

❖ **Moot court** gives students an opportunity to exercise their writing and oral advocacy skills. "Participating in moot court provides excellent training in oral advocacy," says Julie Fenton. The oral arguments presented before a panel of judges in moot court competitions are great practice for thinking and speaking under pressure. Rick Greenberg notes that appellate advocacy classes or clinics can provide excellent practical experience. He adds, "I've done trial work and I've done appellate work and I don't think they are mutually exclusive. I think someone with trial experience will be a better appellate attorney because they understand the process and will know how to read the transcripts. And by the same token, someone with appellate experience will be a better trial lawyer."

❖ **Judicial clerkships and judicial externships** are two of the best ways to prepare for a career in appellate practice. Students can apply for judicial clerkships in their second year of law school. Students who are selected for a judicial clerkship generally work for a judge for one to two years after graduation from law school. Law firms with appellate practice groups are most interested in candidates who have judicial clerkship experience. Students who participate in judicial externships have the opportunity to earn academic credit for working for a judge while in law school. Successful externships can also result in an excellent recommendation (from the judge and judicial clerk with whom you work) for a judicial clerkship following graduation.

❖ **Conducting informational interviews with appellate lawyers** can help you plan a career in the field. Charles Hinkle says, "Talking with appellate lawyers (and judges, if you can) is the best way to find out about the practice. Every city has a certain number of lawyers who are well known to the bench and bar for their expertise in appellate law. Many bar associations now have an appellate law section, and that is a good place to find the names of lawyers who do a lot of appellate work."

❖ If you're interested in working as an appellate defender, consider doing an **internship at a public defender's office**. David Blair-Loy also recommends looking into **law school clinical programs** related to criminal and public interest law. David notes that experiences like these can be good ways to demonstrate your public interest law commitment to prospective employers. Rick Greenberg reiterates the importance of this commitment by saying, "When I hire someone for our office, more than experience, I'm looking for someone who is committed to representing clients, representing the indigent. Not everyone is cut out to be a criminal defense attorney, and I'm looking for the people who are."

APPELLATE ATTORNEYS INTERVIEWED FOR THIS SECTION

David Blair-Loy
Office of the Appellate Defender
New York, New York
UNDERGRADUATE: Brown University
LAW SCHOOL: Northwestern University School of Law

Julie Fenton
U.S. Court of Appeals, Seventh Circuit
Chicago, Illinois
UNDERGRADUATE: Iowa State University
LAW SCHOOL: The University of Iowa College of Law

Theodora Gaitas
Minnesota State Public Defender
Minneapolis, Minnesota
UNDERGRADUATE: University of Minnesota
LAW SCHOOL: University of Minnesota Law School

Richard M. Greenberg
Office of the Appellate Defender
New York, New York
UNDERGRADUATE: State University of New York at Binghamton
LAW SCHOOL: State University at Buffalo Law School

Charles Hinkle
Stoel Rives LLP
Portland, Oregon
UNDERGRADUATE: Stanford University
LAW SCHOOL: Yale Law School

Editor's Note: David Blair-Loy is now employed with the Spokane County Public Defender in Spokane, Washington.

Banking and Commercial Finance Practice

What is Banking and Commercial Finance Practice?

In the classic movie *It's a Wonderful Life*, Jimmy Stewart played George Bailey, the quintessential small town banker, a pillar of the community who bore the burden of running the local savings and loan. If George Bailey were to return to Bedford Falls today, he would likely find the local savings and loan had become part of a national conglomerate that offered numerous financial services beyond the parameters of what we typically think of as banking services.

The banking industry has undergone a wave of merger activity in recent years, with both small and large banks being acquired by national banks and financial services institutions. Banks have also dramatically expanded their services to include the sale of insurance and securities as part of a diversified financial services company. For example, the merger between Citibank and Traveler's Group to form Citigroup resulted in a banking and financial services business with separate business units providing traditional commercial lending as well as selling insurance and securities.

Banking lawyers provide legal services to the financial services industry. Businesses need capital to finance their commercial activities and acquisitions; banking lawyers represent lenders, participants, agents, and borrowers in these financial transactions. For example, a company in the fashion industry might need working capital to finance the cost of designing and developing a new line of clothing, or a company in the construction industry might need a line of credit to finance acquisition of raw materials and land for a housing development. In each of these financial transactions, the lender (a bank or other financial institution), the borrower (the company), and any other participants in the financing (*e.g.*, the suppliers of the goods and materials or the real estate developer) typically would each have their interests represented by one or more banking lawyers.

Such transactions can be highly complex and include multistate or international interests as well as secured and unsecured creditors (secured creditors have rights in a security interest or form of collateral; unsecured creditors have no such special rights). In addition to financing working capital and fixed assets, banking lawyers are involved in refinancings, leveraged (or debt-based) acquisition, and recapitalization financings and tender offer financings, which involve offers for the purchase of the stock of a company as a means to acquire control.

Banking and commercial finance attorneys may become involved in restructuring troubled financings (often called "workouts"), planning bankruptcy buyouts (the sale or purchase of assets or loans in bankruptcy proceedings; *see* the Bankruptcy Law chapter for more information), and assisting either the debtor or the lender in connection with troubled acquisitions. Banking lawyers also assist their clients in assessing the many structures of financial transactions available, including highly specialized transactions which involve complex offers of cash and securities in exchange for the stock of the acquired company. Banking and commercial finance attorneys also become involved in securitizations, or offers of packages of mortgages or other debt obligations in a private or public securities offering (*see* the Securities Law chapter for more information).

Life as a Banking or Commercial Finance Lawyer

Where do banking and commercial finance lawyers work?

Banks and other financial institutions, whether trust companies, credit unions, or commercial finance companies, generally have in-house counsel as well as outside counsel who work for law firms. All lawyers who work for banks and commercial finance institutions must be aware of the stringent regulatory requirements to which their institutions are subject. However, a number of the lawyers who work as in-house counsel, as well as those who work as outside counsel, may be involved in a corporate practice that is similar to that of any corporation (*see* the Corporate Practice chapter). These in-house corporate practice attorneys may advise the bank on employment issues, litigation, general business issues such as the management of subsidiaries, purchasing matters such as the purchasing of computer systems, or tax issues. Lawyers may also play other roles in banks, such as working as trust officers. (*See* the profiles of Jennifer Johnson Rahn in the Trusts and Estates Law chapter and Maureen Mosh in the Civil Litigation chapter.)

Many attorneys who specialize in banking and commercial finance work in law firms, often in large and mid-size firms with banking/commercial finance departments. There are also some "boutique" banking law firms in which all of the attorneys specialize in the banking field. Still other attorneys working in this field work for state and federal regulatory agencies, such as the Federal Reserve Bank or state commerce commissions.

Who are their clients and what types of cases do they work on?

Tiziana Tabucchi is a banking and commercial lending attorney at Davis Polk & Wardwell in New York City. She works with a range of clients, including financial institutions such as JP Morgan, banks such as Chase and Banco Santander, and lenders such as Donaldson Lufkin & Jenrett. She also represents some borrowers, usually large corporations. "My work is transactional work," Tiziana explains. "I'm working on highly leveraged deals. Most often the borrowers are taking on a large debt—the sums often reach hundreds of millions or even billions of dollars."

Cynthia Sellers works as a banking attorney at the law firm of Farris, Warfield & Kanaday in Nashville, Tennessee. "The clients I work with are primarily individual loan officers with large financial institutions," Cynthia explains. "They seek advice on business deals and transactional work." Like many banking lawyers, Cynthia works on deals. "Initially I meet with the client to discuss the terms of the deal, whether it be a loan or a real estate conveyance. Then I draft documents that mirror the terms of the deal as discussed in the initial client meeting. I send the documents to the opposing party and their lawyers for review and spend time with the opposing party's lawyers negotiating the terms of the deal. I revise documents, prepare closing documents, and handle the closing of the deal. The closing occurs when the two parties come together to finalize and sign documents.

A deal reaches its conclusion when I oversee the post-closing work and the transmittal of signed documents."

Commercial finance attorney Neil Goulden works at Heller Financial Inc., in Chicago, where he is the Vice President of Corporate Asset Quality. He was promoted to this position from his position as senior in-house counsel at Heller International, Heller Financial's parent corporation. Heller Financial lends money to businesses; Heller International oversees Heller's financial companies around the world. "'Corporate Asset Quality' is what some other companies call their 'workout' group," Neil explains. "Heller makes loans to such organizations as catalog retailers, heavy tool manufacturers, clothing manufacturers, restaurants, and oil and gas companies. When Heller makes loans that are underperforming, the Corporate Asset Quality group figures out what is going wrong at the borrower's company and how we can best accomplish getting the money we've loaned back. We consider the strategies for 'exiting' the loan. These exit strategies may include liquidation of collateral, whether it's the company's intellectual property, equipment, real estate, inventory, or accounts receivable. Which exit alternatives are best depend on what type of collateral is available and who the other parties are who may have invested in the company. My clients are essentially the business units of Heller from which the loans come and the loan officers of Heller with whom I consult.

"In this practice you have to know the 'game' of lending," continues Neil. "In other words, you have to know what the borrowing company can accomplish in bankruptcy court [*see* the Bankruptcy Law chapter] and what the company can do in terms of borrowing from places other than Heller Financial. Because the companies know the rules, it's a relatively easy game to play. All the parties involved typically know the boundaries and limits. We have an assumption in this business that everyone will act as economically rational beings, and, if they do, things tend to work out. And in fact about 98% ultimately act in a economically rational fashion." Neil says that the 2% who don't act rationally tend to be entrepreneurs or business owners who have a strong emotional stake in their business as well as a financial stake.

What daily activities are involved in banking and commercial finance practice?

Tiziana Tabucchi, a partner at Davis Polk & Wardwell, says, "I spend a huge chunk of the day on the phone. I'm negotiating the terms of documents and helping the clients structure the deals. Usually I represent the lender, and that means I spend time talking with the lawyers representing the borrower. I also spend a great deal of time drafting legal documents on my computer," Tiziana explains. "Today, most of the negotiations involved in deal-making are done over the phone—which I'm on all day long—or via e-mail. As a result, I seldom need to travel."

Farris, Warfield & Kanady attorney Cynthia Sellers tells us that she, too, spends much of her day counseling clients and conducting negotiations via the telephone or by e-mail. "There's really no typical day, but it's fair to say that most of my days involve spending time on the phone or in meetings with clients or in negotiations meetings. I'm also at my desk drafting and reviewing documents." As a partner in her firm, Cynthia plays a role in firm management, as well. "I spend a significant amount of time on firm matters such as client development and management and departmental meetings," she explains.

Neil Goulden of Heller Financial reports that he spends a great deal of time in telephone negotiations, as well. "I'm on the phone or on conference calls or in meetings working on factors involved in our exit strategies. I may work out agreements with the borrowers, work on determining the costs involved in a liquidation, or spend time interviewing the managers of the borrowing company. I would say that about 50% of my discussions are with the borrowers, and the other 50% are with lawyers, accountants, auditors, and outside counsel." Neil's days also include drafting internal reports for Heller as well as letters and memos. "Heller is regulated by the Federal Reserve Bank, so we have a number of standards for internal evaluation," he explains. Neil's job involves frequent travel. "I usually do two or three day trips and one overnight trip per month," he says. "The trips often involve visiting the borrower. For example, if I'm visiting a catalog retailer, I go to the distribution center and actually meet the people who put the retailer's clothing into boxes for shipping. The travel is interesting because I meet a wide range of personalities. Every workout situation in which I'm involved involves its own cast of characters."

What do banking and commercial finance lawyers find rewarding about their practice?

The banking and commercial finance lawyers we talked to enjoy the collaborative nature involved in their work. "I enjoy the challenge of handling complex transactions to the satisfaction of both sides," says Cynthia Sellers. Explains Tiziana Tabucchi, "My work is non-confrontational because everyone has the same goal—completing the deal. I'm working with institutional decision-makers at a high level, and both the borrowers and the lenders have a great deal at stake. All the parties involved make efforts to be accommodating, as it's a good thing for everyone involved to get the deal done."

Neil Goulden says that his job at Heller Financial provides great intellectual challenges. "I like the challenge of taking what looks like a disaster, in which a lot of people are going to lose a lot of money, and turning the situation into one in which no one loses money or in which losses are dramatically minimized."

Neil also enjoys the creative nature of his work. "In my negotiations I have a lot of leeway to structure what will work for a particular client," he explains. "I then do an internal sales job, explaining to Heller why this is the best approach. Though we're working with large sums that may range from $5 million to $30 million, Heller allows me to be creative in my strategies. The executive vice-president or the credit officer of the borrowing company sees our creativity and ends up with a favorable impression of the company even though we are in an exit situation. It's a great creative challenge."

"Banking law is a good fit for me," says Tiziana Tabucchi. "One of the reasons that it's a good fit is that I'm highly organized, and it's work that involves a lot of detail. I enjoy the coordination of activities and people involved in putting together deals. I have good administrative skills, and I get to use them to make the pieces of the deal come together at the right time." Another reason Tiziana says she enjoys banking law is the large percentage of women involved in the field. "I enjoy all the people I work with, but it's especially enjoyable to meet so many women who are clients and who are banking lawyers. They're a great group of people; there's a wonderful sense of collegiality. When I interview female candidates for summer associate positions, I tell them that the large number of women in the field of banking law is a real plus in terms of making this a rewarding practice area."

Tiziana says that another advantage of working in banking law is that the deals she works on have a limited time span, in contrast to litigation work, in which cases may last for years. "There's a lot of turnover in terms of the projects you're working on," she says. "Most of the deals close in six to eight weeks, or, at most, in six months. This means that you're always working on a new project with new people and a new set of relationships."

The Training and Skills Important to Banking and Commercial Finance Law

How do people enter the field of banking law or commercial finance law?

Attorneys who specialize in banking and commercial finance law may begin their legal careers with an eye toward business and finance work. Neil Goulden majored in finance and economics as an undergraduate, and after law school he clerked for a bankruptcy judge. "Clerking for a bankruptcy judge was the best job I ever had. It's such intellectual work. You have the opportunity to think about, discuss, and write about pure legal issues," he comments. The clerkship also helped him become familiar with the issues involved in commercial bankruptcies. Neil then practiced in the finance and reorganization department of a large Chicago law firm for four-and-a-half years before he was hired by Heller.

Other lawyers come to the field of banking and commercial finance in a more roundabout way. Tiziana Tabucchi, who was a literature major as an undergraduate, worked as a summer associate at Davis Polk & Wardwell during law school. "As a summer associate at Davis Polk, you have the opportunity to work in as many different practice areas as you are interested in. My practice group, the banking and credit transactions group, tends to be an area that people either like immediately or don't like at all, as it involves a great deal of detail. I knew it was the right group for me, and I've been in the group since I joined the firm in 1991." Cynthia Sellers became involved in banking law as a result of the firm's needs in the practice group. "I affirmatively chose to practice at Farris Warfield & Kanaday. When I joined the firm, the firm needed lawyers in this area, and that's how I came to practice in this field," she explains.

What skills are most important to banking and commercial finance lawyers?

❖ **Negotiation skills** are important to lawyers who specialize in banking and commercial lending law. "The ability to negotiate successfully is critical, as negotiation is a central part of your work," says Cynthia Sellers.

❖ The **ability to work with details** is particularly important for lawyers specializing in this field. Cynthia Sellers says, "The ability to pay close attention to details is one of the primary skills required of banking lawyers." "There are so many details involved in putting together a deal," adds Tiziana Tabucchi. "To enjoy banking law, you need to enjoy working with details. If detail is not your thing, you won't enjoy this field and you'll find it difficult to be successful in it."

❖ The practice of banking and commercial finance law requires strong **legal drafting skills**. "When you're drafting contracts for these deals, they are contracts that the parties will be bound to for years, and you're likely to continue working with the parties on other matters. When you draft a document, you *have* to get it right, and that requires paying attention to all the details," says Tiziana Tabucchi.

❖ A banking and commercial finance lawyer must also have good **relationship-building skills**. "In my work, I'm dealing with large institutional clients," says Tiziana Tabucchi. "You want those clients to feel comfortable calling on you and relying on you. You want them to like you. You do a lot of deals with the same individuals, so the stronger the relationships you develop, the better. You try to learn how they like things done so that you can better anticipate their needs. You develop an intuitive sense of what is going to work for them and what isn't. Developing such relationships is a big part of my job."

❖ Good **interpersonal communication skills** increase a lawyer's likelihood of success in this field. Neil Goulden's exit strategy work requires him to deal with the owners or managers of companies under financial stress. "There's both money and ego at stake," he explains. "They can be egotistical and difficult to deal with. They are often wealthy graduates of the best schools, and they're in a defensive posture. It takes time to earn their respect." Neil says that being successful requires being comfortable forging relationships with difficult people.

❖ Practicing in this field requires **good business sense**. Says Tiziana Tabucchi, "You intuitively need to know what it's important to get out of the deal. You have to be able to identify the terms of the deal that you must have and the ones on which you're willing to compromise. You also have to be practical. In your negotiations you need to invest your time wisely. You have to do a cost/benefit analysis, making sure that you spend your negotiating time on issues that are likely to arise, as opposed to spending it negotiating on things that theoretically could happen. This is a field in which you earn credibility for being practical." Neil Goulden adds, "You have to think practically and strategically and keep the ultimate goal of the transaction in mind. It's easy to get caught up in all the minutia."

❖ A **knowledge of business** can be helpful to those who plan to practice in banking and commercial transactions law. "In a job like mine, you have to be good at reading financial statements and understanding the numbers," says Neil Goulden. "The people who excel in this work often have accounting experience or experience in credit analysis."

What classes and law school experiences do banking and commercial finance lawyers recommend?

❖ Among the law school classes that can help you prepare for a career in banking and commercial finance law are **business-related classes** such as secured transactions, commercial transactions, bankruptcy, debtor/creditor rights, real estate, corporations, securities, negotiations, and Uniform Commercial Code [Uniform State Laws governing commercial transactions such as banking, securities, and sales of goods] classes. Says Tiziana Tabucchi, "You have to read and know the Uniform Commercial Code. I have a copy in my office and refer to it constantly." Tiziana also recommends a class in legal drafting.

❖ "**Undergraduate business classes in finance or accounting** can be helpful," says Neil Goulden. In addition, most law schools offer an accounting for lawyers class.

❖ Those students who are interested in this field should **gain practical experience** by seeking summer associate positions with firms that have corporate law departments with banks or financial institutions as their clients. "The advantage of working at a large firm," explains Tiziana Tabucchi, "is that such firms have a number of banking clients and a sophisticated specialty in the area. There are some boutique firms that specialize in banking practice, as well, but such firms generally look for lawyers who have experience working in large firms." Many banks and government agencies also offer summer or school year internship experiences.

❖ **Clinical work** can help you develop your skills at working with clients. Find out what types of clinical opportunities your law school offers. Whether the clinic works with indigent clients, immigrants, or battered women, clinical experience allows you to do good while you learn client relations skills, advises Neil Goulden. "Because you're working on real cases, clinical work also helps you learn how to navigate the bureaucracies of the legal system," he adds.

❖ **Working for a judge as a law clerk upon graduation or as a judicial extern while a law student** can help you sharpen your writing skills and gain confidence in your ability to think strategically and to communicate with other lawyers. Says Neil Goulden, "There's no better training for practicing law than working as a judicial law clerk. You sharpen your legal analysis, you learn how to write, you see how people practice, and you watch other lawyers in action. You learn what makes a good lawyer, and you learn how to be persuasive both in speaking and in writing. In addition, you meet wonderful people through your relationship with the judge." Clerks tend to develop strong relationships with the judges for whom they clerk, and those connections last through the years. The relationship he developed with the judge for whom he clerked obviously means a lot to Neil. "I still keep up with Judge Barliant," Neil says with pride and affection. "Working for him was a great, great experience."

❖ Students interested in this field may want to consider **working in a bank or financial institution while in college**. "No matter how lowly the job," advises Tiziana Tabucchi, "it's helpful to work at a bank. You learn how banks fund their loans, and you gain an understanding of the loan process and the banking industry."

❖ **Engage in activities that can help you learn to inspire the confidence of others.** "In banking practice it's important to inspire confidence in your clients. You're judged on your confidence by both clients and the law firm. Clients tend to like lawyers who seem very in charge of themselves and self aware," comments Tiziana Tabucchi, who is active in her firm's hiring process. You might choose to become a leader in a student organization, to participate in bar association activities, or to work as a judicial extern for a judge. Self confidence, Tiziana explains, can help you find your own personal style of negotiating. "When you're negotiating, it's important to stay true to your personality. I'm a pretty casual person. I couldn't replicate some-one else's authoritative or formal style. If you're self-confident, you'll feel comfortable with your own style."

❖   **"Keep up with the latest developments in banking and finance** by reading the *Wall Street Journal*," suggests Tiziana Tabucchi. "Everyone in the financial markets reads it, always, always, *always*. The *Journal* constantly writes about clients, and you want to be sure that you've read what the *Wall Street Journal* says before you get on the phone to your client." Tiziana notes that the *Journal* also does an excellent job of explaining the complex transactions involved in the field, and that law students can learn a great deal about banking law by following the *Journal* daily. "Keeping up with the *New York Times* is also advisable," Tiziana recommends.

BANKING AND COMMERCIAL FINANCE ATTORNEYS
INTERVIEWED FOR THIS SECTION

Neil Goulden
Heller Financial Inc.
Chicago, Illinois
UNDERGRADUATE: Emory University
LAW SCHOOL: Case Western Reserve University School of Law

Cynthia Sellers
Farris, Warfield & Kanaday, PLC
Nashville, Tennessee
UNDERGRADUATE: Meredith College
LAW SCHOOL: University of Tennessee College of Law

Tiziana Tabucchi
Davis Polk & Wardwell
New York, New York
UNDERGRADUATE: Harvard College
LAW SCHOOL: Columbia University Law School

Bankruptcy Law

What is Bankruptcy Law?

The bankruptcy system provides an orderly structure for addressing the inability of an individual or organization to meet its monetary obligations. Whether through liquidation and sale of assets or by restructuring and reorganization to allow an orderly payment of debts, the bankruptcy system governs the obligations and rights of creditors (lenders or others to whom a debt is owed) and debtors (borrowers or recipients of credit, goods, or services). The framers of the U.S. Constitution (Article 1, Section 8) granted Congress the power to establish a uniform bankruptcy law throughout the United States. Bankruptcy law is set forth in the complex federal statutes of the U.S. Bankruptcy Code (Title 11, United States Code) which governs bankruptcy practice. Bankruptcies are processed through the U.S. Bankruptcy Court (part of the federal court system) and cases are appealed to the U.S. District Courts and U.S. Courts of Appeals.

The purpose of the bankruptcy system is to provide overburdened individuals and organizations with an opportunity to resolve and reorder their financial affairs while providing protection for their creditors. In February 1999 the Associated Press reported that more Americans filed for bankruptcy in 1998 than ever before; more than 1.39 million individuals and 44,000 businesses sought protection from creditors in bankruptcy court. Bankruptcy lawyers who represent debtors guide their clients through the statutory framework that provides relief from the lenders to whom their clients are financially indebted. Bankruptcy lawyers who represent creditors attempt to protect their clients' interests by securing the maximum recovery possible from a debtor, whether that debtor is an individual or a business.

The bankruptcy system is intended to be a last resort for individuals or organizations that cannot meet their monetary obligations. Debtors are given a limited opportunity to resolve their financial obligations without resort to the debtors' prisons that were common in England in the days of Charles Dickens (and vividly described in Dickens' novels). However, in order to avoid abuse and overuse of the opportunity the system provides, bankruptcy may only be declared by individuals once every seven years, and bankruptcy of an organization is closely controlled and monitored by the bankruptcy court and trustee (a person appointed by the court to oversee the business involved in the bankruptcy). In opting for reorganization or liquidation, a business is subjected to strict control by the court and trustee and is subject to the intervention of creditors in some daily business decisions.

Some organizations have used bankruptcy as a way to relieve themselves of the burdens of mass tort litigation. For example, Johns-Mansville used bankruptcy to resolve millions of dollars of claims resulting from the sale of asbestos. Similarly, Dow Corning used bankruptcy to provide relief from millions of dollars of potential liability in breast-implant litigation. Texaco sought relief in the bankruptcy system to continue operations in the face of a multibillion dollar verdict in a commercial dispute with Pennzoil. Steel companies and railroads have proceeded through bankruptcy reorganization as a way to manage the large debt owed to unfunded pension plans.

Negotiations Between Debtors and Creditors

Rather than proceed through bankruptcy, lawyers representing the debtor and creditor may try to renegotiate payment terms so that they can be met by the borrower. A renegotiated loan may permit the borrower to repay the debt over an extended period of time (helpful to the borrower in light of his or her ability to pay) but it may require payment at a higher rate of interest (helpful to the lender receiving payment over a longer period of time and at higher risk than anticipated).

Sometimes debtor and creditor negotiations involve a number of creditors who have a financial interest in the transaction. These creditors vary with the transaction—they can include secured creditors (who hold collateral for the loan), unsecured creditors (who do not have an interest in a specific asset of the borrower), and government creditors (including taxing authorities such as the Internal Revenue Service and environmental agencies).

A "workout agreement" avoids the debtor's need to file bankruptcy; such workouts of financially troubled companies are common. Under an "extension agreement," creditors receive full payment of the debt owed, but the debt is paid over time. Under a "composition agreement," creditors agree to receive a percentage of the debt owed. The idea behind a workout is that forgiving the rest of the loan will help the debtor maintain his or her business, yet provide the creditor with a greater return than if the debtor proceeded through bankruptcy.

Reorganization of Debts Under Chapters 11 and 13

The Bankruptcy Code provides several different kinds of protection for debtors. Businesses that are unable to secure a workout agreement may file for Chapter 11 bankruptcy relief in order to reorganize their company. Chapter 11 allows a business in financial trouble to continue to operate and has specific provisions that offer relief for creditors. The business must submit a "reorganization plan" for approval by creditors and then by the U.S. Bankruptcy Court. The bankruptcy trustee, appointed by the court, is represented by counsel. The trustee may oversee the operation of a complicated business reorganization or liquidation. The reorganization plan specifies how the business will restructure its debt. Chapter 11 has offered protection for many large and well-known business entities, as described earlier.

Chapter 13 of the Bankruptcy Code allows individual debtors to reorganize their debts. Debtors repay creditors in installments, in full or in part, over a period of years, without losing their personal assets through liquidation.

Liquidation Under Chapter 7

When restructuring the debt is not an option, Chapter 7 allows individuals and businesses to obtain a "discharge" or release from their debts. Individuals filing under Chapter 7 can keep a limited number of their possessions and assets but must liquidate most of their assets and give the proceeds to creditors. Businesses that file under Chapter 7 must liquidate their assets and cease business operations.

While bankruptcy is governed by federal statute, some states provide limits on what can be seized by the creditor. For example, the state of Florida provides a substantial homeowner's exemption, which permits a once-wealthy homeowner to retain a high-priced mansion even when he or she is forced to liquidate assets. Other states protect personal possessions, such as a car or even a family Bible, from seizure by the creditor.

Some debts cannot be discharged in bankruptcy. For example, student loans are specifically exempted from discharge (a fact recent law school graduates should remember as they write their monthly checks for student loan payments!). Also, fraudulent conveyances, or transfers of money and assets to avoid the reach of the court, can be voided or annulled by the court.

Life as a Bankruptcy Lawyer

Where do bankruptcy lawyers work?

Many bankruptcy lawyers work in private law firms. They represent individual and corporate debtors, individual and corporate creditors, creditors' committees, and bankruptcy trustees. Large and mid-size firms may have departments that specialize in bankruptcy and creditors' rights, and some small firms are bankruptcy "boutiques," in which all members of the firm specialize in bankruptcy.

Other attorneys work at banks, title companies, utilities and corporations, where they may be part of a corporate legal department; they may deal with matters such as bankruptcy issues or creditor/debtor rights issues. The government also employs bankruptcy lawyers. They work for agencies such as the Internal Revenue Service, the Securities and Exchange Commission, the Pension Benefit Guaranty Corporation, and state and municipal tax authorities.

Who are their clients and what types of cases do they work on?

Robert Soriano and John Lamoureux are bankruptcy attorneys at Carlton Fields in Tampa, Florida. Carlton Fields is a large firm, with a commercial bankruptcy/creditors rights department of about 10 attorneys. Robert has nearly 20 years of experience; John has 12 years of experience. Robert explains, "I generally represent lending institutions, mostly large banks. I sometimes represent corporate debtors, and, on rare occasions, individual debtors. In recent years I have represented certain mutual fund companies who purchased bad loans from the FDIC [Federal Deposit Insurance Corporation], the RTC [Resolution Trust Corporation], or banks. The amounts involved in the matters I work on can range from a million dollars to $325 million. Conflicts often arise between the debtors and my clients or between other creditor constituencies (usually unsecured creditors) and my secured creditor clients. When I represent the debtor, it feels like me against the world." John, too, generally represents creditors. "Most of my clients are generally secured creditors, such as banks and insurance companies. These clients are located primarily in large money center cities, and they need to retain local counsel in the jurisdiction of the pending bankruptcy case," he says. Secured creditors, such as banks or financial institutions, generally have an interest in a particular asset of the debtor that was used as collateral for the loan. In contrast, unsecured creditors cannot point to a particular asset of the debtor, and are thus left to receive proceeds from any remaining assets after the payment of the secured creditors.

Shannon O'Toole, a partner at Oppenheimer Wolff & Donnelly LLP, a large firm in Minneapolis, Minnesota, describes herself as "a litigator who works very often with cases in the bankruptcy court or arising out of bankruptcy." Shannon always represents creditors. She often represents indenture trustees—trustees who look out for the interest of small investors who hold notes, bonds, or debentures issued by corporations or municipalities. "For example, I worked on a casino default case. The source of money for building the casino was a public offering, but the casino defaulted on its loan. The indenture trustee sued to work out the best deal for the bondholders." She adds, "All bankruptcy work is in federal court. This has given me wonderful opportunities. I recently argued a case in the D.C. Circuit Court in Washington, D.C. Another case I'm working on involves the standing [jurisdictional right] of the indenture trustee to bring certain claims. That case is in the Fifth Circuit Court of Appeals."

Chicago attorney Paul Gaynor specializes in bankruptcy law at the law firm of Schwartz, Cooper, Greenberger & Krauss. "I represent all types of debtor businesses—including entrepreneurs, national retailers, finance companies, manufacturers, wholesalers, distributors, service organizations, trucking companies, labor unions, and owners of hotels, shopping centers, office buildings, and apartment complexes. I also represent creditors—both secured and unsecured creditors of troubled entities. I help creditors recover pledged collateral, prosecute claims against debtors, and realize their liens or security interests. I assist the creditors in working out payment plans for Chapter 11 debtors. I also represent creditors' committees. In a Chapter 11 bankruptcy involving a business entity, the United States Trustee appoints a committee of seven to nine creditors—often out of thousands of creditors— to look out for the creditors' interests."

What daily activities are involved in bankruptcy law practice?

The bankruptcy attorneys we talked to described a wide range of daily activities. "There's no typical day, thank goodness!" says Paul Gaynor. "Every day unfolds differently. I'm on the phone a lot, and I attend a lot of meetings. The tasks vary with whether I'm representing a debtor or a creditor corporation." Paul notes that a good bankruptcy lawyer has to be familiar with numerous areas of the law. "You really have to be a general practitioner to be an effective bankruptcy lawyer," Paul says. "I feel like bankruptcy law is an umbrella for the practice of every area of law—my practice involves leases, contracts, and loan documents as well as employment issues, tax issues, and financial transactions." Paul also notes that his practice is a blend of transactional work and litigation. "If you draft a plan of reorganization under Chapter 11 for your debtor client, it's a contract with your creditors. If the creditors contest the reorganization, then you find that you're handling a trial." Paul says that he's constantly on the phone, negotiating with the debtor or creditors on the other side of the case. "What you're really doing is arguing about the future rather than fighting about the past. You're trying to create a plan for moving forward, for resolving the issues that arise in the bankruptcy. As a debtor, you're figuring out how to satisfy the obligations to the creditors. You may try to give them stock in the company, or get them to agree to a payment of 10 cents on the dollar, or ask them to accept a percentage of future profits. Whatever the solution, you're trying to move the business forward. And that's a lot of fun," Paul adds.

John Lamoureux told us that his activities also vary day to day. "Often I go through periods where I have a lot of court hearings, and at other times a majority of my time is spent in business meetings or general office work. I generally spend a significant portion of my time at my desk in negotiation on behalf of my clients, responding to inquiries, or drafting and revising pleadings to be filed at court." John adds, "Now that I've practiced 12 years, the amount of research I do in the library has decreased significantly." The bankruptcy-related research at the firm is left to attorneys with less seniority.

Communicating with clients is an important part of a bankruptcy attorney's work, explains Robert Soriano. "There are always telephone conversations discussing case strategies and advising clients on a variety of matters," he reports. Most of Robert's clients are out of state, so he meets with them only occasionally. "We communicate by telephone or through correspondence. Periodically, however, I attend meetings here in Florida or out of state. These meetings tend to be large because they include different constituencies of a bankruptcy case. For example, I often represent bank groups; their meeting will include members of the bank group, perhaps some other advisers to the group (accountants, environmental experts, industry experts, etc.), representatives of the debtor company and its advisers, and sometimes members of a creditors' committee and their advisers." Robert usually attends several court hearings each month. "These hearings can involve long, evidentiary trials; arguing motions on primarily legal grounds when the facts are not in dispute; or merely observing what is occurring in a case." Robert adds that though he's practiced for 20 years, he continues to be a student of the law and works hard to keep abreast of the latest legal developments. "I still spend some time in the library doing research in connection with litigation, with articles and speeches, and as a contributing editor of two treatises. I also keep up with advance sheets and newsletters."

As a bankruptcy litigation attorney, Shannon O'Toole is involved in the myriad tasks that challenge corporate litigators. "Right now, I have a number of cases in the discovery phase," she says. "I compose interrogatories, issue and respond to document requests, and take depositions. I spend time reviewing discovery responses and analyzing how they affect the case. I assess whether the information will motivate my client to move toward settlement. I spend time talking to clients, drafting letters and locating witnesses to the case." As a litigator, Shannon is also in court to argue motions, attend hearings, and conduct trials. (*See* the chapters on Corporate Practice and Civil Litigation for more information on these types of activities.)

What do bankruptcy lawyers find rewarding about their practice?

The bankruptcy attorneys we talked to enjoyed helping their clients solve their business problems. "What's most rewarding," says Paul Gaynor, "is representing a debtor, someone who has been in business 30 years, has run into huge financial problems, and thinks that their life is coming to an end. You help them reorganize their business, and they get a fresh start." Paul adds that he also enjoys the creative aspects of representing debtors. "You have to come up with creative reorganization plans. Representing debtors helps you more effectively represent creditors, because you're better familiar with the debtor's options."

John Lamoureux also enjoys the creative problem-solving involved in bankruptcy practice. "The most satisfying aspect of this job is having a client come in with a problem, and then sitting down with that client to determine how to resolve that problem." He adds, "I enjoy formulating a strategy to accomplish the goal the client and I have set and then executing that strategy successfully for the client."

"It's very satisfying to come into a situation where legal and economic relations between the parties are strained and chaotic and attempt to bring order and resolution to the situation," explains Robert Soriano. In recent years Robert has represented a not-for-profit hospital chain as debtors-in-possession in Chapter 11 bankruptcy cases. "The hospitals were in dire financial straits and at war with not only their creditors but also the local government for the county in which they were located. The hospitals ultimately decided to attempt to impose an involuntary repayment plan on the creditors. The creditors told us we would eventually have to accept their terms (*i.e.*, surrender), but bankruptcy is a great equalizer. The hospitals are now running well, have good relations with the community, and have accumulated approximately $27 million in cash. Their chances for reorganization are excellent. The cases are not yet resolved, but it will be satisfying to have been involved in a situation where the hospitals will be able to continue operating and creditors will be repaid to the greatest extent possible."

Shannon O'Toole says that her bankruptcy-related work has brought her in touch with remarkable people. She explains, "I work with wonderful and bright associates at the firm. They help me along with my cases. I work with high caliber opponents. It's fun to work with—and against—smart, reputable, and conscientious people. This makes the practice of law a lot more fun." Because bankruptcy cases are in federal court, Shannon travels frequently. "Meeting new friends and colleagues is one of the great rewards of travel," she says. "I have met all sorts of interesting people and some really wonderful women attorneys during my travels. One of those women is on the Board of Governors of the American Bar Association. I met her in 1991, when I was doing a bankruptcy in New Orleans, and we've stayed in touch all these years."

Shannon also mentions how much she enjoys the excitement of being in the courtroom. "I love the fast pace of litigation, the thrill of being in court. I love appellate arguments and the requisite back and forth debate with the judges." Shannon also enjoys the intellectual challenge of her practice. "So much preparation is involved in appellate arguments. You look at every case cited by either side and try to find all the pitfalls. You try to anticipate the opponent's arguments, determine which are likely to be strongest, and carefully craft your responses." (*See* the chapter on Appellate Practice for more information on this type of practice.)

The Training and Skills Important to Bankruptcy Law

How do people enter the field of bankruptcy law?

Some attorneys develop an interest in bankruptcy law while law students and decide to pursue the field upon graduation. For these students, the best preparation is clerking for a bankruptcy judge upon graduation from law school. Shannon O'Toole explains that her large Minneapolis firm looks for associates with judicial clerkship experience. "All of our associates in this area of practice clerked for a bankruptcy judge before they came to work for us. This is a crucial stepping stone that we look for when we hire bankruptcy associates."

Students interested in starting out as bankruptcy attorneys can also gain valuable experience by working as a summer associate in a law firm that specializes in the field or a large firm that has a bankruptcy department. "I originally envisioned myself as a corporate lawyer," says John Lamoureux. "After clerking for a summer at a prominent Texas bankruptcy boutique firm, I decided to make a legal career in the field of bankruptcy. I found this area of the law to be business oriented and a practice where parties make decisions based upon sound business rationale."

Other lawyers enter bankruptcy practice once they develop experience in litigation or another field. "I came into this area almost by accident," explains Robert Soriano. "I had clerked for a federal district court judge in New York after graduating from law school and was very impressed by one attorney who was arguing a bankruptcy appeal before my judge. After my clerkship I became a litigator at a firm, but I was approached about an opportunity to go to another firm that had just begun a bankruptcy practice headed up by the lawyer with whom I had been so impressed." Robert further confides, "At the time, I actually viewed bankruptcy as a not very prestigious or interesting area of the law. I was so impressed with the attorney, however, that I decided to work with him. To my delight I found that bankruptcy was a fascinating area, and I was fortunate to learn it from a national expert."

Shannon O'Toole began her legal career as a tax attorney. The firm she worked for assigned her a bankruptcy case. The case culminated in a lawsuit against a Chapter 7 trustee, and Shannon argued the case up through the Eighth Circuit Court of Appeals. Shannon also became involved in the bankruptcy section of the Minnesota State Bar Association. "It's a very small bar, very collegial, and it gave me great exposure. I monitored legislation. I did some pro bono work for debtors." Shannon handled her firm's bankruptcy work while also litigating business and employment cases. By the time she joined Oppenheimer Wolff & Donnelly after five years of practice, she had developed strong litigation skills and acquired a sophisticated knowledge of bankruptcy issues.

What skills are most important to bankruptcy lawyers?

❖ **Negotiation skills** are critical to bankruptcy practice," says John Lamoureux. "I believe that you acquire these skills by actually litigating and trying cases and taking on the responsibility of a case," he adds. Robert Soriano explains why negotiation skills are so important: "In a bankruptcy there is only so much money to go around, and part of the job of the bankruptcy lawyer is to make rational assessments as to who is entitled to what portion of that 'pot' and to convince the parties to accept that portion. In most cases compromise is in the best interests of the parties. Obtaining a compromise sometimes requires convincing not just your adversaries, but also your client, to give in on certain issues. This requires understanding of human nature, the peculiar dynamics of bankruptcy, and the law."

❖ **Creative problem-solving skills** are key to success as a bankruptcy attorney. "Bankruptcy practice involves tremendous creativity," says Paul Gaynor. "You have to figure out economical and easy ways to move the parties from point A to point B. You have to think of creative solutions to people's problems without fighting. Bankruptcy cases should settle. Creative solutions move the parties toward settlement." Robert Soriano agrees on the important role creativity plays in this area of practice. "The skills most important to a bankruptcy lawyer are pragmatism, flexibility, and creativity. I think you learn these skills by experience and by remaining a student of the law, economics, and, especially, human nature," he says.

❖ Bankruptcy attorneys need excellent **writing skills**. "As a bankruptcy lawyer, you do lots of brief and motion writing. You must be clear and persuasive in your writing—whether you're drafting a document or writing to a client," says Shannon O'Toole.

❖ A bankruptcy lawyer needs strong **oral advocacy skills**. "Advocacy skills are important in any area of law, but especially important in bankruptcy law," explains Paul Gaynor. "Bankruptcy is a form of litigation," says Shannon O'Toole. "Bankruptcy attorneys are in court all the time. You need to be comfortable in a courtroom. You have to be comfortable being in front of people."

What classes and law school experiences do bankruptcy lawyers recommend?

❖ Take a **bankruptcy law course**. A basic bankruptcy course will help you determine whether you're truly interested in the field. Your law school may also offer additional courses or seminars in bankruptcy law. **Business law classes** are also helpful, including courses dealing with the Uniform Commercial Code. The lawyers we talked to recommended courses such as tax, accounting, employee benefits, real estate, business organizations, and securities regulations. "Probably the most helpful class for me in preparing for bankruptcy practice was **secured** transactions," says Robert Soriano. "Many of the commercial issues discussed in that course arise in bankruptcy. In fact, most of the current case law in secured transactions is being developed in the bankruptcy courts."

❖ **Moot court** gives students an opportunity to develop strong oral advocacy skills. In moot court competition, students make appellate arguments in front of a team of judges (usually faculty members, experienced practitioners, or local judges). Students must respond extemporaneously to the judges' challenging legal questions. **Trial advocacy** classes, in which students actually conduct a trial, complete with a mock jury, also provide students with an opportunity to sharpen their oral advocacy skills.

❖ Gain practical experience by **working as a summer associate or a law clerk** in a firm that has a bankruptcy practice. Most large firms hire entry-level attorneys through summer associate programs. Smaller firms sometimes hire law clerks that work during the summer or throughout the academic year. Working in a firm can help you determine whether or not you really enjoy bankruptcy practice. "Find an area of practice you like," says Paul Gaynor. "You're going to spend as much time at the office as you are with your family. I'm lucky—I've found an area of law that's very exciting and that lets me use my creativity."

❖ Work as a **judicial clerk for a bankruptcy judge**. While a second year law student, you can apply for judicial clerkships that begin upon graduation from law school. Bankruptcy judges generally hire judicial law clerks, and as Shannon O'Toole mentioned above, this is one of the very best ways to begin a career in bankruptcy law. Large firms often seek entry-level attorneys who have worked for judges.

❖ If your school has a **bankruptcy law clinic**, consider participating. In a clinical setting, you have the opportunity to work with real clients facing the kinds of issues you will encounter in practice. There's no better way to develop client contact skills.

❖ **Become active in bar association activities**. "Get involved in the numerous business law sections of the American Bar Association, the state bar associations, and the American Bankruptcy Institute," advises John Lamoureux. Earlier in this chapter Shannon O'Toole mentioned the "great exposure" her involvement in bar association activities gave her early in her career. Another benefit of involvement in bar association activities? Developing good relationships with the bankruptcy lawyers you meet means that you have people to turn to for advice (and for leads!) in the job search.

❖ **Follow local, national, and international economic developments.** Read newspapers, magazines, and financial journals. "Read the *Wall Street Journal*," advises Robert Soriano. "It will keep you apprised of business developments which drive the bankruptcy practice."

BANKRUPTCY ATTORNEYS INTERVIEWED FOR THIS SECTION

Paul Gaynor
Schwartz, Cooper, Greenberger & Krauss, Chartered
Chicago, Illinois
UNDERGRADUATE: University of Wisconsin-Madison
LAW SCHOOL: Northwestern University School of Law

John Lamoureux
Carlton Fields
Tampa, Florida
UNDERGRADUATE: Fordham University
LAW SCHOOL: Fordham University School of Law

Shannon O'Toole
Oppenheimer Wolff & Donnelly LLP
Minneapolis, Minnesota
UNDERGRADUATE: Colorado College
LAW SCHOOL: University of Minnesota Law School

Robert Soriano
Carlton Fields
Tampa, Florida
UNDERGRADUATE: Rutgers University
LAW SCHOOL: Syracuse University College of Law

Civil Litigation

What is Civil Litigation?

If you talk to successful trial lawyers, they will typically agree that most cases are won or lost before the trial ever begins. It is the pretrial process—in which evidence is gathered, facts and case theories are developed, witnesses are interviewed and deposed, and various motions are filed, argued, and decided by the judge—which occupies the vast majority of the time and effort of civil litigation attorneys (known as "litigators") and has the greatest influence on the outcome of a case or trial.

Litigation involves the process of preparing cases for trial and, if necessary, presenting the case at trial and conducting appeals. Over 90% of all civil cases are settled without having a trial. As an advocate for a client, the litigator must develop the best legal theories possible and gather the facts to support those theories; the litigator's goal is to achieve the best result at trial or a favorable settlement without a trial. Successful litigators typically proceed on the theory that the best settlements are achieved on the strength of the case developed during trial preparation.

Some litigators are generalists who work in diverse areas of the law. Others are specialists in particular practice areas, such as tax, patent, antitrust, labor and employment, and torts. No matter what their specialty area, litigators must have strong oral and written communication skills; must be able to work effectively with their clients, expert witnesses, and opposing counsel;

and must have strong analytical skills that allow them to take creative approaches in representing their client's interest. Because such a large percentage of cases settle, it is also critically important that litigators have excellent negotiation skills.

Investigation and Discovery

The civil litigation process officially starts with the filing and service of a complaint, the statement of the plaintiff's (or aggrieved party's) cause of action and request for relief. The plaintiff usually seeks monetary damages or some type of court intervention. Court interventions can include an injunction prohibiting a certain type of behavior (such as an order that striking airline pilots return to work) or an action (such as an order to prevent the demolition of an architecturally significant building). Long before the official start of the process, however, the parties have typically been involved in negotiations through letters, phone conferences, and meetings to resolve the dispute without resorting to legal action.

Litigation proceedings in federal court are governed by the Federal Rules of Civil Procedure; most state courts have similar rules that govern the actions of the parties and the litigation process. Rule 11 of the Federal Rules of Civil Procedure requires that an attorney make a good faith investigation of the facts before filing a complaint and that the legal theories chosen be well-grounded in both fact and law. Therefore the pre-filing stage of litigation involves extensive investigation, review of documents, and interviews with potential witnesses.

The defendant responds to the plaintiff's complaint in a formal pleading known as an answer. The defendant may also file counterclaims, which are the defendant's own claims or requests for recovery. The parties then engage in a process called discovery.

Written Discovery: Document Requests and Interrogatories

Typically, parties first engage in written discovery. Written discovery includes requests for documents and for written responses to questions (interrogatories) about the matter in dispute. In a commercial litigation case, the parties will seek copies of all correspondence, including letters, memoranda, and even e-mail messages, that relate to the dispute. For example, in the highly publicized antitrust case involving Microsoft Corporation, the government sought copies of literally thousands of internal e-mail messages. In a securities fraud case or a breach of commercial contract case, the written discovery requests may seek to review tens of thousands of pages of documents that include the accounting, sales, and marketing records of the transaction(s) at the core of the dispute.

Interrogatories, an important type of written discovery, are questions to be answered in writing, under oath, by a party in the lawsuit. Interrogatories often seek a written description of a company's organizational structure or its system of accounting and record keeping. In addition they usually seek the details of the other party's contentions of facts or theories of the case. For example, in an action for breach of contract, the defendant may issue interrogatories seeking the details of the alleged contract breach, such as the extent of the economic harm the plaintiff incurred as a result of the breach.

Preparing and responding to written discovery requests such as interrogatories can consume a substantial part of a litigator's time. New attorneys at civil litigation firms or in civil litigation departments of large firms may spend a good portion of their first few years of practice searching for and retrieving documents in response to discovery requests. Successful litigators know that the outcome of a case may depend on their ability to undertake a thorough review of the essential documents and piece together the various threads that will form the fabric of their case.

Oral Discovery: Depositions

Oral discovery involves placing witnesses under oath and obtaining their testimony by deposition. A deposition is a proceeding at which attorneys for each side take turns asking questions of a witness while a court reporter records the questions and answers. Depositions are typically conducted at the attorneys' offices without the presence of a judge. Depositions allow the attorneys to learn the expected testimony of each side's witnesses and enable each side to establish facts under oath and authenticate or explain the details of written documents. Large civil litigation cases which involve numerous parties, such as environmental site clean-up litigation or anticompetitive conduct cases, may require hundreds of depositions that result in tens of thousands of pages of deposition transcripts.

Motion Practice

During the discovery process and before trial, numerous motions are filed before the court in an effort to resolve certain issues or narrow the issues for trial. If a witness refuses to answer questions in a deposition or if a party fails to cooperate in the discovery process, a motion to compel discovery may be filed. In a motion to compel, one party asks the judge to require another party to cooperate with discovery or face sanctions.

Another type of motion that arises as a result of discovery is the motion for summary judgment. In a motion for summary judgment, a defendant argues that, based on the uncontested facts that have been revealed via discovery, the plaintiff is not entitled to prevail on a certain issue as a matter of law. For example, in a breach of contract suit, a party may move for summary judgment on the ground that the plaintiff delayed for too long in bringing the lawsuit. In a product liability suit, a defendant product manufacturer may move for summary judgment on the grounds that it acted in accordance with all of the product warning requirements of the law and therefore the plaintiff is not entitled to any recovery.

Trials

Once the pre-trial tasks are completed, if no settlement has been reached, the case proceeds to trial. This phase and the appeals phase which may follow raise additional issues for attorneys. For example, there are certain requirements that must be met before attorneys can present evidence in a trial. Admission of evidence and witness testimony at trial in federal court are governed by the Federal Rules of Evidence; each state has its own rules regarding evidence and testimony in state courts. Litigators must be very familiar with the rules that govern presentation of evidence and other courtroom behavior.

In addition to state and federal procedural rules, judges may have rules concerning particular behavior within their courtrooms. Many judges have strict prohibitions against inflammatory language or overly-dramatic behavior in the presence of the jury. Some judges even restrict the location from which the attorney must stand and require the attorney to request permission to approach the bench or hand the court clerk a photograph or other exhibit to be shown to the jury.

Appeals

When a trial has reached its conclusion, the verdict or judgment is often subject to an appeal. Part of the challenge in trying a case involves developing a complete record for appeal. Failure of the attorneys to make and renew objections at appropriate times may result in waiving the right to appeal certain rulings. Prompt objections must be made so that the trial court judge can modify or correct a ruling at the time it is made.

Not all rulings and decisions are subject to appeal. Some rulings and determinations, such as credibility of witnesses, are left to the discretion of the trial judge and can only be reversed upon a finding of an abuse of discretion. Other issues are subject to review on standards such as "clearly erroneous" findings or "legal error." The skilled trial lawyer will make sure a complete record is made on all the issues that are necessary for appeal. There are so many nuances involved in appellate practice that some litigation attorneys devote their entire practice to appellate work (*see* the Appellate Practice chapter for more information on appeals and attorneys specializing in appellate work).

Life as a Civil Litigator

Where do civil litigators work?

Most civil litigation attorneys work in law firms. Sometimes they are employed by boutique firms that specialize in a particular type of litigation, such as employment litigation, patent litigation, or business litigation. Other civil litigation attorneys work in the litigation departments of mid-size or large law firms.

While many government attorneys are involved in criminal litigation, some government attorneys work as civil litigators. They may work for federal government offices such as the U.S. Attorneys' offices, for the civil division of a county prosecutor's office, or for a municipality such as the city of San Diego (*see* the Government Practice chapter).

Other civil litigation attorneys work in-house for corporations, insurance companies, financial institutions, and other business entities. Some in-house attorneys handle litigation, while others supervise the litigation work of outside firms hired to do litigation for the organization. (Note that there are several profiles of in-house counsel in the Corporate Law chapter and throughout this book.)

Who are their clients and what types of cases do they work on?

Civil litigation attorneys often represent business entities. "Many of the clients I work with are very large multistate and international corporations, and I represent them in regulatory litigation involving the federal government," explains Anthony Shelley of Miller & Chevalier in Washington, D.C. "These are often companies that have had a long association with the firm. A typical case on which I will work involves judicial review of a federal agency order or regulation. The cases will usually be in federal district court, with an appeal to follow in one of the federal circuits."

As a general litigation and health care partner at Potter Anderson & Corroon LLP in Wilmington, Delaware, Jennifer Gimler Brady works with a wide variety of business clients. "Most of my clients are businesses, both large and small, and several are health care providers. They require a broad range of legal services," she explains.

Joseph G. Eaton is a litigator at Barnes & Thornburg in Indianapolis, Indiana, where he specializes in toxic tort litigation. He says, "A typical toxic tort case involves a claim of personal injury as a result of exposure to chemicals in a residential or occupational setting. The claims include chemical sensitivity, brain damage, immune system dysfunction, neuropsychological impairment, cancer, and birth defects," Joseph explains.

Lisa Schmidt specializes in corporate litigation at Richards, Layton & Finger in Wilmington, Delaware. Her clients are business entities that "range from Fortune 500 companies to smaller privately held companies to local business owners." Adds Lisa, "Their needs can also vary from seeking advice on matters of Delaware corporate law to requiring lead representation in actions filed by stockholders against a corporation in the Delaware Court of Chancery to needing 'local' representation in Delaware proceedings."

Deborah Palmer, a partner at Robins, Kaplan, Miller & Ciresi L.L.P. in Minneapolis, Minnesota, heads the litigation department at her firm. Most of Deborah's cases are large and complex, involving numerous parties. "I've done a little bit of all kinds of litigation, including employment, contractual relations, antitrust, securities fraud, and even patent litigation," she says. Most of Deborah's clients are businesses, such as accounting firms, insurance companies, and publicly held companies, though she also works on suits in which the firm represents individuals.

Maureen Mosh is a litigation attorney and Assistant General Counsel at The Northern Trust Corporation, the Chicago flagship subsidiary of a multi-bank holding company. The Northern Trust's legal department has about 27 attorneys; Maureen and another attorney are the two litigation attorneys in the department. "I work on any litigation in which the bank or any of its affiliates are named as a defendant. This can include real estate cases, breach of fiduciary duties cases, banking cases, securities cases, and employment cases. The only cases I don't handle are tort cases, which are handled by our insurance company." (*See* the Tort Law chapter for more information on tort practice.) Maureen explains that an important part of her job is managing litigation. "When we have to go to court, we hire outside counsel to handle that. I actively manage the work handled by the law firms we hire." Although Maureen's client is always the bank, she works with numerous bank employees in managing litigation. "Generally, I am conferring with senior managers of the bank about litigation issues—whether current or potential litigation."

What daily activities are involved in civil litigation practice?

Like most litigators, Lisa Schmidt says that her activities vary from day to day. "Corporate litigation at our firm has become a truly diverse practice area, and as a result there is no typical day. For example, you could find yourself working with a team of attorneys on an expedited corporate proceeding, drafting a brief in support of a motion for summary judgment, taking a deposition, making an oral argument, or preparing for a trial. It's this variety which makes this practice area challenging and exciting." Lisa recalls a memorable experience early in her career. "At the end of my second year of practice, I returned from my honeymoon expecting to spend my first day back at work going through my mail—instead I found train tickets to Washington, D.C. waiting on my desk. I spent the day participating in a meeting with a new client and 10 months (and several deposition trips) later was sitting second chair in a federal court trial for this same client."

Jennifer Brady also told us that her activities vary widely from one day to the next. "I generally spend several hours each day on the phone with or on behalf of my clients. Sometimes my clients need help on an expedited basis, so I realized early in my practice that any 'plan for the day' must be flexible enough to accommodate emergency research projects. I also spend a good portion of each day drafting letters, pleadings, motions, and briefs."

Anthony Shelley says that as a junior partner at Miller & Chevalier, his duties have changed from what they were as an associate. "My activities have now begun to focus on interfacing with clients and managing cases, rather than simply doing research and writing." Less experienced attorneys are likely to handle most of the research and writing in a large firm. "On a typical day," explains Anthony, "I spend about an hour on the phone with clients or co-counsel or opposing counsel in ongoing cases. I spend four or five hours drafting, reviewing, or editing briefs, other court materials, and legal memos. Two or three hours are spent on fact development or discovery matters in ongoing cases, and I devote an hour or two to firm non-billable work, such as interviewing attorney and summer associate candidates, handling pro bono cases, or business development. I am at my desk most of the day; court appearances are occasional, but not frequent."

For toxic tort litigator Joseph Eaton, "A typical day usually involves managing approximately 50 to 75 toxic tort cases, including negotiating with plaintiffs' counsel, meeting with and conferring with clients, considering strategy with respect to each individual case, and deciding on strategy with respect to future discovery in each case. A large percentage of my time is spent preparing for and taking depositions of plaintiffs and plaintiffs' expert witnesses in toxic tort cases. Like most practice areas, a typical day also involves responding to various crises and emergencies that arise in each case on a day-to-day basis."

Much of Joseph's work on his cases is related to the discovery process. "We typically conduct affirmative discovery [discovery requests directed to the plaintiff or plaintiffs] relating to the alleged exposure, employment history, medical history, lost wages, and liability theories, and we depose the plaintiff. We also conduct extensive research on the plaintiff's expert witnesses and then depose them regarding their opinions. Once we have obtained the opinions from the plaintiff's expert witnesses, we retain our own expert witnesses and prepare motions to exclude the plaintiff's experts based on their failure to comply with the standards for admissibility."

Joseph knows firsthand the powerful role discovery plays in civil litigation cases. He recalls a situation where effective discovery resulted in a favorable settlement for his client. "In a case involving claims of immune dysfunction, we obtained copies of deposition and trial transcripts where a plaintiff's expert stated that he had passed the examination for the board of internal medicine on the first try. We requested and received copies of the examination records from the relevant medical board and discovered that the expert had in fact taken the examination on five occasions and failed on every occasion. More significantly, the expert received a letter from the board indicating that one of the areas he was deficient in was immunology. This information was extremely helpful during the deposition regarding the expert's prior testimony and his qualifications relating to immunology, and it was not well received by the expert. The case settled after the expert's deposition."

As manager of the litigation department of her firm, Deborah Palmer says that 25-30% of her time is spent on administrative matters. "We have five litigation groups with a total of over 100 litigators," she says. "I keep an eye on the costs involved in the practice—where the money is going, how the attorneys' billable hours look, what billing rates to charge—as well as deciding which lawyers get to handle which cases. I have a special interest in our young lawyers and when assigning work I try to even out the case load and the experience level and make sure that even the least experienced attorneys are working on interesting and challenging matters." Much of Deborah's work involves working on the matters that every litigation attorney handles. "After 25 years of experience as a litigator, I know that the best partners have a hands-on approach. They're the partners who carry the boxes into the courtroom, review the documents involved in discovery, draft motions and briefs, and take the discovery depositions."

Deborah goes on to explain the role that less experienced lawyers play. "Much of our legal research is handled by attorneys who recently graduated from law school. They're the attorneys who are most effective when it comes to research; they get the correct answer in the most efficient way." Deborah says that new associates also participate in such activities as brief writing. "Though I still do a lot of brief writing, I also edit what younger lawyers write. Associates, even first year associates, usually write the first drafts of briefs."

In addition to writing and editing, Deborah spends time preparing witnesses for depositions and taking depositions. "I work on huge cases that go on for years and years before they are tried; many of the cases ultimately settle. I don't get into the courtroom except on motion practice. I travel in spurts, depending on where the client is located and what court has jurisdiction over the case."

As an in-house litigator, Maureen Mosh spends much of her time working with bank employees. "I'm constantly fielding questions from people inside the bank who are managing potential problems. I also work closely with the outside counsel who are handling litigation for the bank on matters such as strategy and day-to-day defense issues. I spend a lot of time on the phone with outside counsel, and I edit the writing done by outside counsel. I'm also involved in litigation prevention, as my job involves risk management as well as litigation management. I make presentations to people at the bank advising them how to prevent litigation." Maureen also prepares a number of written reports for the bank. "I prepare reports for auditors and members of the board of directors of the bank, and I keep bank management apprised of the status of all litigation."

What do civil litigators find rewarding about their practice?

Litigation attorneys report that they enjoy the relationships they develop through their work as litigators. They find satisfaction in their work advising clients. "The most personally rewarding aspect of my job," comments Jennifer Brady, "is client counseling. I get great satisfaction out of helping clients avoid problems." Lisa Schmidt agrees. "Although the most professionally challenging cases often involve the firm's larger clients, the most personally rewarding cases are those involving the smaller local clients. In those cases, the outcome usually has a greater impact on the individual or individuals with whom you are working," says Lisa.

Toxic tort litigator Joseph Eaton says that he develops close relationships with both clients and expert witnesses. "The aspect of my practice which I find to be the most personally rewarding is the relationships that I have developed with clients and expert witnesses across the country," he says. "Clients have come to rely on the expertise we have developed in this area and are genuinely appreciative of our efforts on their behalf. Also, the focus of most toxic tort litigation is on expert witnesses; we have developed a database which contains information on more than 200 expert witnesses and have developed ongoing relationships with various experts from across the country."

As the head of the litigation department at her firm, Deborah Palmer finds reward in the working relationships she develops with the firm's young attorneys. "That's what I enjoy most about my work. I love to see the young lawyers come in as new associates, watch them grow in their experience and expertise, and then see them become my partners." When we talked to her, Deborah explained that the firm had just named a new group of partners from the ranks of their associates. "Sometimes a new attorney will have a rocky start, but then grow and develop as a lawyer under the guidance my partners and I are able to provide. There's nothing so exciting as seeing a young lawyer become a partner!"

"This is the best job I've ever had," Maureen Mosh says emphatically of her position as a bank litigation manager. "I like being part of a team effort to resolve the bank's problems. I like the people I work with because they're very intelligent and highly responsible. The people at the bank really appreciate the advice you give them. They see me as part of the team—as someone who is on their side."

Anthony Shelley likes the intellectual challenge of his job as a litigator. "I get the most pleasure from my job when I am writing briefs on complex issues. It is always satisfying to win a case and, in the opinion, see your brief adopted in large measure by the court."

Deborah Palmer notes that litigation offers an attorney the unparalleled opportunity to learn about different industries. "I have the opportunity to learn about different industries, whether the aluminum business or the wine business. I have the chance to learn how accounting firms operate and how a certain chemical product is made in a small town in Japan or how semiconductors work." Deborah's interest in business and industry is longstanding. "I remember having lunch with a partner when I was a new associate. He told me about a case he was working on that involved the construction of a warehouse with cement blocks. He went on to explain, in detail, how cement blocks were manufactured. I was impressed that the partner knew so much about the manufacturing process. I remember thinking, 'How on earth did he ever learn that?'"

The Training and Skills Important to the Civil Litigator

How do people enter the field of civil litigation?

"I knew in law school that I wanted to be a litigator," says Jennifer Brady. Like Jennifer, many law students decide that litigation is the right specialty for them as a result of their first year law school class in civil litigation, their interest in legal writing and research, or their experience in moot court.

Most law firms hire litigators directly out of law school. Explains large firm attorney Deborah Palmer, "We mainly hire through our summer associate program. New attorneys have worked as a summer associate for our firm or have worked for a year or two as a federal judicial law clerk. For our litigation department, we hire students interested in litigation. Students don't need to know exactly what type of litigation they're interested in, but it's helpful if they have some idea. Are they interested in business or technology or medical malpractice? The most important thing is to have an interest in litigation and in civil procedure. The large cases we work on involve a lot of procedure—a lot of pre-trial maneuvering—before the attorneys see the courtroom."

Joseph Eaton began his career as a litigator immediately after graduating from law school. "I started working in toxic tort litigation when I first started at the firm and have enjoyed the interaction with clients and the first chair responsibility at an early stage in my career. The opportunity to conduct plaintiff and expert witness depositions on a regular basis and participate in hearings and trials influenced my decision to pursue this area of practice."

If you are interested in working as an in-house litigator in a corporation, it's generally important to gain litigation experience in a law firm first. "You have to build your career in the direction of becoming an in-house attorney," advises Maureen Mosh. "I had 12 years of litigation experience at a large firm before I came to the bank," she explains. "It's important to develop a good record in a particular practice area, such as litigation, before you seek to move those skills to an in-house position in a corporation."

What skills are most important to civil litigators?

❖ Civil litigators agree that strong **writing skills** are critical to success in the field. "Good writing is the most important skill. I chose to go to law school because I thought that the legal profession would offer substantial writing opportunities. I have not been disappointed," says Anthony Shelley. Deborah Palmer agrees that writing is key. "Motion practice is a big part of cases," she explains. "In large, multimillion dollar cases, the parties often bring all motions possible. There's a lot of writing involved."

❖ **Oral advocacy skills** are also important to the litigator. "Oral advocacy skills are essential in this practice area," says Lisa Schmidt. "I acquired these skills in law school, but I continue to refine them through working with more experienced attorneys." Though it may be a while until recent graduates try a case, they may be called upon to go to court to argue a motion that they've written. "It's my position that the person who writes the motion and the brief supporting it should argue it. If it's an associate who wrote the brief, they should argue it where possible, as they know the arguments best," says senior litigation attorney Deborah Palmer.

❖ Because so many cases ultimately settle, **negotiation skills** are very important. "There are many skills important to litigation, but of particular relevance is the ability to be an advocate for your client while negotiating with plaintiff's counsel, whether in the deposition of a witness or at trial," notes Joseph Eaton. "Negotiation skills are extremely important in this practice area," agrees Jennifer Brady. "Many legal problems can be avoided or minimized through negotiation and diplomacy. Although it may sound trite, the best way to acquire negotiation skills is through experience—yours and others'. Take advantage of opportunities to observe the negotiation methods of other lawyers—you will quickly learn what works and what doesn't."

❖ Litigators need to be **detail-oriented**. "Litigators need to be able to apply details to the big picture," says Deborah Palmer. "In complex litigation details are very important. For example, if you're looking at a business litigation case in which a company is being sued by a distributor, it helps if the attorney on the case can pick up on the details of what happened in the company's other relationships with distributors. An attorney should be able to look at all those details and see how they fit in the big picture of the case." Maureen Mosh agrees, commenting, "The ideal litigator pays attention to the details and minds the store— yet never loses sight of the big picture. Just being a big-picture person isn't enough. You have to mind the details."

❖ Because litigators are often working closely with their clients, expert witnesses, and other attorneys, they must be **skilled at working with people**. Explains Joseph Eaton, "The cases we work on require daily contact with clients, expert witnesses, and plaintiff's counsel. All of my experiences in dealing with people in various situations have been invaluable to my litigation practice."

What classes and law school experiences do civil litigators recommend?

❖ Take **civil procedure and evidence classes** in law school. Beyond those classes, take **classes related to the areas of litigation in which you're interested**. "A basic corporations class is helpful, especially if you specialize in corporate litigation," notes corporate litigator Lisa Schmidt. Because litigation clients are often business organizations, a corporations class can be great preparation for any type of litigation in which you're interested. Joseph Eaton advises students interested in toxic tort litigation to take classes relating to complex litigation and environmental law. And Anthony Shelley believes that most aspiring litigators will benefit from administrative law, federal courts, and federal jurisdiction.

❖ A **negotiations class** in law school can help you prepare for the constant negotiation you're involved in as a litigator. Explains Maureen Mosh, "A negotiations class helps you look at litigation in a new way. You see beyond the 'winning the war' aspect of litigation and see the other creative ways to obtain results."

❖ A **wide range of undergraduate liberal arts classes** can be helpful in preparing for your career as a civil litigator. Says Anthony Shelley, "If you want to be a litigator, the preparation starts, in my view, with a strong background in literature and writing classes." "Law school can be very narrow in focus," says Deborah Palmer. "Having some breadth to your undergraduate education gives you a better outlook on life. It helps you better understand people and how they interact and it gives you a historical perspective on things." Deborah's undergraduate degree was in economics, but she also studied music. "Music has been a marvelous background for being a lawyer. Students do better in classes and learn more in classes when they study subjects in which they're interested," she observes.

❖ A basic **accounting class**, whether at the undergraduate level or at law school, can be useful training for any litigator. No matter what your specialty within litigation, monetary damages are frequently a hotly contested issue. "You need to know how to read a balance sheet," says Deborah Palmer.

❖ Strengthen your legal writing skills through **writing classes** and advanced law school seminars that require writing papers. "No litigator can be successful without the ability to communicate effectively orally and in written form," says Anthony Shelley. Participating in your school's **law review or entering a writing competition** can also provide excellent writing experience, as well as providing an opportunity to develop an excellent writing sample for interviews.

❖ **Moot court** gives students a chance to hone their courtroom skills. Students enrolled in moot court write appellate briefs and argue their position in front of a panel of judges. "Moot court gives you a chance to actually practice litigation skills," says Maureen Mosh. **Trial advocacy classes** can also help sharpen your oral advocacy skills. In trial advocacy, students prepare and then try a case in front of a mock jury. "Any courses that build litigation skills are very helpful," says Maureen. Adds Jennifer Brady, "Trial and appellate advocacy courses are valuable, as they provide an opportunity for law students to develop useful litigation skills before entering the 'real world.'"

❖ Gain practical experience by becoming involved in your **law school's clinical programs**. Clinical programs allow you to work on real cases, with real clients, under the supervision of a professor. "When we hire, I like to see that someone has an idea of what litigation practice is all about," says Deborah Palmer. "A good clinical program can show you what litigation is all about. It can help you see what going to court is like and what navigating the system requires."

❖ Another way to gain experience is to seek a **summer associate position** at a law firm specializing in litigation or at a law firm with a litigation department. As a summer associate working on litigation matters, you'll gain an insider's view of the litigation process. This is the best way to determine whether litigation is for you. Explains toxic tort litigator Joseph Eaton, "The best way to develop contacts in this practice area is to seek out a law firm which specializes in toxic tort litigation or related areas and pursue every opportunity you can to become actively involved in the cases." Explains Deborah Palmer, "When we hire, I look for someone who has an interest in our firm, an interest in the practice, and an interest in life. I look at the summer associate positions as a 10-week interview for an associate position. We're only going to make a certain number of offers for associate attorney positions. We're naturally predisposed to someone who acts like they are really interested in our firm and our practice."

❖ Investigate **federal judicial clerkship** opportunities. Many federal judges hire recent law school graduates to work as law clerks for a period of one to two years following graduation. Working as a judicial law clerk gives future litigators a chance to see litigation from the bench's point of view, an extraordinarily valuable opportunity. Deborah Palmer points out that an additional benefit of working as a judicial law clerk is the contacts you make. "They're contacts that last a long time and that you'll find helpful in practice."

❖ It's never too early to **develop contacts** within the litigation field. Even as a law student, you can participate in bar association activities. "Join and participate in local and national bar associations such as the American Bar Association," advises Jennifer Brady. Jennifer also suggests keeping an organized list of professional contacts. "Develop a contact list that includes the person's name, company or firm affiliation, address, phone number, and a brief description of the person's position or background." Anthony Shelley reminds students that their law school class is a great place to begin developing contacts. "Keep in touch with your law school classmates," he suggests. "They can be, in the long run, a very good source, not only for friendship, but for contacts and referrals."

CIVIL LITIGATION ATTORNEYS INTERVIEWED FOR THIS SECTION

Jennifer Gimler Brady
Potter Anderson & Corroon LLP
Wilmington, Delaware
UNDERGRADUATE: The College of William & Mary
LAW SCHOOL: Dickinson School of Law of the Pennsylvania State University

Joseph G. Eaton
Barnes & Thornburg
Indianapolis, Indiana
UNDERGRADUATE: Butler University
LAW SCHOOL: Indiana University School of Law-Indianapolis

Maureen Mosh
The Northern Trust Corporation
Chicago, Illinois
UNDERGRADUATE: Kean University
LAW SCHOOL: University of Chicago Law School

Deborah Palmer
Robins, Kaplan, Miller & Ciresi L.L.P.
Minneapolis, Minnesota
UNDERGRADUATE: Carleton College
LAW SCHOOL: Northwestern University School of Law

Lisa Schmidt
Richards, Layton & Finger, P.A.
Wilmington, Delaware
UNDERGRADUATE: Drew University
LAW SCHOOL: Dickinson School of Law of the Pennsylvania State University

Anthony Shelley
Miller & Chevalier, Chartered
Washington, D.C.
UNDERGRADUATE: Canisius College
LAW SCHOOL: Harvard Law School

Corporate Practice

What is Corporate Law?

Whether negotiating the acquisition of a multibillion dollar company or assisting a small Internet start-up company, corporate lawyers are involved in advising businesses on their numerous legal rights, responsibilities, and obligations. General corporate practice involves handling a wide range of legal issues for businesses.

Many corporate lawyers work in law firms, particularly large or mid-size firms, where they counsel clients and handle business transactions including negotiation, drafting, and review of contracts and other agreements associated with the activities of the business, such as mergers, acquisitions, and divestitures; they also advise business clients on corporate governance and operations issues such as the rights and responsibilities of corporate directors and officers and the general oversight of the legal activities of the company. In addition, corporate attorneys assist business clients with the financial information they must provide to their owners, employees, and shareholders, including reports that must be filed with the Securities and Exchange Commission (SEC) and other government agencies.

Other corporate lawyers are employed directly by corporations as in-house corporate counsel. In-house counsel act as internal advisers on myriad business and legal issues, including labor and employment issues, intellectual property issues, contractual issues, and liability issues.

Counseling Publicly Held Companies

One role of a corporate lawyer is counseling publicly held companies. A publicly held company is a company with shares of stock that are traded on public stock exchanges like the New York Stock Exchange. Shares of stock represent an investment in a business; members of the public who own stock thus have an ownership stake in the business. Corporate lawyers must be familiar with many state and federal securities laws that govern publicly traded securities. They assist publicly held companies with matters regarding the issuance of securities as well as the detailed reporting requirements of state and federal agencies such as the SEC.

Public companies are held to strict standards with regard to disclosure of information that may have either a positive or adverse material effect on earnings and may therefore affect the price of their stock. Thus corporate lawyers advise publicly held companies with regard to issues such as the public disclosure of disappointing financial results, an adverse judgment in a litigation matter, or the initiation of a government investigation regarding the company. The company may, for example, need to advise the public about an impending product recall, litigation that has been initiated due to an environmental problem, or an unfunded pension liability.

Corporate lawyers also advise their clients on issues concerning trade secrets and other types of intellectual property such as patent and trademark licensing (*see* the Intellectual Property Law chapter); antitrust issues (*see* the Antitrust Law chapter); international transactions such as the acquisition of foreign businesses or real estate (*see* the International Law chapter); and contractual matters such as technical assistance agreements between the company and outside consultants hired to provide computer and other information technology assistance.

Counseling Privately Held Businesses

Corporate lawyers also counsel privately held businesses, in which the stock or ownership is "closely held," meaning that it is owned by a limited number of shareholders, with none of the stock being traded on a public stock exchange. A large number of companies are privately held and may be structured as corporations or partnerships. Some large corporations are privately held, as are many investment banking firms, accounting firms, Internet start-ups, hospitals, churches and other religious institutions, medical practices, and family businesses. Not-for-profit organizations and foundations, such as professional and trade associations and charitable organizations, may also be privately held.

Closely held companies or organizations have many legal needs and represent an increasingly larger share of corporate lawyers' clients. Corporate lawyers provide advice on issues such as creating the company (the "start-up"); obtaining loans and lines of credit or venture capital money; obtaining office space; hiring, firing, and treatment of employees; instituting financial controls over the operation of the business; merging with and acquiring other businesses; divesting, or selling off parts of the company; and selling the ownership interest to a single company (buyout). Privately held companies also seek advice on the formulation and enforcement of contracts, on tax matters, and even on succession issues, in which attorneys help plan for the orderly transfer of ownership or management to the next generation of owners.

Business Start-Ups and Joint Ventures

New businesses are typically faced with numerous business decisions, including whether to structure the business as a corporation, a partnership, a limited liability company, a sole proprietorship, or even as a joint venture (a partnership arrangement with an established company). Determining the appropriate business structure requires a thorough analysis of how to raise initial capital; how to finance the business; the implications of federal and state tax requirements; and how to limit liability for the stakeholders. As part of determining how to structure the business, corporate attorneys also assist the start-up venture with matters such as developing a business plan and finding sources of financing.

Some corporate lawyers specialize in the area of providing advice on new business ventures. These corporate lawyers often work closely with investment bankers and venture capitalists. Business owners with an idea or business plan usually need "seed money" or some type of financing to pay for equipment, employees, supplies, and other materials until a product is finally sold and revenue is generated. Venture capitalists are typically looking to find the next Microsoft, Yahoo!, or Amazon.com in which to invest and eventually cash out when the company is taken public. However, acceptance of seed money often comes with a price—the business owner must typically cede control to the financiers.

Mergers, Acquisitions, and Divestitures

Most chief executive officers of public companies (and even privately held companies) are under pressure from their shareholders to grow the business and thereby increase earnings and revenues and, hopefully, the price of the stock. Often the easiest way to expand manufacturing capacity, add a new product line, or expand market share is through merging with or acquiring another business. Similarly, business units may be divested, or sold, as a result of poor performance or because the company decides to focus on a different product strategy. For these reasons corporations are often involved in merging with other businesses, acquiring other businesses, or divesting portions of the existing business. Corporate lawyers assist their clients with the appropriate financing for mergers and acquisitions and provide advice concerning the drafting, negotiation, and performance of contracts for the sale of portions of the business.

In acquisitions the corporate lawyer participates in "due diligence" checks concerning the company that is to be acquired in the transaction. This means that the attorney reviews the company finances, employee agreements, intellectual property, environmental liabilities, real estate leases, and pending litigation involving the company and then advises the buyer or seller about these risks. Attorneys are also involved in structuring the deal. They help the entity determine what portion of the company will be sold and whether the sale will be structured as a sale of the company's assets or a sale of the stock of the company. They may draft non-compete agreements stipulating that the seller cannot immediately compete with the buyer's newly acquired business. They may assist with matters such as the transfer of technology and intellectual property licenses from one entity to another.

In-House Corporate Counsel

Lawyers who work as corporate in-house counsel advise their companies on a wide range of legal and business issues. In fact large corporations may have full departments of in-house lawyers. A large pharmaceutical company, for example, may have in-house counsel who specialize in litigation, health and safety issues, intellectual property issues, labor and employment issues, regulatory issues, and general corporate issues. These lawyers provide advice on legal as well as business issues relating to the activities of the company.

Besides those in-house attorneys profiled in this chapter, there are several other corporate in-house counsel featured throughout this book. Following is a list of in-house corporate counsel profiled in other chapters:

Admiralty and Maritime Law — Arthur Mead (Crowley Maritime Corporation)

Banking and Commercial Finance Practice — Neil Goulden (Heller Financial Inc.)

Civil Litigation — Maureen Mosh (The Northern Trust Corporation)

Entertainment and Sports Law — Nancy Rinehart (Unapix/Miramar)

Health Care Law — Susan Blackwell May (American Health Network); Suzanne Mitchell (PennState Geisinger Health System); Kim Otte (Allina Health Systems)

Insurance Law — M. Lauretta Barreca (American Continental Insurance Company); Donna Rosemeyer (Allstate Insurance Company); Ann Triebsch (Anthem Blue Cross & Blue Shield)

International Law — Arthur Acevedo (McDonald's Corporation)

Telecommunications Law — Maria Arias-Chapleau (AT&T)

Trusts & Estates Law — Jennifer Johnson Rahn (Bank One)

Life as a Corporate Lawyer

Where do corporate lawyers work?

Most corporate lawyers work in law firms, often in large or mid-size firms that have corporate law departments. Corporate law departments may include attorneys with subspecialties, such as mergers and acquisitions work or venture capital work.

Corporations of all types, from insurance companies to airlines to manufacturers, often hire in-house counsel, with large corporations generally having a larger number of in-house counsel than smaller companies. A limited number of attorneys who specialize in corporate work, particularly securities work, work for the government, most often for agencies such as the Securities and Exchange Commission.

Who are their clients and what types of cases do they work on?

Lisa Maloney is a corporate attorney at Ballard Spahr Andrews & Ingersoll, LLP in Philadelphia, Pennsylvania. "A large percentage of my work involves representing financial institutions; the remainder involves representing various kinds of corporations. Except in my pro bono work [see the Public Interest Law chapter for a definition of pro bono work], I rarely represent individuals. I spend most of my time drafting and revising various agreements, talking to and meeting with clients, and negotiating with opposing counsel. Most of my time is spent in my office or in the offices of opposing counsel," she explains.

Corporate attorney Anne Falvey specializes in project finance work at Kelley Drye & Warren LLP in New York City. "My clients are typically project finance sponsors who specialize in developing infrastructure projects throughout the world," says Anne. "For example, I might represent a power project developer in all aspects of the development, construction, financing, and operation of a project, whether in the United States or elsewhere."

Like Anne, Audrey Roth is also a corporate lawyer at Kelley Drye & Warren in New York. Audrey, however, specializes in working with venture capital funds and emerging growth companies. "My clients range from entrepreneurs in the process of raising funds to start their businesses to multimillion dollar venture capital funds looking to make investments, raise funds, or liquidate their holdings in various portfolio companies," Audrey explains. "The needs of the entrepreneurs are quite varied—from employment issues to intellectual property issues to financing strategies to strategic alliances to the more mundane contract work."

Los Angeles attorney Janis Salin specializes in mergers and acquisitions in the corporate law department of Riordan & McKinzie. Janis says that most of her clients are corporations in the service businesses. "This includes environmental consulting and engineering firms, merchandisers, and product distributors," she explains. "Almost all my clients are based in California and most are located in the greater Los Angeles area." Janis assists her firm's clients with a wide range of matters. "I provide these clients with advice concerning the issuance of securities; the acquisition of other businesses; securing public and private financing; executive compensation matters; and contracts."

Neil Reisman is Assistant General Counsel and Assistant Secretary for Burns International Services Corporation in Chicago. Burns International is North America's largest provider of physical (guard) security and related services. As an in-house attorney, Neil's clients are Burns International's employees. "My clients are essentially everyone in the company, from the chief executive officer down. I advise them on a range of legal issues; I have to be a generalist. I have to be prepared to work on any legal matters in which the company is involved, from corporate issues to finance issues to litigation management to executive compensation," Neil explains. "When you're in a fairly small law department of a corporation, you have to be a generalist. In our Chicago office there are two lawyers, including myself. There are five attorneys at our company's main subsidiary in New Jersey."

In-house corporate attorney John Dirks works in the corporate law department of State Farm Mutual Automobile Insurance Company in Bloomington, Illinois, which, as a national insurance company, is owned by its policyholders. "For the in-house counsel, the client is the corporation. At an insurance company this would include the underwriters and the actuaries and the claims specialists who need assistance with legal issues." Much of John's work involves advising State Farm concerning contractual matters. "The company enters into contracts for many different products and services. We're heavy users of computer software and hardware, and the majority of contracts the company enters into are for computer products, from hardware and software to computer maintenance and training. When you're advising the company about these contracts, you consider all the risks, all the possible pitfalls, and then draft the contracts accordingly." John says that it's the purchasing department's responsibility to handle negotiating the contracts. "I develop and review the contracts, which can involve significant dollars."

Before working on in-house transactional issues, John worked on the insurance side of State Farm's legal department. "As an in-house counsel working on the insurance side of the business, I worked mainly on regulatory issues related to insurance. The insurance industry is highly regulated and requires extensive filings with state departments of insurance. I worked with the actuaries to prepare rate filings and represented the company at hearings before the state departments of insurance. In that capacity I also advised with respect to the statutory interpretation of insurance regulations and laws." (*See* the Insurance Law chapter for more information on this type of practice.)

What daily activities are involved in corporate law practice?

Lisa Maloney finds that each day brings an array of challenges. "Every day and every deal is different," she says. "In a loan transaction, you first must review and analyze the term sheet [which defines the terms of the loan]. Then you prepare the agreement and ancillary documents, negotiate the terms, and prepare for and attend the closing of the deal. In a merger or acquisition, the documents have different names but the process is basically the same. Although it may sound rather uneventful, the process almost never runs smoothly." Lisa comments that it's the unpredictable nature of every deal that makes each day an adventure.

Anne Falvey says that as a project finance specialist, she takes on a role in the early stages of the development of the project. "My work includes everything from formation of a project entity to drafting power purchase agreements and construction contracts to negotiating the terms of financing with project lenders and/or equity participants," explains Anne. "Most of my work is done from my office. I talk with clients on the phone, review and draft correspondence and documents, read industry publications, and occasionally I do a bit of legal research."

Mergers and acquisitions attorney Janis Salin explains her role: "An acquisition transaction begins with conferences with the client to draft a letter of intent that contains the basic terms of the purchase. This letter of intent serves as a basis for drafting the definitive agreement. The attorneys at the firm also perform 'due diligence.' Due diligence essentially involves reviewing the acquired company's agreements, books, and records, as well as completing the required antitrust compliance [filings with the Department of Justice and the Federal Trade Commission which disclose information about the businesses of the acquiring and acquired companies]. After drafting the definitive agreement, I assist the client with the negotiations concerning the terms of the agreement, including the representations and warranties to be made by the acquired company, the conditions to closing, and the indemnification provisions. I also assist the client with the legal work necessary to procure financing to fund the transaction. Prior to closing the transaction, we prepare the documents required to satisfy the closing conditions, which typically include the board of directors and shareholders resolutions, officers' certificates, and legal opinions."

Janis says that most of her day is spent within the confines of her office. "I'm on the phone with clients or preparing documents in connection with the transactions on which I am working." She also spends time with lawyers in other departments of the law firm. "I consult quite often with attorneys in the firm who practice in the litigation, intellectual property, real estate, and tax departments of the firm. These attorneys assist me in providing a full range of services for our clients," Janis says. Such a team approach to providing legal services for clients is common in large law firms.

Janis, who has practiced law since 1979, can recount numerous stories about the intensive work required before a deal closes. For example, "In 1986 Congress enacted substantial changes to the tax laws which were scheduled to take effect January 1, 1987. Our firm served as counsel on several deals which had to close by the year end to take advantage of the then-existing tax laws. Since our firm is based in Los Angeles and most of these closings were scheduled to occur in New York, many of the attorneys in our corporate department spent the two or three weeks preceding Christmas in New York City negotiating, documenting, and closing one deal after another. Thinking that I would be home well in advance of Christmas, I convinced my husband not to begin decorating our Christmas tree, as I wanted to participate in the festivities with him and the children. However, the last deal I was working on did not close until 11:00 a.m. on Christmas Eve. Flying home that evening, I realized that many of the people on the plane were lawyers from our 'team' and our clients. Our families met us at the airport late on Christmas Eve. We made it home for Christmas—but just barely."

Anne Falvey recalls a similar experience—spending Thanksgiving Day at the firm. "My most memorable meal as a lawyer," she says, "was the Thanksgiving dinner I shared with clients in a conference room. We were there on Thanksgiving attempting to get the transaction to close. That night the clients slept on the floor underneath the same conference room table where we shared our Thanksgiving dinner."

As an attorney servicing venture capital funds and emerging growth companies, Audrey Roth assists her clients with all types of transactions. "A typical transaction for an entrepreneur or a venture capitalist would be the offering and sale of the company's securities to institutional investors in a private offering. The offering might range from a seed financing in the one to two million dollar range to a late-stage financing of $20-40 million. Issues that arise most often in these transactions include ownership of intellectual property, protective provisions [which typically provide protections for the investors], and veto rights [the question of which party makes final decisions]." Audrey reports that she puts in long, but satisfying, days. "On any given day (which frequently stretches long into the night), I spend much of the day speaking on the telephone with clients and opposing counsel, engaged in negotiating transactions, troubleshooting, and advising and counseling clients. As a partner I also spend a significant part of the day training the associates who work with me on client matters."

Audrey's days may be long, but they're never boring. With good humor, she recounts a particularly memorable experience. "I once spent an 18-hour day traveling from New York to St. Louis to negotiate a deal. On the airplane ride, the clients gave me information that required a change in the structure we had carefully constructed with the other side over weeks of negotiations. I felt that I couldn't endanger the deal by leaving the clients alone with the opposition in our meeting room. Unfortunately *nobody* called for a break in the meeting, so I was unable to escape, even to use the restroom—thereby personally proving Henry Kissinger's maxim that bladder control is the strongest negotiating tool! Ultimately, we put the deal back together and flew back to Newark, New Jersey, where we landed at 1:00 a.m."

Like most corporate attorneys, Burns International in-house counsel Neil Reisman spends much of his time counseling his clients, the employees of the corporation. "I meet with Burns International personnel both in person and by phone. I also spend a good part of my time drafting and reviewing legal documents. In addition, I oversee various projects. For example, if Burns International is involved in an acquisition, I would oversee the legal aspects of the acquisition, including the due diligence checks." Neil says that his duties extend beyond purely legal tasks to involve business advising. "I have to wear more than one hat," he says.

Counseling clients is also a central part of John Dirks's job as an in-house counsel at State Farm. "Like any corporate lawyer, we develop our clientele and get to know their needs," he says. "I attend company meetings as the corporate law department representative. When a legal issue arises that involves State Farm, we educate other members of the company about the legal implications of the case. As an in-house counsel, I also explain to employees why they should talk to me about legal issues and when they need to pick up the phone and call me for advice. For example, our staff members who write brochures and other publications for State Farm need to know about copyright and trademark issues. We also teach employee courses on topics such as contracting and copyright and trademark law. The employees attending these classes are non-lawyers; they may come from the purchasing department or from the advertising, public affairs, human resources, marketing, or creative services departments."

John also spends a great deal of time on contractual issues. "In the legal department, we review a lot of contracts. I view a contract as a puzzle. When I receive a vendor's contract, I carefully review it to see what the problems are and then brainstorm solutions. I've seen vendor contracts with fine print so small that you have to get a magnifying glass just to be able to read it. An average consumer might just give up on reading such fine print, as it would be a daunting project, but to protect the company, and in turn our insureds, we must look at it and see what it says. When we're working on a contract for our purchasing department, we make the necessary changes and then explain to the purchasing department why we made the changes. They need to know why the changes were made so that they can effectively handle negotiation with the vendor." John says that his role is an advisory one. "In doing contracts we act as advisers to State Farm. Our opinions are couched in the form of a recommendation. It's rare that a vendor proposes something illegal, so our advice is more about the risk inherent in a particular contract."

John explains that other lawyers in the corporate law department oversee litigation involving the company. "If State Farm is sued, the corporate law department retains outside counsel to act as trial lawyers for the corporation. The corporate law department then supervises the litigation. Our attorneys may help in the drafting of briefs and other legal documents." John says that an important role played by these in-house lawyers is acting as a contact for outside firms and State Farm business areas. "State Farm's law department is also responsible for monitoring and coordinating state and federal legislative and regulatory affairs," John adds.

What do corporate lawyers find rewarding about their practice?

Corporate lawyers enjoy the intellectual nature of their work. Says in-house corporate counsel John Dirks, "The issues on which I work, especially the contractual issues, are intellectually challenging." Corporate attorney Lisa Maloney adds, "I find it interesting to see how a deal is structured. I am not yet at a level where I am the one structuring the deal, but I am challenged by the prospect of one day being able to do so." Lisa says that her firm encourages her to continue developing her professional expertise through professional education seminars and community services. "As an extension of my job at Ballard Spahr Andrews & Ingersoll, I am active in the local bar association. My focus in bar association work is professional development and community service, both of which I find personally rewarding. My bar association involvement is fully supported by the firm."

Janis Salin and Anne Falvey tell us that their relationships with clients make their work fulfilling. "The most satisfying and personally rewarding aspect of my job is the relationships I have built with executive officers and directors of companies I represent," comments Janis. "Through these relationships and my attendance at board of directors' meetings, I have learned about their industries and gained exposure to their management techniques." Anne adds, "I enjoy working with the same clients on a number of projects and participating in the growth and development of their businesses over time."

"Our corporate law department is very collegial," says John Dirks. John also enjoys the relationships he develops with outside lawyers and vendors. "We buy a large volume of computers, which means we're working with some of the largest computer companies in the country, which is very interesting. Working with outside law firms is a lot of fun, too. When you're working on a high profile case, you meet fascinating attorneys with exceptional legal expertise. It's a pleasure to work with such outstanding lawyers."

Not surprisingly, Audrey Roth, who specializes in working with venture capitalists and entrepreneurs, enjoys helping her clients' businesses grow and prosper. "Representing early-stage companies is incredibly rewarding. The entrepreneurs look to us as business as well as legal advisers and truly consider us an integral part of their companies," Audrey says. She adds, "I also love the idea of helping to put deals together and helping to build the company. The most rewarding stage of the company's development is when the company, with our help, grows to the stage where it 'goes public'—often the company's major goal!"

Lisa Maloney likes the fact that she's continually learning new things. "'Deal-making' involves not only knowing corporate law well, but having a working knowledge of many other areas of the law, such as environmental law, employee benefits, tax, etc. I find the constant learning process to be personally rewarding."

Neil Reisman enjoys the broad scope and high level of responsibility involved in his job as corporate counsel. "To me, the best thing about being an in-house attorney is that it gives you the chance to expand your area of expertise outside of the law. My ultimate goal is to be chief executive officer of a company. It's difficult to get to such a position while working at a law firm. My in-house counsel job allows me to gain experience I need to advance my career. For example, last year I had the opportunity to work as the interim president of one of our subsidiaries for a period of five months. It was an invaluable experience," he explains. Neil also finds satisfaction in working for a company with high ethical standards. "When I complete a project, I can feel good about the end product and how it was accomplished. Ethics do matter. Results are good, but feeling good about how you got those results is better," he says emphatically.

There are additional benefits to working in-house, according to Neil and John Dirks. One advantage, says John, is that he doesn't have to worry about billable hours. "I have the luxury of devoting the time I need to devote to a project, and I don't have to keep a record of how I spend my time. I can prioritize my work in the way I believe is most beneficial to the company." Neil adds that in-house work means that "I generally have better hours and a better lifestyle [than I did in private practice]."

The Training and Skills Important to Corporate Law

How do people enter the field of corporate law?

Some law students discover before or during law school that they're interested in corporate practice. Audrey Roth was such a law student. "I became interested in venture capital while a second year student, while conducting research on the firms I wanted to interview with," she reports. "One firm wrote compellingly about its venture capital practice and that piqued my interest. I began reading more and more about the industry. Venture capital work has been a perfect specialty for me—I've been practicing in the area since I graduated from law school in 1986."

Janis Salin decided in high school that she wanted to be a lawyer. "In high school I participated in a 'Girls' Day in the Community' program. I was assigned to serve as a Los Angeles county public defender." Janis reports that it was an inspiring experience. "I went to court and sat at the counsel table and even had lunch with the lawyers. After that experience I knew I wanted to go to law school. I was intrigued by the daily activities involved in practicing as well as the intellectual challenges offered by the profession." It wasn't until she entered law school that Janis learned that corporate law was her primary area of interest. "While I was in college and law school, I worked in several law offices. This gave me a better understanding of the various practice areas available and offered me the opportunity to evaluate the area which best suited my personality."

Anne Falvey knew when she entered law school that she was interested in corporate practice. "I decided to go to law school after working during the summers in college in the general counsel's office of a large, public corporation. Once I decided to practice corporate work at a firm, I quickly gravitated toward project finance work."

Other law graduates work for a law firm in another practice area before becoming part of a corporate law practice. Upon graduation from law school, Lisa Maloney joined a general practice firm. "I wanted a diverse experience in the law before actually choosing a field. I spent a number of years as a litigator and realized that my interest and my heart was in 'putting the deal together,' not in arriving on the scene after the deal was falling apart." Lisa clearly found the right match in corporate practice.

In-house lawyers generally work in law firms or for the government for several years before joining in-house corporate legal departments. Neil Reisman majored in accounting as an undergraduate. He began his legal career as a tax attorney in private practice, and Burns International initially hired him as an in-house tax counsel. Neil offered to take on additional duties as well. First he managed environmental litigation. Ultimately he managed all of the parent company's litigation. He then started working on corporate matters, including securities and acquisitions. This wide range of experience prepared him for his current position as assistant general counsel, in which he works as a generalist, advising the company on these and other matters. "Our corporate lawyers usually come to us from private practice," Neil says. "Our attorneys need to have at least two or three years of law firm experience or in-house experience. In smaller legal departments, such as the one I work in, you need to be able to work independently." Neil explains that the general rule is that the smaller the legal department, the more experience is needed to qualify for the position, while larger legal departments may be able to hire attorneys with less experience.

John Dirks worked as a judge advocate for the U.S. Navy before joining State Farm's corporate law department. As a JAG attorney, John gained the legal experience that allowed him to hit the ground running when he joined State Farm. "For the most part," says John, "our corporate department hires experienced attorneys. Some of the attorneys have private practice experience, others have worked for the government on regulatory issues, others have worked for corporations or other insurance companies. Often we're seeking someone with experience in a particular area of law, such as tax or lobbying and legislation." A few entry-level attorneys are hired through the company's internship program. Second year law students who participate in the program have the opportunity to work, on a rotation, in different areas of the legal department. "Interns get a flavor of every part of the legal department, including litigation, corporate work, and legislation," John says.

What skills are most important to corporate lawyers?

❖ The corporate lawyers we talked to agree that strong **interpersonal communication skills** are imperative to success in the field. "Communication is without a doubt the corporate lawyer's most important skill: communication with the client, with the other side, with one's law firm partners and associates," says Audrey Roth. Explains Neil Reisman, "As an in-house counsel, you're communicating with people at all levels of the organization, from the senior management on down. You must be able to talk with them, not to them. Management is interested in your advice; however, you must be able to communicate your advice effectively." John Dirks agrees that communication skills are key. "You can be the smartest lawyer in the world, but if you can't communicate your advice to others, you're not going to be successful. Being an in-house attorney requires that you have the ability to express yourself clearly, and, equally important, that you be skilled in building relationships with people within and outside of the organization," says John.

❖ Lisa Maloney cautions that good communication skills go beyond the ability to talk with others. "You **must be able to listen**," advises Lisa. "You must listen carefully to clients, partners, and opposing counsel." Adds Anne Falvey, "Good communication with your client is crucial; that means listening to your client's business goals as well as communicating effectively the legal issues or obstacles and the solutions."

❖ Corporate lawyers need first-rate **writing skills**. Explains Neil Reisman, "You need to be proficient in two types of writing—first, in **legal writing**, because you must draft contracts, briefs, and other legal documents, and second, in **business writing**, as you must be able to communicate with the real world. Business writing should be more conversational than technical, without using jargon and words such as 'heretofore' and 'aforementioned.'" Janis Salin agrees. "One of the skills most important to a corporate lawyer's success is a precise, clear writing style," she emphasizes.

❖ Corporate practice requires that attorneys have effective **analytical and problem-solving skills**. "In corporate practice you face problems that are very different than those on a law school exam. Your clients are relying on you for advice. You have to find out the facts and decide what's important and not important. If you're not analytical, you can waste time going down false paths," explains Neil Reisman. "A corporate lawyer needs excellent analytical ability," says Janis Salin. "Work on developing your analytical skills in both your academic and work experiences," she advises.

❖ **Negotiation skills** are also critical to attorneys in this practice area. "I continually work on my negotiation skills," reports Audrey Roth. "I have become a skilled negotiator by constantly being in the position of talking with all the parties to a transaction. In many ways negotiation skills are learned on the job. Even as a junior associate in a law firm, being present during negotiation and listening to various styles of negotiation is very useful," she explains.

❖ "**Organizational skills** are helpful," advises Lisa Maloney, as corporate lawyers work on highly detailed transactions which often involve numerous parties. "Being organized yourself, and making sure your client is organized, is critical in the field of project finance," says Anne Falvey. "I'm constantly working on both," she admits.

❖ Attorneys who work as corporate attorneys must be **comfortable both working in a team setting and working with non-lawyers**. Attorneys working at law firms may work on deals that involve non-lawyer clients, investment bankers, accountants and financial experts, sales and marketing professionals, and engineers. Interpersonal relationships are critical to the team's effectiveness. In-house attorneys generally work either formally or informally with employees from many different departments of the corporation. "The vast majority of our work is done in teams, and you're the legal member of the team. The rest of the team members are likely to be from other company departments," explains John Dirks of State Farm. "When you're in-house, you must work hard at building solid team relationships," he advises. Part of John's job is educating other State Farm employees about legal issues. "Teaching skills are an important part of my job," says John, who adds that he greatly enjoys teaching non-lawyers about the legal implications of their work.

❖ **Creativity** is a plus for corporate lawyers, according to Neil Reisman. "As an in-house attorney, you can't simply accept the past; you have to be creative in your approach to problems. As in-house attorneys we have access to more information about our own company than outside counsel; we have to be creative in using that information to meet our company's legal and business needs," says Neil.

What classes and law school experiences do corporate lawyers recommend?

❖ **Business-related law school classes** can be helpful to the aspiring corporate lawyer. "Corporations, tax, and accounting for lawyers were important foundations for my practice," says Anne Falvey. Janis Salin seconds Anne's recommendations. "When I realized I would specialize in corporate law, I took all of the business and accounting classes offered by the law school, such as accounting for lawyers, corporate finance, securities, business transactions, and tax," says Janis. "For my work as a venture capital attorney, corporations, securities law, tax, and partnership law were all helpful. An intellectual property class would have been helpful as well," says Audrey Roth.

❖ **Undergraduate or graduate business courses** can be useful, as well. Neil Reisman notes that the more you can learn about business, the better. "Take corporate classes and business classes. Accounting is pivotal—if you don't know accounting, you'll be lost in corporate practice. A finance course can also be helpful," Neil advises. Neil followed his own advice. He majored in accounting as an undergraduate and took advantage of the business courses offered at the Wharton School of Business while he was a law student at the University of Pennsylvania. Janis Salin agrees that business education can be helpful. "In hindsight," she says, "pursuing a J.D./M.B.A. would have been very helpful to my mergers and acquisitions practice, because so much of the work I do requires a clear understanding of a company's financial statements. I would advise others to consider pursuing such a degree or, at the very least, to take basic accounting courses to gain exposure to common business terms and practices," says Janis.

❖ Take law school and undergraduate **classes that will help you develop strong writing skills.** "Legal writing courses and legal drafting courses are important," advises John Dirks. "But any courses that develop your writing skills, such as undergraduate liberal arts classes, are beneficial."

❖ Join your law school's **law review or law journal or participate in a writing competition.** Generally a law school's top students are invited to join law review, where they gain writing and editing experience. "Law review offers great writing experience and it's an excellent credential when you're in the job market," says John Dirks.

❖ **Gain practical experience** by working as a summer associate at a law firm with a corporate practice, as an intern for a corporation with a corporate law department, or for a government office that handles corporate law issues. There's no better way to determine whether corporate law is the right area for you. "Take the best summer job you can possibly find," advises Neil Reisman. "If you are planning to work as in-house counsel, you should focus on developing corporate practice skills rather than litigation skills. Look at firms' corporate departments rather than their litigation departments. Litigators can get in-house positions; however, there are more opportunities for corporate backgrounds. It's important to get all the corporate experience you can, at the best firm you can."

❖ The lawyers we talked to recommend **becoming involved in bar association activities**. Bar associations welcome student members and offer student memberships for a nominal fee. Many bar associations have corporate practice committees. "I would suggest that anyone interested in this field join and participate in professional bar association committees," advises Lisa Maloney. "While you're a summer associate, try to develop a mentoring relationship with someone in the firm or with an attorney you meet through bar association involvement," she adds. Anne Falvey also encourages both students and new attorneys to attend bar association seminars. "I believe the best way to meet people in the field is to attend the multitude of informational and educational seminars available throughout the year," Anne says. Audrey Roth, too, recommends bar association involvement as a way to learn about corporate practice. "Go to professional seminars to meet people and learn about what's going on," she suggests.

❖ **Keep up with the latest developments in business.** Anne Falvey advises that it's imperative to keep up with business trends. "I suggest reading about new developments in emerging markets and new transactions by reading trade publications," she says. "My best advice to an aspiring corporate lawyer is to read, read, read," notes Audrey Roth. "Read trade publications, the *Wall Street Journal*, *Business Week*, etc., etc., etc.," she says. "I also surf the Internet to develop an awareness of the latest trends in the industry in which my clients operate."

CORPORATE ATTORNEYS INTERVIEWED FOR THIS SECTION

John Dirks
State Farm Mutual Automobile Insurance Company
Bloomington, Illinois
UNDERGRADUATE: University of Illinois
LAW SCHOOL: University of Illinois College of Law

Anne Falvey
Kelley Drye & Warren LLP
New York, New York
UNDERGRADUATE: Smith College
LAW SCHOOL: Boston College Law School

Lisa Maloney
Ballard Spahr Andrews & Ingersoll, LLP
Philadelphia, Pennsylvania
UNDERGRADUATE: Fairfield University
LAW SCHOOL: Villanova University School of Law

Neil Reisman
Burns International Services Corp.
Chicago, Illinois
UNDERGRADUATE: University of Illinois
LAW SCHOOL: University of Pennsylvania Law School

Audrey Roth
Kelley Drye & Warren LLP
New York, New York
UNDERGRADUATE: City University of New York
LAW SCHOOL: Columbia University Law School

Janis Salin
Riordan & McKinzie
Los Angeles, California
UNDERGRADUATE: UCLA
LAW SCHOOL: UCLA School of Law

Criminal Law

What is Criminal Law?

The true life of the criminal lawyer differs dramatically from the romanticized versions often portrayed in film and on television. Both public defenders and prosecutors must process numerous cases on limited budgets through an over-burdened and under-funded criminal justice system. Rarely can a defendant afford to present a case with the assistance of a highly paid "dream team" of attorneys. Prosecutors must often rely on informants and other witnesses with their own extensive records of past convictions, who may agree to testify only in an effort to reduce their own sentences and punishment.

Criminal trials are inherently dramatic. Movies and television make the most of courtroom drama—from classics that challenge our notion of justice, such as *To Kill a Mockingbird*, to farces designed solely to entertain, such as the trial portrayed in the last episode of the hit comedy *Seinfeld*. But trials are only a small part of the picture. Well over 90% of all criminal matters are resolved through plea bargains without trial. Thus, both prosecutors and defense attorneys are constantly involved in high-stakes negotiations that will determine the fate of the defendant.

Criminal lawyers work tirelessly—both inside and outside the courtroom, in advance of trial and, if necessary, during trial—in the zealous representation of their clients. Being a criminal lawyer requires a substantial set of skills beyond being a good trial lawyer; criminal lawyers must be good negotiators, investigators, counselors, and even social workers. Criminal lawyers may be a client's only listening ear, so they must be prepared to deal with all of the stressful aspects in their client's life at that moment, not just the accused crime.

Criminal Prosecution

Prosecutors work for the state or federal government in enforcement of federal and state statutes as well as city ordinances that define the criminal code. State prosecutors generally work for the state's attorneys or district attorneys of their counties. Prosecution of federal crimes is typically coordinated through the U.S. Attorney's Office in each federal judicial district.

Departments in these offices are typically organized by the type of crimes they prosecute. Felonies such as murder, robbery, rape, or vehicular homicide, which are crimes that can result in prison terms of more than one year, are typically handled by a group of felony prosecutors. Misdemeanors, or crimes which can include a fine or jail sentence of up to one year, are typically handled by a different group of prosecutors. Enforcement of city ordinances, including traffic offenses, criminal trespass to property, shoplifting, and parking offenses are often handled by a different group of prosecutors. This allows the various cases to proceed in an orderly manner before judges and other court officials, such as magistrates, who are familiar with the statutory requirements and equipped to handle issues including pre-trial detention (bail), evidentiary standards (probable cause for arrest, detention, or searches), and sentencing. Other divisions of state and county prosecutors' offices handle matters such as consumer fraud and environmental standards enforcement. Juveniles are processed through an entirely separate system that emphasizes treatment and rehabilitation rather than punishment.

Prosecutors at both state and federal levels are given tremendous discretion in determining how to proceed against a particular defendant. The prosecutor determines whether to proceed with charges based on factors including the amount and type of evidence, the nature of the crime and its victim, the existence of a prior criminal record on the part of the defendant, and the effect of the crime on the community (for example, vehicular homicide caused by the defendant's drunk driving or crimes in which the defendant acted against the victim because of his or her race, sexual orientation, or religion). Prosecutors may also seek to charge through indictment, which can involve presenting witnesses and evidence to a grand jury for its consideration and evaluation.

Criminal Defense

Criminal defense attorneys may work for the federal, state, or local government or for private law firms. The Constitution provides that anyone accused of a crime, even the indigent, has the right to be defended by an attorney; thus states, municipalities, and the federal government maintain public defenders' offices which provide defense counsel to anyone who needs it. These offices are typically organized by the type of alleged crime— for example, traffic crimes, juvenile crimes, misdemeanors, felonies, and civil crimes (abuse, neglect, dependency, etc.).

Criminal defendants may be accused of any number of crimes or complaints. Retail theft, assault, possession of drug paraphernalia, criminal trespass to real property, or even telephone harassment are just a few of the criminal misdemeanor charges a criminal attorney defends. Numerous traffic violations include driving with a suspended or revoked driver's license, driving without insurance, or driving while under the influence of alcohol. Criminal defense attorneys also assist clients accused of various felony crimes, including possession of a controlled substance, carjacking, kidnaping, and first degree murder.

Criminal defense attorneys serve their client's best interest and have no requirement to present evidence or call witnesses in defense of their case; it is the prosecutor's responsibility, or burden, to prove the defendant guilty beyond a reasonable doubt. This does not mean that the defense attorney has nothing to do on the case. He or she must investigate the scene of the crime, talk to witnesses to establish what may have happened, and research case law to construct the defense and to gain insight on possible arguments to be made by the prosecution. Defense attorneys are often faced with factual situations that are extremely unfavorable to their clients. They work closely with their clients when preparing for trial and generally attempt to resolve the case before trial by seeking dismissal of the case or negotiating a plea agreement with the prosecutors.

The government also uses criminal sanctions to enforce civil laws—whether tax laws, securities laws, banking laws, antitrust laws, or environmental laws. "White collar" criminal defense lawyers represent individuals and businesses that have allegedly violated such statutory provisions. Attorneys specializing in white collar defense defend their clients in civil and criminal investigations and against both civil and criminal charges. These cases may be complicated by additional civil lawsuits brought by the alleged victims of the crime or crimes. White collar defense lawyers are experts in handling the interplay between these civil and criminal investigations and charges.

Types of Cases Handled by Criminal Lawyers

Examples of the types of crimes handled by prosecutors, criminal defense attorneys, and public defenders include:

Crimes Against People

Crimes against people include rape, murder, child abuse, spousal abuse, hate crimes, and assault. Prosecutors, public defenders, and criminal defense attorneys work with experts in the forensics field on such issues as DNA analysis and ballistics analysis, as well as with the coroner or medical examiner. Generally crimes against people are handled at the state level, but they may be prosecuted federally if the crimes are committed against federal officials, such as the murder of a federal agent, or if they involve interstate transport, such as kidnaping or the smuggling of illegal firearms used in the commission of a crime.

Drug Crimes

The federal government has made the war against drugs a priority, with stiff penalties for those defendants proved guilty of importing, selling, and distributing drugs. An ever-increasing number of drug cases are prosecuted, and drug cases therefore account for a significant percentage of the cases handled by public defenders and private criminal defense attorneys. Drug cases include those brought against neighborhood dealers as well as those brought against organizations involved in large-scale drug trafficking and money laundering (the transfer and concealment of large amounts of cash generated through sales of drugs through various bank accounts).

Organized Crime

Organized crime is often glamorized by the movies and television, with few apparent victims other than those who are associated with the crime families. However, organized crime victimizes citizens at large because of its far-reaching economic consequences. When organized crime infiltrates legitimate businesses or labor unions by demanding payments or taking over the business, costs are driven up, and the effect is felt by individual consumers and government entities. White collar criminal defendants, who frequently fall into this category, often have the financial resources to hire private criminal defense attorneys who work in the white collar criminal defense departments in large law firms or who work in small boutique practices specializing in white collar defense work.

Economic Crimes

In an unceasing quest to get something for nothing, defendants commit a wide variety of economic crimes, including counterfeiting, using false documents to obtain loans, and participating in credit card fraud and other types of commercial scams. Defendants may also commit tax offenses, whether failing to file tax returns or filing false returns. Many of the defendants in these cases hire private criminal defense attorneys with experiences in such fraud and tax evasion cases to handle their defense.

Public Corruption

When public officials such as police officers or elected officials engage in wrongdoings (for example, taking bribes or extorting money or services), prosecutors bring charges against them. Such investigations, such as the "Silver Shovel" investigation that resulted in the sentencing of several government officials in Chicago, are often lengthy and complex. They require a sophisticated coordination of efforts between prosecutors and investigators, and highly specialized defense efforts on behalf of criminal defense attorneys.

Life as a Criminal Lawyer

Where do criminal lawyers work?

Many prosecutors work for state government. Prosecutors who work for the state are generally employed by a state attorney's office or a county district attorney's (D.A.'s) office. Each county has one state attorney or one district attorney and some number of assistant state or district attorneys. Highly populated areas, such as Cook County, Illinois (home to Chicago and a number of densely populated suburbs), may have hundreds of assistant state's attorneys, while counties with smaller populations have smaller prosecutor's offices.

Many of the prosecutors who work for the federal government are employed by the U.S. Attorneys for the various federal judicial districts throughout the country, which are part of the Department of Justice. The U.S. military also employs attorneys who are prosecutors (*see* the Military Judge Advocates chapter for more information), as does the U.S. Coast Guard.

Public defenders also work for the state or federal government. Public defenders who work for the state are employed by a county public defender's office. Each county has a public defender, and the number of assistant public defenders employed by the county depends on the county's population. The public defender fills the Constitutional requirement of providing representation by counsel for all. Counties sometimes hire private criminal defense attorneys to assist defendants when the public defenders are overburdened by their case loads.

Private criminal defense attorneys generally work in law firms. Some work in small firms or on their own, but others are associated with mid-size and large firms. Before becoming private defense attorneys, they often gain experience in criminal litigation by working as public defenders or prosecutors. White collar criminal defense attorneys often work in large law firms, where the complex cases on which they work, unique in their mix of criminal and civil issues, can be supported by teams of attorneys and extensive support staff.

Who are their clients and what types of cases do they work on?

Prosecutor Bill Seki, Deputy District Attorney in the Los Angeles County District Attorney's Office, explains, "As a representative of the people, [prosecutors] don't have clients in the normal sense of the word. We serve the community at large by ensuring that laws are enforced and justice is served. Consequently, we represent the entire county of Los Angeles. Victims of crimes often look at us as their lawyers. In a certain respect, we are the only advocates they have in the criminal justice system. We try to ensure that their interests are protected by getting convictions and seeing that the appropriate sentence is imposed." The Los Angeles D.A.'s Office handles a wide variety of cases. "We prosecute all types of crimes," says Bill, "from crimes as simple as driving without a valid driver's license to crimes as serious as murder. The Los Angeles District Attorney's Office has a number of specialized prosecution units, such as the hard core gang unit, the major fraud unit, the environmental crimes unit, the major narcotics unit, and the domestic violence unit, just to name a few. If you have a special interest in a certain area of criminal prosecution, once you've obtained experience prosecuting cases, you can apply to one of our many special units. There's something for everyone."

Elizabeth Dobson is the lead criminal prosecutor at the Office of the Champaign County State's Attorney in Urbana, Illinois, where she is one of 13 criminal prosecutors. "Though my clients are technically the people of the state of Illinois, my clients are truly those who are victims of violent crimes. I work on felony cases, cases involving crimes such as first degree murder, armed robbery, and rape. Our office also handles felony crimes against property, such as burglary, and crimes such as forgery. Among the most rewarding cases to work on, but the most emotionally taxing, are child abuse and neglect cases." She adds, "Less experienced attorneys in the office handle misdemeanor cases, which involve offenses that are punishable for up to one year in jail. New attorneys generally handle traffic cases."

Mimi Wright is a federal prosecutor at the Office of the U.S. Attorney in Minneapolis, Minnesota. "We are ultimately public servants," explains Mimi, an Assistant U.S. Attorney. "We have client agencies we work with, like the Federal Bureau of Investigation (FBI), the Bureau of Alcohol, Tobacco, and Firearms (ATF), the U.S. Secret Service, the U.S. Department of Agriculture (USDA), and the Office of the Inspector General of the U.S. Postal Service. These federal agencies engage in criminal investigations. They investigate crimes and then bring the results of the investigation to us, to prosecute the case or to give them further direction in the investigation." Mimi says that she works on a wide variety of criminal cases. "Sometimes we have joint jurisdiction over crimes such as drug crimes, which may ultimately be prosecuted by a county prosecutor's office. We tend to take the larger, more complex cases with distinct federal interests. These include cases such as bank robberies; crimes against women in which the defendant has crossed state lines; gun cases in which a firearm is possessed by a felon or in which the defendant possesses a firearm that is banned; threats against the President; possession of stolen mail; bank fraud, such as check kiting schemes and fraudulent efforts to obtain government loans; health care fraud, such as physicians or medical equipment suppliers claiming that they have provided a service or supplies that were never provided; and counterfeiting." Mimi notes that the investigations she works on often reveal surprising schemes. Recently, she encountered a number of counterfeiting cases involving technically sophisticated high school and college students who attempted to manufacture currency with their state-of-the-art computers and printers.

Those defendants who cannot afford a private defense attorney are assigned the services of a public defender. Timijanel Boyd Odom is an Assistant Public Defender for Cook County's Sixth Municipal District in Markham, Illinois, just west of Chicago. "I represent indigent clients of all ages," she says. "I work with juveniles, young adults, middle-aged people, and even senior citizens." Timijanel explains that those defendants who can't afford a private attorney are asked to complete an affidavit (sworn statement) of assets and liabilities. Once a judge reviews the affidavit and determines that they are indigent, the defendant is assigned a public defender. Timijanel handles misdemeanor cases and some felony cases. "In the misdemeanor cases, the client may be charged with possession of marijuana, criminal damage to property, possession of alcohol by a minor, or disorderly conduct. My felony cases include armed robbery, home invasion, credit card or check fraud, and cocaine possession." For more information about criminal defense, see also the description of the Office of the Appellate Defender in the Appellate Practice chapter.

Mark Lipton works as a private defense attorney as well as a civil litigation attorney at a 25-person firm in Champaign, Illinois. Half of Mark's practice is criminal defense; the other half of his practice is civil litigation. "Many of my criminal defense clients come to me via referrals from the companies I represent in my civil litigation practice," he explains. "Before entering private practice, I worked as a prosecutor in the Champaign County State's Attorney's Office. Some of the people I previously prosecuted have come to me to represent them. Much of my clientele comes from word of mouth." Mark represents defendants charged with a range of crimes—from murder to speeding. "Many of my cases are felonies," says Mark. "Some of the cases involve the alleged burglary of autos or businesses. I get a fair number of clients who are university students who have been drinking and their subsequent behavior results in their being charged with a felony or misdemeanor. Champaign County aggressively prosecutes cases in which a defendant has been charged with driving under the influence of drugs or alcohol."

Attorney Robert Humphreys handles white collar cases at Howrey & Simon, a large law firm in Los Angeles. Robert comments that it's "almost impossible" to describe his wide range of clients. "We represent individuals, large corporations, small corporations, partnerships, and other business entities. This is fairly typical in the white collar field, because a criminal investigation into a corporation will necessarily also involve the criminal investigation into the responsible officers, directors, and employees of the organization." Robert explains how these very complex cases work. "A case typically begins with a subpoena from a grand jury, the execution of a search warrant, or interview of the employees of a company by federal investigators. This is generally the first indication that a company or individual has that they are being investigated for criminal activity. The white collar attorney generally tries to make contact with the prosecutor to determine whether the client is under investigation personally for criminal activity or is merely regarded as the witness of the possible criminal activity of another. The attorney then attempts to do a factual investigation and to develop the paper trail necessary to determine whether any laws were broken. In federal cases, because of the influence of the federal sentencing guidelines, it is also generally important to begin determining what factors will affect the length of the client's possible sentence if convicted."

At that point, Robert explains, negotiations generally begin. "Once the attorney feels comfortable with the facts, he or she will often meet with the prosecutor to seek a declination of criminal prosecution or a favorable plea agreement. If those negotiations do not appear to be likely to resolve the case, the attorney will generally attempt to reach some sort of agreement with regard to pre-trial release and request that the client be allowed to surrender, rather than be arrested, in the event that he or she is charged with a crime. If the client is charged, the case will proceed very much like civil litigation. The primary exception is that discovery is very limited in criminal cases. Thus a premium is placed on the actual investigation rather than the discovery tactics employed in civil litigation. The other major difference from civil litigation is that criminal cases proceed much more quickly. Even a very complex case can go from indictment to trial within a single year."

What daily activities are involved in criminal law practice?

"Being a prosecutor is never boring. Every day is different," says Assistant State's Attorney Elizabeth Dobson. "You run from crisis to crisis; it's as if you have to keep your finger in the dam all the time. You're in court every day. Every day new cases come in. And every day you're handling guilty pleas and motion hearings." Elizabeth explains that she's involved in her felony cases right from the start and all the way through trial. "One day a week I review police reports and make decisions about what crimes have been committed, and I file charges against the defendants accordingly." In Champaign County criminal jury trials are convened every two weeks. "Every two weeks, I know I'll be on trial for a two-week period. Few of the trials last more than two or three days. During the two weeks between trial periods, I spend as much time as possible preparing for trial and making sure all the evidence is ready. When the two-week jury term convenes, as many as six or seven cases are set for trial each day, so you need to be well prepared." Many cases settle just before trial, but Elizabeth says she can count on having at least two felony jury trials a month.

Los Angeles County prosecutor Bill Seki agrees that life as a prosecutor is hectic and unpredictable. "I don't spend much time in my office," he admits. "My true office is the courtroom." Bill notes that each day offers new challenges. "We arraign new defendants, discuss plea agreements (case settlements), handle search and seizure and other evidentiary hearings, and deal with probation violations. In addition to these activities, we are either preparing for trial or actually in trial," he says.

As an Assistant U.S. Attorney, Mimi Wright reports that she is involved in a variety of tasks. She especially enjoys court hearings and trials, but her job involves far more than courtroom work. For example, she says, "I meet with federal agents to discuss investigations and offer advice. Because cases often involve complex legal and procedural issues, they require extensive brief writing at the district, magistrate, and appellate level. As U.S. Attorneys, we get to research and write our own briefs." Mimi has also done some public speaking for law enforcement officials and county attorneys. "One of the Attorney General's initiatives was the Violence Against Women Act enacted in 1995 and 1996. Domestic violence is generally a local crime handled at the state level. In order to be effective in enforcing the federal act, we needed to work closely with county and city attorneys' offices to get information about potential defendants. I spoke at seminars in which we talked with probation officers, city and county attorneys, and police officers about the new law and its implications."

Public defenders are often assigned to a criminal courtroom, where they work in a team with a particular prosecutor and an assigned judge. "When I arrive at work, I immediately report to my courtroom," says Timijanel Boyd Odom, Cook County Public Defender. "On any given day, as many as 50 cases may be assigned to the courtroom for discovery, negotiations, or trial. Most of the day is spent assisting my clients in negotiations with the prosecutor. A majority of my cases—about 90%—are resolved through negotiated pleas or agreements. I spend about five days per month in trial."

Private defense attorney Mark Lipton says that he spends much of his time reviewing discovery and doing independent investigations for his clients. "I carefully review the police reports and determine what independent investigation needs to be done. I interview the client to get the client's account of what transpired. I also prepare motions and petitions on a regular basis—for example, motions to suppress evidence at trial. I also have constant and regular contact with the state's attorneys' office to negotiate plea agreements. The conferences with the state's attorneys tend to be very informal—sometimes they are by appointment and sometimes I just talk to the state's attorney as he or she is walking into the courthouse in the morning." On the day we interviewed Mark, he had an appointment to talk to one of the state's attorneys about 16 cases scheduled for a docket call on a single date three weeks later. Mark, whose defense clients make up half of his case load, says, "About 98% of my cases settle," but he ultimately tries about one criminal case per year. Mark says that it's not uncommon for private criminal defense attorneys in his county to try anywhere from six to 12 cases per year.

White collar defense work requires that attorneys spend time developing legal strategies to assist their clients in complex, high-stakes cases. Explains Robert Humphreys, "Most of my day is spent assembling and investigating the facts of the case and in the library developing the legal issues that will affect the client's criminal liability and length of sentence. It is generally the objective of the white collar criminal practitioner to avoid going to court at all and to settle the case prior to the filing of the criminal charges. Thus, far more time is spent in negotiations with the prosecutor's offices than is spent arguing in court. There is a fair amount of motion activity in criminal cases after charges are filed, however, and criminal cases are far more likely than civil cases to actually go to trial."

What do criminal lawyers find rewarding about their practice?

The prosecutors we talked to said that they found their role as public servants particularly rewarding. "I always believe that I'm on the right side of things," says Elizabeth Dobson. "Even when I lose a trial, I feel good about the role I've played in the case. If I win, I feel that justice was served. I never have to wrestle with my conscience. It's satisfying when people who have committed crimes against others are convicted and sent to prison. I know I stand for something, for an important principle—I uphold the laws of our state."

Los Angeles County prosecutor Bill Seki agrees. "The nature of the job of being a deputy district attorney is, in itself, rewarding. It may sound corny, but knowing that you are an integral part of the search for truth and justice is what keeps all of us going. You have the ability to take violent predators off the street. You are able to show victims and their families that the system will work for them and that they are not forgotten. You have the responsibility to ensure that no individual is wrongly accused. You are doing something to help better the community."

Prosecutors tend to love their courtroom work. "There's nothing more rewarding than being in the courtroom every day," says Bill Seki. "Everyone who comes to this office wants to be a trial attorney. For me, there couldn't be a better job in the world!" Mimi Wright is equally enthusiastic about her work in the courtroom. "Both going to court and being in trial are fun," she says. "Many of my evidentiary hearings are actually bench trials [trials heard before a judge rather than a jury], and I have the opportunity to use my oral advocacy skills. I also really enjoy the challenge of arguing cases before the Eighth Circuit Court of Appeals. It's very exciting. I generally have the chance to do two or three Eighth Circuit appellate arguments per year."

As an assistant U.S. attorney, Mimi has the opportunity to do extensive legal research and write briefs for her own cases. "Working for the U.S. Attorney's Office gives you the chance to work with victims and law enforcement officials, so you don't miss out on the human dynamic of practicing law. But you also engage in the more academic legal experiences of law practice—research and writing—as well. And it's that combination that makes my job especially rewarding."

Mimi also enjoys working on a team with her colleagues. "I like my colleagues. We have an open door policy; we get to know each other well. They're extremely talented and very competent. I enjoy my work with a varied group of attorneys, from former JAG attorneys [*see* the Military Judge Advocates chapter] to former county prosecutors to attorneys formerly in private practice. I also work with federal investigators, developing case strategies; we think about the type of evidence we want to develop for a trial, talk through admissibility of evidence issues, debate what approach is most persuasive to a jury, and brainstorm about what we think we need to present a very good case. Then we concentrate on lending that perspective to the entire investigation. It's truly a team approach. I also work with victim witness coordinators who work with the victims of the crimes as well as the witnesses whose testimony we will use during the course of the trial or the hearing."

As a public defender, Timijanel Boyd Odom finds her work with her indigent clients immensely rewarding. "I provide people who can't afford a private lawyer the best defense possible. Just being a good defense attorney is a reward in itself," she says. Timijanel also says that her love of people makes being a public defender the perfect job for her. "I love people. I love the fact that I have a relationship with the other people in the courtroom, that we're working together to make the system work." Timijanel says that she enjoys the relationships she develops with her clients. "There's a very important social work aspect of my job," she says. "I try to help those struggling with alcohol and drugs find treatment programs. I try to help my clients find employment. And with juvenile offenders, I try to be a role model. I tell my young clients that they can do anything. They often come to visit me months or years later, to let me know how they're doing. 'Mrs. Odom,' they'll tell me proudly, 'I'm going to school now!' And they send me their graduation announcements and graduation pictures. My office is filled with pictures my young clients have sent me. Just looking at those faces, knowing those kids have moved on with their lives, is incredibly rewarding."

Most criminal defense attorneys delight in being at trial. "It's rewarding to go to trial and win," says private defense attorney Mark Lipton. Timijanel Boyd Odom is extremely enthusiastic about her trial work. "I love being on trial," she says. "As a defense attorney, you get to be very creative. You brainstorm with your colleagues and come up with ideas and strategies for defense of your client. Jury trials just give me a rush," she confides.

The Training and Skills Important to Criminal Law

How do people enter the field of criminal law?

Some attorneys become convinced that they want to be criminal lawyers at an early age. Public defender Timijanel Boyd Odom says that she knew she wanted to be a criminal defense attorney from the time she was 12 years old. "I come from a single-parent family. My mom raised six of us, including my two brothers, who had juvenile delinquency problems. When I was 12, I met the public defender who was representing one of my brothers. He was great! My mother explained to me what a public defender was—how they represented people who couldn't afford private attorneys and how they were paid for through our taxes. I made up my mind right then that I wanted to be a public defender, and I never changed my mind. I always tell my young clients that, in spite of all the obstacles in my way, I pursued my dream career, and I encourage them to do the same."

Other attorneys who pursue the field are inspired by experiences as student interns in state's attorneys' offices or public defender's offices. "I worked at the state's attorney's office as a student intern," says prosecutor Elizabeth Dobson. "That did it for me—I was hooked. I couldn't ever imagine wanting to practice any other type of law." As an intern, Elizabeth tried her first cases under the supervision of a licensed attorney, which is permitted in some states. "The internship experience was invaluable. As a third year student, I handled traffic trials, including DUI cases. I was working under the supervision of the traffic prosecutor. When I was hired after graduation, I *became* the traffic prosecutor."

Some law students find that working in a prosecutor's office offers them an opportunity to engage in public service while gaining trial experience. Such is the case with Bill Seki, who says, "Two things influenced my becoming a deputy district attorney. First of all, I wanted to give back to the community. I wanted a life in public service. Secondly, I wanted to be a trial attorney. Not just a litigator, but a real trial attorney [*see* the Civil Litigation chapter to contrast civil and criminal litigation]. I knew that only in the criminal justice system could a young attorney get a lot of trial experience." Bill adds that once he knew he wanted to work as a criminal attorney, he faced the decision of whether to work as a prosecutor or as a defense attorney. "After speaking to several prosecutors, I learned that as a prosecutor, I could be an advocate for victims, individuals whose rights had truly been violated by other individuals. I also learned that as a prosecutor, my main role was to seek justice. Although I continue to have great respect for what defense attorneys do, I knew that a prosecutor was what I wanted to be, and I have never regretted that decision."

Many attorneys who pursue this field are inspired by criminal law studies in law school. "I found that the cases in my criminal law classes were the only ones that were actually interesting to read," confides Robert Humphreys.

Assistant U.S. Attorney Mimi Wright worked as a judicial law clerk after graduation. "I clerked for Judge Damon Keith of the Sixth Circuit Court of Appeals," explains Mimi. "While I was clerking, I began to think about becoming an Assistant U.S. Attorney. I watched the Assistant U.S. Attorneys in action, and I was impressed. I saw that they had intellectually challenging jobs that allowed them to research and write about interesting legal and procedural issues. I knew they had frequent opportunities to use their oral advocacy skills. And I liked the idea of being in public service. I also heard about the collegial atmosphere in the U.S. Attorney's Office—and that has proven to be true." Mimi worked as a litigation associate at a large firm for several years before pursuing a job at the U.S. Attorney's office.

It's common for private defense attorneys such as Mark Lipton to begin their careers as prosecutors. Mark worked as a prosecutor for seven years before becoming a private defense attorney. "If you want to do litigation of any kind, working in a state's attorney's office is one of the best training grounds. It's the best way to get into criminal defense work and a good way to get into civil litigation." As a prosecutor, says Mark, "I liked being the good guy and wearing the white hat. But shortly after I decided to leave the state's attorney's office, I was assigned a death penalty murder case that went to trial. That experience provoked my liberal sensibilities, and I shifted into the role of looking out for individual rights. My client in the murder case, rather than being sentenced to death, was sentenced to 80 years, of which he will have to serve 40. That doesn't minimize the fact that 40 years is a long time, but it's much better than the death penalty. That case was a real turning point for me."

What skills are most important to criminal lawyers?

❖ Criminal law attorneys need to have **excellent communication skills**. "The ability to effectively communicate with others is without question the most important skill any trial attorney must possess," asserts Bill Seki. "Some people are naturally blessed with this skill. I, however, was not," Bill admits. "So before law school, I worked hard to develop my public speaking skills. In college I took a number of speech communication classes in which I studied the great orators in history. In law school I participated in moot court and trial advocacy classes. As a law clerk and as a young prosecutor, I carefully observed many experienced and successful attorneys. All of these experiences have helped me to become an effective and persuasive communicator."

❖ The ability to **read and analyze vast quantities of information** is a skill especially valuable to prosecutors. "I know that many prosecutors would argue that public speaking skills and writing skills are the skills most important to the field. But I believe that careful reading is the most important skill a prosecutor can have," says Elizabeth Dobson. "As prosecutors, we handle a staggering volume of work. We review awesome amounts of written information. We're constantly taking in many versions of the same story from different sources—from police records, from witnesses, from investigators. We're also reviewing statutes, case law, and jury instructions. It's a challenge to get through all the information, organize it, analyze it, and decide what crimes to charge. And your decision to charge a defendant with a particular crime or crimes is dependent on what you glean from your reading and analysis of the information."

❖ Because an overwhelming percentage of criminal cases settle before trial, criminal attorneys must have sophisticated **negotiation skills.** Says white collar defense attorney Robert Humphreys, "The attorney's ability to get the best result for his or her client generally depends on his or her ability to either negotiate with the prosecutor or to persuade the court or jury." Federal prosecutor Mimi Wright says, "Negotiation skills are critical. We're often seeking to settle cases. It's important to be able to assess the strength of your case and figure out your goals for settlement as well as how to achieve those goals."

❖ Criminal attorneys need strong **analytical skills.** "You must be able to perform legal analysis and think through investigative strategies and trial strategies," says Mimi Wright. "You have to think carefully about the evidence you'll present at trial," adds Elizabeth Dobson. "Contrary to conventional wisdom, closing arguments aren't the determining factor in a jury trial," she says. "Juries listen to the evidence. And you have to analyze your case carefully to know how to best present the evidence. You're working from the very beginning of the case, from the time the defendant is charged, to present an effective case. This takes strong legal analysis." As a criminal defense attorney, Mark Lipton must analyze his client's options and share that analysis with his clients. "My clients generally say, 'I'll do whatever you tell me to do.' And I have to explain to them, 'That's not how it works. You have to understand that whatever decision you make is your decision. But I can tell you about your options and give you my analysis of the best course of action.'"

❖ The **ability to build relationships** is critical to criminal attorneys. Prosecutors and defense attorneys must work to develop a rapport with their clients, with juries, and with opposing counsel. Public defenders and state prosecutors are often assigned to courtrooms where they work with the same team day in and day out. "The prosecutor assigned to my courtroom and I are able to get a lot done, because we understand the judge and we understand each other," says Timijanel Boyd Odom. Mark Lipton adds, "Establishing a rapport with clients is something that comes naturally for me. People tell me that even my voicemail message is soothing. But maybe it's when my clients meet me that they know I'm approachable. I'm 52 years old, but I wear my long hair in a ponytail and I sport an earring," Mark confides. A few minutes spent chatting with Mark make it obvious that meeting new people is one of his favorite parts of the job.

❖ The prosecutors we talked to emphasized the importance of **management skills**. "You need to be very self-motivated," says Mimi Wright. "You need to work well with others, but you also need to encourage others in terms of management—you're managing the investigators, giving them positive feedback, and explaining why you need the information you're asking them to get—why the information is useful or admissible in the case. You're really leading a team and working on building team spirit."

❖ Good **organizational skills** are helpful to all litigation attorneys, particularly those specializing in criminal litigation. "In a way, building a case is all about information processing," says prosecutor Elizabeth Dobson. "As a prosecutor, you're working with a high volume of cases. In order to roll with the flow of your wildly hectic days, you have to be very organized—organized in terms of your thinking and organized in terms of your case files."

❖ Most criminal attorneys we talked to mentioned the importance of having **empathy for others—whether victims or criminal defendants**. "As a prosecutor, you deal with so many types of people, you must be able to relate to individuals from all walks of life. You have to understand how and why different people react differently in certain situations," says Bill Seki. "You must have sensitivity to the victims of a crime so that in the investigation and prosecution of the crime, they are not further victimized," says Mimi Wright, adding, "It's important to present a human face to victims and families of victims. Part of my job is encouraging citizens' confidence in our justice system. Developing that level of trust is extremely important to me." Timijanel Boyd Odom says, "As a public defender, you're representing the underdog. You have to have strong empathy for your client as well as a strong constitution; you have to be willing to be the underdog."

❖ **Counseling and social work skills** are critically important skills to the public defender. "I'm truly looking out for the client's legal interests, but you can't do that without considering the whole person," explains

Timijanel Boyd Odom. "I spend a great deal of time soothing and reassuring my clients. I help them navigate the justice system, but I also help them seek drug treatment, employment opportunities, and educational opportunities. When I have clients looking for work, I've been known to copy down phone numbers from help wanted signs I spot on my commute to the courthouse! I make every effort to get clients to focus on the future." Timijanel points out that another important skill in working with her clients is **patience**. "My clients sometimes tell me five different versions of the same story. I try to listen to each version as if it's the first time." Timijanel has four children, and she says that she finds herself calling upon her mothering skills to encourage clients to be patient while they await their appearance in court. "When clients have to wait for a couple hours for their case to be called, they sometimes believe that it's because they have a public defender rather than a private defense attorney. I have to reassure them that this isn't the case, and get them to adjust their attitudes. If they're angry when they are in front of the judge, their attitude can adversely affect their case."

❖ **Common sense and good judgment** are helpful to any attorney, particularly the criminal law attorney. "The best white collar practitioners have a combination of good judgment and good communication skills. The white collar defense attorney is often faced with difficult decisions," explains Robert Humphreys. "For example, when the prosecutor offers a plea bargain, the attorney must decide whether to advise the client to go to trial; to reject the offer, taking the risk that the client will spend a longer time in prison; or to concede criminal responsibility without a fight in exchange for leniency. This is an extremely difficult decision and often the advice must be given before all the facts are available. It is the lawyer's judgment and common sense that allows him to anticipate where the facts will likely lead and how they would appear to a neutral fact-finder when presented in trial."

❖ A certain amount of **"street smarts"** can be useful to both prosecutors and criminal defense attorneys. Timijanel Boyd Odom explains, "Sometimes new street scams evolve, and judges and other attorneys aren't aware of the scams. For example, a recent scam is the 'hype rental.' In this situation, a person rents their vehicle out in order to get drug money, then calls the police to report that their car has been stolen. The person who rented the car is then arrested for auto theft. When they tell the judge that they 'rented' the car, the judge thinks that the defendant is playing dumb. 'I find the defendant's story totally incredulous,' said one judge I worked with. 'Who could possibly think that they were renting a car for $25 in cash?' You have to know the practices of the street. You have to know the crimes occurring in the neighborhoods in which your clients live. And you have to talk to your clients and your neighborhood contacts to know that such crimes actually do occur."

❖ Criminal attorneys also need a **sincere commitment to their work and a good sense of humor.** "You have to be passionate, but sincere," says Bill Seki. Elizabeth Dobson agrees. "Your opposing counsel must know that you are an honest person. They must know that you can be trusted to keep your word," she says. Because criminal attorneys are often dealing with cases where the stakes are high, a sense of humor is important for keeping it all in perspective. "You're under a lot of pressure," says Elizabeth. "You have to be able to take a step back and find humor in your day. And, most importantly, you have to be able to laugh at yourself."

What classes and law school experiences do criminal lawyers recommend?

❖ The lawyers we interviewed for this chapter recommended taking **criminal law, criminal procedure, and evidence classes** in law school. Because criminal law is a field that involves extensive negotiations, they also recommended a **negotiations class.**

❖ **If you are interested in white collar crime, take business-related law school courses,** as well. "Because white collar crime involves business issues, a good understanding of corporations, securities, tax, and administrative procedure is very helpful. And because white collar criminal litigation often gives rise to parallel civil litigation, the white collar practitioner should also be very familiar with civil procedure," advises Robert Humphreys.

❖ The criminal lawyers we talked to strongly recommended taking as many **trial advocacy classes** as possible. "Trial advocacy was the most helpful class I took in law school," says Elizabeth Dobson. Timijanel Boyd Odom took three trial advocacy classes in law school. "They were excellent preparation for my work," she says. Students interested in appellate advocacy or seeking to develop their oral advocacy skills should also consider participating in their law school's **moot court competition,** in which students draft an appellate brief and then present oral arguments before a team of judges. The judges are often state court judges and experienced practitioners. Elizabeth Dobson says, "Moot court competition requires you to think on your feet and respond to judges' extemporaneous questions. This helps you learn to be composed even under the most intense questioning."

❖ **Improve your writing skills** by taking legal research and writing classes and participating in law review or other journals and writing competitions. Mimi Wright, who was editor of one of her school's law journals, highly recommends the law review experience. If you're considering work as a federal prosecutor or as an appellate attorney, take advanced writing classes and seminars that will help sharpen your writing skills.

❖ **Undergraduate courses in speech communications, social work, and psychology** can be helpful. As Bill Seki mentioned earlier, speech classes provide an excellent way to learn about persuasive theory and to practice persuasive strategy. Timijanel Boyd Odom advises students interested in working as public defenders to consider classes in social work and psychology. "The classes help you develop the practical skills you need to counsel clients," she says. She also advises students who have no personal experience with the criminal justice system to take a basic course in criminal justice administration. "Such a course helps you begin to understand the complex issues underlying the relationship between the urban community and the justice system."

❖ **Gain practical experience in criminal law settings.** Seek out internships in state's attorney's offices, public defender's offices, and U.S. Attorney's offices, or consider participating in your law school's criminal law clinic. "The most helpful way to prepare to work as a prosecutor is by working as an intern in a prosecutor's office," says Elizabeth Dobson. "Working as an intern allows you to be an apprentice. There's no better way to learn a job than to spend time watching someone who's really good at it." Explains Timijanel Boyd Odom, "Clinical experience gives you the chance to work with real clients on real cases. You also have the opportunity to work under the supervision of a clinical professor who is both an outstanding professor and an outstanding clinician." Mark Lipton worked in his law school's Legal Assistance Clinic. "Clinical experience allows you to learn about the attorney-client relationship," he says. "No other law school classes deal with that issue." Adds Robert Humphreys, "Law students who are interested in white collar crime should get involved in clinics and other activities that offer hands-on litigation experience."

❖ If you hope to become a federal prosecutor, consider working as a **federal judicial extern** while a law student or a **federal judicial law clerk** upon graduation. Federal judges hire law students to work as law clerks for one to two years after graduation. A good stepping stone for learning about judicial clerkships and for obtaining one upon graduation is working as a judicial extern during law school. As judicial externs, students work closely with a federal judge's law clerks, gaining excellent writing experience as well as an opportunity to learn about the merits of seeking a judicial clerkship position. Mimi Wright is generous in her praise for judicial clerkships. "A judicial clerkship gives you a view of the legal system you'll never see again. You get to learn firsthand what's important to judges in terms of written and oral presentations. You get practical, hands-on experience in civil and criminal procedure. And you develop personal relationships with seasoned jurists—not just the judge you're working for but other judges as well—which is extremely valuable in terms of mentoring opportunities. You also have the opportunity to improve your legal research and writing skills. It's an outstanding credential that all legal professionals value." Mimi still maintains a close relationship with the judge for whom she clerked after law school.

❖ **Talk to people who are working as criminal law attorneys.** Advises Bill Seki, "I think that the only way you can determine if a career as a prosecutor is right for you is to talk to prosecutors and to others in the criminal justice system. You have to find out if being a prosecutor fits your personality and ideals." Best of all, says Bill, is that "the one thing you'll learn after talking to several prosecutors is that they all love what they're doing."

CRIMINAL ATTORNEYS INTERVIEWED FOR THIS SECTION

Elizabeth Dobson
Office of the Champaign County State's Attorney
Urbana, Illinois
UNDERGRADUATE: University of Illinois
LAW SCHOOL: University of Illinois College of Law

Robert Humphreys
Howrey & Simon (now Howrey Simon Arnold & White LLP)
Los Angeles, California
UNDERGRADUATE: University of Colorado
LAW SCHOOL: Georgetown University Law Center

Mark Lipton
Meyer, Capel, Hirschfeld, Muncy, Jahn & Aldeen, P.C.
(now Meyer Capel P.C.)
Champaign, Illinois
UNDERGRADUATE: Knox College
LAW SCHOOL: Northwestern University School of Law

Timijanel Boyd Odom
Cook County Public Defender's Office
Markham, Illinois
UNDERGRADUATE: Western Illinois University
LAW SCHOOL: Chicago-Kent College of Law, Illinois Institute of
Technology

Bill Seki
Los Angeles County District Attorney's Office
Los Angeles, California
UNDERGRADUATE: California State University
LAW SCHOOL: Southwestern University School of Law

Mimi Wright
Office of the U.S. Attorney
Minneapolis, Minnesota
UNDERGRADUATE: Yale University
LAW SCHOOL: Harvard Law School

Editor's Note: Bill Seki now works for a private law firm.

Entertainment and Sports Law

What are Entertainment and Sports Law?

The field of entertainment and sports law covers a remarkably broad and varied practice area. The practice involves such substantive areas of the law as contracts, labor, corporate finance, intellectual property, and antitrust. Lawyers in the sports and entertainment fields are specialists because of their knowledge of their clients' worlds (entertainers, athletes, and organizations related to the entertainment and sports industries) and how the relevant legal issues intersect with their clients' interests.

Contract Negotiations and Labor Issues

Entertainment and sports law includes negotiation of performance contracts on behalf of an entertainer or athlete or management. These contracts often involve terms of employment. An athlete, for example, might want to renegotiate her contract in light of a record-setting season, or a news anchor, reporter, or disc jockey, courted by a rival network, might seek to alter his current contract. Because these contracts involve the entertainer's or sports figure's compensation, attorneys must be familiar with the standard performance contract requirements in the relevant field or sport, as well as the details of any collective bargaining agreement or union requirements. Attorneys working on these special employment contracts need to understand estate planning, employee benefits (such as retirement plans), and tax law.

Many athletes and performers are union members, which requires attorneys to be familiar with labor law. Union members may file grievances (complaints) claiming that an employer has violated an agreement with the union relating to any number of issues, such as the dates and numbers of performances; disciplinary procedures; medical care and rehabilitation of sports injuries; or the right to demote a musician or trade an athlete. Unfortunately, lawyers specializing in sports and entertainment law must also sometimes be knowledgeable about criminal law and procedure and the effect of arrest or indictment on the contractual obligations of management (for example, the issues raised by a professional athlete's gambling or a musician's drug use).

Attorneys are also involved in negotiating complex marketing and endorsement contracts. When Michael Jordan appears in a cartoon film, a motivational video, a book, or a magazine photographic piece, attorneys were involved in negotiating contracts with the producers or publishers. Entertainment and sports law thus may require knowledge of right to publicity issues (use of an athlete's photograph or likeness); right of privacy issues (paparazzi photographs of entertainers in compromising situations); defamation and media law; and First Amendment rights of free speech and a free press. Attorneys must have a working knowledge of industry standards and the client's marketability as they assist their clients in making difficult judgment calls. Athletes and entertainers must decide whether association with certain products or even political causes will enhance their opportunities to market other products such as athletic shoes or breakfast cereal or could result in "overexposure" that lessens the value of their endorsements.

Corporate Finance, Distribution, and Marketing

Sporting events, including tournaments, and entertainment projects, such as Broadway musicals and films, require financing and marketing. Some events may be financed by major studios (think of the immense capital investment required for Disney's Broadway production of *The Lion King*) or corporations. Independent filmmakers and event producers must seek their own financial support. Attorneys practicing in this area work with event planners, studios, filmmakers, producers, banks, and other financial organizations to put together complex financial deals to support the development of the project. If the project is a film or an album, negotiations for distribution, both nationally and internationally, become very important. Attorneys working on distribution issues need to understand commercial law, secured financial transactions, intellectual property (copyright and trademark) rights, and tax issues.

Marketing includes substantial revenues related to the licensing of products, such as clothing with team logos and colors. Attorneys for rock musicians and country music stars, as well as ballet companies and symphonies (*e.g.*, the Chicago Symphony, which has its own gift shop) may need to be familiar with law and procedures for seizing counterfeit t-shirts and merchandise at concert events or performances. Marketing of sports events, such as the Winston Cup racing circuit or "official" sponsorship of stadiums and college bowl games, also requires contractual negotiations and an understanding of these relevant substantive law areas.

Life as an Entertainment and Sports Lawyer

Where do entertainment and sports lawyers work?

Attorneys who practice entertainment and sports law work in a wide range of environments. A number of them work in private law firms, where they represent individual performers and athletes, athletic teams, filmmakers and producers, studios, opera companies, dance companies, bands, and symphonies. Some large firms, particularly those in entertainment and sports capitals such as New York City, Los Angeles, Nashville, Chicago, and Miami, have entertainment and sports law departments. Smaller "boutique" firms may specialize in sports and/or entertainment law. A number of athletic teams, music companies, film companies, and other organizations have in-house lawyers. These lawyers may work with outside law firms on matters that necessitate teams of attorneys, such as litigation.

Who are their clients and what types of issues do they work on?

Attorneys practicing entertainment or sports law may work with a wide range of clients. Kevin Sweeney, a sports lawyer at Shook, Hardy & Bacon

L.L.P. in Kansas City, Missouri, explains, "A sports lawyer may represent a professional league or a collegiate conference, an individual team or school, a professional athlete or amateur sports star, or a television syndicator or sports merchandiser. The clients that I have worked for include a professional sports team, a major collegiate sports conference, several horse and dog race tracks, and a golf course operator." He adds, "I also have been involved in structuring the financing for new stadiums and arenas and in negotiating stadium leases." Kevin's firm generally represents institutions rather than individual athletes. A typical matter for Kevin? "I might negotiate a master rights agreement between an amateur sports client and a merchandiser, who would seek to commercialize the client's product through television syndication, radio syndication, pay-for-view telecast, on-line and computerized distribution, and sponsorships."

"My clients," says Lawrence (Larry) Ulman of Gibson, Dunn & Crutcher LLP in Los Angeles, "are primarily film studios. I represent the studios with regard to financing and distributing a film." He also represents a number of international film companies. Larry works on business transactions, many of which have an international component. "A lot of countries offer tax benefits and subsidies if you film in their location. Canada, for example, has taken a lot of film and television production from the U.S. Vancouver can look like any city in the U.S." Larry explains that his work involves a great deal of negotiation. He negotiates film distribution agreements with foreign buyers who are buying the right to distribute a film in their country. "Foreign film companies are always looking for product. And the biggest source of product is still the U.S.—American movies, American film stars."

In-house attorney Nancy Rinehart is Vice President of Unapix/Miramar in Seattle, Washington. Miramar, a 15-year-old video and audio production and distribution company, was bought by Unapix, a larger entertainment company, in 1997. The range of the company's activities is huge, Nancy explains. "We have a nonfiction entertainment product division involving videos, TV broadcasts, and distribution of those works; we have a footage division, which licenses out footage—such as nature footage—that may be included in a TV show or movie; we license musical artists' scores that may be used in the production of animation or in commercials; we have a direct response division that's involved in sales via TV and the Internet; we're involved in emerging technologies such as DVD; and we have a record label and a publishing department." As one of two in-house attorneys, Nancy's client is her company. She gets hands-on experience in every department, including the human resources department. She's involved in business operations, distribution, new product acquisitions, and strategic business partnering. She handles copyright and trademark issues, as well.

Bruce Sostek, an entertainment and intellectual property lawyer at Thompson & Knight L.L.P. in Dallas, Texas, explains that his clients cover a broad spectrum. "Most of them have in common the fact that they are involved in one type of creative enterprise or another, which may involve creating a Web page or an Internet game, painting a picture, taking a photograph, illustrating a magazine, designing a t-shirt, writing a song, performing on television or radio, or running a professional sports team." His firm has over 300 attorneys and represents both institutions and individuals. "Most of our clients are located in Texas or the southwest, but some are in Silicon Valley, Washington, D.C., New York City, Europe, and the Pacific Rim. Most of them come to us to develop, protect, or evaluate their creative ideas, in one form or another."

What daily activities are involved in an entertainment and sports law practice?

Kevin Sweeney explains that his sports law practice involves many of the same activities as any commercial lawyer (*see* the Corporate Practice chapter for more information). "My day is much like that of any corporate finance lawyer—except that I read the morning sports page as a part of my job and not as just an avocation. I also watch ESPN and read *Sports Illustrated*, not just for the scores, but to determine the business practices of and future trends for the industry." He adds that he also spends a great deal of time in negotiations with "sponsors, television syndicators, and the representatives of businesses that interact with the sports industry, as well as the professional teams and universities that provide the 'product' that fuels the economics of both professional and amateur team sports." He typically does not go to court. "I rely on my litigator partners for those skills," he says. Though he doesn't litigate, Kevin emphasizes that he acts as a forceful advocate for his clients. "On any given day I might serve as an advocate for my clients' interest in the cutting-edge areas of bowl alliances, next-century telecast agreements, intellectual property license agreements, corporate sponsorships, and Internet agreements."

Nancy Rinehart of Miramar explains that she spends most of her time discussing and negotiating new audio-visual projects. She is also involved in risk management. "When you work in-house, preventative medicine is important as far as the company's risk management is concerned. You need to keep an open ear as to what is going on around you. I'm working with non-lawyers. They're wonderful, very creative people, but they are people who tend to go at 500 miles per hour. I sometimes have to slow them down and remind them to get things in writing." Nancy adds that in the entertainment industry, lawyers are often seen as the people who slow deals down. "You don't want to be seen as the person who drives the nail in the coffin. You don't want to hear that you don't understand 'the vision.' You want to be the facilitator."

Larry Ulman reports that his transactional work is communication intensive. "I spend my time talking with people, meeting people, reading trade papers. I have a heavy phone practice; I probably spend five hours a day on the phone. I'll often have 30 or 40 phone messages a day. It's very important to return all the calls for client relationship purposes and to keep up with what's going on." His laptop and cell phone ensure that he's available to clients even when he's on one of his frequent international trips. Larry says that it's the international side of his practice that is growing, and this requires many international trips per year. "In developing the international side of the practice (film distribution) you have to get out there. I go to the Cannes Film Festival, the Berlin Film Festival, and other festivals. During my travels I work to establish contacts with other lawyers in other countries. My time at Cannes is spent talking and meeting with people, not putting on a tuxedo."

Other entertainment lawyers are involved in intellectual property issues (*see* the Intellectual Property Law chapter for additional information). Bruce Sostek says, "The theme in my cases is generally how to protect ideas that people have reduced to a tangible form of expression in one way or another. One of our typical goals would be to try to identify the best way to create value for those ideas and to develop a plan to maximize the impact of those ideas as successfully as possible. Sometimes we seek patents, sometimes we counsel clients as to trade secrets, other times we file for a copyright or engage in extensive licensing and royalty negotiations. Each case is different, but they all stem from some type of creative spark."

What do entertainment and sports lawyers find rewarding about their practice?

Lawyers who practice entertainment law said they enjoy the role they play in making artists' ideas come to life. Nancy Rinehart explains, "It's really rewarding to be involved in the process—from the time the idea is a spark to seeing the concept come to fruition and then evolve into something tangible." Larry Ulman and Bruce Sostek echo her sentiments. Says Larry Ulman, "The work I do with the film industry is project-oriented. Although I'm not making the movie, the work I am doing enables the producer to make the film. When it's all done, there's a movie that was made. Though you, as the attorney, aren't behind the camera, you are involved, integrally involved, in the making of the film." Bruce Sostek puts it this way: "I get a great deal of satisfaction from starting out with an individual who has both a great idea and the unshakeable belief that it will work. Watching an idea develop from its original conception into something tangible is very rewarding—as is seeing the resulting product grow and obtain wide scale acceptance and approval."

Bruce adds that he enjoys working on projects that go beyond the familiar notion of entertainment—projects that share practical information with a wide audience. "Because some of the work I do involves access to a large audience, through radio and television broadcasting, books, movies, and the Internet, I have had a number of experiences that were rewarding because of the opportunity to get information out to a much broader segment of the population. For example, I negotiated a television movie deal for the author of a book whose main objective was not to get rich, but rather to inform as wide a segment of society as possible about the advances that are being made toward finding a cure for paralysis. Negotiating the deal with lawyers and Hollywood producers was interesting and challenging, but knowing the author's ultimate goal and working toward that objective made the experience much more satisfying."

The lawyers we talked to also mentioned that they enjoy putting together deals which enhance their clients' interests. Says Kevin Sweeney, "I find it most rewarding when I can take an active and positive role in helping my clients achieve their business and financial goals. Most times, this requires a 'win-win' scenario where both my clients and I understand the other parties' goals and help structure a solution where both sets of primary goals can be achieved. I am most satisfied when I can help 'add value' to achieving a mutually beneficial solution to a challenging business situation." Larry Ulman states simply, "I like negotiating. It's fun to work with other people and put together a deal that's good for your client."

These attorneys enjoy the challenge of working within the extremely complex realm of the sports and entertainment industries. Nancy Rinehart says her favorite part of the job is working on music rights issues. "The issues are so complicated, and they involve so many people—musicians, songwriters, record labels, music publishers, bands. I like getting to know these people and learning what everybody wants to do, where everyone sees the direction of the music going." Kevin Sweeney talks about the inside knowledge he's acquired about the sports industry. "Over the last two years," he says, "I've had the privilege of assisting in structuring and forming one of (if not *the*) major amateur sports conferences in the U.S. In this process, I have had direct discussions with the CEOs of 12 of the major sports universities in the nation, the heads of three major sports conferences and the legal counsel for several more, all of the major football bowl games, most of the major television broadcasts and syndicators, the major sports representation agencies, and the major sports merchandisers. This once-in-a-lifetime opportunity to build a conference from the ground up has allowed me to gain a much greater understanding of the business dynamics of the amateur sports industry." He adds, "It's fun to get to meet and work on a professional basis directly with the CEOs of professional sports organizations and major national universities, nationally known coaches and athletes, and celebrities of the sports industries."

Attorneys in this field also enjoy the "cutting edge" nature of their work. Explains Larry Ulman, "The fun thing about the film industry is that the business changes every year or so. There are always new marketing schemes, new ways of financing films. Technology has a dramatic impact on the film business; my practice evolves with the changes in technology. One of the films I worked on recently, *What Dreams May Come*, starring Robin Williams, used many new technologies for special effects [in the movie, Williams' character visits heaven and hell in search of his deceased wife]. An enormous part of the budget was devoted to special effects. In movies like *Twister* and the asteroid movies *Deep Impact* and *Armageddon*, the story often seems secondary to the special effects. The software game industry has become much more sophisticated, too. New video games involve characters with personalities and behavioral traits. The characters may be derived from films." Larry explains that as a result of the changes in game software, he's becoming more involved in intellectual property issues such as copyright and licensing.

Nancy Rinehart says, "I learn so many new things every day. Everyone I work with is trying to think of new ways to do things. I have to push copyright law to keep up with Internet uses and emerging technologies. There are no form agreements for most of the projects I work on. It's fun to work with existing terms in new contexts." She adds, "I can't imagine being any other kind of attorney. I like really helping to shape the new direction of the entertainment industry."

The Training and Skills Important to Entertainment and Sports Law

How do people enter the fields of entertainment and sports law?

Most attorneys grow into the field of sports and entertainment law through their commercial and corporate law practice experience. Kevin Sweeney offers sounds advice: "Become an excellent substantive attorney, develop contacts in the sports industry, and look for opportunities to become involved in and add value to their activities. Beyond this, luck and persistence can't hurt." He adds, "I did not become a sports lawyer by design, but only because I became a good corporate attorney and some of my clients happened to be involved in the sports industry. Without being a good substantive attorney, you cannot be a good sports attorney."

Larry Ulman grew up in Los Angeles and always enjoyed film as an art form. Larry says two areas have always fascinated him—finance and entertainment. Entertainment law is a field that allowed him to marry his two interests. He began his legal career working for Bank of America. He assisted the bank's media and entertainment group on some projects, and entertainment law issues became a big part of his day-to-day practice. He then left to join a private law firm. "Finance and banking provide a good background for a lawyer to have," he says. "Finance is a good, marketable skill." Larry makes sure that summer associates at his firm who are interested in entertainment law get broad, business-related experience. "I insist that they do traditional corporate work a good part of the time," he says. "This is a narrow area. I want someone who understands the basics of the U.C.C. [the Uniform Commercial Code], the basics of corporate practice, the basics of mergers and acquisitions. New associates have to spend time doing bread and butter corporate and commercial work."

Bruce Sostek didn't start out in entertainment and intellectual property law; he developed his practice in that area. "I took one or two intellectual property courses in law school and enjoyed that subject matter more than anything else I studied. When it came to choosing a law firm, Thompson & Knight didn't have a formal intellectual property practice, but I chose the firm anyway, based upon its people rather than its practice areas. While an associate I actively sought out intellectual property cases being handled by many different lawyers at the firm and volunteered to work on those cases in addition to my own docket. After four or five years of this type of practice, I went to the firm's management with a proposal to create an intellectual property practice group. This proposal was accepted and approved, and we now have 20 full-time and several part-time intellectual property lawyers in the group and are continuing to expand."

In-house attorney Nancy Rinehart took a more unconventional route—she set up a solo practice in Portland, Oregon, immediately after law school (*see* the chapter on Solo, Small Firm, and General Practice for more information on this topic). She had a long-standing interest in the arts, having played the guitar since she was 11, and says she never considered a career other than entertainment law. "I knew I wanted to do this. Starting a practice is a personal sacrifice in terms of start-up costs and time. You have to really want to do it. I found everyone in Portland who was involved in music and the arts. I learned everything I could about the industry. I did lots of reading. I attended seminars. I called people. I conducted informational interviews with experienced attorneys—picking their brains, asking them how they got started in entertainment law. As a result of my informational interviews, I hooked up with a mentor. He was a great teacher who taught me everything he could." Nancy's commitment and persistence paid off. Her clients included art galleries, bands, record labels, a CD-ROM developer, and music and video producers. After two and half years of solo practice, she met the president of Miramar through one of her clients, and she was recruited to join Miramar as in-house counsel.

What skills are most important to entertainment and sports lawyers?

❖ An **understanding of corporate and financial issues** is critical to the sports and entertainment lawyer. "When hiring an experienced attorney to work on entertainment matters, I would really prefer a lawyer who has spent several years in a corporate or commercial practice. The entertainment part of this field can be picked up—it's a matter of understanding how things work in the industry, picking up jargon, and establishing contacts," says Larry Ulman. Kevin Sweeney, who specializes in sports law, agrees. He sees himself as a "corporate finance lawyer whose clients are involved in the sports industry."

❖ An **interest in and understanding of the entertainment and/or sports industry** is key to success in this area of practice. Kevin Sweeney says, "The most important skill for *any* business lawyer is to understand your client's business and their business and financial goals. It is crucial that an attorney read about his clients' business and spend time talking with his clients about the risks involved with their business and their business strategies, their competitors, and the future of their industry to be able to help them reach their goals." Nancy Rinehart says that her training as a guitarist and her experience making videos when she was younger helps her relate to her clients. "You want your clients to feel comfortable with you. My background in guitar helps me talk with my clients. When an artist is turning over their project to you, it helps to have similar interests. You have to believe that the integration of art and commerce can work. And you have to project that confidence to your client."

❖ **Excellent communication skills** are important to those in the field. "The skills I use day to day are reading and writing," says Nancy Rinehart, noting that whether you're writing to lawyers or non-lawyers, you have to communicate in plain English. "Legal writing skills are necessary to drafting linguistically balanced contracts—in other words, if you're getting a right, you need to be giving a right." Finally, she notes the key role that reading plays in her practice. "Reading with attention to detail is critical," she says, whether she is reviewing a business plan or a distribution contract. All of the attorneys we talked to mentioned that they spend a significant amount of time reading trade papers and journals to keep up with developments in the entertainment and sports industries.

❖ Attorneys practicing sports and entertainment law need **outstanding relationship-building skills**. "Interpersonal skills are the foundation of a transactional practice," says Larry Ulman. "In entertainment law you are building on a network of relationships. It's a small bar. There's a very limited number of film studios. You can't alienate anyone—you need to get along with everyone. Of course, you must still vigorously represent your client, but you must be very professional and never burn bridges. In this area of practice, you run into the same people over and over again." "True appreciation for people is an invaluable asset," adds Bruce Sostek. "People are what my practice is all about. Courtesy and kindness to others will redound to your benefit, even if it isn't obvious how that might happen. If you work at trying to understand and appreciate other people and their perspectives, that effort will enhance your ability to evaluate situations, clients, witnesses, lawyers, and judges."

❖ Attorneys working in the sports and entertainment law fields must possess **strong negotiation skills**. Nancy Rinehart cites listening as the number one negotiation skill. Larry Ulman agrees, commenting, "When you're talking with a group of lawyers, it's difficult not to want to make the first point and the last point. Sometimes it's beneficial to let the other person get their two cents in."

❖ **A flexible and creative approach to problem-solving** is necessary to succeed in the rapidly evolving field of entertainment law. Says Nancy Rinehart, "You have to find creative solutions to an ever-changing array of problems. This means you have to be open-minded and willing to change your approach." Bruce Sostek adds, "I regard flexibility as essential. As John Lennon once wrote, 'Life is what happens to you while you're busy making other plans.' This is a very apt description of legal practice in this field. You never really have control over where you will be or when, and, lately, with the incredibly dynamic changes in technology and their impact on intellectual property rights, you can't even be sure what the legal landscape will look like from month to month, or even daily. Maintaining a flexible attitude toward these rapid changes (and a sense of humor to go with it) will help to avoid unnecessary wear and tear on your psyche."

What classes and law school experiences do entertainment and sports lawyers recommend?

❖ **Take a core curriculum of business-oriented classes** in law school. Consider classes in secured transactions, international business transactions, antitrust, corporations and partnerships, corporate finance, negotiations and telecommunications. Also consider taking intellectual property, computer law, labor law, and estate planning. Tax classes—including corporate tax, international tax, and personal income tax—are also helpful, notes Larry Ulman. "A lot of the business practice is tax-oriented, and even though you're not a tax lawyer, you have to be able to identify the tax issues."

❖ **Gather information about and make contacts in the industry**. Nancy Rinehart recommends reading as much as you can about the music industry. Two books that she has found particularly helpful (she still keeps them next to her desk) are M. William Krasilovsky, Sidney Shemel, *This Business of Music* (Billboard 1990) and *The Musician's Business and Legal Guide* (Mark Halloran, ed., Prentice Hall 1996). Nancy also suggests making contacts with lawyers and non-lawyers through involvement in the arts community. "The best way to develop contacts," says Bruce Sostek, "is by doing. Attend performances, volunteer for arts societies, create your own home page, watch athletes in competition, go to shows where artists exhibit. In general, get your hands dirty in the business of those you want to get to know and represent. The most important thing is to work with people who are the source of creative new ideas," he says.

❖ **Consider learning a foreign language.** Several years ago, Larry Ulman observed that the U.S. film market was mature and that the big growth market for American films was in foreign countries, so he began to establish international contacts. Currently, he says, Germany is a big growth market. When we talked to Larry, he was preparing to speak at the Berlin Film Festival. Larry advises that those students interested in entertainment law could find the knowledge of German, French, or Spanish helpful in developing business contacts. Larry notes that knowledge of a foreign language, and the ability to talk with a contact in their native tongue, makes the nonbusiness part of the relationship flow more smoothly. "Foreign language study also helps you identify the ways in which different cultures respond to law-related problems," says Larry.

❖ **Liberal arts classes** can be helpful in preparing for the practice of entertainment law. Bruce Sostek comments, "Oddly enough, the classes that have helped me the most in my practice include philosophy, psychology, and sociology—not what you would expect, perhaps, but they are classes that trained me to examine the motivations, needs, and drives of people, and to appreciate the subjective nature of the world around us and the value and power of commonly shared symbols. For a lawyer dealing with trademarks and copyrights, this has proved to be very valuable information." Nancy Rinehart recommends English, political science, and sociology classes. "My English classes were helpful because they required extensive reading, detailed analysis, and careful writing. The best class I took was a poetry writing class. It challenged me to write concisely." Political science and sociology classes "get you to think about how other cultures think and express themselves. They also help you acquire a familiarity with the legal systems of other countries," says Nancy.

ENTERTAINMENT/SPORTS ATTORNEYS
INTERVIEWED FOR THIS SECTION

Nancy Rinehart
Unapix/Miramar
Seattle, Washington
UNDERGRADUATE: Vassar College
LAW SCHOOL: Chicago-Kent College of Law, Illinois Institute of
Technology

Bruce Sostek
Thompson & Knight L.L.P.
Dallas, Texas
UNDERGRADUATE: Union College
LAW SCHOOL: Emory University School of Law

Kevin Sweeney
Shook, Hardy & Bacon L.L.P.
Kansas City, Missouri
UNDERGRADUATE: University of Notre Dame
LAW SCHOOL: University of Missouri-Columbia School of Law

Lawrence J. Ulman
Gibson, Dunn & Crutcher LLP
Los Angeles, California
UNDERGRADUATE: University of Southern California
LAW SCHOOL: University of Southern California Law School

Environmental Law

What is Environmental Law?

Today's children grow up with a keen awareness of environmental issues. Grade school children participate in community efforts to clean up creeks and rivers and spend class time studying the causes of global warming. Preschoolers, coached by sophisticated teachers as well as a certain purple dinosaur, remind family members to recycle. The parents of these savvy kids—whose own childhood knowledge of environmental issues may have been limited to planting a tree in the schoolyard on Arbor Day—find themselves facing an ever-increasing array of environmental challenges in the workplace. Whether employed in real estate, manufacturing, construction, banking, or health care, they grapple with environmental issues, many of which touch upon the law.

Environmental law is a relatively new legal specialty. Since the 1970s—often referred to as "the environmental decade"—the U.S. Congress has passed a number of major environmental statutes. The Environmental Protection Agency (EPA) and other federal agencies have adopted hundreds of thousands of pages of regulations under those statutes. State and local governments have also enacted regulations in response to environmental concerns. Thus a vast range of environmental issues intersects with the law—from the generation and disposal of hazardous waste to the transfer of property that may be contaminated to the protection of land, water, and air from future contamination.

Environmental Permitting

When entities build, expand, or transfer (through sale of real estate) any industrial property, they must consider federal, state, and local environmental laws. Federal statutes such as the Clean Air Act, the Clean Water Act, and the Toxic Substances Control Act, as well as state and local laws, come into play. A major part of this practice involves "permitting"—obtaining the proper federal, state, and local permits and operating licenses.

When a new facility, such as a chemical plant or an auto manufacturing plant, is constructed, the operating entity needs to obtain air permits, water permits, solid and hazardous waste permits, and other permits and operating licenses to ensure that the facility will meet environmental standards. The procedures for obtaining these permits and operating licenses can be extremely complex. Environmental attorneys help guide business entities through this complicated process of obtaining the necessary permits and licenses from regulatory agencies.

A business, a community group, or a municipality can challenge the issuance of a permit if, for example, they believe a regulatory agency has issued a permit that fails to adequately protect the environment, or if they believe the permit violates the agency's own regulations. These challenges result in an administrative hearing.

As environmental laws change and become increasingly restrictive, businesses must comply with the changed regulations. This may involve upgrading their facilities or even changing the design of their products. For example, a neighborhood gas station may have to upgrade its storage tanks to comply with federal, state, or local regulations. Federal regulations require automobile manufacturers such as Ford and General Motors to produce vehicles producing fewer emissions. Attorneys guide businesses in developing plans to comply with these laws.

Superfund and Brownfields Practice

To fight the problem of hazardous waste, Congress passed the Superfund Program (The Comprehensive Environmental Response Compensation and Liability Act of 1980, as amended in 1986). Superfund allows the federal government and private parties to bring cost recovery actions for the cleanup of chemical contamination to property. Such cleanups may cost millions of dollars. Superfund litigation generally involves numerous parties, including those who deposited the chemicals and prior owners of the property, seeking to apportion the high cost of cleaning up this toxic waste.

There are many industrial sites that are contaminated, but not heavily contaminated. The EPA defines these sites as "brownfields." According to the EPA, brownfields are "abandoned, idled, or under-used industrial and commercial facilities where expansion or redevelopment is complicated by real or perceived environmental contamination." These sites are often in low-income areas and contribute to urban blight. Potential buyers and redevelopers of the sites fear an unknown amount of liability due to cleaning up hazardous waste. Brownfields programs have been developed at the federal, state, and local level to clean up these sites and make them available for purchase by private industry. The Clinton administration developed the Brownfields Redevelopment Initiative, designed to spur cleanup and redevelopment of thousands of brownfields sites around the U.S.

Real Estate Transactions

Many manufacturing plants are located in areas with high concentrations of industry, but commercial redevelopment and movement toward a service economy and lighter industrial processes are causing this to change. Old industrial sites, such as steel mills and petrochemical plants, may be converted into offices, shops, and entertainment facilities, or they may be converted to light industrial facilities, such as package distribution centers. When these properties are sold, the buyers and sellers are often required to negotiate each party's responsibility for any potential liability for environmental hazards related to the property. For this reason, most of today's commercial real estate transactions involve environmental assessments or environmental audits. This means that a professional person reviews the real estate as well as the state of environmental compliance of the business being sold. Environmental lawyers then evaluate the results of the audit and assess the legal risks and liabilities related to the transaction. Environmental lawyers advise their clients on how to structure the real estate deals to minimize environmental liability.

Life as an Environmental Lawyer

Where do environmental lawyers work?

Environmental lawyers work in many different settings. Those employed by the government work to enforce environmental law statutes and develop and enforce regulations, whether at the federal, state, or local level. In law firms, environmental attorneys represent the corporations and industries subject to environmental regulations. In corporations, in-house attorneys advise their employers concerning compliance with environmental laws. Some environmental lawyers work for public interest organizations, assisting residents and community groups with the environmental problems that may plague low-income areas. Others work for environmental advocacy organizations.

Who are their clients and what types of cases do they work on?

Environmental attorneys who work in law firms generally represent corporate clients. Kevin Bruno, formerly of Hannoch Weisman in Roseland, New Jersey, explains, "My practice involves large corporate clients, most of which are Fortune 500 companies. At least 90% of my clients are from outside of New Jersey, most in the Midwest or along the Atlantic Coast." He adds, "These corporations are either suing or being sued for environmental contamination, or they may be pursuing their insurance carriers for coverage of those environmental costs. The damages are frequently in the tens of millions of dollars."

James Collier is an environmental attorney at Dykema Gossett PLLC in Detroit, Michigan. James has worked with corporate clients from a wide variety of industries—oil and gas, waste management, retailing, auto parts, and other manufacturing industries. He represents clients in environmental litigation. A typical case might involve a leaking underground storage tank that has contaminated surrounding soil and ground water. Sometimes the cases involve contamination that happened years previously, resulting in the interesting, but arduous, task of investigating events that occurred as long as 50 years ago.

Ignacio Arrazola works as Associate Regional Counsel for the Environmental Protection Agency regional office in Chicago, Illinois. "My clients," he explains, "are the various program offices in the EPA that are charged with enforcing environmental laws. For example, an engineer who works for the EPA who inspects a plant and finds evidence of violations of the Clean Air Act would refer that case to our office. I work on cases involving civil enforcement of federal environmental laws, including the Clean Air Act, the Clean Water Act, the Comprehensive Environmental Response Compensation and Liability Act, the Federal Insecticide, Fungicide, and Rodenticide Act, and others."

Mike Thrift, an attorney for the Office of General Counsel of the U.S. EPA in Washington, D.C., works on the regulatory side of environmental law. He advises EPA headquarters and regional program staff who are assigned to regulatory rule-making projects. He writes notices that justify the regulations the EPA adopts. When the EPA is sued by state agencies, environmental groups, or industry, he works with Department of Justice attorneys to defend or settle the litigation. This litigation arises when petitioners allege that a part of a federal statute or regulation is not stringent enough, is overburdensome, or is otherwise illegal.

"The issues I work on are of a national scope," says Mike. "They can be abstract and are rarely of local or specific immediate consequence. We almost never save single places from destruction here in Washington, but we do set up the rules so that regional and state agencies can."

Some environmental attorneys work for non-profit organizations. Vickie Patton is an attorney for the Environmental Defense Fund (EDF), an environmental advocacy group. Vickie works in Boulder, Colorado, at one of the group's five regional offices, and her clients are the members of EDF. She works on air quality and climate change issues, especially those affecting the western United States. "The issues I work on may range from intense local controversies to international policies. There may be an issue that affects air quality in Boulder, or there may be an issue that affects a multinational protocol to address reduction of greenhouse gases. Most of my work involves broader policy issues. I spend a considerable amount of time advocating for EPA and state agencies to adopt sound environmental policies."

A limited number of environmental law attorneys work in the public interest sector. Keith Harley is the Director of the Environmental Law Program of the Chicago Legal Clinic (CLC). "As an attorney at CLC, my clients are people who cannot otherwise find or afford an attorney. I assist individuals and community groups who are facing urban environmental problems." Keith works on the remarkably wide range of environmental issues that affect residents of low-income areas. Most issues are related to "living space," such as use of lead-based paint, indiscriminate use of indoor pesticides, and improper demolition and renovation activities. Other issues, such as nuisance conditions and brownfields issues, concern the larger community.

What daily activities are involved in environmental law practice?

Those environmental attorneys at firms report dividing their time between meetings, telephone conferences, and drafting written materials. Explains Kevin Bruno, "On a typical day, telephone calls and conferences consume one-third of my time, meetings another third, and preparation and review of written materials the last third." An experienced veteran with over 14 years of experience, he reports that he is seldom in the library. James Collier reports that his environmental litigation practice requires him to spend about 20% of a typical month out of the office—taking depositions, arguing motions, or attending the occasional trial. His in-office time "is spent heavily on the telephone with clients, in drafting agreements and litigation documents, and in holding internal meetings."

Ignacio Arrazola reports that his role as a Regional Counsel for the EPA requires that he spend a great deal of time in conferences or on phone calls with opposing counsel. "I spend a good deal of my time negotiating settlements. It's an important part of the job," he says. "Most environmental cases tend to settle. I've only tried one federal case in the last six years—the others have settled." Ignacio also conducts internal training sessions for new EPA attorneys.

Mike Thrift, who works on the regulatory side of the EPA, reports that he spends much of his time writing. He writes Federal Register Preamble Notices that justify the regulations adopted by the EPA, as well as writing briefs and drafting written responses to congressional inquiries. He reviews and edits the written work of staff at other EPA offices. He also drafts what are called "guidance documents," which discuss how the EPA will implement a particular program. Mike adds that he spends "endless" hours on the phone, whether engaged in settlement negotiations, advising staff at other EPA offices, or providing program clients with legal and policy advice.

In her work for the Environmental Defense Fund, Vickie Patton participates in a wide variety of activities. "This job involves rolling up your sleeves and doing all kinds of things. I do the nuts and bolts things such as legal research and writing. But I also meet with and advocate before senior officials in state and federal government. I engage in both written and oral advocacy. I litigate. I work on press and public outreach strategies to engender public support for important environmental issues. I meet with representatives of other environmental organizations to strategize about how we can work together to shape policy. I also have fundraising responsibilities. I do my share of traditional legal work, but it is balanced by advocacy work and work outside the office."

Keith Harley explains that as an environmental public interest lawyer, "I spend most of my time talking to people confronting problems and helping them devise strategies for dealing with those problems. That sometimes involves legal action, but more often involves implementing change in nontraditional ways." He notes that facilitating change requires going beyond traditional lawyering. "I do a lot of community education. I write manuals and newsletters. I look for ways to educate our target population. If people understand their rights, they can exercise them without resorting to the legal system."

What do environmental lawyers find rewarding about their practice?

Whether working for law firms, the government, or non-profit organizations, the environmental lawyers we talked to report that their greatest satisfaction comes from proactively solving environmental problems. Ignacio Arrazola explains, "It's satisfying to negotiate cleanup settlements. When a company that's responsible for hazardous waste comes to an agreement with us, and bears the costs of cleanup—that's rewarding. For example, in 1997 we negotiated with Union Carbide to provide $50 million to clean up a hazardous waste site in southern Ohio. It's a good feeling to know that a large environmental problem is actually being addressed."

Kevin Bruno, who is in private practice, finds it rewarding to "negotiate a fair resolution of these matters in a way both favorable to the clients and timely enough to allow for the prompt remediation of the environmental problem at issue."

Keith Harley explains that, though working to solve the problems is rewarding, so is working with the people who work to solve the problems. "One of the very best parts of the job is working with good people. I live in this network of people in business, government agencies, and community groups, and they have a common goal—solving problems. These are people I respect very much. They have all points of view, yet they come together with creative solutions. One of the best people I work with works with a local landfill company. I also work with 60 volunteer attorneys, as well as with law students who work on our projects. I tend to see the very best side of the legal profession."

The attorneys we talked to were enthusiastic about their clients and colleagues. James Collier reports that interacting with people is one of his favorite parts of the job. "I like the clients I work with," he says. "They are decent, honest, and capable." Mike Thrift claims that there are no better people to work with than his colleagues at the EPA. "They are the best as far as human beings are concerned. They aren't out to make a quick buck. There's no competition and no backstabbing. There's tremendous collegiality."

The attorneys we talked to also mentioned the intellectual challenge of their work. Vickie Patton says, "It's challenging to influence decision-makers. When you are successful, you've convinced someone to take into account some environmental consideration or viewpoint that they weren't otherwise considering. And best of all, this ultimately makes a difference in the environment."

Mike Thrift enjoys the academic challenge of his work at the EPA. "Intellectually, it's a pretty cool job. I handle issues of first impression under the Clean Air Act. This is heady stuff. It's neat to see the broader philosophical legal issues that exist beyond the technical standards at hand. I have the opportunity to actually influence national environmental policy."

The Training and Skills Important to Environmental Law

How do people enter the field of environmental law?

Many of the attorneys who enter environmental law report that they've been interested in environmental issues for as long as they can remember. Explains Keith Harley, "I've always had an interest in environmental issues. All of these issues have been unfolding during my lifetime. I even remember participating in the first Earth Day when I was a kid." Mike Thrift reports, "I grew up in California, watching the destruction of paradise.

Once-beautiful towns turned into pavement because of no planning, no zoning, and no control. I knew at an early age that I wanted to get into the environmental field somehow." Vickie Patton had a similar experience. "I had a long-standing interest in environmental issues. I grew up in the southwest, where you could see the stresses of rapid growth take their toll on the environment." Ignacio Arrazola adds that his interest in the outdoors was his primary motivating factor to pursuing a career in environmental law. "I'm into rock climbing, and it takes you to all kinds of really neat places. Seeing those places heightens your appreciation and concern for the environment."

Summer employment during law school often tends to pique student interest in environmental law. Ignacio Arrazola clerked at the EPA in Chicago following his first year of law school. This summer job ultimately led to his attorney job at the EPA. "Clerking is a common way into the EPA," he explains, noting that he still sees the people he worked for during that first summer at the EPA. Mike Thrift worked at the Natural Resources Defense Council for two summers during law school. He, too, was hired by the EPA directly out of law school, but he notes that the EPA now hires a number of experienced attorneys who have worked at law firms and for environmental groups.

Other attorneys report that they entered the environmental law field through opportunities that came to them once they began practicing. "Although I took the only environmental law class offered in my law school, it was merely fortuitous that my firm was just beginning to expand its practice into the environmental area when I joined in 1984," says Kevin Bruno. "Since then, I've had the opportunity to develop an environmental practice that is a mix of litigation and counseling." James Collier reports that he started as a tax lawyer; he then developed a business and litigation practice. Then, he says, "Several years ago I decided the environmental area presented an opportunity for interesting and challenging work, while the business practice was suffering from a deep recession. During the 1980s, when the environmental law field was assuming greater and greater importance, my practice began to tip more in that direction."

What skills are most important to environmental lawyers?

❖ Environmental law attorneys need to have **creative problem-solving skills**. Mike Thrift comments, "Problem-solving skills are the most critical talent in environmental law. They are what your clients turn to you for and what they are most disappointed and disbelieving about when you fail." "I constantly push myself to think creatively to solve problems. My clients want a solution, not a lawsuit," says Keith Harley. One of the most rewarding issues Keith remembers working on was solving the problem of the Chicago Housing Authority's (CHA's) use of lead-based paint in public housing. "The case started with a single lead-poisoned child," he says. "It resulted in a complete overhaul of how the Chicago Housing Authority handles the problem. The CHA progressed from handling the problem worse than any other organization in the country to handling it better than any other organization in the country. We had people—law firm attorneys, CHA representatives, mediators, residents—who came together with goodwill to solve a problem."

❖ **Writing skills** are important to environmental lawyers. "They're paramount," asserts Ignacio Arrazola. Kevin Bruno adds that "a well organized and concise written work product" is invaluable to the practitioner and notes that he spends about one-third of his day drafting and editing written work. The writing skills required often go beyond legal writing: Keith Harley uses his writing skills to draft newsletters and manuals that will be meaningful to community groups and to clients who may not have a great deal of formal education.

❖ **An interest in and understanding of science** are helpful to environmental lawyers. Vickie Patton, who came to the field with an undergraduate degree in hydrology, says "You need to understand the science *and* understand the law." However, says Kevin Bruno, "There's some misconception that a strong engineering or science background is a prerequisite to succeeding in this area. Although it's helpful, it's not necessary." Ignacio Arrazola adds, "Knowledge of science helps, but if you have natural curiosity, an ability to focus, and a good eye for detail, you can learn enough science to get along. Most of the attorneys in our EPA office have a liberal arts education. We focus on lawyering and we leave the science to our engineers." Mike Thrift agrees. "It's not necessary to have much of an understanding of science," he says, "especially if you work for scientifically competent and reasonably articulate clients."

❖ A **willingness to learn new things** is also important to the field, since environmental law is so complex and changes constantly. "You have to be able to spot lurking issues or issues that haven't been raised," says Mike Thrift.

❖ The lawyers we talked to also emphasized the critical nature of **negotiation and oral advocacy skills**. Vickie Patton says that at the EDF she must often persuade a decision-maker to see things from her point of view. "You must present the most cogent and persuasive argument you can in a limited amount of time," she says. Mike Thrift's EPA job in Washington, D.C., requires him to constantly exercise his oral advocacy skills. "You have to jump into the snakepit of argument," he says. "In D.C. people are outspoken and opinionated. You must keep your cool. Because you're representing the government, you must maintain an unemotional, objective demeanor. It's a challenge," he adds.

❖ All of the attorneys we interviewed agreed that **interpersonal skills** are of primary importance to environmental lawyers. James Collier explains that when you work in a law firm, "You must be sensitive to clients as people and deal with them in a way that is satisfactory to them. You must understand people to negotiate with them. People skills provide the foundation for persuasion, and as lawyers, we are often called upon to persuade others to accept a point of view." Vickie Patton explains that to further the interests of the EDF, she must focus on forming coalitions with colleagues and decision-makers who have other interests. She notes that this requires good listening skills as well as an astute political ear. "You need to be aware of the politics of the situation and aware of where there are opportunities or lack of opportunities to make a difference," she says.

❖ Environmental lawyers, particularly those who work in non-profit organizations, need an **ability to communicate with and relate to different sectors of society**. Keith Harley explains that his advocacy work for the Chicago Legal Clinic requires him to work with diverse populations. "On the same day, I may attend a meeting in a church basement in the Altgeld Gardens housing project and a meeting of corporate advisers in an elegant conference room in the Loop. Few people are comfortable moving between those different worlds." Keith has a master's degree in divinity, and it has served him well in working with community groups, as many of them are church-based. Vickie Patton has the opportunity to work firsthand with people adversely affected by environmental hazards. She recalls an EDF trip to Mexico during which she met with citizens to gain an understanding of the air quality problem at the El Paso border. "There was incredible pollution. I talked with the citizens about the air pollution problem and its effect on their lives. It was a very humbling experience."

What classes and law school experiences do environmental lawyers recommend?

❖ Take your law school's **environmental law survey course**. If your law school offers additional environmental law classes, consider taking those as well. **Get to know your school's environmental law professors.** As Keith Harley noted earlier, environmental law professors can introduce you to the vast array of opportunities in the environmental law field. These professors also know alumni who are working in the field. Professors and alumni can be valuable mentors for those students who are committed to an environmental law career.

❖ Environmental lawyers strongly recommend taking an **administrative law course** in preparation for dealing with the numerous regulatory agencies involved in this field. "Administrative law is a class that is at least as important as environmental law," explains Ignacio. Attorneys also recommend that students take courses in corporations, federal courts, torts, and evidence.

❖ Attorneys also recommend **courses that will sharpen your litigation and oral advocacy skills**, such as trial advocacy and appellate practice. **Participating in your school's moot court program** is one of the best ways to develop your ability to think on your feet, both inside and outside the courtroom. But in the end, says Mike Thrift, "the best training is to force yourself to actively and orally participate in discussions and argument of any kind—whether it's in large lecture classes, small seminars, or study groups. As Mr. Jordan says in the Nike ads, don't be afraid to lose—failure is critical to learning how to win. You must learn to listen and to argue, and argue a lot, and then to listen again, and hang fire, and then make your point quickly and clearly and demonstrably."

❖ **Pursue a judicial clerkship during your second year of law school.** A judicial clerkship provides you with the opportunity to work for a federal judge upon graduation from law school. Kevin Bruno says, "I found my clerkship experience to be invaluable when entering private practice." Adds Mike Thrift, "Although I never clerked myself, there seems to be no better training for litigation. Working with a judge helps you assess legal risk. And at the EPA, a judicial clerkship allows you to start your job at a higher grade—and thus a higher rate of pay—than those graduates who haven't done judicial clerkships."

❖ If possible, take advantage of your law school's **judicial externship program**. These programs allow students to work as "junior" law clerks for federal judges while in law school. Students generally receive several hours of credit for their work.

❖ **Acquire clinical and/or externship experience** during law school. If your law school has a clinical program that allows you to work on environmental law issues, become involved. "An externship with the U.S. Attorney's office, specifically its environmental task force, would be very valuable," explains Kevin Bruno. Mike Thrift recommends "any administrative agency experience, even if it's not environmental. It will help you understand regulatory issues." **Consider clerking for a law firm or organization that does environmental work.** Part-time work provides you with a more balanced law school life and widens the circle of people you know in the environmental law field. Vickie Patton worked for the Natural Resources Defense Council and for EDF while in law school and reports that she is still in contact with many of her former colleagues.

❖ **Do volunteer work related to environmental issues.** "Volunteer with grassroots groups or with national environmental groups. Student organizations on campus can also be very valuable," Mike Thrift advises. "Most law students don't get as lucky as I did and land summer or school-year jobs with major national environmental groups. But that need not put anyone behind, since there are needy grassroots organizations everywhere that want and appreciate any help they can get. They, in turn, can provide you with real life experience and can reaffirm the validity of your career choice." This is particularly important if you're interested in a public interest career. "Public interest organizations look for people who show a demonstrated commitment to the public interest," Keith Harley explains.

"You can demonstrate this commitment by showing a lifetime of trying to make your values work. When we hire we look for whether someone has an aptitude for public interest work. Be able to show that you've worked in a number of different public interest settings and that you've had success working for those organizations."

❖ **Recognize the rewards and challenges of public interest work.** If you're considering a public interest career, be aware that you're entering a sector with more competition for jobs and a lower rate of pay than the private sector. "There are very few jobs in the public interest sector and they are incredibly difficult to get," says Keith Harley. He adds that it's important to "solve the money question." Even after years of practice, public interest work attorneys generally find their salaries lag significantly behind those of attorneys in government and private practice. "You have to somehow make sense of that," explains Keith, who in addition to his public interest work teaches as an adjunct professor at a Chicago law school. "Even though I have 10 years of experience, I make half as much as my former students completing their first year of private practice." (*See* the Public Interest chapter for more information about this type of practice.)

❖ **Join student groups dedicated to environmental issues.** Explains Vickie Patton, "It's always helpful to spend time with students with similar interests to keep your focus. If you really want to pursue environmental law, it helps to have support from other students." Ignacio Arrazola says that he joined student environmental organizations in college and in law school. "I helped form a student environmental organization when I was an undergrad at Tulane," he says. "I did everything from organizing protests to distributing information about how to recycle to selling t-shirts." He adds that he also helped establish an environmental student group at his law school.

❖ **Become part of the environmental law community** by joining national, state, and local bar associations. The American Bar Association has a section on Environment, Energy, and Resources, for example. Bar associations often make student memberships available at discounted rates. In addition, consider joining or volunteering for national environmental organizations such as the National Wildlife Federation, The Nature Conservancy, The Sierra Club, or the Environmental Defense Fund.

ENVIRONMENTAL ATTORNEYS INTERVIEWED FOR THIS SECTION

Ignacio Arrazola
U.S. EPA
Chicago, Illinois
UNDERGRADUATE: Tulane University
LAW SCHOOL: Northwestern University School of Law

Kevin Bruno
Hannoch Weisman
Roseland, New Jersey
UNDERGRADUATE: Rutgers University
LAW SCHOOL: Rutgers University School of Law

James Collier
Dykema Gossett PLLC
Detroit, Michigan
UNDERGRADUATE: University of Michigan
LAW SCHOOL: University of Michigan Law School

Keith Harley
Chicago Legal Clinic Environmental Law Program
Chicago, Illinois
UNDERGRADUATE: Moravian College
LAW SCHOOL: Chicago-Kent College of Law, Illinois Institute of Technology

Vickie Patton
Environmental Defense Fund
Boulder, Colorado
UNDERGRADUATE: University of Arizona
LAW SCHOOL: New York University School of Law

Mike Thrift
U.S. EPA, Office of the General Counsel
Washington, D.C.
UNDERGRADUATE: UCLA
LAW SCHOOL: UCLA School of Law

Editor's Note: During development of this book, Hannoch Weisman dissolved. Kevin Bruno is now employed with Robertson, Freilich, Bruno & Cohen, LLC in New Jersey.

Family Law

What is Family Law?

The issue here is the deceptively simple question, "What is a family?" We might answer that question differently now than we did even 20 years ago. Today's family members negotiate a web of relationships far more complex than those depicted by the ever cheerful step-family on *The Brady Bunch.* Our families may include birth parents and adoptive parents, gay and lesbian partners, and step-siblings from multiple families. Our notion of what it takes to create and re-create a family has changed over the years, as well. We cast a skeptical eye as we watch *Brady Bunch* reruns, knowing it's unlikely that any newlyweds (whether married for the first or third time, with no children or six children) could create a new family with as little effort and as much bliss as Mike and Carol Brady did.

Family lawyers handle a wide range of matters—divorce; child custody, support, and visitation; prenuptial and postnuptial agreements; guardianships for the elderly, infirm, and mentally disabled who cannot care for themselves; domestic and foreign adoptions; termination of parental rights; and the establishment of paternity. As our society's definition of family continues to expand, so does the range of issues faced by attorneys specializing in family law. For example, when an unmarried gay couple adopts a child, which partner receives custody of the child if the couple splits up? If a couple undergoing fertility treatments decides to divorce, who retains frozen embryos? Are grandparents entitled to visitation rights in a divorce?

Our society's changing notion of what constitutes a family means that family lawyers have the opportunity to make creative arguments and "think outside the box." In addition, family lawyers have the chance to develop and draw upon business expertise. When working on issues related to a party's assets, a family lawyer needs a working knowledge of tax law, real estate law, employee benefits law, and estate planning.

Divorce

Divorce cases make up the majority of most family lawyers' practices. Divorcing spouses must decide how to divide their property, what type of custody and visitation arrangements to make for the children, and whether child support or spousal support is warranted. Family lawyers work closely with their clients, encouraging them to reach an agreement. If no agreement is reached, the case will result in a trial. Because family lawyers are working with clients at one of the most emotionally difficult points in their lives, they must have outstanding counseling skills and employ those skills with sensitivity and empathy.

Division of Property

Spouses may accumulate a broad range of assets during their marriage—such things as real estate, securities and investments, businesses, pension and profit-sharing plans, and insurance. In addition, the family may have property that is especially difficult to divide, such as antiques, family heirlooms, and works of art. Family lawyers must be knowledgeable about the tax and financial implications of dividing these assets.

Child Support and Spousal Support

Family lawyers help divorcing spouses work through issues concerning their own financial needs and those of their children. This involves an analysis of the income of the payer and the needs of the payee. These issues can be complicated. Consider the situation in which a husband may be self-employed and therefore not have a predictable income, or a wife may be paid on a commission basis, or one partner may work with the other partner in a family business. In the case of a young couple, the husband or wife may have chosen to give up a career to be a stay-at-home parent. In the case of an older couple, a wife may not have used her skills in the labor market for a number of years, making it difficult to find a job after the divorce. Computing child or spousal support may begin with a mathematical accounting, but it requires remarkable negotiation skills on the part of the family lawyers involved in the case.

Custody and Visitation

The interests of the children are paramount in determining both custody and visitation arrangements. Lawyers try to help their clients avoid the turmoil involved in a contested custody battle. This requires creative lawyering; again, masterful negotiation skills are required. If an agreement cannot be reached, the case will proceed to trial—family lawyers must therefore have excellent courtroom skills.

Post-Decree Modification and Enforcement

After a divorce decree, one party may seek to modify the custody arrangement or the visitation provisions. For example, a custodial parent may decide to move out of state or out of the country, or a non-custodial father with visitation rights may decide to seek shared custody instead. A spouse may fail to comply with the support or custody arrangements, refusing to allow the child to spend the agreed-upon holiday with the other parent or failing to pay child support. The other spouse may, in this case, seek to enforce the support agreement. Both modification and enforcement of the decree involve litigation. If an agreement cannot be reached, the matter proceeds to trial.

Prenuptial Agreements

Clients who have property and/or children from a previous marriage or who have substantial personal assets may wish to protect their assets in the case of a divorce. Before marriage, they ask the future spouse to sign a prenuptial agreement that sets forth how the property will be divided if the marriage should end in divorce or in the death of the spouse.

Adoption

In recent years, adoption has become a specialty in and of itself. As it has become more difficult to find American infants available for adoption, prospective parents have pursued international adoptions. Interstate and international adoptions require attorneys who are specialists in the laws of other states and countries. Some adoptive parents are extremely concerned about the risk of contested adoptions and thus seek out attorneys who are experts in the field.

Guardianships

A court may appoint a guardian ad litem to represent the interests of a child whose parents are divorcing or for an adult who appears to be legally incompetent due to senile dementia or mental illness. In the case of a child whose parents are divorcing, the guardian ad litem talks with the child to determine the child's desires and concerns about custody and visitation issues. This helps the court determine which arrangement is truly in the best interest of the child.

In the case of an adult, the court appoints a guardian ad litem to help determine whether the person is mentally competent to function on his own or whether he needs a legal guardian (generally, the legal guardian is a family member). The guardian ad litem visits the person in question (often at a hospital or health care facility) and interviews the person in order to determine their competency. The guardian may also ask a doctor to interview the person and to render a medical opinion as to competency. The guardian ad litem then makes a recommendation to the court concerning the person's need for a legal guardian.

Parental Rights in the Case of Child Abuse and Neglect

Just as a court may appoint a guardian ad litem, it may appoint a private attorney to represent children or their parents in cases of abuse or neglect. When a child is abused, neglected, or without supervision, the child may be removed from his or her home, and a trial determines whether the child is in fact neglected. At that point, a change in custody arrangements, an adoption, or the termination of parental rights may be sought.

Life as a Family Lawyer

Where do family lawyers work?

Most family law attorneys practice in small firms or on their own. Some large firms employ a family law attorney or two to handle high-stakes divorce cases for their clients. Government attorneys may work on issues such as guardianship; courts may appoint private attorneys to work on guardianship and parental rights cases, as well.

Who are their clients and what types of cases do they work on?

In divorce cases, family lawyers represent individuals. Hanley Gurwin, of Dickinson Wright PLLC in Detroit, Michigan, says that his typical client has "been married 10 to 30 years, has one or more minor children, and has assets in excess of one million dollars." Jeffrey Warchol, of Machulak, Hutchinson, Robertson & O'Dess, S.C. in Milwaukee, Wisconsin, works with clients at a different end of the economic spectrum. "My clients," he says, "are middle to low-income people from all areas of Milwaukee."

Harry Schaffner, of Schaffner & Van Der Snick, P.C. in Geneva, Illinois, who has been practicing since 1967, reports that as he's grown older, his client base has grown older. He explains that older clients seeking divorces feel that he can understand the problems that are unique to those in their age group. While they may have an empty nest, they may be experiencing stress due to the physical problems of a spouse or the financial downturn from a corporate shakeout. He notes that his practice reflects other societal changes—for example, currently as many as one in eight of the divorces he works on involves extramarital relationships developed via the Internet.

Adoption attorneys generally represent adoptive parents. Kathleen Hogan Morrison, who has her own practice in Chicago, Illinois, explains that though she usually represents adoptive parents, on rare occasions she represents birth parents. As an adoption attorney, she is sometimes called upon to give adoption-related advice to child welfare agencies. At other times attorneys ask for her assistance in adoption-related litigation. She reports that, in spite of the public's impression, "Contested adoptions are rare." Currently between one-fourth and one-third of Kathleen's cases involve international adoptions—the countries involved are determined by which countries have the borders open for adoption at a particular time.

Attorneys handling guardianships in the role of guardian ad litem are appointed by the court to represent the interests of those individuals thought to be incompetent due to senile dementia or organic brain disorders such as paranoid schizophrenia. Jeffrey Warchol explains that 50% of his practice is adult guardianship law. "As a guardian ad litem, I look out for a person's best interests. It's a fascinating area of law, very people-oriented," he explains. (*See* the profile of Sherryl Fox in the Public Interest Law chapter for more information on guardianships.)

Sharon Gibson, a solo practitioner in Washington, D.C., assists the indigent. "I am appointed by the court to represent a parent, a child, or a group of children from the same family in cases of abuse or neglect. Generally my clients receive public assistance and food stamps. They often have part-time or seasonal jobs, if they can find work at all." In many of Sharon's cases, the city brings a case alleging abuse or neglect, and a trial is held to determine whether the child is in fact neglected. Depending on the trial's outcome, Sharon may assist her clients with custody issues or adoption proceedings or she may represent the parent's or child's interest in termination of parental rights. "One case may last until a child reaches the age of majority or it may be resolved in a matter of days," says Sharon.

What daily activities are involved in family law practice?

Most family law attorneys divide their time between client counseling, court appearances, and legal work related to their current caseload, such as drafting pleadings and briefs, taking depositions, and handling phone calls related to the case. Harry Schaffner says, "Being a divorce attorney is like being a dairy farmer. It's not like growing crops, where there's a period of minimal activity in the summer and then things get busy in the fall. Like a dairy farmer, I have to attend to my cases on a daily basis."

For attorneys specializing in family law, keeping in close touch with their clients is a top priority. Explains Jeffrey Warchol, "The number one complaint about lawyers in general is that they don't return their phone calls. Talking with my clients is my top priority. Each call gets a call back. Every case has to be your most important case. Even when you're exhausted after a trial, or you've had a horrendous day, you make it a point to get back to your clients no matter what."

Explains Beverly Pekala, of the Law Offices of Beverly Pekala in Chicago, "Your clients are at the most distraught point they will ever be in during their lifetime. That client may call you 12 times in one day. Lawyers in other areas of practice may not think that talking to the same client 12 times in one day is part of their job. But for a matrimonial lawyer, handling a case is as much about listening and counseling as it is about substantive legal issues."

What do family lawyers find rewarding about their practice?

Family lawyers report that the opportunity to work closely with their clients makes this area of practice extremely rewarding. Hanley Gurwin explains that he takes satisfaction in knowing that he has helped someone "get through one of the saddest and most emotionally traumatic times of his or her life. The phrase 'attorney and counselor' is especially applicable to a matrimonial lawyer, who frequently serves as a therapist as well as an attorney." Jeffrey Warchol agrees. "You feel like you are not just a lawyer, but a counselor. I help people get through the system with respect and dignity."

Explains Harry Schaffner, "I feel as if my role is helping people find a new future. It's ironic that my last name means 'train conductor' in German. It's as if I work on the train of change—I call out the stops, and the client decides at which stop to depart. The reward is the thrill of seeing someone come in with a heavy heart, and then, by the time we end the journey and part ways, this person, my client, stands erect and has clear eyes and a different view of life." These close relationships even lead to friendships. Says Hanley Gurwin, "Over the years many of my former clients have become good friends and have invited me to their subsequent weddings."

Kathleen Hogan Morrison explains that she works with clients during a joyous but nerve-racking time in their lives. As an adoption attorney she has the privilege of "helping in the formation of new families. It's rewarding to have the opportunity to make life better for children, especially those children in the foster care system. The older a child is, the less likely he or she is to be adopted into a home, so it's wonderful to see adoptions of older children."

There are highly personal rewards for being a family lawyer, as well. Says Sharon Gibson, "I deal with children, families, and government bureaucracies every day, and these encounters bring me laughter, frustration, sadness, anger, friendships, self-reflection, and so much more." Sharon Kelly, of Dykema Gossett PLLC in Ann Arbor, Michigan, enjoys having appreciative clients. "In the family law work I do, I have a chance to do something important for ordinary people. Although there are some clients who are impossible to satisfy, there are also very many who actually say 'thank you' and who appreciate the work I do for them."

Jeffrey Warchol notes that the community-based nature of his practice and the work he has done with children in divorce cases have led him to become an active volunteer in the work of the Milwaukee Bar Association. Jeff participates in the Teenage Alcohol Prevention Program, in which he and members associated with the Milwaukee Bar Association go to area high schools to speak about the ramifications of drunk driving. An additional benefit of his work with the bar association is that he has met a group of supportive colleagues and made professional contacts that can lead to client referrals.

Beverly Pekala says that her job as a matrimonial lawyer has allowed her to pursue exciting opportunities outside the law. She does a great deal of public speaking and conducts workshops at corporations on such topics as violence in the workplace. Her public speaking has led to television appearances on *The Oprah Winfrey Show*, CNN, *The Today Show*, and *Good Morning America*. And her TV appearances led to a book deal—she recently authored *Don't Settle for Less*, a book addressing the topics of divorce, custody, and family law issues for the non-lawyer.

Family lawyers also mention the satisfaction of working in an area of law in which every case is different and in which every case comes to a unique resolution. "Family law is one of the most interesting areas of law because it's so unrepetitive. Each case represents a unique intertwining of economics and humanity," says Harry Schaffner. Family lawyers also mention the creativity it takes to resolve the complex issues involved. "There simply is no typical divorce case," says Sharon Kelly. "If there is anything 'typical' about a divorce case, it is the creativity one must bring to resolving disputes given the reluctance of judges to actually try these matters." Beverly Pekala adds, "At any given time, I have amazingly interesting cases. I constantly have opportunities to create new law and to be creative in my lawyering."

The Training and Skills Important to Family Law

How do people enter the field of family law?

Some attorneys report that a long-standing interest in family law issues led them into the field. Jeffrey Warchol says, "Even as an undergraduate business administration student, I was always 'big' on the family. I took every sociology of the family class I could." Jeff worked for a large manufacturing corporation immediately after college. No matter how much his company sold, it didn't give him a feeling that he was making a difference in the world. "Because I like helping people, solving problems, and using my communication skills, I decided to go to law school. I knew that family law was an area of law where you get a sense that you're helping people."

Several of the family lawyers we talked to were inspired by their prior careers as teachers and by their own family experiences. Harry Schaffner was a high school English teacher. He explains that the tumultuous family life with which he grew up gives him a special empathy for his clients. Like Harry Schaffner, adoption attorney Kathleen Hogan Morrison was a high school English teacher; she also did private tutoring. She reports that her interest in adoption issues was piqued by her two sisters and her late mother, all social workers. Sharon Gibson, who works with indigent children and their parents, comments, "As a former teacher, I have always been interested in child welfare issues. In the District of Columbia there are a lot of neglected children who need representation in order to secure the basics—food, housing, and a safe environment."

According to Beverly Pekala, "Family law tends to attract people who are entrepreneurial, people who want to hang out their own shingle. Family law gives me the unique opportunity to use my interest in business and finance as well as my communication skills. I have an LL.M. in Taxation, and family law lets me draw upon that expertise. In many ways matrimonial law is less about social work and more about the Internal Revenue Code. Divorces are really business dissolutions between individuals." Jeffrey Warchol adds that he loves having his own practice. "I knew I had to be able to do my own thing. I have the ability to come in when I want and leave when I want and to spend as much time on matters as I think they warrant."

Some attorneys enter family law practice in a more roundabout way. Sharon Kelly explains, "I have done medical malpractice work from the beginning of my career. However, statutory reform made these cases more difficult and less lucrative to prosecute, which caused my firm's business in this area to decrease. In order to generate my own client and billing base, I looked at burgeoning areas of practice which my firm had not exploited. Family law was one such area, and I began to take on such cases under the tutelage of one of my partners."

Kathleen Hogan Morrison warns that it can be difficult to enter the field of adoption law because there's a limited amount of work available. Her background as litigation attorney, teacher, and tutor led to a position with a 14-person firm that was specifically seeking an attorney with a background in social services and litigation. Her clients, satisfied with her work, referred friends and family members to her. She now has her own firm. She advises law students and attorneys interested in adoption law to work with experienced adoption attorneys. "The best preparation for this field is working on cases directly," she says.

What skills are most important to family lawyers?

❖ Family law attorneys agree that the **ability to empathize** with the problems of others is critical to success in the field. "Sensitivity to other people's problems is the single most important skill," says divorce attorney Harry Schaffner. Kathleen Hogan Morrison agrees. "Intelligence, compassion, and sensitivity . . . they're all important," she says. "Who I am as a person in my life radiates to my clients," says Jeffrey Warchol. "I'm a people-oriented person, and clients sense that. I have to be able to meet someone and earn their trust within an hour."

❖ Another important skill is the **ability to remain objective** about highly sensitive matters, even when the client is facing a life crisis. "You must remain dispassionate while everything around you remains passionate," says Harry Schaffner. Kathleen Hogan Morrison, who works on highly emotional adoption cases, adds, "You must be able to be objective about family matters." Says Jeffrey Warchol, "I work hard to guide people through the initial shock involved in the divorce process. I help clients get to a point where they engage in a rational thinking process."

❖ **Counseling skills** are key to this area of law. Hanley Gurwin explains, "The most important skill for a good family lawyer is being a good listener." Sharon Kelly adds, "A family law attorney must advise, take direction from, and persuade a client who has probably never been in a worse position in his or her life. If you can't recognize and care about the vulnerability of your client in this situation, this area of practice is not for you."

❖ Nearly every family lawyer we talked to mentioned the need for an extraordinary degree of **patience**. Beverly Pekala lists patience as the primary factor in developing a successful family law practice. "You must be able to deal with your client's need to talk with you at all hours of the day," she says. "People who don't succeed in this area are those who lack the patience to work closely with people who are under extreme stress. Patience is much more critical to success than how smart you are or where you went to law school."

❖ Family lawyers need excellent **negotiation skills**. Explains Jeffrey Warchol, "Nine out of 10 cases settle. I tell my clients that they usually do better by settling. In order to do what's best for the client, you have to negotiate with the attorney on the other side of the case." Sharon Kelly agrees. "The 'hardball' negotiation skills I picked up in my personal injury defense work have served me well in family law, which is heavily influenced by negotiation," she says.

❖ Because family lawyers are often in court, a family lawyer needs the **ability to think on his or her feet**. According to Sharon Gibson, "The most important skill for success is thinking on your feet! This means knowing the law that applies and being able to apply it on the spot in court or in an emergency situation." Beverly Pekala explains, "When you walk into court at 10:00 a.m., the event about which you may end up arguing may have just happened at 8:00 a.m. There's no time to look at the statute and no time to interview witnesses. You have to assimilate the facts, consider the law as you know it, and argue orally without a written motion." Beverly explains that you must also think quickly when clients call you in an emergency situation. "I sometimes get a call from a client who says their spouse is at the door with a weapon. And I can hear the doorbell ringing over the phone. These situations arise more often than you might think. In order to help your client, you have to think fast and make decisions quickly."

What classes and law school experiences do family lawyers recommend?

❖ Take **family law and business law classes** in law school. Jeffrey Warchol explains that because you are working with the division of people's assets, classes relating to business—such as tax, employee benefits, corporations and partnerships, and accounting—are extremely helpful. A conflict of laws class can help prepare you to work on divorces in which the parties or property are in different states and to work on interstate adoptions. The family lawyers we talked to also suggested taking a negotiations course.

❖ Work to develop strong **writing skills**. "You have to make articulate legal arguments in your pleadings and in briefs," says Beverly Pekala. She adds, "You must also engage in an extremely high level of written communication with clients. You must be able to explain complex legal issues to nonlawyers."

❖ **"Any class that helps you get comfortable in the courtroom** is worth taking," says Beverly Pekala. Moot court gives students an opportunity to exercise their ability to make oral arguments under intense questioning by judges. "Moot court forces you to be able to think on your feet and articulate quickly," says adoption attorney Kathleen Hogan Morrison. Trial advocacy classes give law students a chance to actually try a case before a mock jury and are thus one of the best ways students can sharpen their courtroom skills.

❖ The attorneys we talked to believe that a **wide range of liberal arts classes** can be helpful in preparing for your career as a family lawyer. "Family law is really made for liberal arts students, because it covers every human endeavor," says Harry Schaffner. While a law student, he was inspired by a library plaque inscribed with the words of U.S.

Supreme Court Justice Felix Frankfurter: "Exhort the law student to study everything other than the law." Harry particularly recommends taking a class in comparative world religions. "By understanding other people's religions, you will understand their values and the perspective from which they view life," he says. Many family lawyers recommend classes in psychology, counseling, or social work. Classes in speech communications and persuasion can also be helpful.

❖ **Gain practical experience by working as a law clerk** for a family lawyer. Attorneys often hire law students for the summer or during the school year to assist them with legal research and drafting. The practical knowledge you gain by working on actual cases will help the principles you learn in your family law class come to life. You'll see what goes on behind the scenes and in court. "Whenever possible, sit in on court proceedings," urges Sharon Gibson.

❖ **Clinical experience** can be helpful in developing your client counseling and courtroom skills. Law schools often have clinics that work with indigent clients. In return for working in the clinic, you earn credit hours and an opportunity to engage in real-world lawyering. Other clinical experience programs are associated with government offices. While in law school, Jeffrey Warchol participated in a program associated with the City of West Allis, Wisconsin. Wisconsin Supreme Court rules allowed him to try cases under the supervision of a city attorney while still a law student. "The experience greatly increased my confidence in the courtroom," he says.

❖ **Develop relationships within the community of family lawyers**. Family law is a specialized field; family lawyers in a particular geographic area know each other well. Developing good relationships with the lawyers you clerk for and the lawyers you meet in bar association activities can be very helpful when you begin your search for an attorney job after graduation. Sharon Gibson advises, "Join the family law section of your local bar association." Many bar associations have student memberships, and the benefits, including educational programs and networking opportunities, far outweigh the minimal student membership fee.

FAMILY ATTORNEYS INTERVIEWED FOR THIS SECTION

Sharon L. Gibson
Law Offices of Sharon Lynn Gibson
Washington, D.C.
UNDERGRADUATE: Texas A & M University
LAW SCHOOL: Emory University School of Law

Hanley Gurwin
Dickinson Wright PLLC
Detroit, Michigan
UNDERGRADUATE: University of Michigan
LAW SCHOOL: University of Michigan Law School

Sharon M. Kelly
Dykema Gossett PLLC
Ann Arbor, Michigan
UNDERGRADUATE: Nazareth College
LAW SCHOOL: University of Detroit Mercy School of Law

Kathleen Hogan Morrison
Law Offices of Kathleen Hogan Morrison
Chicago, Illinois
UNDERGRADUATE: Saint Louis University
LAW SCHOOL: The John Marshall Law School

Beverly Pekala
The Law Offices of Beverly A. Pekala
Chicago, Illinois
UNDERGRADUATE: DePaul University
LAW SCHOOL: Chicago-Kent College of Law, Illinois Institute of
Technology

Harry Schaffner
Schaffner & Van Der Snick, P.C.
Geneva, Illinois
UNDERGRADUATE: University of Illinois
LAW SCHOOL: University of Illinois College of Law

Jeffrey Warchol
Machulak, Hutchinson, Robertson & O'Dess, S.C.
Milwaukee, Wisconsin
UNDERGRADUATE: Marquette University
LAW SCHOOL: Marquette University Law School

*Editor's note: Sharon Gibson now works for Ross, Dixon & Bell, L.L.P. in
Washington, D.C.*

Government Contracts Practice

What is Government Contracts Practice?

Government contracts, and the processes involved in the award and performance of those contracts, play a major role in events of great significance to our country. During the U.S. military actions in Yugoslavia and Iraq, the American public became intimately familiar with advanced air weapons systems such as Patriot missiles, Stealth bombers, and "smart-guided" cruise missiles. Yet before any of those weapons systems could become a working part of the military, defense contractors were required to complete a complex process of bidding, negotiating, awarding, and implementing one or more government contracts for each system.

During the 1999 crisis in Kosovo, reporters revealed that the U.S. suffered a shortage in its supply of cruise missiles because the government had miscalculated the number of missiles needed for a sustained air war. The U.S. government had contracted with defense contractors for only a limited supply of the remarkably accurate cruise missiles, which brought to public awareness the importance of the many government contracts behind the scenes of the U.S. military action. Such contracts involve not only defense contractors, but also medical and health care delivery systems and numerous other kinds of private businesses.

Attorneys who specialize in government contracts work represent clients in all aspects of negotiating and securing contracts with the government, as well as in disputes that arise out of these contracts. Their practice therefore includes both client counseling and litigation. While their clients are often U.S. companies such as defense contractors and health care organizations, they may also represent foreign clients dealing with U.S. government agencies, as well as U.S. clients dealing with foreign governments. They may also work for federal, state, or local governments or agencies reviewing and negotiating contracts with outside vendors.

Private companies that wish to bid for contracts with federal, state, or local governments must meet a host of regulations, such as compliance with special U.S. labor laws, before they are eligible to enter into such contracts. Attorneys specializing in government contracts guide their clients in submitting a proposal to do the work or supply the goods sought by the government, whether those goods are planes, ships, trucks, or coffee makers, and then help their clients in the contract negotiation process with the government. If a company is unsuccessful in its bid for the government work, the attorney may assist the client in protesting the bid. If the company is successful in bidding for the work, it may have to defend against allegations from other companies that the bid was gained unfairly or inappropriately. Government contracts attorneys provide advice at every stage of this litigation, which may be heard as an administrative hearing in the U.S. General Accounting Office (GAO), in federal district court, or in the Court of Federal Claims.

Government contracts attorneys may also advise their clients concerning issues relating to performance of the contract. For example, the government has certain rights to terminate the contract, or the client may run into cost overruns in completing the work for the government. These issues, too, may result in litigation. Numerous submissions to the government must be made throughout the performance process. They may also assist clients with the many complex issues that arise in performing the contracted work in compliance with environmental regulations and export regulations.

In addition to assisting with performance issues, government contracts attorneys may assist clients with the acquisition, divestiture (selling off), or financing of companies that perform government contracts and with the special circumstances involved as a result of the existence of such a contract.

Another growing area of work for government contracts attorneys involves what are called *qui tam* actions under the False Claims Act. In a *qui tam* action, an employee of the company under the contract, who is known as a "whistle-blower," alleges that his or her company has committed fraud against the government and brings suit against the company on behalf of the government (*see* the Legislative Practice chapter for more information on whistle-blowers). The False Claims Act allows a whistle-blower to recover up to 30% of what the government collects in such an action, a measure that encourages whistle-blowers to pursue such actions. Government contracts attorneys represent the companies accused of wrongdoing and defend against the claim.

Attorneys specializing in government contracts work may also become involved in international issues. They may represent international defense contractors on matters related to foreign military sales and technology transfer, or they may represent defense contractors that sell to foreign governments and foreign companies. Numerous questions relating to export control laws may arise in such circumstances. Government contracts attorneys may also handle issues that arise out of the ownership or control of U.S. companies by foreign governments or foreign corporations.

Life as a Government Contracts Attorney

Where do government contracts lawyers work?

Many government contracts lawyers work for law firms. They may work in large or mid-size law firms that have departments specializing in government contracts, or they may work in smaller "boutique" firms that specialize in such work. Some attorneys who specialize in government contracts law may work as in-house attorneys at companies that make defense or aerospace products or other companies, such as U.S. auto companies, that engage in large contracts with the government. Still other government contracts lawyers work for federal, state, or municipal governments.

Though government contracts lawyers practice throughout the country, there is a particularly large concentration of them in Washington, D.C. because of the large amount of federal contract work performed there, as well as on the West Coast due to the location of the aircraft and defense industries.

Who are their clients and what types of issues do they work on?

Peter Hutt is a member of the law firm Miller & Chevalier, a large firm in Washington, D.C. Miller & Chevalier has over 20 lawyers in its government contracts department. "The clients I work with are primarily corporations that do business with the federal government. The contracts in which the clients are involved may involve goods or services, or they may involve federally funded programs, such as Medicare. As a result my clients represent an extremely broad range of both individuals and organizations," Peter explains.

Peter reports that his firm handles the full range of issues that arise in government contracting. "When an organization first seeks a government contract," he says, "our lawyers assist the organization in making sure they are in compliance with the government regulations that must be met before entering into a government contract. When the government issues a request for proposals, we assist our clients with putting together a proposal. We then assist with negotiations with the government that may lead to the formation of a contract."

When a contract is not awarded to a certain company, Peter says, the disappointed bidder may file what is called a bid protest. "We may file a bid protest for a disappointed bidder or defend against bid protests on behalf of our clients who are successful bidders," Peter explains. "Bid protests result in litigation which is quickly resolved. Some such cases are heard in the General Accounting Office, others are heard in federal district courts, and others in the Court of Federal Claims. These multiple forums make the decision-making process involved in the litigation especially exciting. At the beginning of the litigation, we make decisions concerning the jurisdiction of the case that can make a big difference in the outcome of the case. This type of strategizing makes government contracts litigation unique.

"We also handle litigation that develops out of contract performance problems," Peter continues. "There may be a breach of the contract, or the government may decide to terminate the contract. Sometimes the contractor submits claims for cost overruns. Such issues are often litigated. There are numerous statutes and regulations that govern contracts; attorneys who specialize in this field must be familiar with them—they are one of the aspects that make government contracts litigation different from contract litigation involving purely commercial entities."

Over 95% of Peter's practice is litigation, and about 30% of the litigation he handles involves the False Claims Act. Amendments made to the False Claims Act in 1986 have dramatically increased claims by whistle-blowers alleging that the companies involved in government contracts have committed fraud against the government. "The amendments allow a whistle-blower to bring a *qui tam* case, in which he or she can recover up to one-third of the amount awarded to the government. There's been a proliferation of such cases, as they are a good way for whistle-blowers to vindicate what they see as fraud against the government and make money by doing so," Peter explains. "In such cases, we represent the defense contractors, health care contractors, or other businesses accused of making false claims. Because of the 1986 amendments to the False Claims Act, the statute has only been litigated in the past 10 years. This means that the law in this area is changing rapidly. We actually witness the creation of the law regarding the False Claims Act, and that is endlessly fascinating and challenging."

Brian Caminer was formerly an Assistant Corporation Counsel for the City of Chicago's Contracts and Commercial Law Division and is now Director of Contract Administration for the Mayor's Office of Workforce Development (MOWD). "When I was in the Corporation Counsel's office," says Brian, "my client was the City of Chicago and the over 40 departments of the City and, occasionally, not-for-profits established by the city. My role was to facilitate the business deal by ensuring compliance with policy, practice, and legal requirements. The City is involved in a wide range of contracts and privatizes more services yearly, allowing attorneys to work on a variety of contracts. I was involved on contracts as diverse as the security system for O'Hare International Airport to the property management contract for the City's main library." Most of the contracts that Brian worked on began in the City's Purchasing Department. "The Purchasing Department started working on the contract and then came to the Law Department when it needed further assistance. The contracts generally required minimal drafting, but might involve a significant amount of negotiation. The negotiations were often conducted by phone," Brian explains. "Now my role is to manage the unit responsible for procuring goods and services for MOWD and to assist the City's Workforce Board on contractual issues. While my work is now much more business oriented, I still do a lot of drafting and negotiating of contracts."

What daily activities are involved in government contracts practice?

Peter Hutt explains that his daily activities are similar to those of any litigation attorney. "I do legal research and a great deal of legal writing, including drafting briefs. I interview witnesses and take and defend depositions. I am also involved in negotiations, whether they are negotiations with the government concerning the formation of a contract or settlement negotiations. Our firm handles cases from cradle to grave. This means that we counsel clients before they enter into contracts, handle litigation that arises during contract performance, and handle appeals as well."

Brian Caminer says that his days are also spent counseling his client, the City of Chicago. "Most of my days are spent with clients, either on the phone or in meetings. I spend little time actually drafting contracts, although I do write and edit numerous memoranda and letters. When I was in the Corporation Counsel's office, occasionally I was responsible for supervising outside counsel. Now my time is spent providing advice on contractual matters and reviewing and negotiating contracts in which the City is involved."

What do government contracts lawyers find rewarding about their practice?

It's not surprising that government contracts lawyers, who spend much of their time counseling clients, greatly enjoy this part of their practice. "I love working with my clients," says Peter Hutt. "They are exceptional. They tend to be engineers or doctors or medical professionals. They are straightforward, intelligent people, and I enjoy working with them. I work with clients such as Lockheed Martin and Hughes Electronics, which means that I work with many engineers. I find it fascinating to learn about engineering issues from the engineers themselves. I spend a great deal of time talking with them about, for example, the construction of weapons systems, how satellites are constructed, and the mechanics of how these systems work. I usually talk to the principal designers of such systems and learn every detail about what the systems do and how they work. If you're a science junkie, government contracts is the place to be—it's just fascinating!"

Peter says that he also appreciates the intellectual challenge his work offers. "Government contracts work is truly intellectually interesting and stimulating. The issues are complex; they are difficult to understand and difficult to resolve. The practice requires extensive knowledge of regulations and statutes and also requires sophisticated strategic decision-making regarding jurisdictional issues. On almost every case, with almost every client, there's a consistently high level of intellectual content in the work."

Brian Caminer says that his position with the City of Chicago provides him with the opportunity to work on behalf of the public's interest. "It is really rewarding to be able to help people and contribute to the civic good," says Brian. "And it is very satisfying to see the City embrace a project you've been personally involved in."

The Training and Skills Important to Government Contracts Law

How do people enter the field of government contracts law?

Some lawyers may enter law school knowing that they are interested in government contracts work, due to experience in the military or in the corporate sector. Serendipity leads others to the practice of government contracts law. "Government contracts is a field that many people enter by accident," Peter Hutt observes. "Many people start in another area of law, such as commercial litigation, and then discover the field of government contracts through some aspect of their work experience, as I did." After graduating from law school in 1989, Peter worked as a federal judicial law clerk for a judge in California. After his clerkship he worked in the litigation department of a large firm in Washington, D.C. "The first two cases I worked on as an associate were a government contracts case and a False Claims Act case. Working on these two cases convinced me that government contracts was the right area of practice for me. I then looked at firms that had specialty practices in government contracts, and that's how I came to join Miller & Chevalier."

Brian Caminer knew when he entered law school that he was interested in business-related practice. "I always had it in the back of my mind that I wanted to do something related to corporate law—I majored in business as an undergraduate and received my C.P.A. I've always had some civic interest, and I chose the City of Chicago because of the mix of responsibility and experience available."

What skills are most important to government contracts lawyers?

❖ **Writing skills** are critically important to the government contracts attorney. "Communications skills, particularly writing skills, are invaluable to the government contracts lawyer," says Brian Caminer. "An integral part of the writing process, which is frequently neglected, is editing. Improving your writing skills requires daily practice under the watchful eye of a good writer. My judicial clerkship helped me hone my analytical and writing skills."

❖ Government contracts attorneys must have good **negotiation skills**. The attorneys we interviewed stressed that the practice involves negotiation skills both in creating a contract and in the subsequent settlement of any litigation relating to the contract.

❖ Attorneys in this field must **enjoy complex intellectual challenges**. "To enjoy this field, you really have to like intellectual challenges," says Peter Hutt. "You're constantly dealing with complex accounting issues and complex technical issues."

❖ Another skill required by government contracts attorneys is an **understanding of the facets of government decision-making**. Explains Peter Hutt, "You must recognize the many aspects of the government decision-making process and understand how they work. This includes how Congress works, how the administration works, and how the different agencies involved in the procurement work, not to mention understanding the inner workings of the government bureaucracy. You have to have enough patience to work with the many parts of the government involved in decision-making. You have to know what's happening on Capitol Hill, and know how what you're working on will affect what's happening on the Hill, and what the administration would think about what you're working on. You have to understand the realities of working with the government."

❖ If you work for a firm, it's very important to be comfortable **being a generalist**. "You have to be comfortable handling a full range of legal services, including negotiation and litigation," says Peter.

What classes and law school experience do government contracts lawyers recommend?

❖ Taking a **wide range of law school classes** can be helpful preparation for the government contracts attorney. "Contracts, federal jurisdiction, administrative law, negotiations, and classes about government regulations and statutes, such as environmental law or labor law, are helpful," advises Peter Hutt.

❖ **Litigation-oriented courses** can provide you with sound training for a government contracts career. Consider taking such courses as evidence, civil litigation, and trial advocacy. Peter Hutt says, "In this field litigation cases tend to go to trial or hearing more frequently than in other fields of litigation. Trial advocacy classes go a long way in helping you prepare for trial work. Moot court, too, can be a good experience. It requires you to get on your feet and present an oral argument, and this is something you are going to do the rest of your career."

❖ **Participating in your law school's law review, a law journal, or a writing competition** is a good way to sharpen your writing skills. "Legal writing requires a great deal of skill," says Peter Hutt. "In government contracts cases, you are often required to explain in writing extremely complex and often poorly drafted statutes. You must explain these statutes in plain English to an agency board of contracts appeals or to a district court judge or—occasionally—to members of Congress. This requires excellent writing skills, which law journals can help you develop."

❖ **Consider working as a judicial law clerk upon graduation from law school or as a judicial extern while a law student.** Most federal and some state judges hire law clerks to assist them in drafting their opinions. Judicial law clerks work closely with judges and see the inner workings of the judge's courtroom. In addition, they review legal briefs filed by parties and assist the judge they work for in drafting opinions. Some law schools have programs through which students can work as judicial externs and receive academic credit for doing so. Attorneys who have worked as judicial law clerks highly recommend the experience. "My judicial clerkship was more valuable to me than any law school class," says Brian Caminer. "It gave me some understanding of government and how it works, and it helped me hone my analytical and writing skills."

Peter Hutt is equally enthusiastic in his praise for the clerkship experience. "There's no such thing as a bad clerkship," Peter says. "If you have the opportunity for a clerkship, take it. No matter what you want to do with your career—even if you eventually want to work on Wall Street rather than work as a lawyer—you'll do a better job of whatever you do professionally because you worked as a law clerk first." Peter says that his clerkship was particularly helpful in preparing him for his litigation practice. "When you work side by side with a judge, you learn what truly persuades judges. If you want to work as a litigator, it's an invaluable experience to work as a judicial law clerk before you begin your career as a litigator. It's the best thing in the world to do. If you have the opportunity, you're nuts if you don't do it!"

❖ **Work as a summer associate or as a law clerk** at a firm that has a government contracts practice **or as a summer intern** at a government office. Large and mid-size firms that hire government contracts lawyers often have summer associate programs through which they hire second year law students to work at the firm between their second and third year of law school. Some government employers, such as the City of Chicago, also have summer programs for second year students, and other government offices have summer interns or student externs who work for academic credit during the school year. "A summer associate position in the field will help you learn whether government contracts is for you," says Peter Hutt, who participates in his law firm's hiring committee. Brian Caminer recommends working as a law clerk for a government office. "Whether you clerk for a state's attorney, a judge, the U.S. Attorney, or the public defender, all of those positions are very good learning experiences. The experience will help you shorten your learning curve in the field of government contracts or any other area of law."

❖ **Make yourself part of the legal community and the broader community.** State, local, and national bar associations welcome student members, and offer student memberships for a nominal fee. "The legal community is really relatively small, even if you live in a large city. Be active in the community, including bar associations and community organizations," advises Brian Caminer.

❖ **The Public Contract Law Section of the American Bar Association** can be a good place to make contacts within the field. "The ABA Public Contract Law Section is extremely active," says Peter Hutt. "It includes attorneys who are in private practice, corporate in-house counsel, and a significant number of government lawyers. It's a true community of lawyers working together to promote statutes and regulations that will do better for the country. As I've gotten more involved in the section, I've been impressed with the determination and altruism of the attorneys involved."

GOVERNMENT CONTRACTS ATTORNEYS
INTERVIEWED FOR THIS SECTION

Brian Caminer
Mayor's Office of Workforce Development, City of Chicago
Chicago, Illinois
UNDERGRADUATE: University of Michigan
LAW SCHOOL: Northwestern University School of Law

Peter Hutt
Miller & Chevalier, Chartered
Washington, D.C.
UNDERGRADUATE: Yale University
LAW SCHOOL: Stanford Law School

Government Practice

What is Government Practice?

Attorneys seeking a career in public service will find a multitude of opportunities in government practice. Many of our public officials at the federal, state, and local level, including presidents and members of Congress and, of course, judges, are lawyers. The proliferation of media coverage of criminal and civil trials and government investigations on Court TV, on CNBC, and on programs such as *20/20* has drawn much attention to government attorneys, especially prosecutors and judges. Yet there are countless lawyers in all branches of government who work to enforce and administer our systems of law and justice.

In addition to federal and state judges and prosecutors, government attorneys include U.S. Attorneys (who, as part of the Department of Justice, handle both criminal and civil cases), public defenders, and judicial law clerks. The Department of Justice, which is supervised by the U.S. Attorney General, employs attorneys working on issues as diverse as federal drug trafficking law, computer crime, and tort law. Attorneys also work for federal agencies, such as the Internal Revenue Service, the Food and Drug Administration, the Equal Employment Opportunity Commission, the Federal Communications Commission, and the Securities and Exchange Commission. These agencies employ hundreds of attorneys to assist with investigations, enforcement, interpretation of regulations, and litigation, as well as to provide assistance to judicial officers within these organizations. Each branch of the U.S. military has attorneys who work as judge advocates, providing advice to military officers around the world.

Attorneys also work for regulatory and enforcement agencies at both the federal and state level, such as the Environmental Protection Agency (EPA) and state pollution control boards. State governments hire attorneys to work for state departments of mental health, human rights, public aid, public health, and insurance; public transportation entities; boards of education and elections; and myriad other boards and commissions. Local governments, including cities, villages, townships, park districts, and water reclamation districts, also employ attorneys.

Life in Government Practice

Where do government attorneys work?

Government attorneys work for all three branches of the government at the federal, state, and local level. There are government attorneys who work in most every substantive legal area described in this book. Besides the profiles of the four government attorneys described in this chapter, review the profiles of government attorneys in other chapters of this book, listed below, for a well-rounded picture of some of the opportunities available to government lawyers.

Admiralty and Maritime Law — Rachel Canty (U.S. Coast Guard); Mark Skolnicki (U.S. Coast Guard)

Appellate Practice — David Blair-Loy (Office of the Appellate Defender); Julie Fenton (U.S. Court of Appeals, Seventh Circuit); Teddie Gaitas (Minnesota State Public Defender's Office); Richard Greenberg (Office of the Appellate Defender)

Criminal Law — Elizabeth Dobson (Champaign County State's Attorney); Timijanel Boyd Odom (Cook County Public Defender's Office); Bill Seki (Los Angeles County District Attorney's Office); Mimi Wright (U.S. Attorney's Office)

Environmental Law — Ignacio Arrazola (U.S. EPA); Mike Thrift (Office of the General Counsel, U.S. EPA)

Government Contracts Practice — Brian Caminer (Chicago Mayor's Office of Workforce Development)

Immigration Law — Annette Toews (U.S. Immigration and Naturalization Service)

Labor and Employment Law — Maryl Rosen (U.S. Postal Service Law Department)

Legislative Practice — Charles Clapton (House Committee on Commerce)

Military Judge Advocates/JAG — Mary Card (U.S. Army); Robert Taishoff (U.S. Navy); Barbara Zanotti (U.S. Air Force)

Public Interest Law — Sherryl Fox (Cook County Office of the Public Guardian)

Securities Law — John Reed Stark (U.S. Securities and Exchange Commission)

Telecommunications Law — Howard Griboff (Federal Communications Commission)

Who are their clients and what types of cases do they work on?

Joan Humes is an assistant U.S. Attorney for the U.S. Attorney's Office in Minneapolis, Minnesota. Joan works primarily on civil rights cases. "My client is the Department of Justice," she explains, "and in the larger scheme of things, like anyone who works for the government, U.S. citizens are my clients. One of the rewards of doing civil rights work is the feeling that you are advocating for the victim in a particular case. The beauty of working for the government is that your interest extends in scope beyond the victim, to include all citizens. I tell the victims that I work with that I want to do what would be best for them as well as what would be best for anyone in their circumstances. Even though the individual claimant may only want a certain level of relief, our job in the U.S. Attorney's Office is to look out for anyone who might find themselves in similar circumstances."

Joan works on several different types of civil rights cases. "The first category of cases I work on are civil cases related to acts such as the Americans with Disabilities Act [ADA] and the Fair Housing Act. These cases concern the access of disabled people to public accommodations and public health services, as well as complaints alleging housing discrimination due to religion, familial status, etc. The second category of cases on which I work are criminal civil rights cases, which are generally hate crime cases. I'm currently working on a huge project on hate crime prevention and awareness. As part of that project, I meet with and talk with law enforcement people about how to investigate and prosecute these crimes. These criminal civil rights cases also involve allegations of excessive force. The third category of cases I work on concern mental health commitments to the federal mental health center in Rochester. These cases involve criminals whom we argue are too dangerous to be released at the end of their criminal sentences. I work with a superb psychological staff at the mental health center in preparing these cases, some of which we win and some of which we lose."

Gail Johnson is an attorney for the Civil Division of the U.S. Department of Justice in Washington, D.C. Gail handles Federal Tort Claims Act (FTCA) litigation, in which she defends U.S. agencies against allegations of tortious conduct. A tort is a civil (non-criminal) injury, other than a breach of contract, that results in damages. Plaintiffs in these cases allege that an agency or a person employed by the federal government itself has committed a tort by acting or failing to act in circumstances in which they had some obligation or responsibility toward another and that the government is therefore liable for the resulting injury. The FTCA, enacted in 1946, spells out the necessary conditions for plaintiffs to bring tort claims against the U.S. government.

"My clients," Gail explains, "are the various federal agencies with headquarters in the Washington, D.C. metropolitan area. A typical case involves an allegation of medical malpractice on the part of a government employee while working in a military hospital. For example, parents of a child with cerebral palsy might file an administrative claim with a branch of the military alleging negligence on the part of a treating physician at a military hospital during the delivery of the child. If the administrative claim is denied, the parents can then bring suit in federal court. I become involved once the suit has been filed in federal district court."

Mary Foster is senior counsel for the Attorney Registration and Disciplinary Commission (ARDC), an agency of the Illinois Supreme Court which investigates and prosecutes lawyers for professional misconduct. "Technically," Mary explains, "my client is the chief administrator of the ARDC, who functions as the agency's chief executive officer. But in actuality my role is that of an adviser to the Illinois Supreme Court regarding issues of attorney discipline." Mary says that most states have a disciplinary commission, but notes, "In some states the disciplinary commission is part of the state bar association or under the supervision of the legislature as opposed to the state's high court." Illinois has over 70,000 lawyers; the ARDC has over 30 attorneys charged with lawyer discipline.

"We prosecute lawyers for ethical misconduct," says Mary. "We investigate lawyers in every legal setting, so our attorneys are exposed to a wide variety of substantive issues on a wide variety of law. Complaints against lawyers usually come from an attorney's client. There's also an Illinois law that affirmatively requires lawyers and judges who know of illegal or fraudulent attorney conduct to report such conduct to the commission. Most of the complaints against attorneys involve a lack of communication between the attorney and his or her clients. The cases that result in prosecution generally involve fraud or conversion of the client's funds, misconduct before a court, or criminal conduct." Even after 14 years of prosecuting wayward attorneys, Mary notes with amazement that "lawyers are always finding novel ways to get into trouble."

Other government attorneys work for municipalities. Gretta Tameling is the Acting City Attorney of the City of Naperville, Illinois. Naperville is a burgeoning suburb in the high tech corridor west of Chicago. "The population of Naperville is 128,000, and it's growing rapidly. Naperville has 1,000 municipal employees, including the five of us who are in-house city attorneys," she reports. Gretta explains that her clients are the city's elected and appointed officials, as well as all of its employees. "Our city attorneys must be familiar with local government law, as the city is a municipal corporation. Part of the job involves budgeting and then carrying out the charge of the elected officials within our city budget. We are constantly trying to think of innovative ways to do the public's business and ways to deliver better service. Our city manager is a wonderful man who is very energetic and interested in reinventing government. He is working hard to bring this community, which is over 150 years old, into the 21st century. It's a momentous day-to-day challenge."

The wide scope of activities in which the city is involved requires Gretta to be a generalist. "There are so many different facets involved in working as a city attorney. My job is almost like that of a general practitioner. I advise our city manager regarding how to conduct city council meetings and advise him concerning resolutions and ordinances. Land use concerns are a big part of my job. Naperville is growing so rapidly that there's tremendous pressure to keep up with the private development community. I also work on utilities issues and public works issues, as well as environmental issues. We have our own sewer, water, and electric systems, and a public works department responsible for roads and public improvements such as sidewalks. The city has a large purchasing department that enters into contracts with vendors, and I assist the purchasing department with legal issues. Because we have 1,000 municipal employees, we have a large human resources department with complex employment issues. Employment and labor law are a growing area of my practice. We also have over 100 police officers and a huge fire department. Civil rights issues arise out of police interactions with the citizens, generating constitutional law issues."

Gretta's work also includes real estate matters. "The city buys and sells property for its own use. For example, we recently purchased property to build our eighth fire station. If we are unable to negotiate the purchase of property for fire stations, public utilities, or parking lots, we become involved in condemnation actions. Naperville is a particularly interesting city in that the heart of old Naperville—where our downtown is still located—was developed in the 1800s and the property interests were set at that time, when surveying equipment was imprecise. We thus work to establish property boundaries that have never before been properly delineated. This requires researching real estate interests and allows me to delve into some fascinating but arcane areas of the law."

Naperville's in-house legal staff also defends some tort claims made against the city. "When the stakes in tort litigation are extremely high, we work with splendid outside counsel to defend these cases. For example, we had a recent case in which a city employee driving a city vehicle profoundly injured a child. In such a case, the plaintiff's counsel may have armies of attorneys working on the case. Outside counsel are a tremendous help to us in such cases." Naperville also has one attorney who specializes in prosecuting municipal violations, which include parking and traffic offenses, cases involving driving under the influence of drugs or alcohol, and building code violations.

What daily activities are involved in government practice?

Assistant U.S. Attorney Joan Humes's days are highly varied. "I do a great deal of research and writing," she reports. "When we get a complaint from a citizen regarding access issues under the ADA, I conduct research to determine what the ADA requires as far as access. Or if hearing-impaired patients need to be accommodated in a hospital, I do research as far as what kind of interpreters are required under the ADA. Once the research on access or housing issues has been done, I draft notice letters to a facility, notifying them of the complaint and explaining that we're conducting an investigation. In these cases I have the opportunity to do a fair amount of the investigation, while in the criminal cases our office handles, the FBI generally conducts the investigation. Generally, we focus our efforts on public facilities and larger commercial enterprises as opposed to small businesses. We may focus our accessibility investigations on hotels, movie theaters, and large stores instead of small restaurants or shops. As part of the investigation, I actually go out and take a look at the facility.

"In the hate crimes cases in which I'm involved, I do a lot of brief writing," Joan continues. "The courts are unfamiliar with the status of hate crimes laws and the rules concerning admissibility of evidence in such cases. Working on the civil side of the U.S. Attorney's office involves educating and updating the judge as to the law." Joan's litigation also requires that she make court appearances. "I make fewer court appearances than a traditional prosecutor, but I am in court for motions, hearings, and settlement conferences. A substantial majority of our civil cases settle. In our office only about one or two of our civil cases go to trial per year."

Gail Johnson's work as a tort litigation attorney in the Civil Division of the Department of Justice varies depending on the status of the litigation in which she's involved. "Because the practice in my office is national in scope and most of my cases involve intensive discovery," she reports, "the first few months of case preparation involve lots of travel, witness and document identification, and depositions. When I travel I conduct business over the phone, on the plane, and in hotel rooms across the country. After the formal discovery period is closed, most of my work is conducted at my office in Washington. This work includes the preparation of pre-trial briefs or motions and trial preparation."

When she's in trial, Gail's routine changes dramatically. "When I'm in trial, the pace of my day is more akin to a fast ride on a roller coaster. To date only one of my trials has been in Washington, D.C., so this means living out of a hotel for days at a time. The trial day starts early, with perhaps a breakfast meeting with co-counsel and witnesses, review of direct and cross-examinations, and exhibit preparation. Upon arrival at the courthouse, the roller coaster ride continues. Being in trial is both exhilarating and exhausting. Developing the ability to listen during the examination of a witness by your opposing counsel and also keep track of what you need to do when you examine that witness is difficult, to say the least. You are juggling so many things—when to object and when not to; forcing yourself to remain poker-faced when the judge rules against you or when something funny or dramatic happens in court; rewriting in your head your cross-examination of the witness who just spun opposing counsel during questioning. Your days can be long or cut short due to an emergency matter that the court must hear. By the time you are finished for the day, you have enough time to eat a quick dinner, check to see if your witnesses for the next day have arrived from the airport, return to the hotel, prepare the next day's witnesses, review or edit the next day's work, grab a few hours of sleep, and prepare for the next day's roller coaster ride."

Gail's roller coaster adventures are often exhilarating. She shared the story of an especially memorable case. "The case involved a very sad set of facts—the unfortunate drowning of a young child in a man-made swimming lake located on government property. The parents of the child sued the United States for $5 million. Discovery in the case lasted over six months and resulted in 40 depositions. As trial neared, the plaintiffs' counsel filed four separate motions for partial summary judgment on four of the defenses raised by the United States in its answer. In response to these motions, the United States filed a notice of non-opposition as to one motion but filed opposition briefs as to the remaining three.

"The trial date was quickly approaching and plaintiffs' counsel was concerned that the trial would interfere with his plans to go on a cruise. He filed an uncontested motion for continuance of the trial. This motion, as well as the other three for summary judgment, was pending when I received a phone call from the judge's secretary just two days before the trial was scheduled to begin. The secretary informed me that the judge had granted the motion and that the trial would not be going forward as scheduled. I thanked her, assuming all along that she was referring to the grant of the plaintiffs' motion for continuance, and I therefore asked her to give me the new trial date. The judge's secretary then interrupted, insisting, 'No, Ms. Johnson, you don't understand. The court granted the motion for summary judgment in your favor. The United States is dismissed from the case.' At that moment, I actually jumped out of my shoes and ran out of my office shouting, 'We won! We won! We won!' It then dawned on me that the judge's secretary was still on the phone. I hurried back to my office, picked up the receiver, and calmly said, 'Thank you very much for calling. Please thank the judge for me.' The loss of the child was heartbreaking, but nevertheless, the court did the right thing in dismissing the United States as a defendant. I've never forgotten the excitement of that day."

In her work as an attorney for the Attorney Registration and Disciplinary Commission of Illinois, Mary Foster investigates complaints against attorneys, determines whether disciplinary hearings can be brought, and prosecutes the cases before hearing panels. "My work is similar to that of a civil litigation attorney," Mary explains. "Once an attorney's client files a complaint, we ask the attorney to respond to the complaint in writing. Over 6,000 complaints are filed each year. Each complaint marks the beginning of an investigation. Our agency has subpoena power. We subpoena the attorney's files as well as banking records and any other records that may show fraud or misconduct. The case then goes to an inquiry panel. The panel is composed of volunteers, including two lawyers and one nonlawyer—the nonlawyer may be a member of any profession, and may be a banker or a bricklayer. The panel determines whether to 'vote' [or file] a formal complaint before the hearing board. Cases are ultimately tried before hearing panels. Attorneys in our office generally handle 40-90 investigations and eight hearing matters at one time. Each of our staff attorneys concludes about 12 hearing matters per year. We ultimately prosecute about 120 lawyers per year."

Gretta Tameling says that as city attorney for Naperville, "Every day I do a little bit of everything." Much of her day involves client counseling. "There's so much client contact in my job. On an hourly basis, the city department heads and people on the city staff come to me for advice— 'How should I do this? How should this controversy be handled? What information should I give this councilman?'" Gretta dispenses legal advice to the scores of city employees who depend on her expertise. "The trend is for the city government to be more responsive to the public, and we're in the process of teaching our staff members how to do their jobs while interacting with the public to a greater and greater degree. One of the chief roles of the city attorney is that of handling organizational change. The human needs of my clients—the city's officials and employees—have multiplied."

Gretta continues, "On any given day, I might review four or five contracts. I also review research reports from my staff as well as building development agreements and property damage claims filed against the city. Naperville has its own claims manager who essentially functions as a claims adjuster for whenever the city damages someone's property. I supervise the claims manager's work and advise him regarding whether or not the city should pay on particular claims. I also spend a good deal of my time supervising the other city attorneys on our staff. I delegate work to them, review their work, and provide guidance."

What do government lawyers find rewarding about their practice?

The government attorneys we talked to are enthusiastic about the public service aspect of their jobs. Joan Humes says that she enjoys being a citizens' advocate. "I've always loved the civil service side of government work," she enthuses. "It's a privilege to advocate for the citizenry and to represent the interests of the public. Public policy issues are incredibly important, and I believe that I'm advocating justice in a 'capital J' kind of way." Adds Mary Foster, "My work at the Attorney Registration and Disciplinary Commission is very gratifying. I'm protecting the public and protecting the legal profession from disrepute. Unfortunately, I can't make a client who has been bilked by an irresponsible attorney whole. But I can work to seek justice for the harm that's been caused. It's a privilege to wear the white hat."

"The most personally rewarding part of my job," says Gail Johnson, "is simply the fact that I am representing the people of the United States. Because I have no financial stake in the outcome of a case, I can participate in the pure practice of the law. I have never defended or brought a lawsuit that I did not believe in or where I felt that was on the wrong side. When I wake up in the morning, I can look myself in the mirror and say without hesitation, 'You've done good, Gail.' After 11 years on the job, I still get excited about what I do and that makes me very happy and content."

Gretta Tameling says that she, too, finds reward in the public service aspect of her work. "I went to law school to change the world," she explains. "I came out of the women's movement; the women's movement convinced me that going to law school would give me the tools I need to make a difference in the world. In my job as city attorney, I work with huge public policy issues. I have the opportunity to influence—sometimes in significant ways and sometimes in the smallest ways—the development of public policy."

The government practice attorneys we interviewed said they enjoy their colleagues immensely. "At the Commission, we have a very pleasant working environment," says Mary Foster. "The atmosphere is very open and I have simply wonderful colleagues. Because our investigations of attorneys are confidential and we can't discuss them outside the office, we tend to talk with each other. There's also a sense of teamwork. I work closely with investigators and paralegals. I've worked on a team with the same investigator since I started working at the Commission in 1985. These relationships mean a lot to me and to all the attorneys in our office. I also enjoy the opportunity I have to supervise and assist less experienced attorneys, as well as my role in hiring new attorneys for our office."

"I really like my colleagues," says Joan Humes. "There's a tremendous sense of teamwork within our office. I solicit my colleagues' views, and we truly seem to work in a coalition. Our office is an office in which everyone is passionate about the law. It's the type of office that when a Supreme Court opinion comes down, you can run out into the hallway and ask people what they think about it—and you know that you're surrounded by people who enjoy talking about Supreme Court opinions and all kinds of legal issues."

Mary Foster finds that her work at the Commission is intellectually challenging. "Even after 14 years of handling attorney investigations, I find the cases endlessly fascinating. The nature of the cases means that I'm always learning new areas of law, depending on the area of law in which the attorney being investigated practices. It's often said that the worst lawyers—those with the most egregious conduct—hire the best lawyers to defend them. That means that my opponents are some of the best lawyers in the state. I generally have a collegial relationship with my opposing counsel, and because they are such outstanding attorneys, I learn a great deal from working with them. The cases I work on are interesting from a human interest standpoint, as well. In an increasing number of cases, the respondents claim that they engaged in fraudulent conduct due to substance abuse or mental illness. This means that I'm frequently dealing with experts on areas such as drug abuse, depression, schizophrenia, and bipolar disorder, and working with these experts is exciting."

Joan Humes, too, enjoys the intellectual challenge of her job. "I really like research, writing, and the study of the law. My passion isn't courtroom drama. My passion is resolution and mediation and finding the middle ground, finding the commonalities so that the case can move ahead. And in my job, my research and writing means that I'm likely to have an opportunity to move the case ahead and get it resolved."

"The variety of matters I handle in my job makes the job exciting," says Gretta Tameling. "I work on issues related to so many different areas of law. I have a really high energy level, and I have a broad range of interests. My job gives me the opportunity to use all I learned in law school and all I've learned through my years of practice experience. I grew up in the area, and I find special satisfaction in my work because it allows me to view, firsthand, the growth and change of the city from a historical perspective. DuPage

County was largely an agricultural community when I was growing up. Now Naperville and other DuPage cities are large communities with urban rather than rural concerns. There are storm water issues and transportation issues to deal with. There are sustainable growth issues—how to sustain a viable tax base past the point of buildup. There is the question of how to support Naperville's large infrastructure." It's clear that Gretta enjoys the role she plays in addressing these monumental challenges.

Gretta says that her job as city attorney has given her a chance to work close to home so that she can attend to her family's needs. "I live in Wheaton, just two or three miles away from the Naperville office. Practicing in the government sector has allowed me to be with my family when I need to be with them, without being stressed out. And it's a joy to work in the community in which I live."

The Training and Skills Important to Government Practice

How do people enter the field of government practice?

Gail Johnson's government career began immediately upon graduation from law school, when she worked as a federal judicial law clerk. A judicial clerkship can be an excellent stepping stone for attorneys seeking to further their careers in the government sector. "My federal judicial clerkship greatly influenced my decision to practice tort law with the Justice Department. While I was clerking, I used to watch the trials and hearings in tort cases and I found them interesting and exciting. I used to say to myself, 'I can do that!'" Gail confides that she decided she wanted to be a lawyer when she was just eight years old. "I am a lawyer today for one reason: I watched entirely too much television as a child. I loved watching now-defunct TV shows about lawyers such as *Owen Marshall, Counselor at Law* and *Judd for the Defense*. I must admit that I still catch an occasional 3:00 a.m. showing of *Perry Mason*."

Mary Foster says she never dreamed of doing disciplinary law while in law school. "When I was in law school, I knew more about what I didn't want to do than what I did want to do. I knew I didn't want to practice criminal law or family law. I was active in Moot Court, and I knew I was interested in litigation. But I had no clear career path in mind." Mary's first job after graduation was as an insurance defense lawyer with a mid-size firm, in which she handled numerous bench and jury trials. "After a year of trial experience, I knew that I loved litigation, and through a law school classmate I heard about opportunities at the ARDC. The Commission was interested in my trial experience, and they knew I could hit the ground running."

Assistant U.S. Attorney Joan Humes entered law school after working as a social worker and businesswoman. "My undergraduate degree was in child psychology and social work, and I was a social worker in Hennepin County for five years," she explains. "I left social work to run a wholesale arts business for seven years. When you run a business, you live it and breathe it. I wanted to learn more about the legal aspects of business and decided to enter law school. At that time I had no intention of practicing law; I simply thought I would use the degree in my business. I loved law school. During law school I worked as a teaching assistant for a constitutional law professor. After graduation I worked as a law clerk for a trial court judge in Minnesota. I then joined the Minnesota State's Attorney's Office, where I worked on labor enforcement and wage fairness issues. I liked the service aspect of the work. It was rewarding to help people who had been cheated by their employers get the wages that were owed them."

Joan then joined the U.S. Attorney's Office in Minneapolis. When she joined the office in 1994, she handled civil fraud cases. "They're fascinating and very complex cases. They involve grant fraud, Medicare fraud, and so forth." She began handling civil rights work in 1998, and the work has proven an excellent match for her talents. Joan cautions students that there is keen competition across the country for positions in U.S. Attorneys' offices. "Most of the offices hire attorneys with at least three years of litigation experience. We tend to hire people with experience because our attorneys have to be able to walk in and handle a case load from the beginning. There's no time for learning litigation skills on the job."

Gretta Tameling returned to law school as a full-time student when she was 38 years old. "I was attracted to government service, as I knew I could get hands-on courtroom experience early in my legal career. I clerked in the DuPage County Public Defender's Office while in law school. Though I liked the challenge of the courtroom, I decided I didn't want to be on the defense side of things. Jim Ryan (now Illinois attorney general) was seeking election as DuPage County's State's Attorney, and I worked on his campaign. He won the campaign and needed new assistant state's attorneys, and I was able to join the DuPage County State's Attorney's Office."

Gretta prosecuted crimes for a year and a half before becoming involved in the civil division of the State's Attorney's Office. "The civil division represents the county government, the elected and appointed officials, and the employees of the county. An opening occurred in the public works department, which handled sewers, water, and garbage. This was in the early 1980s, a time in which there was a shortage of landfill space in Illinois as well as a rash of flooding that catapulted public works into a high profile area of government service. I was provided with remarkable opportunities. I drafted legislation concerning storm water regulations, proposing that counties, rather than the state, be responsible for storm water management. I rewrote much of the state law concerning garbage management. In addition to drafting legislation, I lobbied the state legislators and represented the public works department in all its dealings with the government. Working in this area also required me to develop an expertise in environmental law."

In the meantime, Gretta explains, the DuPage County city of Naperville had experienced phenomenal population growth. Naperville had used a large Chicago law firm as its counsel, but the city decided that it was time to develop an in-house legal department. Naperville first hired a city attorney and then hired Gretta as second in command of their legal department in 1991. In 1999, when the city attorney left, Gretta was appointed Acting City Attorney. Gretta speaks enthusiastically about her work. "I want to remind students that often your career takes a direction you had never imagined. Where you go after graduation may be beyond your wildest imagination. I love working as City Attorney; when I joined the staff, it was as if the planets aligned perfectly, allowing me to find the ideal job for me. I never expected to be a municipal government lawyer; it's not something I dreamed about in law school. But it's been a wonderful life and a great, great practice."

What skills are most important to government lawyers?

❖   The government lawyers we interviewed agreed that the best government lawyers have a **passion for their work**. "The work I do is very emotional and personal because an American citizen is alleging an injury and they are looking to assess blame or fault," says Gail Johnson. "As a lawyer for the United States, I am expected to represent my client zealously. And just as important, as a public servant I am expected to treat the opposing side in a manner that is professional, fair, respectful, and humane."

Gretta Tameling says, "A passion for learning is key to this type of work. Every day the city manager comes to me with a question that I can't answer off the top of my head, something that I need to research. This happens every single day—to be happy in this type of work you must have a real love for learning new things."

Mary Foster says that working for the Commission requires a passion for litigation. "To do this type of work, you really need a desire to do litigation. This work requires a thick skin, as you run into harsh criticism from the lawyers being investigated as well as the clients who have complained to the Commission about their lawyers. When you're investigating lawyers for wrongdoing, they are upset and threatened, as their very livelihood is threatened. And the clients you are seeking to assist sometimes come to believe that you've taken the guise of looking out for them but are really working to protect lawyers—because, after all, you're a lawyer too. To survive in this field, you must be highly committed to the mission of protecting the public and the legal profession."

Joan Humes adds, "You have to love what you do. When you listen to lawyers advocate in the courtroom, it's so clear when someone really believes in their cause. When you believe in your cause, it's easier to communicate your arguments, and your persuasive strategy is much more effective. In Minneapolis we have a small bench and bar. It's easy to lose credibility. It's important that judges know that they can rely on me to tell the truth and to know the law. It's a huge, huge positive to be passionate enough about your cause, and well enough prepared, to set aside your sword and talk. Judges learn they can count on you."

❖ All of the attorneys we talked to stressed that strong **research and writing skills** are critical to the government practitioner. "My disciplinary work requires good legal writing and business writing skills. I'm writing briefs and drafting pleadings as well as communicating with the respondent's client who initiated the complaint process," explains Mary Foster. Says Joan Humes, "In my civil practice, I've learned that the court relies on me, as an Assistant U.S. Attorney, to know what the rules are with regard to the civil issues I work on. Much of our advocacy in civil practice is written. The government is generally the plaintiff, and the court looks to me to learn the government's position. It's important to explain the statute and why we need to enforce it in a particular situation. I have to be meticulous in my research, as I need to clearly communicate the government's position." City attorney Gretta Tameling adds, "In local government work, a lot of what you do must be committed to writing. Persuasive writing is especially important, as you have to be able to persuade the city council or city manager of your position and have to be clear and concise as well as persuasive."

❖ **Interpersonal skills** are also important to those attorneys who enter government service. "As a government lawyer, you are dealing with clients just as you are in private practice," says Gretta Tameling. "Some of those clients you deal with have strong personalities and big egos, so good interpersonal skills are a must. I've found that it's not necessary to be a star public speaker; exercising good communication skills on a day-to-day basis is what counts."

❖ **Self-confidence** helps government lawyers advocate effectively. "I'm obsessive about being well prepared," says Joan Humes, "but my preparation gives me confidence. Federal practice is formal and intellectual. Judges expect you to be well prepared. You must be confident at the podium. I know that by spending an extra four hours preparing for a court appearance that I'll be well prepared, that I know and can articulate my position. Preparation and confidence go hand in hand."

❖ **A sincere interest in and commitment to the area of law in which you practice** is also helpful to government attorneys. "My tort work is discovery-intensive," says Gail Johnson. "Natural curiosity is a big plus. I love to get fact-intensive cases where you have to dig and dig to get to the nitty-gritty of the case." Adds Mary Foster, "In disciplinary work you are making judgments about the behavior of other legal professionals and making decisions that may impact a professional's ability to make a living. You have to be committed to the task and be confident that you have the information you need to make effective and fair decisions."

What classes and law school experiences do government lawyers recommend?

❖ Take a **wide range of law school classes** to ensure that you're prepared for the broad scope of issues you may face as a government lawyer. "A sound law school education is important," says Gretta Tameling. Advises Joan Humes, "Go heavy on the substantive law courses, such as civil procedure, constitutional law, federal jurisdiction, etc. These classes teach you to think creatively and thus build your understanding of all areas of law."

❖ Take **classes in the area of government practice in which you're interested**, whether criminal law, tort law, environmental law, tax law, or any other area. "If you're interested in litigation, take course work related to litigation, including evidence and trial advocacy," advises Mary Foster. "Another course helpful to many lawyers is accounting for lawyers, as it teaches you to read balance sheets." Joan Humes adds, "I took a federal taxation course and found it to be incredibly helpful, because tax and financial concepts are involved in most every area of law practice." Gretta Tameling suggests that students interested in municipal law may want to take a local government course, as well as classes in land use and environmental law.

❖ **Legal writing classes** and a **legal drafting course** are also important. "The attorneys we hire must be able to advocate effectively both orally and in writing," says Mary Foster. Many law schools offer advanced legal writing courses as well as seminar courses that involve writing lengthy papers.

❖ Several of the lawyers we talked to also recommend taking a **negotiations course**. "My work requires me to negotiate every day, whether I'm negotiating with my staff, the city manager, or city employees. I negotiate with department heads, for example, asking them to complete a project within legal bounds," says Gretta Tameling.

❖ Take a **trial advocacy class and participate in moot court competition**. "Trial advocacy helped me develop the skills I needed to be an effective litigator," says Mary Foster. Gail Johnson recommends participating in moot court, in which students prepare and argue an appellate brief in front of a panel of judges. "Experience is a great teacher," Gail says. "I am a strong advocate of involvement in experiential learning—moot court is a great place to start."

❖ Develop client counseling skills through **working in your law school's legal clinic**. Legal clinics allow law students to work on legal cases with real clients. Clinical work is closely supervised by a clinical professor, who provides personalized guidance with regard to your client counseling skills. "Clinics give you the opportunity to experience what life in law practice will be like," says Gretta Tameling. "You learn practical things about how to work with clients, how to file things at the courthouse, how to manage written case records."

❖ **Work as a judicial law clerk after graduation from law school or as a judicial extern while a law student.** Many federal and some state judges hire law students to work as law clerks for a period of one to two years after graduation. Law clerks work closely with the judge and assist the judge in drafting opinions. Judicial externs work as junior law clerks, assisting the judge's clerk or clerks, and often receive academic credit for their work. A clerkship helps strengthen your writing skills and offers you an unparalleled opportunity to learn about the legal procedure and meet and observe attorneys who specialize in many different fields of law.

"It wasn't until my judicial clerkship that I knew that I had an interest in tort work," says Gail Johnson. "That's why I'm a strong advocate of judicial clerkships and judicial externships." Joan Humes is enthusiastic in her praise of the clerkship experience, commenting, "My clerkship experience has colored my whole legal career and continues to affect my practice daily. It affects how I write my pleadings and briefs, how I present my case to the court, and how I approach my work. My clerkship made me tremendously conscious of the intelligence of the court and respectful of the court's time constraints."

❖ During law school, **work as an intern or law clerk in a government office.** "Working in any government legal office shows that you have a commitment to public service and an understanding of the work government lawyers do," says Mary Foster. U.S. Attorneys' offices often have summer internship programs, and state agencies may hire summer interns or law clerks for academic year positions. Mary tells us, for example, that the ARDC generally hires several law clerks to work through the summer and the school year, and Gretta Tameling reports that Naperville generally hires one or two law clerks each year.

❖ **Gain all the practical experience you can during law school,** whether through volunteering, working as a judicial extern, or working in a government office. "The more practical experience you get, the better prepared you are to practice law," advises Gail Johnson. "I was the first attorney in my family and I did not know the importance of moot court, clinical experience, externships, and judicial clerkships. Hindsight is always 20/20. Now I can see very clearly how those experiences enhance my ability to do my job for the Justice Department."

❖ **Acquiring work experience in a professional field before entering law school** can help you develop the skills that will allow you to be an outstanding public servant. "My social work background has proved to be valuable in my work as an Assistant U.S. Attorney," says Joan Humes. "The work experience makes a huge difference in the way I approach my work. As a social worker, I gained experience interviewing clients, working with families, and working with people in crisis situations. I developed a high tolerance for crisis—and that allows me to remain calm and professional and keep my work in perspective. I am able to remind myself that I am working on fascinating legal issues that are going to be resolved and that emotional outbursts won't move the matter further along. My counseling experience also taught me how to connect with people and helped me to develop speech and intonation that engages people, even those who are suffering or traumatized."

Joan says that her business management experience has also helped her legal career. "My years running a business gave me an immense respect for people in business. When the U.S. Attorney's Office sues people in fraud cases, I have empathy for the defendants. I know what it feels like to be the defendant. And I'm able to discern the difference between people who have truly erred and people who have aggressively looked for a loophole and then driven a truck through that loophole. I can recognize when defendants are truly confused versus situations in which they know how to comply with the law and have the resources to comply but nevertheless choose not to comply."

❖ **Begin to build government contacts** while you are a law student. "Make all the contacts you can as soon as you can," advises Gretta Tameling. "Meet your friends' parents, and your parents' friends, and friends' friends. Don't be shy about telling people what type of work you're interested in—they may be able to refer you to someone who works for the government doing that type of work. Most of the government lawyers I know are thrilled to talk to students about their work and why they find it rewarding," says Gretta. "Another way to meet people in this field is through working in political campaigns. You learn about the pressures government officials work under and meet government attorneys firsthand."

GOVERNMENT PRACTICE ATTORNEYS
INTERVIEWED FOR THIS SECTION

Mary Foster
Attorney Registration & Disciplinary Commission of the Illinois
Supreme Court
Chicago, Illinois
UNDERGRADUATE: Drake University
LAW SCHOOL: University of Illinois College of Law

Joan Humes
U.S. Attorney's Office
Minneapolis, Minnesota
UNDERGRADUATE: University of Minnesota
LAW SCHOOL: University of Minnesota Law School

Gail Kimberly Johnson
U.S. Department of Justice, Civil Division
Washington, D.C.
UNDERGRADUATE: Howard University
LAW SCHOOL: UCLA School of Law

Gretta Tameling
City of Naperville
Naperville, Illinois
UNDERGRADUATE: Wheaton College
LAW SCHOOL: Chicago-Kent College of Law, Illinois Institute of
Technology

Health Care Law

What is Health Care Law?

The award winning television program *ER*, with its fast pace, hand-held camera angles, and heart wrenching plot twists, won over both viewers and critics. It follows Dr. Mark Greene, nurse Carol Hathaway, and a host of doctors, nurses, interns, medical students, orderlies, and administrators as they attempt to provide quality care at an inner city emergency room.

An equally compelling drama, however, takes place behind the scenes of every American hospital and health care organization. This drama involves legal professionals who are every bit as dedicated as the medical professionals depicted on *ER*. They work on myriad issues, from ethical matters involving patient care to labor issues with hospital staff members to business deals involving hospital mergers and acquisitions.

Health care lawyers often represent hospitals and other health care providers, such as nursing homes, psychiatric centers, and acute care centers, as well as health maintenance organizations (HMOs). These organizations, like other corporations, seek legal advice regarding general corporate matters such as corporate reorganization, capital financing, employee benefits, tax, and antitrust issues. They also seek legal advice concerning issues that are unique to health care providers, such as physician recruitment, the acquisition of physician practices, and numerous medical staff relations issues—including the review of staff bylaws, credentialing issues, disciplinary matters, the development of faculty/staff practice plans for teaching hospitals, and the formation of physician-hospital organizations. Health care lawyers also provide guidance concerning Medicare and Medicaid fraud, abuse, and payment issues; HMO and insurance regulation; telemedicine; and health reform issues. In addition, health care lawyers deal with bioethical issues such as assisted reproduction and death and dying, and advise hospital clients concerning risk management, informed consent, and confidentiality issues.

The health care industry is highly regulated, and hospitals and other health care facilities must therefore carefully monitor legislation affecting the industry. Lawyers represent health care providers before federal agencies such as the Department of Justice, the Federal Trade Commission, the Food and Drug Administration, and state agencies that regulate issues such as licensing, reimbursements, and other administrative issues. They also help hospitals develop legislative strategies, draft legislation and supporting documents, meet with legislative leaders, and prepare witnesses for testimony before legislative committees. (*See* the Legislative Practice chapter for more information on these types of activities.)

Health care lawyers may also assist hospitals and health care organizations with many types of litigation, such as the defense of medical malpractice cases, as well as commercial disputes, breach of contract disputes, intellectual property cases, real estate issues, and labor disputes. Health care organizations may also be involved in antitrust litigation, health care fraud and abuse litigation, and litigation involving Medicare and Medicaid reimbursement.

Health care attorneys also work with a wide range of additional clients. Physicians are often involved in professional groups that form corporations or partnerships; health care lawyers provide advice concerning the formation of such entities. Health care attorneys may represent physicians, hospitals, and physician/hospital joint ventures in negotiating with health insurers concerning provider networks. They can also work for health insurance companies, including HMOs and preferred provider networks. Health care attorneys also represent dental practices, ambulatory surgical centers, and laboratories, as well as nurses, dentists, podiatrists, and chiropractors. In addition, health care lawyers work for corporations such as pharmaceutical companies, providing assistance on regulatory compliance with state and federal agencies such as the Food and Drug Administration.

There are five health care attorneys profiled here; you can learn more about this practice area by also reviewing the profiles of Ann Triebsch and Lauree Barreca in the Insurance Law chapter and Toby Singer in the Antitrust Law chapter.

Life as a Health Care Lawyer

Where do health care lawyers work?

Many health care lawyers work for law firms, often in large or mid-size law firms that have departments specializing in health care law. Some health care lawyers work for hospitals and other medical corporations, pharmaceutical companies, and companies that develop and manufacture medical equipment. Still other health care lawyers work for insurance companies, whether negotiating contracts with physician groups or handling legislative and regulatory issues or handling tort litigation brought against physicians and other medical professionals.

Government agencies, including federal or state health and human services and social services agencies, also hire health care attorneys. Other employers of health care lawyers include professional and trade associations, such as the American Hospital Association or the American Dental Association.

Who are their clients and what types of issues do they work on?

Suzanne Mitchell is the Associate General Counsel of PennState Geisinger Health System in Danville, Pennsylvania. "I work for a health system as opposed to a single hospital," Suzanne explains. "This system has a number of different components, including three hospitals. Each of the hospitals in the system is very different: one is a small community hospital, one is a rural regional referral tertiary care center, and the third is an academic medical center (the major teaching site for the Pennsylvania State University College of Medicine) where residents can obtain advanced training. All of the hospitals operate differently, they evolved differently, and, to a certain degree, different government regulations apply to each of them. The PennState Geisinger Clinic employs about 1,000 physicians practicing at about 75 sites in over 60 Pennsylvania communities. The PennState Geisinger Health System also operates its own not-for-profit HMO, which is licensed in 31 Pennsylvania counties. We have for-profit subsidiaries that provide contract management, consulting, and maintenance services; and we operate a Medicare-certified home health care agency. These entities are spread throughout the state of Pennsylvania.

"As a lawyer for the health system," Suzanne continues, "my clients include any employee of any of those entities, as well as people who provide services on our behalf. Any of these people can pick up the phone and call me when they have a legal concern. As a result, I am a legal generalist." The issues on which Suzanne works cover a wide range. "Some issues are patient care issues. For example, a patient who comes into the emergency room and is in and out of consciousness and therefore can't give permission to receive treatment. Or a child born to a Jehovah's Witness family may need a blood transfusion, which is contrary to the family's religious beliefs. I also work on regulatory issues, such as OSHA [the Occupational Safety and Health Act, a federal law enacted in 1970 establishing occupational safety and health standards] regulatory matters. If, for example, a fire were to occur in one of our hospitals, we would have to report on how we handled the incident. Regulatory work involves both handling discrete incidents within the relevant regulatory framework and preparing for routine reviews by regulatory and accrediting bodies.

"In addition, I handle general operational issues concerning the health system," Suzanne explains. "If a surgeon appeared to be intoxicated upon entering the operating room, I would help decide what to do in the short term and in the long term. My job involves numerous labor and employment issues. We are proactive in documenting and handling disciplinary actions. We respond to complaints filed by discharged and disciplined employees, as well." Suzanne says that other lawyers on the health system's staff oversee medical malpractice litigation pending against the health system. The health system also employs law firm attorneys to assist in-house counsel on a variety of matters, including commercial litigation, tax, real estate, antitrust, labor, intellectual property, etc.

Julie Robertson is a health care attorney at Honigman Miller Schwartz and Cohn, a large law firm in Detroit, Michigan. "Our clients are health care providers, typically hospitals and their affiliates and provider groups such as professional corporations or physician hospital organizations. Most of my clients are located here in Michigan, but I consult with clients across the country," she explains. As an example of a case, Julie describes a recent matter on which she worked: "We helped a university medical school and a hospital in establishing a joint program to provide specialty medical services. Our work included analyzing the reimbursement and tax impact of various legal structures, establishing a new corporation, and negotiating and drafting the agreements between the parties."

Health care attorney Jack Schroder, Jr., practices at Alston & Bird LLP, a large Atlanta law firm. "Most of my clients," he says, "are health care providers (primarily hospitals) or entities which serve the provider industry, such as hospital associations, suppliers, etc. Typically a client needs assistance in complying with or obtaining a ruling or directive from an administrative agency. For example, health care providers must obtain a 'certificate of need' from a state agency before they can add a new service or piece of equipment." Jack helps prepare the materials and documentation needed to persuade the state board to issue the certificate allowing the hospital to add new medical equipment, add or reduce bed capacity, add a new service, or make significant capital expenditures such as adding a wing or remodeling.

Susan Blackwell May is a health care attorney with American Health Network in Indianapolis, Indiana. American Health Network is a large primary care network that employs doctors in Ohio and Indiana. Susan is one of two attorneys employed by the network. "My clients are the physicians in our network, as well as employees of the network who have legal questions," she explains. "I handle a wide range of issues. I buy insurance for the physicians and handle contractual issues. Among the contracts I handle are the employment contracts with the physicians, the contracts we have with insurance companies, and the contracts we have with hospitals and specialists. I also manage the litigation involving our primary care network; this involves monitoring tort cases and also employment and contracts disputes."

Kim Otte works for Allina Health System in Minnetonka, Minnesota, where she is one of 12 in-house attorneys. "Allina is an integrated health system, composed of a health maintenance organization and numerous hospitals, clinics, and health care delivery services. Allina, which is a Minnesota-based organization, has over a million insured members." Kim specializes in legislative affairs, and tells us that her number one client is the health system's public affairs department. "I advise our public policy team and help link them with the legal department. I monitor the many changes in state and federal law that relate to health care. I monitor legislation from the time it is first proposed as a bill. I assess whether it's bad or good from Allina's standpoint. I sometimes draft bills. I also negotiate with other parties who are interested in a bill. I assist Allina's two full-time lobbyists. During the legislative session, I'm often at the Capitol, drafting legislation and promoting good bills." (*See* the Legislative Practice chapter for more information on these activities.)

Kim explains that her job involves educating Allina employees about new laws. "Once a bill becomes law, I let the relevant portions of the company know about the change in the law. I tell them about the history of the legislation, the legislative intent, and the implications. I get calls from company employees on an ongoing basis about how to interpret the law. Allina staff call and suggest changes in the laws, and I work with the lobbyists on these issues. I also work with state professional and trade associations, such as the American Association of Health Plans (AAHP). The professional and trade associations often make comments as a group concerning pending legislation or regulation. For example, at the state level, new HMO rules were recently promulgated. I spent time negotiating the language for the regulations and attending the final hearings. Now I'm communicating with my clients about that law. It's exciting to see the legislative procedure from beginning to end and to help Allina with the implementation of the new law."

What daily activities are involved in health care law practice?

"On any given day," reports Suzanne Mitchell, of the PennState Geisinger Health System, "I can work on 20 different things. There's a lot of variety in my job. I spend a great deal of time fielding questions that come to me via telephone and e-mail. The person contacting me often needs short term advice and asks for help with 'just one quick question.' I can be asked, for example, to assess the consequences of terminating an existing contract with a vendor. A physician may want to end a relationship with a non-compliant patient. The Infection Control Program may need advice about how to handle an employee who is HIV-positive. The Human Resources Department may ask about how to manage an employee's performance problems. The Public Relations Department may be wondering about the legal implications of marketing health care services on the Internet. An injured employee from a nearby company may come to the emergency room and object to substance abuse testing. Often I can answer the question quickly, but sometimes the issues are more numerous and complicated than the requester realizes. Then I may have to do additional research or ask the requester for more information in order to provide sound legal advice."

In addition to the daily variety of questions Suzanne encounters, she works on more comprehensive, long term issues. "We may consider, for example, a unified set of medical bylaws that will apply to all three of our hospitals. As mentioned earlier, I also work on a number of regulatory issues which can involve, for example, Medicare and Medicaid regulations. I also review, revise, and develop system-wide policies and procedures in a wide range of areas."

Julie Robertson says that her practice at Honigman Miller requires her to work closely with her clients, which are hospitals and provider groups. "I spend most of my time in my office, either talking on the phone with clients, meeting them in person, or working on legal projects for them. My work generally consists of reviewing contracts between health care providers and other providers or entities; analyzing the impact of various federal, state, and tax laws and regulations on health care providers' business arrangements; handling general corporate law matters; and analyzing issues raised in structuring affiliations among health care providers."

Alston & Bird's Jack Schroder says that his days are spent attending to client needs. "When I'm in the office, most of my day is spent on the phone providing quick-response advice to health care providers who have questions about compliance due to the overwhelming statutory and regulatory schemes governing their operations," Jack explains. He comments that each day brings new challenges. "Every day I work on something that I've never encountered before in the state of Georgia and sometimes never encountered in the country. This means that I'm developing new 'war stories' every hour of every day!"

Susan Blackwell May, of American Health Network, says that her days involve fielding numerous questions via phone and e-mail. "I'm connected with all of our company's Ohio and Indiana offices via e-mail. We have over 1,300 employees, resulting in a large number of phone and e-mail questions. I also draft contracts and work on contractual issues across the board. My work requires working with the company's business people, including the head of computer services, the head of provider relations, and our marketing department. Employment issues also arise. For example, we might have a non-physician employee writing prescriptions for himself. I also monitor health care legislation. In addition, I may counsel the doctors who are involved in litigation, though the litigation itself is handled by the attorneys hired by our insurance companies."

Kim Otte, of Allina Health System, says that her legislative work involves both formal and informal communication. "Any new law requires a formal written bulletin explaining the law, which is then distributed throughout the company. I also make the required changes in client manuals. I do oral presentations concerning changes in the law at meetings on the delivery side of the company—the part that delivers health care services—as well as at meetings on the health plan side of the company." Kim also fields a number of questions over the phone. "I get lots of phone calls. Sometimes I field as many as three or four 'quick questions' a day. They might involve the interpretation of a new regulation, such as HMO rules defining 'experimental treatment' in a new way."

Kim says that about half of her time is spent in meetings. "In internal meetings we're figuring out our positions on legislative issues, such as coverage for special education services or changes in the insured's grievance process." Kim also attends meetings outside the company. "In external meetings I communicate and negotiate our position with outside parties, including legislators, regulators, and the consumer advocacy groups who often sponsor proposed acts." The other half of Kim's time is spent doing research and writing. "It's important for me to keep up with trends in the industry. Every day I receive a stack of mail five inches high, including journals and industry publications. I do a great deal of legal research, which is similar in nature to the legal research a health care attorney in a law firm does."

What do health care lawyers find rewarding about their practice?

"At some level I feel I am making a difference in people's lives," says Suzanne Mitchell. "I feel that if I can make a difference to one individual, by helping out one of our doctors or one of our social workers, that I can have an impact on patient care and patient satisfaction and, ultimately, patient quality of life." Another rewarding part of her job, Suzanne tells us, is the risk management work she does. "Risk management involves identifying risks before they happen, and that's very rewarding. For example, it might be easy for a nurse to give a patient the wrong medication because two medications are in the same color bottle. Risk management tracks such incidents numerically. You then help to set up a system to put the medications in different color bottles, and the chance of a mix-up is much less. You can actually see the positive results of the steps you've taken to decrease risk, and it's satisfying to know that you've made a difference."

Julie Robertson especially enjoys working on new ventures. "I particularly enjoy using my knowledge of the health care business environment in conjunction with my knowledge of the health care legal environment to assist clients in structuring new ventures," she says. She also enjoys working with her non-profit clients. "Working with non-profits is particularly rewarding," she comments, "as they provide valuable services to members of my community."

Jack Schroder reports that he enjoys the role he plays in health care legislation. "During the past 17 years, I have either drafted or been involved in revising most of Georgia's health care legislation, including some rather innovative statutes which have been imitated in other states."

Susan Blackwell May tells us that she enjoys the ever-changing nature of health care practice as well as the intellectual challenge it offers. "In this field, there are always good opportunities to get involved in new things. There's always more to learn. The field is intellectually challenging, and you feel as if you're involved in cutting edge issues."

Kim Otte reports that she loves the research and writing work that her job requires and the unique vantage point that her legislative work provides her within the health care industry. "Instead of seeing just a single research project, I see the whole company—including the doctors, the finance people, and all our employees—and how the company is affected by the research I'm doing. I also enjoy the role I play in long term strategy decisions. The ultimate goal to work toward in health care is universal access, and I get to play a role in moving toward that goal. I also enjoy being part of the public policy team, which defines legislative priorities and sets an agenda for the company." In addition, Kim says that her work is intellectually stimulating. "Every piece of legislation is loaded with ethical issues and public policy issues. Nothing is simple. I love theory and ethics, and I appreciate the fact that I have a job that lets me contemplate and work on these types of issues." Kim's job also allows her to work on cutting edge issues. "There's no repetition and no precedent for what I do. There's nothing that tells you how to do this job. Some people might find that unsettling, but I find it exciting. Every day is different from the last."

The Training and Skills Important to Health Care Law

How do people enter the field of health care law?

Often a lawyer's academic training, work experience before or during law school, or family background will spark an interest in the health care field. Kim Otte, who specializes in legislative health care issues at Allina, has a master's degree in philosophy with a focus on bioethics. "Bioethics has always been my interest. Even as an undergraduate student, I took lots of philosophy and bioethics classes. Like many lawyers who enter the health care field, I come from a family of health practitioners. My father is a doctor; my mother is a nurse. One of my sisters is a doctor. I've really had a lifelong interest in health care."

Like Kim, Jack Schroder's interest in health care developed through growing up in a medical family—his father was a physician. "My interest in health care really evolved when I was a child. My uncle, a medical malpractice defense lawyer, would come to our house to talk to my physician father about specific cases on which he was working. When I chose to join Alston & Bird, one of the attractive things about the firm was that it had a very active health care practice which dated from the 1940s. During my first eight years at Alston & Bird I worked as a medical malpractice defense lawyer [see the Tort Law chapter]. My experience in medical malpractice defense was great training for my subsequent role as an adviser to providers on other regulatory issues. In short, I learned how providers *worked*, which made my subsequent advice to clients much more practical."

Julie Robertson also had a long-standing interest in health care when she entered law school. "I had even considered non-legal careers in the health care field. After I entered law school, I started clerking for a law firm with a significant health care practice. That experience helped me determine that health care law was the right field for me," Julie explains.

Susan Blackwell May returned to law school while she was working full-time for a county health department in Illinois. "I was an administrative assistant to a public health administrator. I was exposed to legislative affairs and other aspects of health care. It was a great experience, as I gained both legal knowledge and administrative skills by working for a wonderful public health administrator who became one of my mentors. My second mentor was a female attorney in the public health department. She was an outstanding role model."

Susan continues, "I moved to Indiana and, while I was studying for the Indiana bar, I met someone in the bar review class who worked for a hospital. She was leaving her job and told me that I might be interested in it. I landed the job at Methodist Hospital in Indianapolis, where I worked as an in-house attorney and risk manager for 12 years. My experience at the hospital led to my current position working for American Health Network."

Suzanne Mitchell became interested in health law during law school, when she took a seminar that explored medical-legal problems. "I went into the health care field because I perceived it to be an area of law where your human instincts can merge with your legal knowledge," says Suzanne, "and that has proven to be true." Suzanne has worked for a number of hospitals, including the University of Chicago Hospitals. "At U of Chicago, all of the work I did concerned the doctors, nurses, social workers, other clinicians, and patients at the hospitals. My focus in that job was patient care and operational issues, as opposed to traditional business issues. Other attorneys on the U of Chicago legal staff handled labor issues, reimbursement questions, and finance and business matters.

"In my current position at PennState Geisinger Health System, I'm more of a generalist," Suzanne explains. "It's a lot like being in a solo or small group practice. This isn't the type of job you can get straight out of law school. A lot of what I do requires having basic legal knowledge and expertise. You can't run to the library to research every question you're asked. You have to be mature enough and experienced enough to be able to rely on your instincts, your experience, and your good judgment."

Suzanne, who previously worked as Assistant Dean and Director of Career Services at the University of Chicago Law School, encourages students who are interested in health care law to begin their careers in a law firm. "Most hospitals and health care organizations will not hire law students right out of law school because these legal offices are usually very small (*i.e.*, too small to devote a lot of resources to training a brand new lawyer), very busy (and therefore need someone who can hit the ground running and work quickly with minimal supervision), and possess few resources (*i.e.*, few or no standard legal research materials). Working for a hospital can be a nerve-racking practice in some ways, since you are often just 'making up an answer' based on your best guess and your general knowledge of health law principles. That's why hospitals hire lawyers with significant experience. Working in a firm allows you to gain a wide variety of health care experience," says Suzanne.

Suzanne worked as a federal judicial law clerk, then practiced at a large Chicago law firm for two years and spent two years as an attorney at the American Hospital Association before landing her first job as a hospital attorney. Some law schools have externship programs in which hospitals have students work for a limited number of hours for credit. These positions offer great experience and give students a chance to make excellent contacts.

There are numerous law firms that have excellent health care law practices. A number of health care lawyers spend their entire careers at law firms, while others move on to work for a hospital, corporation, or pharmaceutical company. Many of the law firms with health care practices hire summer associates to work between the second and third year of law school, and then hire entry-level associates from the ranks of the summer associate program. Some firms with health care law practices hire law clerks to work during the school year or during the summer.

What skills are most important to health care lawyers?

❖ Excellent **writing skills** are key to success as a health care attorney. "Writing is important in this line of work," says Susan Blackwell May. "I write contracts, write letters to our physicians, and write articles for our medical ethics group. The legal meaning of words is so important; you have to be very careful in drafting contracts," Susan explains. While still in private practice, Kim Otte interviewed many first year candidates. "I always asked for a writing sample and reviewed it carefully. Attorneys must write well. A writing sample reveals a great deal about someone's writing as well as their level of attention to detail," she explains.

❖ The health care attorneys we talked to stressed the importance of **interpersonal skills**. Explains Julie Robertson, "My clients depend on me to advance their interests by working cooperatively with other parties and their lawyers and also with government regulators." Says Suzanne Mitchell, "You must be facile with both the spoken and the written word. You must be able to translate legal concepts into lay language at a wide variety of levels. For example, in my job, I talk with people at every level of education, from those who have an associate's degree in nursing to M.D.'s to people who have Ph.D.'s in biomedical engineering. You're constantly communicating with people who have different backgrounds and different perspectives."

❖ The ability to **think on your feet and act with good judgment** will help you be a successful health care attorney. "You've got to be smart and confident, and you've got to think on your feet. Good judgment is a huge part of the job," says Kim Otte. "I have to make split-second judgments. I may be at the Capitol and a floor amendment is added to a bill. I have to make a quick judgment call—What is our position? Is the amendment objectionable from a policy standpoint? Is it financially objectionable?"

❖ "Health care lawyers must be able to **juggle a number of projects at the same time**," advises Suzanne Mitchell. "Because I'm a generalist, the many projects that I'm working on often involve different areas of law," she explains. "My clients often want immediate answers." Adds Susan Blackwell May, "Good **administrative skills** are important. You must be organized; you must maintain careful records. In-house staffs are often small, so you must know what you can delegate to your administrative assistant, and you must be able to train support staff to separate what's important from what's not so important."

❖ **Creative problem-solving skills** are valuable to attorneys in this field. "In my regulatory work, clients value the ability to offer imaginative approaches to often constrictive regulatory regulations. It's something you learn to do by doing it! But you can't be trained to have an imagination—you have to bring a good imagination to the practice," says Jack Schroder.

❖ Well-developed **analytical skills** are critical. "You must be able to spot business issues as well as legal issues," says Julie Robertson. "This is especially important because issues affecting health care providers span a wide variety of fields of legal practice." Adds Suzanne Mitchell, "When I review legal issues, I try to envision how the various issues could eventually manifest themselves in litigation. A good health care lawyer must also learn to distinguish the law from the business decisions. This takes time and experience."

❖ Health care lawyers need to **enjoy working in a team with non-lawyers**. Teamwork is an important part of Kim Otte's job. "Every issue

I work on at Allina involves an internal operations team. There's an internal implementation team for each provision that becomes law," Kim explains. Suzanne Mitchell says that teamwork is one of the most important aspects of health care law. "In a health care setting, a lawyer is part of a team—and not always a key part of the team. Students interested in this area need to get used to working with—and *respecting*—people with backgrounds and perspectives that are different than their own. Multi-disciplinary collaboration is a fundamental aspect of hospital and health care lawyering."

❖ Health care lawyers must be **comfortable working in a field that's constantly changing**. "The health care field is not the place for people who like to master a body of law in a relatively short period of time. I have never seen a legal area in which the political, legal, economic, and ethical issues change so rapidly," says Suzanne Mitchell.

What classes and law school experiences do health care lawyers recommend?

❖ Health care lawyers recommend taking a **broad range of law school classes**. "Health law encompasses a variety of traditional practice areas, and therefore a broad range of classes is quite helpful to practicing in this area," says Julie Robertson. Helpful law school classes include torts, labor law, negotiations, legal drafting, administrative law, legislation, and bioethical issues.

❖ "Take at least one **introductory health law class**," advises Suzanne Mitchell. "Advanced health law classes can be helpful as well." Jack Schroder recommends taking a health law seminar in which you can write a paper on a topic "that gives you a chance to sharpen your knowledge about a specific subspecialty of health care law."

❖ **Business-related law school classes** will also help you prepare to practice in this field. The lawyers we talked to recommended corporations and partnerships, contracts, business transactions, personal income tax, and corporate tax.

❖ Suzanne Mitchell recommends taking **undergraduate classes that develop analytical and problem-solving skills,** such as engineering, business, and science classes. "These classes require you to do rigorous problem-solving, which is excellent training for health care practice," says Suzanne. Suzanne majored in English as an undergraduate, and she tells us that English and liberal arts classes that require students to hone their writing skills are also good preparation for the practice of health care law.

❖ **Gain practical experience in the health care field** by working as a summer associate or law clerk at a law firm with a health care practice or as an intern for a federal or state agency that does health care-related work. Says Kim Otte, "Any practical experience in the health care field is helpful, whether it's working for a firm or a state or federal health-related agency, such as a state department of health or a state attorney general's office."

❖ Some law schools have **externship programs** through which you can work for professional associations or government agencies and earn credit. "Working for the American Medical Association or the American Hospital Association may not result in an entry-level job, but it may result in something better—you may earn a 'mentor for life,'" Suzanne Mitchell sagely advises.

❖ **Volunteer for a health care-related organization.** "Students should consider exploring the many volunteer opportunities available with health and human service organizations such as AIDS-related organizations or Planned Parenthood," advises Suzanne Mitchell. "Volunteering in such organizations shows a demonstrated interest in health care and human services, which gives students a head start." Adds Susan Blackwell May, "Giving back to the community makes your life more balanced. Start giving back while a law student and continue your volunteer efforts once you begin practicing law. You'll meet wonderful people, and your efforts will make a difference."

❖ Become part of the health care community by **becoming active in bar associations** while a law student. "I recommend that anyone interested in this field join the health law section of their state and local bar associations as well as national bar associations such as the American Health Lawyers' Association," says Julie Robertson. Most bar associations have student memberships available for a small fee. "Bar association programs allow you to hear speakers talk about the latest health care issues. And bar associations provide a great place to network. An easy way to meet attorneys is volunteering to help put together a health law committee program," suggests Suzanne Mitchell.

❖ **Keep up with the latest developments in the health care field** by reading general interest newspapers, legal newspapers, bar journals, and association newsletters. "Reading health law publications is a way to become familiar with health care issues and a way to learn more about the opportunities available in the field," says Julie Robertson.

HEALTH CARE ATTORNEYS INTERVIEWED FOR THIS SECTION

Susan Blackwell May
American Health Network
Indianapolis, Indiana
UNDERGRADUATE: Eastern Illinois University
LAW SCHOOL: Northern Illinois University College of Law

Suzanne Mitchell
PennState Geisinger Health System
Danville, Pennsylvania
UNDERGRADUATE: The University of North Carolina at Chapel Hill
LAW SCHOOL: University of Michigan Law School

Kim Otte
Allina Health System
Minnetonka, Minnesota
UNDERGRADUATE: Baylor University
LAW SCHOOL: University of Minnesota Law School

Julie Robertson
Honigman Miller Schwartz and Cohn
Detroit, Michigan
UNDERGRADUATE: University of Michigan
LAW SCHOOL: Wayne State University Law School

Jack Schroder, Jr.
Alston & Bird LLP
Atlanta, Georgia
UNDERGRADUATE: Emory University
LAW SCHOOL: University of Georgia School of Law

Immigration Law

What is Immigration Law?

Immigration law involves issues related to immigration (leaving one country to live in another) and naturalization (becoming a citizen). The federal government has exclusive control over immigration issues. The Immigration and Naturalization Service (INS) is part of the Department of Justice, under the direction of the Attorney General. Along with the Department of State, INS administers and enforces our immigration and naturalization laws. The INS has a broad role, including processing visas (permits to be in the U.S. temporarily or as a permanent resident) and applications for naturalization, investigating fraud related to immigration and naturalization, and arresting those who violate immigration laws. Hearings concerning these matters are conducted by immigration judges in an administrative court system. The immigration court is supervised by the Executive Office for Immigration Review, another part of the Department of Justice. The INS also works with U.S. Attorneys to prosecute noncitizens and citizens involved in criminal activity; these cases are heard in federal district court.

Noncitizens (referred to as "aliens" in immigration law) may seek to live, work, visit, or attend school in the United States. Those noncitizens who seek permanent residence in the U.S. may be sponsored by a relative who is already a citizen or by an employer who is in need of the specialized services of the noncitizen worker (*e.g.*, a person's language or technical expertise).

U.S. law also has residency provisions for noncitizens who seek political asylum from their native countries. In addition, Congress has authorized "temporary protected status," which is available to a resident of a country in crisis who is currently in the U.S. when that person would face danger upon return to his or her country due to a natural disaster or an ongoing armed conflict.

Other noncitizens, such as tourists, students, diplomats, and temporary workers, may seek to enter the United States for a limited amount of time. People who seek to come to the U.S. temporarily are issued "non-immigrant" visas. By far the largest number of noncitizens entering the U.S. are tourists, but the non-immigrant category also includes people engaged in teaching, research, and consulting; radio and television journalists; members of the press; foreign government officials; and executives employed by international companies who come to the U.S. on temporary work assignments.

Deportation refers to a noncitizen's removal from the United States. Those who enter the country illegally are subject to deportation. Noncitizens who enter the country legally but remain longer than their visa allows or violate the work provisions of their visa may also be subject to deportation. Those noncitizens granted permanent residency in the U.S. may be subject to deportation under certain circumstances, such as conviction of a serious crime.

Life as an Immigration Lawyer

Where do immigration lawyers work?

Attorneys working in the immigration law area work in several different practice settings. A number work in private law firms doing business immigration work, in which they assist domestic and international corporations in transferring noncitizen employees from foreign offices to the United States and hiring noncitizens as employees for the U.S. corporate offices. Business immigration attorneys generally work in mid-size or large firms. Those attorneys who work in smaller law firms may do business immigration work, or they may assist individuals with personal or family immigration issues. Indigent individuals faced with immigration concerns often turn to public interest lawyers who specialize in immigration. These lawyers work in immigration clinics related to law schools or for public interest organizations. Some immigration lawyers work for the INS or other government agencies in enforcement or administrative roles.

Who are their clients and what types of cases do they work on?

Attorneys who practice business immigration generally have corporate clients. Douglas Halpert, an attorney at Frost & Jacobs LLP in Cincinnati, specializes in business immigration. "The majority of our clients are corporations, ranging from large, 'brand-name' multinational corporations to mid-size and small corporations. We handle cases for companies requiring the services of skilled foreign nationals in cities from coast to coast. Many of our corporate clients are U.S. companies owned by Japanese, German, or Canadian parent corporations. Many of our immigration clients are computer manufacturers or software services companies that need the services of computer engineers and programmer/analysts. Our practice is large, however, and our work brings us into contact with almost every type of human enterprise and every type of professional and skilled employee—including scientists, actors, researchers, professors, athletes, and film directors. We even handled a case for a Chinese national whose occupation was working as a cashmere fiber identification specialist." Douglas adds that his firm also represents individuals. "Most individuals we represent are professionals such as computer scientists, professors, and others who receive job offers from U.S. companies, universities, or other institutions."

Harry Joe, an attorney and shareholder at Jenkens & Gilchrist in Dallas, also practices business immigration. He explains that his clients tend to be major domestic and international corporations that operate in a large number of countries. "Many of our large corporate clients are engaged in the technology and telecommunications industry. Others are engaged in oil and gas exploration and production, marketing, finance, real estate, steel manufacturing, and other industries. These companies may transfer alien employees to the United States," he explains. "Their domestic operations typically employ many alien students graduating from schools in the United States."

Public interest attorneys who specialize in immigration provide services to noncitizens who cannot afford private attorneys. Ben Casper works as an immigration attorney at Centro Legal Inc., a non-profit community law office in St. Paul, Minnesota. Centro Legal's mission is to serve low-income, Spanish-speaking clients from across Minnesota. Most of Ben's clients are from Mexico, Central America, and South America. Centro Legal has three immigration attorneys; other attorneys in the office work with clients on housing, consumer, and family issues. "My work is divided between clients who are documented and those who are undocumented. I represent immigrants in both groups in deportation hearings before the immigration court," he explains. Ben works as his clients' defender, helping them pursue remedies so that they can remain in the United States and avoid deportation. INS attorneys act as prosecutors in such cases.

Alberto Benitez is Associate Professor of Clinical Law and Director of the Immigration Clinic at George Washington University Law School's Immigration Clinic in Washington, D.C. Alberto has a diverse group of clients. "My clients are the full range of people who happen to be aliens. They are from everywhere in the world. They have all types of immigration status—including no immigration status. A significant portion of my clients are indigent, but a large percentage of them are middle class working professionals." Alberto says that clients are referred to the clinic by the INS, the immigration court, and by attorneys who practice in other areas of the law. Clients pay an administrative fee and remain responsible for court costs. George Washington University Law School students who participate in the clinic assist Alberto in handling the clients' cases.

The U.S. government also employs immigration lawyers. Annette Toews is Assistant District Counsel for the Immigration and Naturalization Service in St. Paul, Minnesota. Annette's client is the United States government, which acts on behalf of the citizens of the United States. As an assistant district counsel, Annette advises government representatives involved in the prosecution of immigration cases, including investigators, border patrol agents, and immigration inspectors. She also advises the INS district office management on legal issues, such as personnel issues involving INS employees. For example, if an INS employee lodged an equal employment opportunity complaint, Annette would advise and represent INS management. Another part of Annette's job is working with U.S. Attorneys. "We work with and advise U.S. Attorneys representing the INS in federal court under the immigration laws, as well as under other laws such as the Federal Tort Claims Act," she explains. (*See* the Government Practice chapter for more information on the Federal Tort Claims Act.) These tort claims often stem from automobile accidents. Investigators and border patrol agents, for example, do a significant amount of driving while on duty. When they are involved in accidents which injure a member of the public, the injured party can sue for damages in federal court. Annette explains that the INS also has attorneys in regional offices that provide assistance to field offices and to the administrative centers that process applications for visas and other immigration benefits. "District counsel for the INS deal with more pure immigration issues," she reports, "while regional counsel are more like general practitioners of the federal government."

What daily activities are involved in immigration law practice?

Attorneys practicing business immigration spend the majority of their time counseling clients, often by phone. "A typical day involves a substantial number of phone conversations with clients and (to a lesser degree) government officials, a significant amount of time drafting case documents of clients, and continual informal conversations with the other members of our firm's immigration practice," explains Douglas Halpert. "The pace is very fast," he says. He also represents clients at administrative hearings at the offices of the INS, but he notes that immigration law has become more of a "paper practice," so he makes few appearances at the INS.

Harry Joe, also a business immigration lawyer, reports that he spends most of his day advising clients on issues relating to securing visas and employment authorization for alien employees. "Typically, we work directly with the corporation's human resources or personnel department and with their alien employees." Harry's cases generally begin with efforts to gain temporary employment visas for alien employees, followed by efforts to acquire permanent resident ("green card") status for the alien employee and his or her family. "These are usually administrative proceedings requiring preparation and filing of petitions with required supporting documentation to several U.S. administrative agencies, including the INS and the Department of Labor," Harry says. Harry also counsels clients regarding employment sanction cases. "These cases involve the unauthorized employment of alien workers and civil fine proceedings against employers for failure to comply with employment verification requirements," he says.

Public interest attorneys specializing in immigration law also spend a significant amount of their time counseling clients. Alberto Benitez adds that he also spends time writing petitions, applications, and motions and supervising a team of law students engaged in these activities on behalf of the immigration clinic.

Ben Casper says that he spends at least 30% of his time doing client intake interviews and assessments. "I talk to hundreds of people a month who are seeking our services," explains Ben. "We are one of just two offices in the Twin Cities that handle calls from people who are detained by the INS. The office has 'intake days' once a week where I spend the day talking to people who have been arrested by the INS and are waiting for a hearing date with the immigration court." Ben assesses the prospective clients' cases to determine whether Centro Legal can take on their case. "We only open cases for about 10% of those people we interview. The clients must be low-income and Spanish-speaking. They must also appear to have a legal remedy for their situation. For example, a client might not have appropriate paperwork to stay in the United States but might be married to a U.S. citizen. In this case the client has a remedy. Because they're married to a citizen, they can immigrate right away. Or you may have a client who can seek asylum in the United States because he or she fears political persecution in his or her native country. Another example of a remedy is hardship-based remedy. In this case a client who has been here illegally for many years can seek to avoid deportation because so much of their life and family is in the U.S. and deportation would cause exceptional hardship for the family." Ben reports that he spends about 65% of his time developing opened cases and working on applications for remedies. He spends one to two days a week at immigration court, where he attends hearings on the merits of his cases. About 5% of his time is spent in public education and outreach. He speaks at community centers and churches, telling people about Centro Legal and its work.

Annette Toews counsels and advises law enforcement officers, senior-level and mid-level supervisors, and administrators of the INS. Her job as an adviser requires her to be familiar with a vast array of issues—from understanding constitutional law issues to knowing how to handle (collect, process, and track) employer sanction fines. She advises officials on such things as investigations, arrests, and detentions; management issues; and personnel issues. Another part of Annette's job involves training and development—she has trained INS attorneys, law enforcement officers, and administrative personnel. She has developed training materials and conducted training sessions on myriad issues, from search and seizure to new immigration laws to case prosecution and strategy.

What do immigration lawyers find rewarding about their practice?

The immigration attorneys we talked to said they found great satisfaction in making a difference in people's lives. Says Alberto Benitez, "Being able to help aliens get what they want, whether it's immigration status or the prevention of deportation—I personally find that very satisfying." Explains Harry Joe, "One's immigration status is so personal. Finding a way to enable an alien to reside legally in the United States on a permanent basis is very rewarding. Aliens who secure immigration to the United States through our efforts show great appreciation for the work we have performed on their behalf." Adds Ben Casper, "The personal stakes for our clients are always quite high. When you succeed the result has profound consequences in the individual's life—someone may be able to remain in the U.S. with their family, and continue the life that they've known for years. Winning means a lot to our clients."

Douglas Halpert mentions the satisfaction he receives from working with the remarkable group of people seeking to become immigrants. "Yearly, I am able to assist individuals from dozens of countries around the world. All of them have interesting backgrounds. I believe that bringing professional, bright, and enthusiastic individuals here from abroad enriches our culture and stimulates our economy." He adds that the immigrants he meets sharpen his appreciation for life in the United States. "The keen interest in securing U.S. status that I see and hear on a daily basis makes me realize how lucky we are to be U.S. citizens. We possess the freedom and opportunities that many cannot take for granted." Ben Casper, too, enjoys the relationships he develops with his clients. "My job involves getting involved in people's lives on a personal level. You have to show the judge that they deserve to stay in the United States. You have to make the judge understand the client's life, show the judge the client's connections to the community, and help the judge see the personal aspects of the client's life," he says.

Annette Toews finds working on behalf of U.S. citizens immensely rewarding. "My work is very public service-oriented. To be happy as a government attorney, no matter what entity you work for, you need to be very public service-oriented. That's why we're there—we're doing the public's work." Part of her work involves removing aliens who have engaged in criminal acts. "Our INS resources are limited. One of our priorities is removing criminals. We deal with criminals who have harmed U.S. citizens, who have ruined lives. I have the chance to do my part to protect U.S. citizens."

Annette also enjoys the intellectual challenge of her work. "Because I advise officials on such a broad range of issues, my brain is on high gear. It's quite intense and never boring. I especially enjoy the training aspects of my job. Training INS officials is very intellectually challenging." Ben Casper also mentions the intellectual rewards of his work. "It's fast-paced," he says, "and in a public interest organization, you're the underdog. Our resources are much more limited than those of the INS. Being the underdog is a challenge, but one I greatly enjoy," he says.

His position as a clinical professor allows Alberto Benitez to supervise law students earning credit for working in the immigration clinic. He comments, "I really enjoy the mentoring aspect of my work. I love working with the law students who are enrolled in the clinical program. It's rewarding to teach them fundamental lawyering skills and then watch them apply those skills as they talk to clients and work on cases. It's exciting to watch their self-confidence blossom."

The Skills and Training Important to Immigration Law

How do people enter the field of immigration law?

"My parents are Mexican immigrants," says Alberto Benitez. "I went to law school so I could do immigration work. It's all I ever wanted to do." Many immigration lawyers are, like Alberto, influenced by personal experiences with immigration. Alberto says that most of the law students he works with who plan immigration law careers are either immigrants themselves or have immigrant families. "The bulk of the students in our immigration clinic and in the immigration class I teach have an immediate connection with the experience of immigration—whether their parents' or grandparents' experience or their own experience."

Harry Joe was similarly influenced. "My parents were aliens and successfully obtained permanent resident status in this country. I recall the difficulties they went through. Many of their friends encountered the same problems. I actively chose to specialize in the field of immigration law. I came to realize the greatness of this country through the eyes, thoughts, and hearts of these aliens."

Those lawyers who work on the public interest side of immigration law are often interested in human rights and international issues. "People who are on the legal services side of it tend to have had connections with other countries and an interest in international issues," says Ben Casper. Before he began law school, Ben spent time traveling in Australia and Latin America. His travels heightened his interest in international issues. In law school he knew he wanted to do public interest work and became involved in his law school's clinical programs. His law school, University of Minnesota, had a program that assisted Minnesota prisoners. He ended up working on the immigration and deportation cases. He then became involved in the law school's Asylum Law Project in south Texas, in which students assisted people arrested for coming into the U.S. from Mexico. Between his second and third years of law school he worked with migrant farm workers in Minnesota. He also became involved in the law school's immigration law clinic, where he worked on cases involving political asylum. The extensive range of practical experience Ben acquired in law school helped him land a public interest job.

The guidance of mentors leads others to the practice of immigration law. While a third year student at Hamline University School of Law, Annette Toews did an internship at the INS Regional Counsel's office. She was impressed by the attorney she worked for and respected him so much that she remembers thinking he would make a great boss after she graduated from law school. In the meantime, she applied for the Department of Justice Honors Law Graduate Program, a highly competitive program through which the Department of Justice hires entry-level attorneys for its divisions. She was hired as an Honors Law graduate to work for the INS Regional Counsel's office. And her supervising attorney? He was the same wonderful mentor who had supervised her as a law student. "Being a known quantity definitely helped me get the job," says Annette. "I learned so much from him," she recalls. "I really enjoyed working with him. He was calm and unflappable, good-natured, and interested in my progress. Even when we disagreed with one another, he listened to and respected my opinions. He was a wonderful lawyer, a great mentor, and a fantastic boss."

Douglas Halpert recalls the role serendipity played in his journey from estate planning lawyer to immigration lawyer. "Upon graduation I went to work for a medium-size corporate law firm in Buffalo, New York, just minutes from the Canadian border. I started out in the estate planning and probate area. However, after less than six months, the associate handling the immigration work for the firm left and the partner who supervised the immigration practice took a leave of absence for several years. The managing partner of the firm visited my office and asked me whether he was correct in recollecting that I took a course in immigration law during my third year in law school. When I said yes, he motioned to a file clerk who brought in about 40 files and knighted me as the firm's new immigration attorney." He adds, "The phone started ringing later that day with calls from the immigration clients. Given that I did not enjoy the estate planning field, I seized upon the opportunity to learn a new area of law."

What skills are most important to immigration lawyers?

❖ Immigration attorneys must be adept at **reading and understanding statutes and legislation.** Harry Joe says simply, "Thorough knowledge of the provisions of the Immigration and Nationality Act and of the applicable regulations is paramount." "This is a statute-based area of law," says Alberto Benitez. "Law schools train students to read and understand cases. But this is not case law. I'm 12 years out of law school, and I still have a dog-eared copy of the regulations and statutes on my desk. I am still fighting my way through Section 8 of the U.S. Code [the Immigration and Nationality Act]." Annette Toews emphasizes the importance of developing the skills of reading and understanding statutory law. "Immigration law can be mind-boggling because it's so complicated—like tax law, it's very technical. A good rule to keep in mind is 'always read the regulations, always read the statute.' The law changes rapidly. So many things intertwine, it's like a big jigsaw puzzle. You have to find all the pieces to put the puzzle together—all the provisions and regulations that are relevant to the case at hand."

❖ **Attention to detail** is critical in this highly technical field of law. "Lack of attention to detail can undermine your case," says Douglas Halpert. "Even a small mistake can create havoc in an immigration case." Adds Harry Joe, "It's important to be thoroughly knowledgeable of the procedures in connection with administrative filings and in immigration court and administrative agency practice." A lawyer's mistake can have devastating consequences for an immigration client.

❖ Immigration lawyers must **remain calm and composed under pressure**. Douglas Halpert explains, "When your client has been detained by INS at an airport or land port of entry or you face a similar pressure-packed situation, where your client is in serious jeopardy, you must act quickly and decisively. You must be a cool clinician who collects the facts, analyzes them, develops the best strategy for the resolution of the problem, and executes the plan." Public interest immigration lawyers have the additional challenge of handling a high volume of clients and cases. "Working in a public interest organization means that you're in a fast-paced, rapidly changing environment. The number of clients you see is high; the law changes quickly. It's very hectic. You have to cope well with the high volume of matters you're handling," explains Ben Casper.

❖ **Foreign language skills** can be an asset to immigration lawyers. Alberto Benitez says that mastering most any language is helpful. He recommends that students consider Spanish, French, German, Russian, Tagalog (the native language of the Philippines), the languages of India and Pakistan, and African languages and dialects. "Studying a language helps you understand culture," says Alberto. "Language opens up sensitivities and helps you develop relationships with your clients. It builds respect, rapport, and repeat business." Ben Casper also recommends studying a foreign language and believes that it's never too late to begin foreign language studies—even if you're already in law school. He suggests that students consider French, Chinese, or Spanish. Ben explains that he still works on the Spanish skills he uses with his clients and reminds students that it takes a great deal of practice to become fluent. Traveling abroad or enrolling in a study abroad program can help.

❖ Lawyers practicing in this field must be **sensitive to the complex emotional issues** involved in immigration cases. Annette Toews puts it eloquently: "You must remember that you're dealing with people and their lives, their loved ones, their families. Their families may be separated or uprooted and facing dramatic change. In immigration law you're not dealing with money or chattels [property], you're dealing with people." She adds that when working on the government side of immigration law, an attorney "needs a certain amount of fortitude" because "but for one fact difference, someone may have qualified for relief, yet you must enforce the laws."

❖ The **ability to build strong relationships** is important to immigration attorneys who work closely with clients, court administrators, and government attorneys. "You have to navigate the inefficiencies of the bureaucracies," says Ben Casper. "You have to be good at gathering information. Strong relationships help you make your way through the Byzantine bureaucracies of the government."

❖ **Strong writing skills** are important to the immigration lawyer. Douglas Halpert says emphatically, "First, and foremost, an immigration attorney must be able to write persuasively." Legal writing classes and seminars in which you write research papers can be helpful in developing strong writing skills.

What classes and law school experiences do immigration lawyers recommend?

❖ **Take an immigration law course in law school.** "The course in immigration law that I took at Fordham Law School clearly proved to be the impetus behind my being selected to do this type of work," says Douglas Halpert. Other classes attorneys recommended included administrative law, legislation, and constitutional law. "We deal with so many areas of law at the INS," says Annette Toews. "More important than any particular class is being a well-rounded student of the law."

❖ **Working in a law school's immigration law clinic** gives students an opportunity to gain practical experience in the field while in law school. Because clinical experience gives you the chance to work with actual clients on pending cases, Alberto Benitez believes it's the very best way to prepare for a career in immigration law. Ben Casper gained experience through the University of Minnesota's immigration clinic as well as its Legal Assistance to Minnesota Prisoners Program. "Clinic is great because you get academic credit for participating. Everyone I know who does the type of work I do participated in clinics in law school."

❖ If you're planning a public interest career, **volunteer for a public interest organization.** "Volunteer work shows that you have the dedication you need to work for a non-profit organization. Volunteering gets you direct, hands-on experience, and that's key to the job search," says Ben Casper. "Immigration is so complicated that unless you know quite a bit about it, a non-profit will not be interested in taking you on. The organizations don't have a lot of resources and can't pay for training. You need to come to these organizations well prepared. It's ideal if you can volunteer for an organization you would ultimately like to work for."

❖ **Get involved with community organizations that do work related to immigration.** Explains Alberto Benitez, "Community organizations often sponsor naturalization drives in which people who are long-term residents of the U.S. are encouraged to become citizens. Volunteers help these residents fill out forms and instruct them regarding the process of seeking citizenship." Alberto notes that these types of programs are often sponsored by local organizations such as the Korean Association of Maryland and the Spanish Catholic Center in Washington, D.C.

❖ **Work for a government agency or a law firm while in law school.** Annette Toews gained invaluable experience as an intern at the INS Regional Counsel's office during her third year of law school. Douglas Halpert recommends that students interested in working in a firm's immigration department clerk at a firm while in law school. "If I had known that immigration law was going to be my calling, I would have made every effort to intern with a firm that practiced immigration law. Experience is the key," he says.

❖ **Become part of the network of immigration lawyers.** Says Ben Casper, "The legal community in this field involves a small and comfortable and well-acquainted group of lawyers. People get to know each other fairly well." Harry Joe agrees that networking is critical. "Become familiar with immigration law practitioners who are well-established," he advises. A good way to meet these lawyers is through involvement in bar association activities. Alberto Benitez notes that bar associations often have immigration law committees. Students can join bar associations for a small fee, and meetings are usually free. "It's a terrific way to meet people," says Alberto. "The field of immigration law as a specialized area is still new. There's not an established, formal way of pursuing a job." Alberto shared the story of a recent graduate who found a job lead—and ultimately a job—through a phone call to a classmate who had graduated the year before. The classmate's firm just happened to be looking for an associate. "That's the way these immigration jobs come up," he says. "That's the way it happens."

❖ Douglas Halpert recommends **conducting informational interviews** with attorneys who are practicing in the immigration field. "I recommend that anyone who has a serious interest in becoming an immigration attorney call a practicing immigration attorney who is willing to field questions about what the practice area is like and what the demands are," he says. Douglas also recommends that graduating students apply to become members of the American Immigration Lawyers Association (AILA), which is based in Washington, D.C.

❖ **Focus on developing good lawyering skills.** Annette Toews emphasizes the importance of the basics. No matter how much clinical experience you have or how many immigration law classes you take, she believes it's the fundamental lawyering skills that are important to success in the field of immigration. "Above all you need to know how to read regulations and statutes and have good analytical skills and good judgment," she says.

IMMIGRATION ATTORNEYS INTERVIEWED FOR THIS SECTION

Alberto Benitez
George Washington University Law School Immigration Clinic
Washington, D.C.
UNDERGRADUATE: State University of New York at Buffalo
LAW SCHOOL: University at Buffalo Law School

Ben Casper
Centro Legal Inc.
St. Paul, Minnesota
UNDERGRADUATE: Carleton College
LAW SCHOOL: University of Minnesota Law School

Douglas Halpert
Frost & Jacobs LLP
Cincinnati, Ohio
UNDERGRADUATE: University of Chicago
LAW SCHOOL: Fordham University School of Law

Harry Joe
Jenkens & Gilchrist, P.C.
Dallas, Texas
UNDERGRADUATE: University of North Texas
LAW SCHOOL: Washington University School of Law

Annette Toews
U.S. Immigration and Naturalization Service
St. Paul, Minnesota
UNDERGRADUATE: Augustana College
LAW SCHOOL: Hamline University School of Law

Insurance Law

What is Insurance Law?

Insurance policies are contracts. They are purchased in an effort to provide protection from monetary assessments that result from large medical bills and from the legal consequences of accidents, mistakes, misjudgments, and disasters. Insurance policies provide a pooling of assets from which medical claims or judgments against one or more policy holders can be paid. For example, doctors, accountants, and attorneys obtain insurance to protect them from monetary judgments relating to professional service. Automobile owners purchase insurance to cover issues ranging from monetary judgments from accidents caused by driver error to vehicle damage caused by a severe hail storm. Businesses also obtain insurance to protect them in the case of incorrectly designed or manufactured products, the wrongdoing of employees, or unsafe conditions on the premises, such as a chemical spill in a factory or a slippery floor in the produce department of a grocery store.

Insurance lawyers become involved in the various issues relating to these contracts. Some insurance lawyers work as the defense counsel on behalf of a doctor accused of malpractice or an automobile owner accused of driving at a speed deemed unsafe for the weather conditions. Other insurance lawyers focus on questions of insurance coverage—for example, whether an insurance policy purchased many years ago covers acts or problems, such as environmental damage, uncovered many years later. Insurance lawyers also work in the health care industry on issues involving claims and payments, regulatory issues, and contracts with physicians and hospitals for managed care. Examples of the various types of insurance law practice follow.

Coverage Issues: Insurance is based on a contract between the policy holder and the insurer. Sometimes a dispute arises between the insurer and the policy holder over whether the contract provides insurance coverage for a particular incident. In this case attorneys specializing in coverage issues work to resolve the issue, which may end in litigation between the policy holder and the insurance company. In recent years, for example, disputes have arisen over whether environmental law issues involve liability for asbestos, lead paint, or compliance with environmental regulations. (*See* the Environmental Law chapter of this book for further description of these types of issues.) The stakes can be high in these cases, leading to complex litigation in which millions of dollars are at stake.

Insurance Defense: When an insurance policy holder is sued by a third party and the insurance company determines that the contract provides coverage, the insurance company will either use in-house attorneys or hire outside attorneys to handle the defense of the insured. This is often referred to as insurance defense work (interviews with insurance defense lawyers are featured in the Tort Law chapter of this book).

In-House Counsel: Insurance companies employ a large number of attorneys. The attorneys have a wide range of duties, from supervising claims and litigation to advising the company regarding legislative and regulatory matters affecting the industry to advising the insurers on the use of computer technology to manage records and claims. Lawyers might work as in-house counsel for health care insurance companies, setting up contracts with physician groups and hospitals. Lawyers also work for the insurance industry investigating cases of insurance fraud and with government consumer protection agencies in prosecuting such suits.

Insurance Counseling: Corporations seek advice from attorneys when determining how much insurance to purchase for a business and its employees, including liability, health, and property insurance.

Life as an Insurance Lawyer

Where do insurance lawyers work?

Attorneys who work as insurance defense lawyers may work for insurance companies or for private firms of all sizes, hired to handle litigation of the cases for the insured. Attorneys specializing in coverage work generally work for law firms, often in large law firms with departments devoted to insurance issues. Large firm attorneys specializing in insurance matters may also provide insurance counseling for corporations in the process of determining their insurance needs.

Insurance companies employ a number of in-house attorneys, whether to manage and supervise litigation or to work as in-house counsel. Some insurance companies specialize in property and auto insurance, others specialize in commercial insurance, and still others specialize in health care. A limited number of insurance lawyers also work for state agencies that regulate insurance issues.

For further information about attorneys working in the insurance field or working for insurance companies, read these profiles:

Corporate Law — John Dirks (State Farm Mutual Automobile Insurance Company)

Health Care Law — Susan Blackwell May (American Health Network); Kim Otte (Allina Health Systems); Suzanne Mitchell (PennState Geisinger Health System)

Tort Law — Rick Foster (Donohue Brown Mathewson & Smyth); Thomas Browne (Hinshaw & Culbertson); Kevin Burke (Hinshaw & Culbertson); Patrick McClarney (Shook, Hardy & Bacon L.L.P.); Margaret Costello (Dykema Gossett PLLC)

Who are their clients and what types of cases do they work on?

M. Lauretta (Lauree) Barreca is the Assistant Vice-President and Regional Director of Claims for American Continental Insurance Company, an MMI Company, with offices in Deerfield, Illinois. "Our clients are our insureds throughout the country. They're all health care-based insureds, including hospitals, physicians, physician groups, clinics, health care systems, and managed care organizations. We insure over 160,000 physicians who are in physician networks or physician health care groups."

Lauree oversees medical negligence cases in which the defendants are doctors and other health care professionals. Many of the cases, says Lauree, stem from care that's given in emergency rooms. "For example, a patient might go to the hospital emergency room for chest pain, be diagnosed as having gastroenteritis, and be discharged. Upon returning home the patient dies of a heart attack. The plaintiff sues, alleging that the emergency room physician failed to properly diagnose and treat the patient's illness. Unfortunately, many such cases are the result of people using the emergency room as a primary care facility, when the people should see a physician familiar with their medical history on a regular basis." The tort cases Lauree oversees also include allegations that physicians failed to properly diagnose cancer, caused birth trauma, performed surgical procedures improperly, or prescribed the wrong medication or the wrong dose of medication.

In addition Lauree's office handles other cases involving the hospital and physician networks. These include the liability of hospital directors and officers, employee liability issues, antitrust issues, and billing issues such as billing errors and omissions. "Business risks are increasing," she says. "Employment law issues are coming to the forefront. Morale issues are important in health services, as they can impact practitioners' ability to provide good care, which can result in a medical negligence case."

Donna Rosemeyer is the Legal Director of Allstate Insurance Company in Northbrook, Illinois. "My clients are all the people who are insured with Allstate who get sued as the result of an accident and whose lawsuit is referred to our staff counsel attorneys for defense." Donna explains that Allstate, which handles both auto and property insurance, has 90 staff counsel offices with over 700 lawyers and 700 support people. Donna supervises the defense attorneys employed in the eastern half of the country. Some cases are referred out to insurance defense attorneys at law firms, but more than half of the cases are handled by Allstate's own in-house staff. "We are working on expanding our staff counsel by another 200 lawyers," Donna says. "We've been taking an increased number of cases to trial and jury verdicts have come down in terms of dollars. We win about 60% of the cases that go to trial; in many cases we are better off trying cases than settling."

The vast number of cases handled by staff counsel means that new Allstate attorneys get a great deal of tort litigation experience early in their tenure. "Our attorneys are litigators. They are trying cases within six months of joining the company. Though we refer some cases out to insurance defense attorneys at law firms, staff counsel is the counsel of choice. More and more major insurance carriers are going to handling cases in-house, as it is more cost effective to do so. It's almost always cheaper for staff counsel to handle a case than retaining outside counsel. We handle half of the litigation for about one-third to one-fourth of what retained counsel charges to handle the other half. This results in keeping insurance rates as low as possible for our insureds."

Carol Proctor is an insurance lawyer at the law firm of Hinshaw & Culbertson, a large law firm in Chicago. "I represent insurance companies throughout the country on various legal issues," she says. "The insurance companies are interested in contract interpretation, contract development, and effective handling of insureds' claims." Much of Carol's work focuses on coverage issues. "A typical case involves determining whether an insurance policy covers a claim presented to an insurer by an insured. It involves issues surrounding the duty to defend and the duty to indemnify. These are issues presented with respect to excess insurance, reinsurance, and bad faith."

Ann Triebsch is an in-house counsel in the Louisville, Kentucky offices of Anthem Blue Cross & Blue Shield, a health insurance company. "My primary duties involve contracting with hospitals and physicians and other providers to be in our managed care networks. I help negotiate and write the contracts and deal with issues that result from the contractual relationships. My clients are the Blue Cross & Blue Shield business people who handle the relationships with the providers. I am also the legal representative on the committee which credentials physicians to join our network, and I work closely with the medical director of Blue Cross & Blue Shield on this issue." Ann says that she's one of five lawyers in the Louisville legal department. One is a litigator; one writes certificates (which are the booklets the insurance company develops describing benefits) and contracts with employers; another handles appeals from physicians and group members and works with quality processes; and one is a lead attorney who oversees the legal department and works with insurance brokers and agents.

Ann explains that Anthem Blue Cross & Blue Shield has contracts with hundreds of hospitals and thousands of physicians. "You begin with standard contracts, but some things are negotiable and some things aren't. When we're working with hospitals, I may meet with the hospital to see what we can work out on the contract. And, of course, numerous issues come up after the contract has been signed. In health care, things are always changing. We try to work closely with physicians and hospitals to improve the quality of health care. Improving quality takes an enormous amount of cooperation on all sides. If you consider a standard surgical procedure, such as the removal of a gallbladder, there are perhaps eight different ways to do the surgery. Doctors are constantly doing research to determine the best ways to perform the procedure, but medicine is both a science and an art. How doctors practice can be unique to a particular geographic area because of the way the physicians were trained. Anthem would like to see physicians and hospitals create national standards of treatment. We try to do quality improvement on a local scale and work with physicians toward this end. But in Kentucky there are two major cities, some mid-size cities, and many rural areas in which medical care is at a premium. Convincing the physicians and the hospitals in the rural areas to change their procedures can be difficult, and because they are the only medical providers in a particular area, it's politically difficult. My job thus requires lots of negotiating and lots of strategizing."

A large part of Ann's job involves regulatory issues. "Tense relationships are inherent in the health care industry," Ann says, "because there is so much change due to technology and because you're talking about an industry that's not just about dollars but also about human lives. Emotions run high." Ann explains that Anthem developed a coronary care network that sent non-emergency coronary care patients to particular hospitals that had high rates of success in their surgeries. When this plan was implemented in the state of Ohio, about 3% fewer cardiac patients died. "In spite of all those lives saved in Ohio, we've had a hard time convincing the Kentucky Department of Insurance and some rural Kentucky hospitals that this program should be implemented. Yet the program saves lives and gets people out of the hospital faster, so it's frustrating to run into these roadblocks."

Ann says that she works with several other Anthem Blue Cross & Blue Shield executives on these regulatory issues. "I work with our medical director, our quality assurance person, our network manager, and our government relations liaison. The five of us are the core team who worked with the Kentucky Department of Insurance on the Coronary Services Network. This has involved testifying before the Banking and Insurance Subcommittee of the Kentucky legislature. We deal with the Kentucky Department of Insurance every day on a variety of issues." (*See* the Legislative Practice chapter for more information on these types of activities.)

What daily activities are involved in insurance law practice?

Donna Rosemeyer supervises hundreds of Allstate staff counsel in the eastern United States. "A staff counsel lawyer has an active tort litigation practice. He or she is in court nearly every day, arguing motions or representing the insured in routine court appearances. A staff counsel also takes or defends depositions nearly every day. Allstate staff counsel try five or six cases a year, and nearly all of them are jury trials. Their case load is about 80% automobile negligence cases and 20% premises liability cases," she says. (*See* the Tort Law chapter of this book for descriptions of these types of cases.)

"As a legal director for Allstate, I travel one to two days a week to visit our offices all across the eastern half of the country; I meet with the staff counsel and their local supervisors. I usually fly to the out of state offices and back to Chicago in the same day," says Donna. When Donna is in her office, she handles a wide range of matters for the legal department of the insurance company. "I handle human resources issues. For example, if an attorney needs to be accommodated under the ADA [Americans with Disabilities Act], I determine what reasonable accommodations we need to provide to comply with the Act. I also handle employee terminations countrywide, whether they involve attorneys or support personnel. I handle some very interesting legal issues, as well." Donna is also responsible for making sure that the legal department is handling its work in a way consistent with that of the entire insurance company.

As an assistant vice president and regional director of claims for American Continental Insurance Company (ACIC), much of Lauree Barreca's work is related to pending litigation. "I evaluate whether the doctor, hospital, clinic, or health care group is covered for the event that has occurred. An insurance policy is a contract, and it's my job to review the contract and tell the client whether or not there's coverage under the terms of the policy." Lauree works closely with her clients. "I tell the hospitals and other clients how to protect their interests. When they are defendants in a lawsuit, I meet with them and help them select defense counsel. We have a good panel of qualified law firm attorneys available to hire to represent our insureds."

Like many of the attorneys hired by her company, Lauree worked as an insurance defense attorney before joining ACIC. She also has a medical background and worked for nine years as a nurse before returning to law school. Her litigation experience and medical knowledge are key to her role as regional director of claims, since, she notes, "I'm selling my experience and knowledge." Lauree handles strategic plans on each case. "I discuss the legal strategy with the clients and explain the benefits of a particular strategy. I also set up the appropriate financial reserves for the case. This requires careful analysis. I have to know the degree of liability of our defendant and what the value of the entire case is likely to be." If the cases do not settle through negotiation, Lauree attends the trials. "I monitor the cases every step of the way," she says. "I began my job here as a consultant. Our Midwest region has 13 professional staff consultants who manage the cases pending against our insureds. These consultants are really strategic managers in managing the cases. They have a higher level of experience than insurance adjusters. Most of the attorneys who work for us have a medical background," she says.

Carol Proctor, of Hinshaw & Culbertson, handles litigation matters and spends a great deal of time both counseling and developing strategies for her clients. "A typical day often involves a court appearance, whether on a 'routine' matter or a substantive matter. Part of my day is spent on the telephone with clients addressing their questions. The bulk of the day, however, is spent analyzing client problems and responding to problems through what are called 'opinion letters,' in which I give legal advice. The day often involves various types of client development activities including talking with current and prospective clients."

As an in-house counsel at Anthem Blue Cross & Blue Shield, Ann Triebsch says she spends time in meetings, on the phone, and communicating with the employees of Anthem who are her clients. "I generally have a couple of meetings every day," Ann reports. "Some days may have as many as eight meetings and others may have none. I'm often meeting with people inside or outside the legal department to make sure that we're making progress on a particular issue. I also have a lot of one-on-one meetings with people. For example, my clients in the network development area may stop by to talk to me about a particular legal issue." Ann also spends time handling the regulatory issues she described earlier. Writing is also an important part of Ann's job. She drafts contracts, writes letters, and edits letters that other Anthem employees have written to make sure that they're legally accurate.

Ann says that when you're an in-house counsel, you inevitably get lots of what she calls "general lawyer" calls—calls for general legal advice. "When someone in the company needs legal advice, they know they can just pick up the phone and call. For example, a clerical supervisor might have a question about an employee's handling of a budget matter. Or a medical director who is on the board of a local charity may want to know if he can send out a letter soliciting charitable funds for the charity but sign the letter with his title as medical director. Often these calls are five minute calls, but being available for these calls and responding to these employees' needs is an important part of being in-house counsel." (*See* the Corporate Law chapter for more information on life as an in-house counsel.)

What do insurance lawyers find rewarding about their practice?

Like many lawyers, Carol Proctor reports that working closely with her clients is the most enjoyable part of her job. Carol's clients are generally insurance companies. "Helping a client resolve a problem or address an area of concern is the most rewarding part of my practice," she says simply and emphatically.

"I love the people part of my job," says Donna Rosemeyer. "I love work-ing with the people employed by Allstate, and it's exciting to travel to our offices to meet them. Whether you're a staff counsel or you have my job as a legal director, 90% of the job is talking with people either on the phone or in person. It's the kind of work where you have to like working with people better than you like handling paper. It's very people-oriented, fascinating, and fun! The people working here are just good people who are a delight to be around—they're wonderful people to work with."

Donna also enjoys the fact that her job as in-house counsel allows her time to spend with her family. "I have three little girls. I love the fact that in my line of work I can easily have a family *and* have a challenging job. Allstate takes the work/family balance issue very seriously, and I can honestly say I don't feel any stress at all between work and family life. As far as the company is concerned, there's absolutely no downside to my having a family life."

Donna also enjoys the opportunity she's had to move ahead in the com-pany. "Working for Allstate I've had a chance to do three very different legal jobs—and that's just to this point in my career. I haven't begun to exhaust the opportunities, and I know that they'll be open to me when I'm ready. Large insurance companies offer a wide range of different opportunities for lawyers. For example, the company has a mergers and acquisitions depart-ment, a research center, and a computer systems area." Donna is equally enthusiastic about insurance law as a practice specialty. "Insurance law is truly interesting; every day brings new challenges. In my current job, I find the human resources issues I face to be incredibly interesting."

Donna says that she's always loved trying cases and, though she isn't in the courtroom in her current job, she has the joy of passing her knowledge to the staff counsel she supervises. "Successfully trying cases is very rewarding," she says. "It's what so many people go to law school to do. Working as a staff counsel allows you to use your skills and talents from the beginning of your legal career." Donna admits that she was nervous when she handled her first few cases. "But after I successfully tried several cases, I fell in love with the challenge."

Lauree Barreca says that she's privileged to work with the medical professionals. "The doctors and nurses we represent are very dedicated. When a doctor or nurse is sued, they are more upset, concerned, and devastated than you can imagine, because they have dedicated their career to giving the best care they can to people. I admire their commitment to the medical profession. It's really inspiring to see that in an era of managed care, in which they are paid less to do more, their performance of their job remains absolutely professional. In short, I really admire and respect my clients," says Lauree.

Lauree especially enjoys the company she works for. "I've been at ACIC for 11 years. The company touts itself as a company where you can learn and grow, and I've had every opportunity to do that. I work with a highly educated and motivated staff and that makes my job a real pleasure. My job gives me a chance to use all my skills sets—my legal skills, my people skills, and my medical expertise."

Ann Triebsch says that there are many rewards to being an in-house counsel. "I've worked at Anthem Blue Cross & Blue Shield for three years. When you're an in-house counsel, you know your client well because your client is the company that you work for. You know who the players are; what the company's history is; what the hot issues are; when, how, and where to go to find out what you need to know; and you even know the things that your clients are forgetting to tell you. When you're advising people in-house, I think you have the best chance of knowing what all the facts are—good and bad—and that allows you to represent your client in the very best way and to offer your client the very best legal advice."

Ann adds that she really likes the team atmosphere of her corporation. "I really know the people here, and I really like being part of the team. When we start a project that the company knows could have significant legal issues, I am on the team from day one. This minimizes the legal risks. It also helps me truly be part of the team. I'm not necessarily viewed as a lawyer—I'm just another person on the team, who happens to have legal expertise. I'm a people person—I'm definitely not someone who could be happy doing legal research all day—and my in-house position gives me a chance to work with terrific people in a team setting."

Ann also likes the fact that she has the opportunity to play a role in both the insurance and the health care industries. "I just happen to be on the insurance side of the health care industry. I like the fact that the issues we deal with are issues that truly affect people's lives. In every case our company thinks about what our obligation is to our member, the insured. In cases in which there's a difference of opinion about whether benefits apply, I may be able to say, 'Our obligation to our member is greater than that. This is how this should be handled.' I can make sure that our member gets everything that's due to them under their contract and also gets the benefit of the doubt, and if we're in the gray area, I generally recommend that we come down on the side of the member." Ann adds that the general public sometimes has a negative impression of managed care. "People think of managed care as denying care. But that's not true. An insurance policy is a contract. We want to give you what you're entitled to, and we try to conduct our business in the most ethical manner possible. I like the fact that I can get involved in decisions in such a way that the result for the member may be better than might have otherwise occurred."

Ann adds that being part of the health care insurance industry is exciting. "It's a vibrant industry," she says. "There's constant change. It can be rather overwhelming—there's so much reading to do and so much information to review. Socially, people are interested in the topic of managed care, and I enjoy trying to enlighten people and help them learn about managed care so that they will hopefully adjust their opinions about what managed care is all about."

The Training and Skills Important to Insurance Law

How do people enter the field of insurance law?

Attorneys who work as insurance defense lawyers at firms or as staff counsel in insurance companies generally begin practicing in the field upon graduation from law school. Often they are attracted to insurance defense work because they know they will get significant trial experience within their first year of practice. Many law firms that do insurance defense work hire summer associates to work for their firms between the second and third year of law school. They hire many of the new attorneys through their summer associate programs.

Insurance companies who have in-house defense counsel often have internship programs or hire law clerks during the summer or during the school year. "At Allstate many of our new staff counsel are hired through their work as interns or law clerks," says Donna Rosemeyer. "Positions are generally advertised through postings in career services offices or through ads in legal newspapers. Most of our law students tend to work year-round as law clerks." Donna says that about half of the attorneys her company hires are recent graduates and half are more experienced attorneys. Many of the experienced attorneys have worked as prosecutors and already have significant courtroom experience.

Donna began working for Allstate while in college. She started as a part-time employee, taking witness statements in a claims office. When she started law school, she continued to work in the same capacity. After graduation from law school, she transferred to Allstate's legal office in downtown Chicago, where she tried numerous cases as a staff counsel. After four years Donna was promoted to the home office in Northbrook, Illinois, where she worked as a supervising claims attorney. In that position, she monitored and supervised complex civil litigation nationwide. After six years in that position, she was promoted to her current position of legal director.

Lauree Barreca, who has a bachelor's degree in nursing, worked as a nurse for nine years before returning to law school. She hoped to find a legal position that would use her medical background and her legal skills. She worked as a summer associate at a large insurance defense firm in Chicago and was subsequently hired as an associate. Lauree worked in private practice for three years before becoming a claims consultant at ACIC. "Most of the attorneys hired by our company have six to eight years of litigation experience. They have generally worked as insurance defense counsel for our company or for another insurance carrier. Attorneys who work in a claims position in a company such as ours need to have enough law practice experience that they have a good understanding of litigation, of the discovery process, and of how to prove up a medical malpractice case," she explains. In her current position as regional claims director and vice president, Lauree supervises the company's claims consultants.

Attorneys like Carol Proctor, who work on coverage issues and insurance contract issues in the insurance departments of large law firms, generally begin their legal careers as summer associates in large law firms. Often these firms participate in fall on-campus interviewing programs in which they interview second year students for summer positions. Carol is very happy with her decision to pursue insurance law, an area in which she's been practicing since 1985. "I chose to pursue a career in insurance law because it is an area that's constantly changing. I wanted the intellectual and legal challenge in my career to come from the legal subject area itself."

Attorneys who work as in-house counsel generally bring several years of law firm experience to their positions. They need law practice experience in order to act as in-house advisers for their employers. Ann Triebsch began her legal career in private practice at a large firm in Washington, D.C. "While an associate, I worked on a variety of matters, including health care issues, litigation, lobbying, environmental work, antitrust law, and corporate matters," she says. From Washington, Ann moved to her home town of Louisville, Kentucky, where she secured her first in-house position. After a year and a half, that company left Louisville and Ann worked at a Louisville law firm for a year before landing her position at Anthem Blue Cross & Blue Shield.

"As an in-house counsel, it's important to have a large base of knowledge and a wide range of experiences so you can serve your company effectively," says Ann. She explains that most insurance companies, and most corporations generally, have tight budgets. "They don't have the resources to train a new lawyer. You have to hit the ground running. Law school teaches you to do legal research, to write effectively, and think analytically, but it doesn't prepare you for practicing law." Ann says that as a general rule, the bigger a company's legal department, the more likely they'll take on someone with just a few years of experience. "But in a small in-house department like we have here at Anthem, we use outside counsel for many things. When we hire an in-house counsel, we tend to look for someone who is more of a jack-of-all-trades with four to six years of legal experience." Often, such attorneys are hired from large law firms or from government positions.

What skills are most important to insurance lawyers?

❖ Good **relationship-building skills** are key to success as an insurance law attorney. Says Lauree Barreca, "Good people skills are critical. You play so many roles when you work as a claims director. You're interacting with clients, defense counsel, and insurance professionals. You have to understand the basis and the nature of insurance relationships." Adds Ann Triebsch, "Relationships are so important in this field. If my in-house clients don't like me and don't feel comfortable with me, they won't bring problems to me, and that's what I'm here for—to help them with those problems. On the other hand, you have to have strong enough relationships that you can say 'no' to your colleagues and openly disagree with them. You have to establish a comfort level with the employees in the company."

❖ **Interpersonal communication skills** are important to all insurance attorneys, whether they work in insurance defense, on coverage issues, or as in-house counsel. As Donna Rosemeyer mentioned earlier, 90% of her job involves communication skills. "In the insurance industry," she says, "you're constantly working with people." Carol Proctor agrees. "The most important skill is communication," she says, advising, "The best communication with clients is often achieved through breaking down complex ideas into smaller units of information which connect in a logical sequence."

❖ **Strategic thinking skills** are paramount. "You can't be a reactive thinker; you have to be a strategic, proactive thinker," says Lauree Barreca. "You have to be creative in the way you approach legal problems. You have to look at things in a new light nearly every day. You have to be able to formulate legal strategies and then partner with defense counsel and senior management to put those strategies into action."

❖ Insurance is an industry in which issues can be highly emotionally charged and stakes are often high; thus attorneys must exercise **exceptionally good judgment**. "You have to have a sense of who the players in the industry are, where they are coming from, and how they are going to react," advises Ann Triebsch. "For example, you may have a law that's not well written, and you have to ask yourself how the company can conduct itself in order to act within the intent of the legislature. You have to look beyond the words on the page and consider the totality of the circumstances, the temperature of the situation, the parties involved. You have to know the history of the relationships between the legislature, the board or commission, and the parties involved on all sides of the table."

❖ Lauree Barreca cautions that part of good judgment is **knowing your limitations.** "You can't be afraid to ask for help. Because the stakes are high, you have to **feel comfortable seeking advice from colleagues and superiors.** The failure to seek advice can be financially devastating. In companies such as ours, there's always someone who is willing to help you." Donna Rosemeyer notes that one advantage of working for a corporation such as Allstate is that there is an emphasis on training. "We make sure that our lawyers have the background and skills they need for the courtroom. We have a rigorous, week-long, in-house National Institute for Trial Advocacy program that all of our lawyers take. There are always people here to help you sharpen your skills and people to address your concerns and answer your questions."

❖ The lawyers we talked to said that **negotiation skills** are imperative. "There's an excellent business book titled *Getting to Yes: Negotiating Agreement Without Giving In* [Roger Fisher et al. (Penguin 1991)]. And at the end of the day, that's what this field is all about. It's about conflict resolution, about coming to a middle ground that all sides feel good about," says Lauree Barreca.

❖ Insurance lawyers of all types need to be able to **think on their feet.** "Every day, unpredictable things happen," says Donna Rosemeyer. "You have to protect your client." Ann Triebsch agrees. "In the insurance industry, and in health insurance in particular, things are very volatile. You've got to be able to think on your feet and keep your head squarely on your shoulders. Matters you face can be highly emotionally charged and sometimes a quick response is required. You must be able to cope well under such circumstances."

❖ Because the insurance industry is one of constant and continual change, insurance lawyers must be able to **deal effectively with change.** Lauree Barreca comments, "Case law is constantly changing. You have to be able to adapt to change quickly." Adds Ann Triebsch, "There are constantly new laws in the industry. Technology is changing, enforcement efforts are cranking up, and you have to be cognizant of these changes. You must be able to anticipate what the next hot issue will be. For example, right now a hot issue in our industry is the sharing of profile information about physicians with other physicians and entities in the health care industry. There aren't any laws on the books right now about this, but I have to help my clients see what those laws are likely to be when they're developed. And in the meantime, I have to explain to my clients how liability could arise under existing tort law."

❖ Insurance lawyers have to **learn quickly from experience**. "You have to be able to learn as you go along," says Donna Rosemeyer. "You can't learn everything you need to know about being in the courtroom from a book."

❖ If you're considering a career in health care insurance, **a knowledge and understanding of medical issues and a sincere interest in those issues** can be helpful. "It's not necessary to have a medical background," says Lauree Barreca, "but an understanding of health care law and clinical issues can help you understand the medicine involved in a particular case."

What classes and law school experiences do insurance lawyers recommend?

❖ If you're considering a career in insurance defense work, **classes such as evidence, civil procedure, torts, insurance law, and negotiations** can be helpful. **Trial advocacy classes and moot court** can help you sharpen your oral advocacy skills. "Moot court, in which you present an appellate argument in front of a panel of judges, is great preparation for the courtroom," says Donna Rosemeyer. "It requires you to think on your feet. Trial advocacy classes are also excellent preparation for trial work."

❖ Lauree Barreca says that once you supervise litigation in an in-house position, additional law school classes prove helpful, including **contract law, health care law, and arbitration and conflict resolution classes**. "Insurance law is all about contracts, so contract law is important. Conflict resolution training is also helpful, whether it's a class you take in law school, as an undergraduate, or in a continuing education setting as a lawyer." In addition, Lauree recommends that anyone interested in the health care area take a basic physiology course at the undergraduate level in order to develop a familiarity with medical terminology.

❖ If you're considering a career as an in-house counsel in a health care insurance company, Ann Triebsch advises taking **health care law, insurance law, and administrative law classes.** "Administrative law is important because all insurance companies are regulated by state agencies and there are numerous federal laws that affect insurance companies as well. Administrative law helps you understand your state insurance regulators, with whom you will need to have a close relationship." Ann says that health care law positions bring you in touch with the entire spectrum of legal issues, including antitrust law, labor law, and tort law. A broad legal education is thus important.

❖ **Summer associateships and law clerkship experiences** are important to those students seeking positions in insurance law. "Pursue opportunities for hands-on experience," advises Ann Triebsch. "You'll know whether this is the direction you want to follow." Donna Rosemeyer recommends summer associateships, law clerking experience, and internships. "These practical experiences give you a solid foundation to build on as an attorney," she notes. Lauree Barreca suggests that students who eventually want to supervise litigation first work as associates in insurance defense firms. "The best way into such a firm is through clerking or working as a summer associate," she says.

❖ **"Don't be afraid to try out your skills in the courtroom,"** advises Donna Rosemeyer. "I wish I hadn't been so frightened of trial law in the beginning of my career," she confides. "You never know how you'll feel about courtroom work until you give it a try. I truly believe that if I can do it and enjoy it, the vast majority of law graduates can do this kind of work and be very happy doing it," she says. When we asked Donna what further advice she had for law students, she offered reassurance. "In law school, some of the things that seem so important at the time, like the grade you get in your evidence class and your class rank, don't turn out to be so important in the grand scheme of things. If you're a good person, a good lawyer, and a hard worker, and if you're bright and dedicated to your clients, good things will come your way."

❖ **Meet and talk to lawyers who are practicing in the insurance law field.** "It's never too early to start networking," says Carol Proctor. Bar associations offer memberships to students at very reasonable fees, and the associations welcome students to attend events and committee meetings. Your school may also offer an alumni adviser program in which you can talk to alumni volunteers about their careers and the advice they have to offer you.

❖	**Start keeping up with developments in the insurance law field.** "Reading advance sheets [recently published opinions] can help you determine which firms consistently practice in your area of interest," advises Carol Proctor. Keeping up with national, state and local bar journals and legal newspapers, as well as with newspapers such as the *Wall Street Journal* and the *New York Times*, can also help you stay up to date on the latest developments in the field.

INSURANCE ATTORNEYS INTERVIEWED FOR THIS SECTION

M. Lauretta Barreca
American Continental Insurance Company, an MMI Company
Deerfield, Illinois
UNDERGRADUATE: College of St. Francis
LAW SCHOOL: Chicago-Kent College of Law, Illinois Institute of
Technology

Carol Proctor
Hinshaw & Culbertson
Chicago, Illinois
UNDERGRADUATE: Aurora College
LAW SCHOOL: DePaul University College of Law

Donna Rosemeyer
Allstate Insurance Company
Northbrook, Illinois
UNDERGRADUATE: Millikin University
LAW SCHOOL: University of Illinois College of Law

Ann Triebsch
Anthem Blue Cross & Blue Shield
Louisville, Kentucky
UNDERGRADUATE: Centre College
LAW SCHOOL: Northwestern University School of Law

Intellectual Property Law

What is Intellectual Property Law?

Intellectual property (IP) law has its basis in the Constitutional imperative (Article II, Section VIII of the U.S. Constitution) that laws should be established to promote science and the useful arts. A body of law that protects inventions and various forms of artistic and scientific expression has been developed through statutes and court interpretation. The range of protectible intellectual property is remarkably broad. It ranges from a sculptor's rights in a sculpture that has been commissioned by a city, to a composer's rights in the performance of and variations in a piece of music, to an inventor's rights in both the hardware and software incorporated in a microprocessor, to a corporation's rights in trademarks in its name, corporate logo, and even the color of its products. The practice of intellectual property law has grown dramatically in recent years as technology has become more important to businesses and services in the global economy.

There are several areas of substantive law within the field of intellectual property, including patents, copyrights, trademarks, unfair competition, and trade secrets. Intellectual property law has also expanded to cross over into other practice areas, such as computer law (negotiation of software licenses and hardware purchase agreements), international law (obtaining and enforcing patents and licenses abroad), and corporate law (mergers and acquisitions involving high technology companies).

Patents

Students with an interest or background in technology may want to explore patent law. A patent is a property right protecting an inventor's interest in a technical development, whether that development is a machine, a pharmaceutical product, an electronic device, computer hardware or software, or, more recently, a living organism (such as the famous cloned sheep, Dolly). A patent precludes others from making, using, or selling the patented invention for 20 years from the date of the patent application. To obtain a patent, the inventor must show that the invention is useful, new, and not obvious in light of previous technology in the same area (defined as "prior art" in the lingo of intellectual property law).

Some patent lawyers specialize in preparing and obtaining ("prosecuting") patent applications before the U.S. Patent and Trademark Office (PTO), based in Washington, D.C. These practitioners must have some technical training, such as an undergraduate degree in engineering, biological, or physical science and must pass a patent bar examination administered by the PTO. Other practitioners, who aren't necessarily technically trained, become involved in the litigation of patent rights belonging to individual inventors or to corporate entities. Patent practitioners may become involved in negotiating and drafting licensing agreements concerning the transfer of technology. Other practitioners may work with corporate attorneys in preparing initial public offerings for technology start-up companies.

Copyrights

Copyright law concerns the rights of creators of works in the entertainment, publishing, and fine arts industries. The federal Copyright Act provides rights in original works of authorship—a book, musical composition, film, recording, theatrical performance, painting, or sculpture. The owner of a copyright can prevent the copying, public display, or public performance of a work without the author's permission. Copyrights are aggressively enforced in the music industry through the efforts of such organizations as the American Society of Composers, Artists and Performers (ASCAP) and Broadcast Music Incorporated (BMI).

Copyright attorneys counsel playwrights, authors, artists, and composers regarding the rights to their works, negotiate contracts protecting their rights, and represent them in lawsuits enforcing these rights. (*See* the Entertainment and Sports Law chapter for additional profiles of attorneys who deal with copyrights.)

Trademarks and Unfair Competition

A trademark is a word or symbol used by a company to identify the origin or provider of a product or service. Examples of well known trademarks include the McDonald's golden arches, the NBC peacock, and the rolling script of the Coca-Cola logo. Trademark rights have also been extended to colors such as the pink of Owens-Corning's fiberglass insulation and to symbols such as the Nike swoosh. Trademark law now also plays a role in the establishment of domain names and other rights on the Internet.

A trademark owner has the right to prevent another organization or an individual from using any mark which would create confusion in the consumer's mind as to the source of the goods. The owner's mark is thus protected from "trademark infringement." The U.S. Olympic Committee, for example, tirelessly enforces the use of its symbols and the rights to use them to ensure that they are used exclusively by official sponsors of the U.S. Olympic team.

Trademark attorneys work with clients on choosing a mark, clearing it for use, and registering it with the Patent and Trademark Office. They also watch the marketplace for unauthorized use of the trademark, litigate against potential infringers of a client's trademark, and defend clients who are accused of infringement. Trademark attorneys also negotiate and draft licenses for use of a particular mark, such as the association of a company's name with a professional sports stadium (for example, the new arena housing the Washington Wizards basketball team is the MCI Center).

Trade Secrets

A trade secret is a secret formula, process, or data compilation with economic value. Its value derives from the fact that only certain people know the information and the owner has taken steps to maintain the secrecy of the information. Well-known examples of trade secrets would include the formula for making Coca-Cola and the "original recipe" for fried chicken that Colonel Sanders developed for Kentucky Fried Chicken. Customer lists can be trade secrets as well. Another example of a trade secret is computer programming code. Source code and object code often are not patented by a company but are kept as trade secrets of the company and are closely guarded from disclosure to outsiders.

The owner of a trade secret can protect against unauthorized use of the information by someone who has improperly acquired the information. Trade secret cases often arise when key employees who have been entrusted with technical or financial information leave a company to form their own company or to work for a competitor.

Attorneys working on trade secret cases advise clients as to how to keep their trade secrets confidential and litigate on behalf of clients when a trade secret has been improperly acquired. They also help clients devise strategies to avoid trade secret litigation, including drafting non-compete agreements so that employees who depart to start their own companies or to work for another company cannot compete by using the secret information.

Computer Law

Computer law draws heavily on other areas of intellectual property law as well as on general contract law. The main focus of this area of law is the protection of software and hardware developed by a client. This may involve protection under all the areas of intellectual property discussed above—patents, copyrights, trademarks, and trade secrets.

Computer law involves the preparation and negotiation of software license agreements and/or hardware purchase agreements and the litigation growing out of these contractual relationships. Attorneys who work in a computer law practice generally work within the intellectual property department of a law firm.

Life as an Intellectual Property Lawyer

Where do intellectual property lawyers work?

Attorneys specializing in patent, trademark, and copyright law often work in the intellectual property department of large general practice law firms or in small to medium-size boutique firms which specialize in intellectual property law. Intellectual property attorneys also work in corporations as part of an in-house legal staff or for the federal government in the Patent and Trademark Office.

Who are their clients and what types of cases do they work on?

Intellectual property attorneys work with a wide array of clients. Says trademark and copyright attorney Ned Himmelrich, of Gordon, Feinblatt, Rothman, Hoffberger & Hollander, LLC in Baltimore, Maryland, "My clients work in almost every industry and range from mothers working from their homes to large corporations. All of them have the same issues in common—concerns about their organization's name, their copyrightable ideas, and their trade secrets." Patent attorney Steven Goldstein of Frost & Jacobs LLP in Cincinnati explains that, because patent services tend to be expensive, most of his clients are corporations or research institutions such as universities, although he does work with some independent inventors as well.

David Callahan, an IP attorney at Kirkland & Ellis in Chicago, works with clients from myriad industries—automotive, aerospace, medical imaging, electronics, building materials, and petroleum. Jean Burke Fordis, a patent attorney with a biotechnology background at Finnegan, Henderson, Farabow, Garrett & Dunner, L.L.P. in Washington, D.C., reports that her typical client is a small, start-up biotechnology company. "These companies come to our firm because the protection of their intellectual property is vital to their continued growth, as these properties are their primary assets," says Jean.

David Callahan explains that a typical case in his firm's intellectual property department might be a patent infringement case involving two large, competitive corporations. "Such a case typically lasts from one to three years and often involves a bench or jury trial in federal court," says David. David reports that in his first five years of practice, he had the opportunity to participate in four trials—exceptional training for his career in patent litigation.

According to trademark and copyright attorney Ned Himmelrich, most of the trademark cases he handles involve a client asking whether a certain name can be used in connection with particular goods or services. Ned explains that clients may also seek his advice on handling copyright and trademark issues when structuring a business deal.

Jean Fordis and Steven Goldstein focus on prosecuting patent applications. An example, explains Steven, is when "a client has a new, commercially important invention which requires patentability evaluation, development of a strategy for commercially valuable proprietary protection, and the drafting and prosecution of patent applications on the invention." Jean Fordis describes the process in more detail: "An inventor will call me with a description of a new invention and I will send him an 'Invention Disclosure Statement' to complete. Together with the disclosure and supporting materials, the inventor sends review articles to provide a deeper understanding of the invention. With this information we prepare the patent application and file it with the PTO. As our understanding of the technology develops, we are able to respond to any actions from the PTO and prosecute the patent through until it is issued."

What daily activities are involved in intellectual property practice?

Most intellectual property attorneys spend a good deal of their time counseling clients, and those we talked to agree that client counseling is their favorite part of the job. Jean Burke Fordis enjoys the close working relationships she develops with inventors. She explains, "Virtually all the inventors with whom we work call me on the phone with a simple 'Hi, Jean—it's me.' We're on a first name basis; the relationships are so well developed that we don't even need last names."

Patent attorney Hugh Abrams of Sidley & Austin, in Chicago, explains that there's a logical reason IP attorneys grow close to their clients. "There is a high learning curve for technology in a particular industry—whether automotive parts, plastics, or fertilizer. Once you have mastered the technology in that area, you tend to continue to work closely with a client." He explains that writing patent applications provides new attorneys with an opportunity to focus on a technology they find interesting and that relates to their technical background. "It's also excellent preparation for handling the complexities of litigation involving that technology," he says.

Intellectual property attorneys spend their days using their communication skills. They have conferences with clients, expert witnesses, and other attorneys. They may visit their clients' research facilities or manufacturing plants. They draft correspondence, pleadings, briefs, patent applications, and opinion letters to clients concerning the validity of a patent or reviewing the likelihood of patent infringement. In intellectual property lawsuits, the discovery, or fact-finding, phase of the lawsuit is intensive. Attorneys review documents, take and defend depositions (witnesses' sworn oral statements), and draft or respond to interrogatories (parties' sworn answers to questions posed by other parties). They go to court to argue motions and to represent their clients in trials and hearings. (*See* the Civil Litigation chapter for more information on these activities.)

Because patent law issues are litigated in federal court, patent attorneys may find themselves traveling to out-of-state depositions, hearings, or trials. Due to the global nature of intellectual property rights, IP attorneys of all types may travel abroad to visit and advise clients. Hugh Abrams travels periodically to Japan to consult with clients in the photographic and automotive industries. So that he could better understand his clients and their culture, Hugh began to study Japanese. His trips are much more enjoyable now that he can readily navigate the subway, chat with office workers and store clerks, and decipher even the most cryptic menu. Clients appreciate his efforts and have taken on a role in his education—with unfailing patience and good humor, they correct his grammar and coach him on the finer points of pronunciation.

The Training and Skills Important to Intellectual Property Law

How do people enter the field of intellectual property law?

A technical background leads some law students to careers in IP law. Steven Goldstein, for example, majored in chemistry. "I decided to go into patent law because it would allow me to combine my interests in law and chemistry," he says. Jean Fordis followed a similar path—she worked as a biologist in the fields of pharmacology, biochemistry, and molecular biology before becoming an attorney. She explains, "While I was working in a laboratory, a respected friend advised me to go to law school because there was a need for biotechnology patent attorneys. He was right!" Hugh Abrams majored in mechanical engineering but was a college and high school debater. A legal career allowed him to merge his technological expertise with his skills in oral advocacy and persuasion.

Other students become interested in intellectual property in a more roundabout way. David Callahan, who majored in political science, chose to pursue intellectual property after he worked at a large general practice firm as a summer associate. "I took assignments in several practice areas but ended up choosing intellectual property because of the people in the practice group and the chance to work on a variety of projects with a broad range of clients," he says.

Trademark and copyright attorney Ned Himmelrich was first inspired to pursue a legal career by his grandfather, who was a lawyer. "Blood makes me woozy," he admits, so medical school wasn't an option. "I became an intellectual property lawyer purely by happenstance. I never took an IP course in law school. While clerking at a law firm during my third year, I worked on two trademark projects for the firm's trademark attorney. When that attorney left the firm three weeks before I arrived as a full-time associate, it was decided that I would be the new IP 'expert' (in fact, I spent my first vacation on the beach reading a copyright treatise). The area interested me and was in line with my retailing and microeconomic background. My involvement and experience in the area merely blossomed from that pivotal point."

What skills are most important to intellectual property lawyers?

❖ Intellectual property attorneys, no matter what their specialty, agree that good **oral and written communication skills** are key to success in this field. Steven Goldstein explains, "Patent attorneys act as translators between the technical world (the inventors) and the legal world (judges and juries)." Because a good portion of an IP attorney's day is spent writing, strong business writing and legal writing skills are important. "Strong legal writing skills are absolutely critical. Equally important, however, is the ability to write clearly and precisely when communicating with clients," says Hugh Abrams. Adds Ned Himmelrich, "Some documents require 'lawyerly' writing, but most written material consists of letters with descriptive and persuasive content."

❖ The large amount of client counseling involved means that IP attorneys must have good **interpersonal skills.** Jean Fordis says, "Most important are the abilities to listen and work well with others."

❖ IP attorneys work hard to help clients resolve disputes before they end up in the courtroom; thus, **negotiation skills** are key. David Callahan observes, "Much of what I do during the course of a day—including discussions with clients, experts and opposing counsel—involves negotiation and compromise."

❖ IP attorneys who work in patent law need **an interest in a broad spectrum of technology.** Many IP attorneys report that the opportunity to work on the latest technologies is one of their favorite parts of the job. Jean Fordis believes having the flexibility and desire to work with a tremendous variety of technical fields is key to success as an IP attorney.

❖ An **understanding of business and economics** is also important to IP attorneys. Attorneys counsel clients regarding the best way to protect their intellectual property assets. Jean Fordis, for example, counsels domestic and foreign clients on patent litigation and prosecution, including issues related to strategy, risk analysis, patent portfolios, and litigation management. Steven Goldstein says one of the most satisfying parts of his job is working on IP issues relating to corporate acquisitions and mergers.

❖ Today's companies look at their intellectual property assets from the perspective of their value in the global economy. This requires an **understanding of international issues.** Hugh Abrams explains, "Protection and enforcement of patent rights in Europe, Asia, and around the globe means that attorneys who have an understanding of international issues provide their clients with an added advantage."

❖ An **awareness of social and consumer issues** can also be helpful to IP attorneys. "The rules of trademark and copyright law depend on what a typical consumer thinks. Thus knowledge of our current culture is helpful," says Ned Himmelrich. "I acquired part of this skill innately, part of this skill (as it turns out now) by forgoing homework and watching TV, and part of this skill by looking at and reading diverse magazines and television shows, plus keeping my eyes open to the world around me."

What classes and law school experiences do intellectual property lawyers recommend?

❖ Intellectual property attorneys agree that any law school experience that improves your writing ability is worth your time and effort. **Law review** provides students with exceptional legal writing experience as well as the opportunity to be published. If you are not selected for law review and your school offers an opportunity to write an article to submit for admission to the law review, take on the challenge. In addition, consider **writing for other journals** or **entering writing competitions** sponsored by your law school or bar associations. Simply participating in these activities will improve your legal writing.

❖ **Clerking for a federal judge** provides an unparalleled opportunity to improve your writing skills, make contacts, and learn how to see things from the judicial perspective. Clerking for the U.S. Court of Appeals for the Federal Circuit, which handles appeals concerning intellectual property cases, provides an outstanding opportunity for students interested in intellectual property. If your school has a **judicial externship program** that allows you to earn credit while working for a judge, take advantage of the program. Most every student who takes on a judicial externship or judicial clerkship remembers it as a profound learning experience. As Jean Fordis says, "My clerkship for the U.S. Court of Appeals for the Federal Circuit has been a highlight of my legal career."

❖ IP attorneys invariably suggest that interested students take a **survey class in intellectual property** and explore the **other IP classes** your school offers. Also consider classes that increase your understanding of federal litigation, such as a course in federal courts or complex litigation. A class concerning business organizations (corporations, partnerships, etc.) can be helpful, as well. Ned Himmelrich reminds students that an accounting course is helpful for any lawyer. As a trademark attorney concerned with consumer issues, Ned also recommends courses that deal with social issues and the law.

❖ While you are a law student, **gain practical experience in the field of intellectual property by working as a summer associate or law clerk**. Working as a summer associate or law clerk gives you the opportunity to develop the skills you need to practice law. "The complex nature of patent litigation means that the sooner you start to acquire on-the-job experience, the better," says Hugh Abrams. Ned Himmelrich adds, "The phrase 'the practice of law' is entirely accurate. You cannot start on your first day as a lawyer being an expert in a field and knowing everything. It takes practice."

❖ **You can also learn more about the field and make important contacts by joining a student organization or bar association** related to intellectual property issues, such as the American Intellectual Property Law Association. Many law schools have student Intellectual Property Law Associations. Bar associations, including the American Bar Association, often have IP sections and may offer a discounted student membership rate.

INTELLECTUAL PROPERTY ATTORNEYS
INTERVIEWED FOR THIS SECTION

Hugh Abrams
Sidley & Austin
Chicago, Illinois
UNDERGRADUATE: University of Illinois
LAW SCHOOL: University of Illinois College of Law

David Callahan
Kirkland & Ellis
Chicago, Illinois
UNDERGRADUATE: University of Chicago
LAW SCHOOL: University of Michigan Law School

Jean Burke Fordis
Finnegan, Henderson, Farabow, Garrett & Dunner, L.L.P.
Washington, D.C.
UNDERGRADUATE: California State University
LAW SCHOOL: American University Washington College of Law

Steven Goldstein
Frost & Jacobs LLP
Cincinnati, Ohio
UNDERGRADUATE: Massachusetts Institute of Technology
LAW SCHOOL: Boston University School of Law

Ned Himmelrich
Gordon, Feinblatt, Rothman, Hoffberger & Hollander, LLC
Baltimore, Maryland
UNDERGRADUATE: Bowdoin College
LAW SCHOOL: University of Maryland School of Law

International Law

What is International Law?

For many years international law was practiced primarily by those attorneys located in branch offices of large U.S. firms in major financial centers, such as London, Hong Kong, Tokyo, or Singapore. But with the increasing globalization of the world's economies, that has changed. Now, increasing numbers of U.S.-based attorneys practice international law. Attorneys who once dealt only with domestic laws regarding taxes, securities, labor, intellectual property, and other concerns today are often required to understand the equivalent laws in other countries. The international expansion of U.S. law firms has been driven by client demand—clients want seamless representation throughout the world as their financial transactions and acquisition activities are no longer restricted to a single country or even a single continent.

As the global economy grows, ventures in countries outside the U.S. raise numerous issues in a variety of areas of law. For example, attorneys assist their clients in resolving issues of ownership and sharing of intellectual property rights relating to technology, as well as product names and trademarks. Construction of an electric power plant requires acquisition and ownership of real estate and can also raise issues of environmental permitting and local government utility regulation. The appropriate corporate structure for joint ownership or lease of real estate and intellectual property rights can also involve consideration of tax consequences in the local country, as well as for the parent corporation in its residence country. As a result, U.S. attorneys must work closely with their colleagues in other countries to provide the necessary advice to complete such a project or transaction.

The growth in international law practice has been driven by the increased number of international corporate mergers and acquisitions and the reliance of businesses on international capital markets for their financial needs. For example, the automobile industry recently saw the merger of Germany's Daimler-Benz Corporation with America's Chrysler Corporation, as well as affiliations between companies such as Ford and Mazda. Attorneys assisting with such transactions must be aware of the impact of the laws on various issues throughout the world. For example, the Daimler-Chrysler merger potentially had far-reaching antitrust implications with regard to the various suppliers, customers, and markets of these two companies in the U.S., Europe, Asia, and even Latin America. Daimler-Benz was listed on a European stock exchange, while Chrysler was listed on a U.S. stock exchange, presenting potential difficulties for both companies in meeting the various accounting and disclosure requirements of the securities laws of different countries. The relations between each company and its various unions as well as the dramatic differences in executive compensation, including employee benefits, retirement plans, and stock options, presented numerous issues with regard to employment and labor law as well as employee benefits law.

Even mergers between two U.S.-based companies can present international legal issues. The merger in the petrochemical industry between Exxon and Mobil required antitrust and regulatory approval in petroleum exploration, refining, distribution, and the gasoline retail industry. Antitrust issues arose with regard to overlap or concentration in market power in the gasoline retail industry in some U.S. states, such as California, as well as the concentration in market power in certain oil field exploration ventures in Asia. The merger between Kimberly-Clark Corporation and Scott Paper required divestiture of certain paper product business lines in Europe as a result of European Union regulatory concerns. In these types of transactions, U.S. attorneys must work closely with their counterparts in Europe and Asia to provide advice with regard to the impact of the transaction on legal issues arising both in the U.S. and abroad. While U.S. attorneys are licensed to practice law only in the United States, their advice to their clients may be impacted by the laws and regulations, as well as the customs and cultures, of many other countries.

Financial transactions also have been a primary force in the internationalization of the practices of many U.S. firms. Companies in the U.S. are increasingly turning to the international capital markets for raising capital. For example, a group of New York-based financial institutions might undertake the purchase and securitization of millions of dollars of mortgages owned by a group of Japanese banks. Those mortgage-backed securities might then be offered for sale through exchanges in other international markets. Such a transaction might be based on New York law, Japanese law, or a combination of both.

Developing countries also seek large investments of capital for infrastructure development, or project finance. For example, construction of electric power plants in India, highways in China, or a new airport in Bangkok, is often financed by arrangements between the governments of those countries as well as investors from inside those countries and around the world. These financial instruments, whether they are bonds or commercial loans, are then sold to raise capital. U.S. attorneys may be involved in these project finance transactions, representing investors, construction companies, financial institutions, or even the local governments. (*See* the Corporate Law chapter and the Municipal Finance chapter for more information on project finance.)

In making investments in developing countries, companies will often seek joint venture partners, which may be local or based in other neighboring countries. For example, U.S. companies seeking to build a manufacturing plant in China might choose to team with a local Chinese company or to work with another Asian-based company, such as a Japanese or Korean company. Such a joint venture between companies from two or more countries, with the intention of undertaking a project in a third country, can raise issues of law in all of the involved countries. In this situation U.S. attorneys may be intimately involved on behalf of U.S. or foreign-based companies in the negotiation and documentation of the partnership arrangement for such a transaction.

Life as an International Lawyer

Where do international lawyers work?

Many international lawyers work in law firms that have departments specializing in international trade or international finance. Such firms tend to be located in large cities. Other international lawyers work for corporations with international interests, for accounting and consulting firms, for financial institutions, or for government agencies such as the Department of Commerce or the International Trade Commission (ITC).

Who are their clients and what types of cases do they work on?

International law attorneys working in law firms generally represent corporate clients. Lisa Bostwick is an international finance lawyer at the Hong Kong office of Clifford Chance, a large, international law firm. "Our clients are generally investment banks or companies seeking to access the U.S. capital markets. Our office has clients from around the world and across an enormous variety of industries," she reports. "In general, the companies seeking to sell securities in the U.S. have been fairly successful in their own countries and are seeking to widen their investor base [*see* the Securities Law chapter for more information on this topic]. As their U.S. counsel, we provide our clients with legal advice based on U.S. law, regarding how to make their proposed transactions comply with U.S. laws and regulations.

"A typical transaction in our securities practice," explains Lisa, "would involve our representation of an investment bank underwriting securities of a foreign company or government to be sold, in part, to U.S. international investors. In addition, to comply with U.S. laws and regulations, a typical transaction may involve country-specific issues, such as different accounting methods, foreign exchange controls, and disclosure issues, that would never arise in standard domestic transactions."

Herbert Shelley is a partner specializing in international trade at Howrey & Simon, a large law firm in Washington, D.C. He, too, represents corporate clients. "I represent predominantly large, commercial companies, both foreign and domestic. The foreign companies I represent are located mostly in Europe and Asia," he explains. "These clients require a variety of international trade services. They might need assistance in importing merchandise into the United States in compliance with U.S. laws and regulations, or they might need representation in bringing a claim when competing imported products may be violating U.S. laws or regulations or infringing a client's intellectual property rights." These cases are often argued before the International Trade Commission.

Herbert says that international trade cases are remarkably varied, but that a common case before the ITC would be a patent infringement case. "We would file the case with the International Trade Commission because our client holds a patent which we believe is being infringed by the importation of another company's product," he explains. "The case would proceed before an administrative law judge [ALJ] and would be conducted on an unusually fast timetable. Initially, we may seek immediate redress by obtaining a temporary exclusion order to temporarily prohibit importation of the infringing goods. The time from the filing of the complaint through a trial, decision by the ALJ, and final decision by the Commissioners is typically between 12 and 15 months. During this period we will conduct discovery, prepare and respond to pretrial motions, conduct a full evidentiary hearing that may last one or two weeks, and file several pre- and post-trial legal briefs. The litigation team will usually include international trade, patent, and litigation attorneys, as well as engineers and other experts. These cases are exciting and rewarding in that they always involve diverse products and industries and a satisfactory resolution can be achieved in a relatively short time period."

Arthur (Art) Acevedo is an in-house counsel in the international legal department of McDonald's Corporation in Oak Brook, Illinois. Art's clients are McDonald's employees. "All of my clients are internal clients," he explains. "They're generally in management, but they may be anyone in the company with a legal question, as we have an open door policy." Art reports that, worldwide, McDonald's has 15-20 attorneys specializing in international law issues. "Many of the issues that I work on are related to contract law. They may be questions about agency/principal relationships, franchising agreements, real estate transactions, corporate law issues, or company law issues. No two days are alike."

What daily activities are involved in international law?

A significant amount of an international attorney's time is spent in client counseling. "During a typical day, I spend a great deal of time on conference calls and answering phone calls from clients," says Lisa Bostwick. Herbert Shelley reports that about 25% of his time is spent in meetings with colleagues and clients. "In those meetings we strategize about such issues as how to present an argument at trial, how to help a client navigate U.S. laws and regulations concerning products it wishes to import into the United States, or the merits of an appeal of an administrative decision."

"I spend a fair amount of time both on the phone and in front of the computer," says Art Acevedo. "Whether it's fax, e-mail, phone, or video conferencing, I try to find the simplest and most efficient way to communicate with my clients." Art counsels McDonald's employees on issues as diverse as real estate transactions, company law issues, and franchise issues. Company law issues generally involve questions about how to establish a corporation or partnership in a particular country. Many of McDonald's restaurants around the world are franchises. "Franchise disclosure laws vary greatly from one country to another. The laws are designed to give prospective franchisees notice of terms of a franchise contract before the contract is executed." The franchise laws are an important factor to consider when negotiating international contracts.

International lawyers at law firms are likely to spend time in negotiation with opposing counsel and in administrative hearings or in court. "About one-fourth of my time is spent negotiating with opposing counsel, attending hearings before a U.S. government agency, and in court," says Herbert Shelley. "My court time is typically concentrated during specific periods, such as for a trial, when almost all my work is conducted in the courtroom."

International attorneys spend a fair amount of time at their desks, as well. As an international finance attorney, Lisa Bostwick prepares and edits securities prospectuses (documents with information about the investment designed to disclose information to prospective investors) for her clients, making sure they comply with federal securities laws. International trade attorney Herbert Shelley prepares and reviews filings related to trade matters.

Many international lawyers find themselves traveling at least a few weeks each year. Herbert Shelley travels approximately 10 weeks per year. "I travel both in the United States and overseas, taking or defending depositions or assisting clients in the preparation of materials for various types of international trade cases, particularly antidumping and countervailing duty investigations," he reports. Art Acevedo travels about one week per month. "McDonald's has plans for growth worldwide," Art explains, and most of Art's travel is therefore international. "On the average, I travel between 20 to 25% of the time," he says.

What do international lawyers find rewarding about their practice?

Not surprisingly, the international lawyers we talked to enjoy interacting with business people around the world. "It's fascinating to see how business operates in other countries, and I enjoy seeing how people in other countries approach business issues," explains Art Acevedo. Lisa Bostwick agrees. "One of the things I enjoy most about my work is the ability to interact with people from around the world on a daily basis. Throughout the course of a transaction, you have the opportunity to get to know people who view the world from a different perspective," she says. She offers the following example. "At the pricing of a bond offering by the government of a newly independent state in the former Soviet Union, cheers—rivaling those of a soccer win—broke out when the investment bankers announced that the deal would be priced at a slightly more favorable price than that of a similar deal issued by the Russian Federation."

Herbert Shelley says that he appreciates the wide variety of issues in which international trade lawyers become involved. "Attorneys can work with foreign clients advising them and preparing the material they need to participate in an antidumping duty or countervailing duty investigation by the Department of Commerce. Or they may work with a domestic client in petitioning for such an investigation where imported products are being sold below fair market prices in the United States or are being unfairly subsidized by foreign governments. They can assist clients in obtaining the proper tariff classification of imported products before the U.S. Customs Service. They may be asked to assist a client in drafting and promoting legislation involving tariff classifications, or amendments to the U.S. trade laws. They may represent a client who has an interest in the outcome of a dispute between the United States and a foreign country before the World Trade Organization and thus might assist the office of the U.S. Trade Representative in preparing the arguments of the United States. And they may represent a domestic or foreign client in a case involving imports of products alleged to infringe patent, trademark, or other intellectual property rights." Herbert says that these are but a few examples of the exciting issues that come up in international trade practice. "Over the course of several years, it is common for an attorney to be involved in all of these and many other types of cases. The opportunities to learn a client's business and product, to learn about other countries and cultures, to travel, to participate in the formulation of laws and regulations, keep this an exciting and dynamic specialty," he says.

"I enjoy the intellectual challenge of the work," says Art Acevedo. "It's satisfying to look at a project that involves complex legal issues and know that you can rise to the challenge and get the project done. Sometimes you're under a great deal of pressure or tremendous time constraints, but you know that you can find a way to complete the assignment and get things done in a practical and efficient way." Lisa Bostwick reports that she, too, enjoys the intellectual challenges posed by international law issues. "I enjoy the problem-solving aspects of my work," she says. "We work closely with our clients to structure transactions that meet their financing needs. We work hard to make sure that we accomplish these goals in the most efficient and effective manner in compliance with U.S. law and market practice."

Art adds that another rewarding aspect of his work as in-house counsel is working with an exceptional group of colleagues. "I have excellent peers at McDonald's," he says. "They're outgoing. They value teamwork. They enjoy their work as much as I do. It's great to know that the people you work with feel as good about their jobs as you do about yours." We couldn't resist asking Art whether he had the good fortune of eating McDonald's products for lunch every day, since his office is at company headquarters. "I just finished a Big Mac at the McDonald's restaurant here in our office building," he confided. "I get to participate in taste panels for new products. And I even see the new toys developed for our Happy Meals."

The Training and Skills Important to International Law

How do people enter the field of international law?

Students who are interested in international law careers should seek out summer associateships with law firms that have litigation or corporate law departments that represent clients in international finance or similar matters. Often, an opportunity to work on international issues arises out of working on business law issues with a particular client that needs advice with regard to international transactions. A sound background in business transactions is often a good way to begin developing an international law practice. Many attorneys who work in fields such as intellectual property, real estate, and securities law find that international law issues become a significant, though not primary, part of their practice.

People who enter the field of international law often have a special interest in international affairs, perhaps as a result of international work experience or employment at a government agency such as the U.S. Department of Commerce. "I have been interested in law and international relations for some time," says Lisa Bostwick. "I sought as many international experiences as possible, including studying for a year in Austria during college, working for a year in Germany prior to law school, working as a summer law clerk in the Federated States of Micronesia, as well as working and studying in London during my final year of law school. In addition, while at Georgetown University, I enrolled in a joint-degree program in law and international relations, to earn my Juris Doctor and Masters of Science in Foreign Service." Lisa says that graduate work in international relations can be helpful to those interested in an international law career, but is not necessary. "My graduate course work in international relations was personally enjoyable, but such additional course work is certainly not necessary for a lawyer practicing in the area of international finance. Nonetheless, I found my courses in international finance and international trade have been helpful in providing the big picture for the work I now do."

Herbert Shelley says that his work in the international arena developed both through his interest in the area and as a result of his adaptations to client needs throughout his 20+ years of practice. "My employment following law school began as an administrator of the antidumping and countervailing duty laws in the Treasury Department of the U.S. government, followed by three years as a U.S. trade negotiator at the U.S. Mission to the GATT [General Agreement on Treaties and Tariffs] in Geneva, Switzerland. This experience was followed by private practice in a boutique law firm specializing in a variety of international trade matters. The boutique firm later merged with Howrey & Simon, where we have been able to expand upon the international trade services we can offer our clients using attorneys with international trade and intellectual property expertise, as well as with broad litigation experience."

Most corporations hire lawyers that have experience in firms, in government, or in a corporate setting. Art Acevedo had significant business and legal experience before joining McDonald's. "My original specialty was tax law," Art explains. "As an undergraduate, I majored in accounting and finance. I was an Internal Revenue Service agent before and during law school. Upon graduation from law school, I worked for Price Waterhouse (now PricewaterhouseCoopers), an accounting firm. I then joined McDonald's. I really fell into the position, but I soon discovered that I really enjoyed international transactions." Art speaks Spanish fluently, and he's currently learning Italian. His language skills and his business experience have proved helpful to his international law career.

What skills are most important to international lawyers?

❖ **Writing skills—both business writing and legal writing skills—**are critical to the international lawyer. "Superior writing ability is paramount," says Herbert Shelley. Adds Art Acevedo, "Writing in general is important in this field, not just legal writing. You need to know when to write as a lawyer and when to write as a layperson."

❖ **Creative problem-solving skills** are especially important in this field. "You need to be flexible, creative, open-minded, and inquisitive," says Art Acevedo. "These are qualities that feed off each other. The approach in this field is, 'Don't tell me no, don't tell me this can't be done. Tell me that we'll figure out a way.' A good lawyer will figure out a way to get the job done."

❖ **Strong analytical skills** are also important to the field. "You need to be able to identify and resolve complex legal issues in order to successfully advocate your client's position," explains Herbert Shelley.

❖ An **interest in and ability to work with people from other cultures** is key to the successful practice of international law. "You have to enjoy working with attorneys from other cultures," says Art Acevedo. "Sometimes American lawyers think they are more creative and better lawyers than lawyers from other countries, and that's simply not true. You have to be the kind of person who enjoys sitting down with foreign lawyers and talking about the differences in our legal systems. Open-mindedness is extremely important."

❖ International lawyers need **strong interpersonal communications skills**. "At the end of the day," says Art Acevedo, "it's all about communicating." Adds Lisa Bostwick, "I spend time focusing on developing the interpersonal skills demonstrated by lawyers that I admire."

❖ A **high level of commitment to the practice** is also important. "When you work in the international arena, you're working in an environment where people are highly motivated. You have to be willing to push yourself, to ask yourself, how can we get this done? How can we solve this problem? What additional resources and solutions are out there?" says Art Acevedo.

What classes and law school experiences do international lawyers recommend?

* **Business-related law school courses** can be helpful to students planning an international law career. "Courses such as contracts, securities regulation, and commercial law are useful for their basic concepts and their theoretical underpinnings," says Lisa Bostwick. In addition, Art Acevedo recommends business organizations, international business transactions, secured transactions, and a Uniform Commercial Code class as important classes to take while in law school. Art adds that classes in intellectual property, antitrust law, international finance, labor law, and accounting for lawyers are also helpful. Herbert Shelley recommends that students interested in international trade take an administrative law and international trade course as well.

* Many law schools offer **classes in international law**. A basic course followed by advanced international courses related to business (as opposed to international human rights issues, etc.) is good preparation for a career in this field.

* **Writing courses** provide excellent preparation for international law practice. "Take as many writing courses as you can," advises Art Acevedo.

* **Moot court and appellate advocacy classes,** which require you to write appellate briefs and defend them in front of a panel of judges, can be helpful preparation for a career in international trade, suggests Herbert Shelley, observing, "They help you develop exceptional oral advocacy skills, which are very important to this practice specialty."

* **Undergraduate or graduate business courses** can be valuable preparation for practicing in this field. Advises Herbert Shelley, "Undergraduate students should try to take courses in basic business law, international trade, finance, economics, and accounting."

* **Foreign language skills** are a plus. Art Acevedo says that after he masters Italian he hopes to learn Japanese or German. "When you learn a language, you inevitably learn about culture," he says.

* Gain practical experience in a **summer associate position** at a firm with an international law department or a **summer internship** with a corporation or government office that works on international issues.

❖ **Talk to people who work as international lawyers.** "There are so many subspecialties within the practice," says Art Acevedo. "Talk to international practitioners to find out what they do day-to-day." Explains Herbert Shelley, "Most international trade law is practiced in large cities, with almost all of the administrative international trade work located in Washington, D.C. Thus a student should begin to develop contacts in these cities."

❖ **Professional associations** provide another way for students to meet lawyers who specialize in international law. You can meet attorneys through the American Bar Association and the International Law Society as well as through regional bar associations. Most bar associations have inexpensive student memberships, and students are welcome to attend most bar association events. "A myriad of international trade seminars are held each year in Washington, D.C. and New York City," adds Herbert Shelley. "Students and young attorneys are welcome."

INTERNATIONAL ATTORNEYS INTERVIEWED FOR THIS SECTION

Arthur Acevedo
McDonald's Corporation
Oak Brook, Illinois
UNDERGRADUATE: DePaul University
LAW SCHOOL: DePaul University College of Law

Lisa Bostwick
Clifford Chance, LLP
Hong Kong
UNDERGRADUATE: University of Notre Dame
LAW SCHOOL: Georgetown University Law Center

Herbert Shelley
Howrey & Simon
Washington, D.C.
UNDERGRADUATE: Columbia College
LAW SCHOOL: Vanderbilt University Law School

Editor's Note: Herbert Shelley is now a partner at Steptoe & Johnson LLP in Washington, D.C.

Labor and Employment Law

What is Labor and Employment Law?

In the documentary *Roger & Me*, director and producer Michael Moore lampoons General Motors' 1980s labor practices, during which GM closed 11 plants in Flint, Michigan and laid off over 30,000 workers. In the film Moore takes on Roger Smith, General Motors' then-president, concerning GM's plant closings. The documentary takes a look at the effect labor practices have on companies, communities, individual workers, and their families.

Roger & Me raised the American public's awareness of the ways in which labor practices affect auto workers and the auto industry. Yet labor practices affect countless other industries in the United States as well. Airlines, hospitals, trucking companies, and even sports leagues are profoundly affected by their relationships with their employees; pilots, nurses, truck drivers, baseball umpires, and their families are likewise affected by their union's relationship with their employer. Ultimately all Americans are affected by the far-reaching economic impact of labor relations.

Traditional labor practice deals with the relations between workers and their employers. Attorneys play an important role in labor relations matters, providing assistance to both labor and management. These lawyers counsel their clients concerning plant closings, unfair labor practice charges under the National Labor Relations Act, and collective bargaining negotiations. Attorneys advise both management and labor unions with regard to union organizing, representation elections, and related campaigns. Labor attorneys also become involved in union and employee grievances and arbitrations of those grievances.

In addition to involvement in the highly charged atmosphere of union/management relations, attorneys advise labor unions and management on day-to-day issues. These might include affirmative action compliance or matters concerning wages and work hours. Attorneys assist with preparation of employee handbooks, employee policies, and employment contracts, as well as covenants not to compete (promises not to work for competitors for a period of time after leaving the company), employee terminations, and severance arrangements. In today's work environment, companies need advice from attorneys on drug and alcohol testing, AIDS-related issues, and immigration matters as well.

An important outgrowth of traditional labor practice is employment law. This practice includes the defense of clients' interests in cases involving the violation of civil rights. Attorneys handling these issues may represent clients who allege employment discrimination based on race, sex, age, disability, sexual orientation, or other types of civil rights violations; they may also represent the employers accused of these violations. Employment lawyers may also defend employee clients who are sued for breach of employment contracts, breach of covenants not to compete, workplace libel, and slander. They may bring suits for employees who claim wrongful discharge, invasion of employee right of privacy, and intentional infliction of emotional harm. More recently employment attorneys have become involved in litigation of claims involving sexual harassment, as well as the institution of "zero-tolerance" policies and other educational programs to eliminate harassment in the workplace.

Labor and employment attorneys represent their clients in state and federal courts as well as in appeals. They may also represent employers and employees before federal and state administrative agencies. These agencies include state bureaus of employment services, bureaus of workers' compensation, the Equal Employment Opportunity Commission (EEOC), state civil rights commissions, the National Labor Relations Board (NLRB), the state employment relations boards, and the Occupational Safety and Health Administration (OSHA).

Life as a Labor and Employment Lawyer

Where do labor and employment lawyers work?

Many labor and employment lawyers work for law firms. Large and mid-size law firms may have departments devoted to labor and employment law practice. Some small and mid-size firms may have specialized boutique practices in which all attorneys specialize in labor and employment issues. A number of employment lawyers work as solo practitioners or in very small law firms (*see* the profiles of Yvonne Owens and Laura Todd Johnson in the Solo, Small Firm, and General Practice chapter of this book).

Unions employ labor lawyers to handle issues concerning their members. Corporations may have in-house counsel who focus on labor and employment issues; they may also employ law firm attorneys to assist them with litigation or other matters.

A number of attorneys specializing in labor and employment issues work for state and federal government agencies such as the National Labor Relations Board, the Equal Employment Opportunity Commission, state civil rights commissions, and many others.

Who are their clients and what types of cases do they work on?

Richard Rabin is a labor and employment attorney at Akin, Gump, Strauss, Hauer & Feld, L.L.P. in New York City. "Most of the clients my firm represents are large businesses, including many Fortune 500 and Fortune 1,000 corporations. One of the tremendous things about working with such corporations is that they do much of their routine work in-house and send to us, as outside counsel, complicated work that requires special attention. The legal issues on which we work tend to be highly sophisticated," he explains.

Richard has represented corporations in a wide range of cases, from those brought by a single plaintiff to those brought as class actions. "We handle cases under a variety of different employment laws, such as Title VII of the Civil Rights Act, the Americans with Disabilities Act, the Age Discrimination in Employment Act, the Fair Labor Standards Act, the National Labor Relations Act, the Occupational Safety and Health Act, and any state or local analogs. All cases require the same basic approach: Gaining an understanding of the facts in light of the relevant law, developing an understanding of any exposure, and thinking of creative and persuasive legal arguments that will lead to a favorable resolution for our client."

Employment attorney David Proctor works for Johnston Barton Proctor & Powell LLP in Birmingham, Alabama. Like Richard Rabin, David represents corporate clients. "Most of my clients are large corporations. They may be located either in Alabama or in other states," he explains. David assists the corporations in navigating their way through complaints filed by employees. "In many cases an employee is fired or does not receive the promotion he or she feels entitled to. The employee goes through the grievance procedure and is dissatisfied with the result. The employee then files a charge with the EEOC and, after a 'right to sue' letter is issued by the agency, a lawsuit is filed. After the charge is filed with the EEOC, I begin to interview our corporate client's managers, supervisors, and other decision-makers. We move quickly to request all EEOC documents and have an initial meeting of the parties. Discovery then commences, with an eye toward filing a motion for summary judgment on behalf of our client [see the Civil Litigation chapter for a discussion of the discovery process and motions for summary judgment]. If our motion for summary judgment is not successful, a trial ensues."

Mary Mikva, of Abrahamson Vorachek & Mikva in Chicago, works on the other side of the fence, representing individual employees in their actions against employers. Mary's firm is a boutique firm of six attorneys specializing in plaintiff's side employment litigation. "My clients are almost exclusively employees. Generally they are people who have either been terminated from employment or people who encounter ongoing problems at their jobs," she says. The largest number of Mary's cases concern employment discrimination due to race, sex, age, disability, or sexual orientation. "Another large group of cases involves pensions and employee benefits," Mary explains. "In these cases my client is terminated because her pension is about to vest, or my client has been terminated and his employer hasn't adhered to the severance or benefit plan the employer promised him. My clients may have been deprived of a bonus, a commission, or some other benefit they are entitled to. Other cases involve such matters as an employer's failure to pay overtime."

Maryl Rosen is an employment lawyer for the U.S. Postal Service in Chicago. "The Postal Service is my client," Maryl explains. "The Postal Service was created in 1971 as an independent establishment of the federal government." Maryl is one of 13 lawyers in the Chicago office. "Most of us do employment work, but there are some lawyers in our office who also litigate torts, contracts, and other business issues, often cases in which employees are injured on the job. There are over 350 people nationally who work in the U.S. Postal Service Law Department." Maryl most frequently works on cases in which the Postal Service is accused of employment discrimination. "The plaintiff may allege discrimination based on race, sex, national origin, religion, age, or disability. The cases generally involve issues about hiring, firing, or promotion. In all cases an administrative complaint must be filed by the plaintiff before they can file a suit against the Postal Service in federal court."

Tom Carpenter is a union side labor lawyer. He works for the American Federation of Television and Radio Artists (AFTRA) in Chicago. "I work as an in-house attorney for the union," he says. "My clients are the union and the union membership. The membership includes broadcast journalists, radio announcers, actors, singers, and other performers. Essentially I represent the union, but in my work I am sensitive to the concerns of the membership and individual members. My work includes contract negotiations for our membership and the representation of our membership in arbitrations and labor board matters with their employers." Tom hasn't always worked in the seemingly glamorous world of TV and radio personalities. He previously worked as a counsel for the Teamsters Union Local 705 in Chicago, where he represented employees such as construction workers and truck drivers. "If a union is run well and operated fairly, members' interests don't conflict with the union's goals," Tom explains.

What daily activities are involved in labor and employment law practice?

Labor and employment lawyers spend much of their time conferring with their clients and drafting legal documents. "I spend most of my time preparing written work product such as letters, memoranda, briefs, and position papers and conferring with clients and colleagues," says management side attorney Richard Rabin. "I spend a good portion of the day on the telephone with clients," reports David Proctor, who, like Richard, represents corporate clients. "I also spend a great deal of time answering correspondence and keeping clients up to date on the progress with their cases." David's work involves the tasks common to civil litigators: reviewing and analyzing documents, responding to discovery requests, and preparing for trials and depositions (*see* the Civil Litigation chapter for details on these activities).

Mary Mikva, who represents employees, tells us that her days are filled with telephone calls and meetings with clients. "It's a field that requires an attorney to spend time hand-holding and seeing the client through the legal process," she explains. Mary's days also involve going to court, attending meetings, and handling the discovery and depositions that are part of any litigation practice. She also does a great deal of written work, including writing pleadings, briefs, demand letters, and letters to clients.

Maryl Rosen gave us a detailed description of her work as an in-house attorney defending the U.S. Postal Service. "Once an employment discrimination case has been filed in federal district court, I begin to gather information on the case. I gather the records that exist and sketch out what happened. I interview the witnesses and draft what is called a litigation report, in which I include the facts, a legal analysis of the claims, and an assessment of mediation and settlement potential. I address whether we should litigate the case and report on potential problems we might encounter in litigation. I draft an answer, and, if appropriate, I draft a motion to dismiss or a motion for summary judgment." If the case isn't dismissed and doesn't reach settlement, it will go to trial. Maryl's litigation work also involves taking and defending depositions and responding to discovery requests. In addition she trains and advises Postal Service management on how to handle various employment issues.

"One of my responsibilities," AFTRA attorney Tom Carpenter reports, "is negotiating contracts for our members, who include broadcast journalists and radio announcers. I meet with the union members before negotiating their contracts to determine what issues may affect their contract. For example, if they work for a radio station, they must be cautious about efforts to sell the station. A new owner might change the radio station format, affecting the union member's job. Another issue might involve a station's use of a TV reporter's interview in other markets. If the TV and radio personnel don't have a personal attorney, we work with them in negotiating their contracts; if they do have a personal attorney, we assist their personal attorney with negotiations with the station."

Tom also represents union members in the arbitration of cases related to their employment contracts. "These cases might involve a dispute about overtime. Perhaps their contract says that they are to be paid time and a half for working on weekends and the station refuses to pay that. The employee would file a grievance, and then the case goes to arbitration, to be decided by a neutral third party. Often the arbitrators are labor law professors, retired personnel managers, or attorneys." Tom also represents members in labor board cases, which concern violations of the National Labor Relations Act governing relations between employers and unions. "In such cases the union member alleges that the employer has engaged in an unfair labor practice, such as firing him or her for engaging in union activity."

Besides Tom's legal duties, he explains, "At least 50% of my work is non-legal work in which I handle the administration of the union organization. I'm AFTRA's only national representative in Chicago; its national headquarters is in New York City."

What do labor and employment lawyers find rewarding about their practice?

Labor and employment attorneys enjoy the intensive client contact involved in their jobs. Says Richard Rabin, "Compared with other fields, I think labor and employment law tends to involve more client contact, which is something I really enjoy." Adds David Proctor, "It's especially rewarding to counsel clients *prior to* there being a lawsuit. I take great pride in helping our clients avert litigation. Often a lawsuit can be prevented if our client's decision-maker simply picks up the phone and calls for advice."

Mary Mikva finds it rewarding to help her clients through a dark time in their lives. "In my work as a plaintiff's employment lawyer, I get to help people through a bad time. Their lawsuit provides them with hope for economic help; I also try to push them to get on with their emotional lives, which is very rewarding." Mary says, "I try to take on clients that I like and enjoy spending time with," another plus of working in this specialized field. "Many of the most compelling cases involve employees with disabilities. One of my clients was a deaf employee of the Federal Deposit Insurance Corporation (FDIC). He was denied promotional opportunities and literally stuck away in a corner. After the suit the FDIC promoted him, and he's still working there."

Tom Carpenter is enthusiastic about the opportunity his job provides to serve union members. "My job gives me a chance to help people who have very difficult jobs to do. Most of the members are really great people, but I often meet them during very stressful circumstances. If a union is run fairly and properly, it provides a good mechanism for co-workers to solve employment problems. If employees don't have a contract that protects them, they can be fired for a good reason, a bad reason, or no reason at all. But if the contract with the employee says that there must be just cause for firing someone, and there is just cause, and I am able to help the person get back to work, that's very rewarding."

Tom told us about one particularly rewarding arbitration case from his previous job. "When I worked with the Teamsters, I helped a union member who believed the employer was violating seniority provisions of its employment contract. The employer assigned the oldest dock workers to lift the heaviest packages. These older employees were worried about taking care of their backs until they retired, and the younger dock workers were more than willing to take on the work. The case went to arbitration. The arbitrator ruled that the employer had violated terms of its contract and reassigned the older dock workers to less physically stressful duties. The union member I represented had worked 30 years for the employer and wanted to keep his job while avoiding injury. He was tremendously grateful for my help."

One of Maryl Rosen's favorite parts of her job is working with her colleagues. "The people at the U.S. Postal Service are very impressive, knowledgeable, committed, and professional—at all levels of employment. They are always willing to work with me on my cases and always willing to sit down and talk with me and explain things. Some of the Postal Service employees started working there before I was born! They've seen so much and know so much, and they're always willing to share their expertise with me."

Labor and employment attorneys also tell us that they're fascinated by the factual situations involved in their cases. "The stories my clients tell are always interesting," says Mary Mikva. "You learn about people's career histories, from how their careers began to how their jobs came to an end. And you learn that there are always two sides to every story." Richard Rabin likes the role he gets to play in excavating those facts. "Whether it's an on-site to learn how airports operate, a tour of a printing press, or an interview to get to the bottom of a tangled factual dispute, I feel like I'm always learning something."

Maryl Rosen has enjoyed learning how the Postal Service moves mail. "It's just fascinating!" she comments. "When I started my job here, I went for a week of training to learn about how the Postal Service operates—the ins and outs of how a letter or package gets from one place to another. Our attorneys tour the Postal Service and learn which machines do what and meet the people who operate the machinery. It's important for us to know all of this so that when we're in court, we can explain these matters to a judge or jury."

The intellectual challenge of labor and employment work is also appealing to lawyers. "I enjoy the intellectual stimulation of the ever-expanding field of employment litigation," says David Proctor. "Although trying to stay abreast of the legal developments in this practice area is at times daunting, there is rarely a dull moment." Says Maryl Rosen, "It's a most interesting practice. It involves tremendous intellectual challenge and sophisticated legal analysis." Adds Richard Rabin, "There's a great deal of strategizing and planning. I'm always asking whether there's an answer to a problem that no one else has considered. There is no better feeling than the moment you realize you've got a creative, winning idea."

Mary Mikva gives a simple but eloquent reason for her fondness for employment law. "It's fun! There are difficult parts of the practice, but they're far outweighed by the fun parts. I'm happier practicing law than most people I know. The cases are interesting, the clients are fascinating, and it can be a lucrative area in which to practice. It's also a field in which you can have a lot of control over which cases you take on, and that helps make it satisfying."

The Training and Skills Important to Labor and Employment Law

How do people enter the field of labor and employment law?

Some students enter law school knowing that they're interested in the labor and employment law field. Maryl Rosen worked as a paralegal in employment law before she began law school. "I later joined the EEOC as an investigator and entered law school as an evening student a year later. I continued to work for the EEOC while in law school and graduated in 1995. I then secured an attorney position at a small firm, where I handled employment law cases as well as general practice matters." Maryl then joined the Postal Service as a contract attorney under a pilot program that hired attorneys to handle administrative work related to EEOC claims. After a year at the Postal Service, Maryl was hired as part of the permanent legal in-house staff.

Tom Carpenter first explored the field of labor and employment law while in college. "While I was an undergraduate, I took a part-time job with a firm that handled employment discrimination cases. My college job gave me the advantage of knowing what labor and employment law was all about." Tom chose a law school with a specialty program in labor and employment law and subsequently developed close relationships with the professors in the program, who assisted him in making contacts in the field. Committed to union side labor work, while in law school Tom worked for two and half years for the American Federation of State, County and Municipal Employees (AFSCME). After graduation Tom landed a job working for the Teamsters before joining AFTRA.

Richard Rabin was introduced to the field while a law student. "I worked as a research assistant for one of my professors. Although I had the professor for constitutional law, his main field of expertise had always been employment law, so that was the field in which I did most of my work. When I came to Akin Gump, the firm needed to add some new associates to the labor and employment law practice section. Since I had some relevant experience, I figured I'd give it a try." Labor and employment law has been an excellent match for Richard's talents. "It was a fortunate chain of events, as I have grown to love the field," Richard comments with satisfaction.

Other attorneys gravitate toward the field after they begin practicing. When David Proctor graduated from law school, he joined his firm as a commercial litigation attorney. "Our firm then went through some internal changes which gave rise to a need for experienced litigators in the area of employment discrimination. With the firm's need and the increasing amount of legal activity in this area, I have moved almost exclusively into employment litigation defense work."

Mary Mikva began her legal career as a criminal defense attorney. She then joined the City of Chicago Department of Law, where she focused on the management side of labor and employment work for four years. She joined a law firm where she handled plaintiff's employment cases in 1991 and has been at her own small firm since 1996. "If you're interested in handling the plaintiff's side of employment law, it's best to begin your career at a law firm that practices on the management side. Management side work allows you to learn the law and learn how management side law firms think."

What skills are most important to labor and employment lawyers?

❖ The practice of labor and employment law requires excellent **writing skills**. "Good legal writing skills are a necessity, as my practice involves writing briefs, letters, and position statements, and drafting contracts," says Tom Carpenter. Mary Mikva agrees. "There's so much writing involved in this field," she says. "You're writing briefs, drafting interrogatories, and constantly communicating with your clients. You have to be able to muster your legal arguments and write about them in ways that are persuasive to the court and to your clients."

❖ Effective **interpersonal skills** also play a critical role in a lawyer's success in this practice area. David Proctor puts it simply but emphatically: "Above all things, a successful labor and employment attorney has to understand people." Says Maryl Rosen, "You have to inspire people's confidence and get them to tell you the truth of what happened. This involves listening carefully and making people feel comfortable." Mary Mikva cautions that part of practicing effective interpersonal skills is setting limits with your clients. "As a plaintiff's employment lawyer, you can't be overly empathetic. You are meeting with some very needy people at a very difficult time in their lives. You must be able to be warm and sympathetic and yet set limits."

❖ Labor lawyers should be **comfortable working with difficult people**. "Labor law can be highly polarized," explains Tom Carpenter. "Most of the union members are really great people. As much as I enjoy them, there are times that some can be difficult. Union members may be in conflict with their employers, the NLRB, or even other members of the union. Opposing counsel can also be overly-contentious where labor relations are concerned. There are sometimes contentious issues in which the difficult personalities become a real problem. If you get hung up on personalities you won't be happy as a labor lawyer. In short, you have to have a high pain threshold for difficult people," he advises.

❖ **Oral advocacy skills** are critical to labor and employment lawyers. Their work involves hearings and trials, and lawyers must be able to advocate forcefully for their client in either situation. "In the labor cases on which I work, there's little real discovery," explains Tom Carpenter. "Most of the work is done in the courtroom or in the hearing.

Proceedings are run fast and loose. This means you have to have a good grasp of the rules of evidence, and you have to be very quick on your feet. You must be able to do hearings off the cuff, without writing down your questions."

❖ Another important skill for labor and employment lawyers is **tenacity**. "Other than the ability to think clearly, I think tenacity is the most important trait. Tenacity in researching the answers to legal issues, in thinking about problems your clients face or potentially may face in the future, in ensuring that your work is the best it can be, and in taking the initiative to follow up with your clients," says Richard Rabin. He adds emphatically, "This is not a field or profession that rewards passivity."

What classes and law school experiences do labor and employment lawyers recommend?

❖ Take **labor and employment classes** while in law school. Most of the attorneys we talked to agreed that these classes give you a head start in this field. "Take all the labor and employment law courses available," advises David Proctor. "Labor law, employment discrimination law, workers compensation law, ERISA—they're all important," says Tom Carpenter, who adds that negotiations, alternative dispute resolution, and corporate law courses can also be helpful.

❖ **Trial advocacy classes** and **moot court** can sharpen your oral advocacy skills and prepare you for hearings and trials. "Trial advocacy class was extremely helpful to me. There's no better preparation for doing trials than actually preparing for and doing one, and that's what trial advocacy gives you the opportunity to do," says Maryl Rosen. Adds Mary Mikva, "Even if you don't get into the courtroom right away, trial advocacy classes and moot court help you think on your feet."

❖ **Undergraduate courses in speech and communications** can also be helpful. "If you decide to pursue labor and employment law, speech and communications classes will serve you well. But the most important thing to remember as an undergraduate is to major in something you really enjoy," advises Tom Carpenter, who majored in radio, TV, and film as an undergraduate. "If you major in something you enjoy, you'll do well in it."

❖ Sharpen your legal writing skills by writing for your school's **law review**, one of your school's other **law journals**, or outside **writing competitions**. "Law review will help you develop excellent writing skills," says Mary Mikva. "In addition, your law review article makes an outstanding writing sample for law firm interviews."

❖ **Gain practical experience** by working or volunteering in the field. Tom Carpenter's work for AFSCME helped him establish his credentials in union side labor work. "If you're interested in working for a union, it's important to demonstrate your interest in working for a union as early in your law school career as possible. You may also want to explore summer opportunities in college. The AFL-CIO has a program called 'Union Summer,' which offers college students an opportunity to work on labor movement issues and see what the labor movement is all about. If you're a union member, or your parents are members of a union, that can be helpful. Don't be shy about exploring opportunities with unions and telling the union how and why you're interested in union side labor law. While you're in law school, be sure to work for a union's legal department or clerk for a union side labor law firm. If you're interested in union employment, such experience is critical." Mary Mikva adds, "Working, as I did, for a large firm on the management side of things or for the government gives you credibility and good habits. Small boutique firms such as mine need attorneys who can hit the ground running. That's why we hire people with large law firm or government experience."

❖ Consider working for a judge as a **judicial law clerk** upon graduation from law school or as a **judicial extern** while a law student. "In addition to developing your writing skills, a clerkship can help you develop important contacts within the legal profession," explains Mary Mikva. Federal judges generally hire law students to work as their clerks for a period of one to two years after graduation.

❖ **Develop contacts in labor and employment law through bar association activities**. "Get involved in state, city, and American Bar Association committees that deal with labor and employment law," David Proctor recommends. "Bar association involvement allows you to learn about the latest trends in the field," says Mary Mikva, adding, "I'm involved in both the Chicago Bar Association (CBA) labor and employment committee and in the National Employment Lawyers Association (NELA). Both of these bar associations offer student memberships."

❖ "Join your law school's **student groups related to labor and employment law**," advises Tom Carpenter. "Sometimes the National Lawyers Guild or minority student groups have programs featuring speakers addressing issues such as racial or sexual discrimination in the workplace. The National Lesbian and Gay Law Association (NLGLA) is a professional association for gay and lesbian attorneys, and it can be a great place to make professional contacts."

❖ **Read widely to keep up with the latest issues and cases** in this rapidly changing field. "Pay attention to news stories about issues facing employers," suggests Richard Rabin. The *Wall Street Journal* and *New York Times* are excellent places to start.

❖ Demonstrate your **commitment to the labor and employment field** through your class work, your work experience, and your knowledge of the field. Says Mary Mikva, "When I'm hiring, it's more important to me that someone has a genuine interest in the field than the number of labor and employment law classes they've taken." Adds Richard Rabin, "Those who tend to be successful in the field of labor and employment law are those who are truly passionate about it."

LABOR AND EMPLOYMENT ATTORNEYS
INTERVIEWED FOR THIS SECTION

Tom Carpenter
American Federation of Television & Radio Artists
Chicago, Illinois
UNDERGRADUATE: Northwestern University
LAW SCHOOL: Chicago-Kent College of Law, Illinois Institute of Technology

Mary Mikva
Abrahamson Vorachek & Mikva
Chicago, Illinois
UNDERGRADUATE: Beloit College
LAW SCHOOL: Northwestern University School of Law

David Proctor
Johnston Barton Proctor & Powell LLP
Birmingham, Alabama
UNDERGRADUATE: Washington & Lee University
LAW SCHOOL: University of Alabama School of Law

Richard Rabin
Akin, Gump, Strauss, Hauer & Feld, L.L.P.
New York, New York
UNDERGRADUATE: University of Michigan
LAW SCHOOL: Georgetown University Law Center

Maryl Rosen
U.S. Postal Service Law Department
Chicago, Illinois
UNDERGRADUATE: Northwestern University
LAW SCHOOL: Chicago-Kent College of Law, Illinois Institute of Technology

Legislative Practice

What is Legislative Practice?

In the aftermath of the Columbine High School shootings in Colorado, a Colorado gun control advocacy group, Sane Alternatives to the Firearms Epidemic (SAFE), led by Denver attorney John Head, organized a "children's march" on Washington, D.C. On July 15, 1999, a group of about 95 Denver area high school students, including six from Littleton, descended on Capitol Hill on a mission to convince members of Congress to adopt more stringent gun control restrictions.

Most lobbyists have to persuade members of Congress to spend a few minutes with them, but the Denver students found politicians willing and even eager to meet with them. They met privately with President Bill Clinton and posed for pictures with Vice President Al Gore and Representative Richard Gephardt (D-MO), House Democratic Leader. They met with Colorado's two senators and six representatives as well as with more than 20 lawmakers thought to be swing voters on the issue of gun control.

Despite their extensive preparation for their meetings with legislators and their warm reception in the Capitol, the students soon learned that lobbying is an arduous process, and that it can be difficult at best to have an impact on a legislator's vote. One of the group's chaperones told the *New York*

Times that President Clinton's advice to the students was to increase the numbers of involved students in Colorado, create similar student groups in other states, and return for another lobbying effort next year.

Lawyers play an important role in the legislative process, working both for the government and for special interest groups at all levels of government. Lawyers work for senators, representatives, city council members, and other public servants, as well as for all types of government committees. In addition, they work for professional and trade associations and special interest groups, monitoring legislation that affects particular industries, such as health care, or interests, such as the environment; they also work as lobbyists. Law firm attorneys may also specialize in legislative and regulatory affairs.

Life as a Legislative Lawyer

Where do legislative lawyers work?

Attorneys specializing in legislative affairs may work for local, state, and federal senators, representatives, and legislative committees, as well as for governors, city councils, school boards, and more. They may also work in law firms, where they advocate on behalf of legislative and regulatory interests of corporations, trade associations, and units of local government. They draft and initiate legislation, participate in committee hearings, and assist in the passage or defeat of particular bills on issues as diverse as labor relations, environmental issues, and tax law.

Legislative attorneys also work for corporations such as insurance companies and auto companies, trade associations such as unions, and professional associations such as the American Dental Association. These attorneys track legislation affecting the industry and advise leaders of the corporation or members of the association of the effects of the legislation. Attorneys also work for special interest groups such as the Environmental Defense Fund, the American Medical Association, and the American Association of Retired Persons.

Three legislative attorneys are profiled in this chapter, but for more information about this type of practice, you can also read the profiles of Kim Otte and Jack Schroder in the Health Care Law chapter, Vickie Patton in the Environmental Law chapter, and Peter Hutt in the Government Contracts chapter.

Who are their clients and what types of issues do they work on?

Janna Day is a legislative affairs attorney at Fennemore Craig, a large law firm in Phoenix, Arizona. About eight of the 120 attorneys at Janna's firm specialize in government relations work. "We represent a variety of companies on legislative issues," says Janna. "Our clients range from international mining companies to defense contractors to local trade associations. For the most part, the clients I work with are headquartered in Arizona." Janna's work involves monitoring legislation and helping the client determine whether to take a position on the legislation. "In addition to the client counseling work we do, clients sometimes ask us to become involved proactively in legislative affairs. In that case we may be involved in drafting legislation and then formulating a strategy for its passage."

Maureen Shick works as the State Society Relations Manager for the American Academy of Dermatology in suburban Chicago. The American Academy of Dermatology (AAD) is a national professional association for physicians who specialize in the skin and its diseases. "My clients are the doctors who belong to the AAD as well as state dermatological societies," Maureen explains. "The academy is governed by a board of directors. Committees composed of physician volunteers advise the academy on all types of matters, including ethical and risk management issues. I staff the academy's medical and legal ethics committee and risk management committee, setting the agenda for the committees, determining what issues they may want to address, and responding to membership suggestions concerning what issues the committee should address."

Maureen says that her work is primarily policy work. "There are always fascinating issues at hand for consideration by the committees I oversee. Right now a big issue for the ethics committee is physician advertising. There's a great deal of debate about what constitutes fraudulent or unbecoming advertising. Advertising claims may be false, or they may be offensive to the profession. Another issue of importance to dermatologists is the issue of office-based dispensing—should medications be distributed from a dermatologist's office rather than a pharmacy? How much dispensing should a physician's office undertake? The risk management committee faces interesting issues, as well. A risk management task force has recommended that the Academy publish a Medicare compliance manual to help smaller dermatologists' offices find a compliance plan that works effectively for them."

Charles (Chuck) Clapton is counsel to the U.S. House of Representatives Committee on Commerce. "I'm one of several attorneys who work on oversight and investigations for the House Committee on Commerce," Chuck explains. "In addition, several other counsels assist the committee by handling policy issues. Those of us who conduct oversight review the actions of government agencies to determine whether there are instances of wrongdoing and work to ensure that the statutes governing agency conduct, including mandatory requirements and specific prohibitions, are complied with. The Committee deals with a broad range of issues, including health care, telecommunications, and energy; the Committee on Commerce has jurisdiction over much of the legislation that is passed by the House."

Though oversight counsels handle a wide array of issues within the jurisdiction of the Committee, Chuck primarily handles health care issues, including issues related to the Department of Health and Human Services, Medicare, and Medicaid. "With health care matters, I'm looking at how the agency bureaucrats implement policy. I investigate instances where policy decisions have left the Medicare and Medicaid programs vulnerable to fraud and abuse. I work with the policy counsels to design initiatives to respond to these problems. The policy counsels then actually write the bills to implement these initiatives and work to get them enacted."

Chuck's position as counsel for the Committee on Commerce is actually his third legislative job. After graduation from law school, Chuck started on Capitol Hill as a legislative aide for a Subcommittee of the Senate Judiciary Committee, which was chaired by Senator Arlen Specter of Pennsylvania. He then joined the personal office of U.S. Representative Harris W. Fawell of Illinois. "When I worked for Senator Specter, my clients were both the Senator and the 11 million citizens of the Commonwealth of Pennsylvania who were the Senator's constituents. In addition to the general committee work, I advised the Senator and his senior staff on important issues, represented the Senator in dealing with constituents, lobbyists, and others, and assisted constituents generally in their interactions with the federal government. For example, I worked on behalf of Pennsylvania residents to get a federal prisoner transferred to a prison in Pennsylvania in order to facilitate visits by aging family members. This project involved working closely with officials at the Federal Bureau of Prisons."

Chuck went from Senator Specter's staff to work as the counsel in Congressman Fawell's personal office. As the only lawyer in the office besides the Congressman, Chuck was called upon to research legal and policy issues relating to pending legislation. In addition, he tracked bills as they were considered by the House of Representatives, advising the Congressman on the underlying issues as well as amendments that had been offered. One of the first issues he handled involved an effort to force the resignation of Speaker Newt Gingrich, based on allegations that Gingrich had violated certain campaign finance laws through the operation of a non-profit educational foundation. Chuck had to review a multi-volume Committee Report, as well as case law on non-profit political activities and the statutory prescriptions of the campaign finance laws. He then had to distill this information into a brief summary memo for the Congressman, along with recommendations on how to vote on the matter.

What daily activities are involved in legislative practice?

Depending on the needs of their clients, legislative attorneys who work in law firms may spend their days advising clients, researching and reviewing legislative issues, drafting legislation, attending legislative hearings, and lobbying. Says law firm attorney Janna Day, "I am usually in and out of the office quite a bit—attending meetings and hearings at the legislature, business lunches with legislators and legislative staff members, and meetings with clients. When I am in the office, I spend a great deal of time on the phone with clients."

Chuck Clapton says that his work for the House Commerce Committee involves a number of different activities. "I spend about half my time writing letters to agencies involved in investigations asking them to produce documents relating to their actions. I also meet with special interest groups who advocate for the Committee to support their policy positions. This support could include writing to an agency, holding a hearing, or even introducing a bill that would attempt to address their particular concerns. One example of such a special interest group would be an association representing a particular field of health care providers, such as surgeons, chiropractors, or anesthetists, who believe that the reimbursements they receive from government funded health care programs are inadequate.

"Another major portion of my time is spent preparing for investigative, fact-finding hearings. For example, if there's a hearing concerning Medicare fraud, the whistle-blower [usually an employee alleging wrongdoing] comes to the hearing and testifies. The accused organization also testifies concerning their version of what transpired. The Members of the Committee will usually then subject all of the witnesses to rigorous questioning, which sheds additional light on the scope and nature of the problem and hopefully identifies potential solutions. We then work with the policy team to try to create more effective policies, to help address the problem and prevent the situation from recurring." (*See* the Government Contracts Practice chapter for more information on whistle-blowers.)

Chuck says that politics do play a role in his work for the Committee. "There are both Democrat and Republican staff members, and each side is trying to advance their partisan vision. So there is a lot of negotiating between Democrat and Republican staff regarding what will actually go into a bill. In some cases both parties will support passage of a bill but will disagree on the actual terms of the proposed legislation. In this case, the policy attorneys negotiate and fine-tune the provisions of the proposed bill."

"My job is tremendously varied in what I do from day to day," says Maureen Shick. "I focus on state legislative issues affecting our members. I constantly monitor legislation. I read lots of journals and news clippings to keep up, and I subscribe to a legislative search service that keeps me informed about legislative developments in all 50 states. As State Society Relations Manager, I am the liaison between the Academy and 47 state dermatological societies. I communicate with the state societies about what the academy is doing for them, and I go to as many state society meetings as possible, which means that in the spring and the fall, I'm on the road traveling from state to state. At the state society meetings, I am usually a speaker on the program, so some of my time is spent planning my speeches. I speak about what the academy is doing concerning government relations issues. I also listen to the concerns of our members and answer their questions. Though my focus is state issues, I have to know the federal issues—such as the federal controversy concerning a patients' 'Bill of Rights' concerning medical care—well enough to discuss them with the doctors and other professionals I meet at conferences and talk to over the phone." Maureen says that her job also involves providing leadership training to the volunteers who lead state societies. "I coach the state members concerning how they can better organize their society and how they can encourage their members to volunteer. I also speak at an annual national leadership conference for all state society leaders."

What do legislative lawyers find rewarding about their practice?

Many legislative attorneys find great satisfaction in the relationships they develop in their work with clients, legislators, government officials, and colleagues. "The most rewarding aspects of my jobs are the variety of issues I work on and the variety of people I meet on a daily basis," says Janna Day. "The legislative bar is a relatively small group of attorneys and everyone is very friendly, which makes the work especially enjoyable," she adds. Maureen Shick says that the dermatologists she works with are wonderful clients. "The doctors I work for are so appreciative of my work. They're vocal in their appreciation, which is especially rewarding. It's a pleasure to work with dermatologists—they're just particularly nice people!" Chuck Clapton says he has exceptional colleagues at the House Committee on Commerce. "The people I work with are great," he enthuses. "It's simply a superb staff. My colleagues are some of the brightest and hardest working people I've ever met, but are also very fun and exciting outside of the office as well."

Chuck reports that he finds tremendous satisfaction in working on public policy issues. "My job for the Committee on Commerce is really the most exciting and rewarding job I've ever had, because of the variety of issues I deal with and the fact that I'm in the midst of major policy debates. I can really feel at the end of the day that I've made a difference. It's especially rewarding to work on an issue as important as Medicare fraud, which has a major impact on American taxpayers, as well as the senior citizens who rely upon it to meet their health care needs." Chuck says that his work for Senator Specter and Representative Fawell were satisfying as well, in that they offered a chance to assist constituents with real-world problems and an opportunity to craft legislation as well as monitor legislative developments.

Maureen Shick enjoys the collaborative nature of her work. "One of my strengths is working in a team. Legislative work, with its emphasis on collaborative efforts, suits my personality," she says. Maureen also enjoys the opportunity to work on policy issues. "I love the legislative work that I do," she confides. "I became interested in legislative issues in high school, and I've been fortunate to find a career that involves something that I'm passionate about."

The Training and Skills Important to Legislative Practice

How do people enter the field of legislative practice?

Some attorneys who pursue this career path know from the time that they enter college that they want to pursue a career in legislative practice. Janna Day's goals were clear from the beginning. "I was always interested in the political arena—my family has long been involved in politics. I majored in political science as an undergraduate and did a college internship for a U.S. Senator in Washington, D.C. I entered law school with the intention of practicing government relations." Janna's legislative experience gave her the foundation she needed to begin law practice as part of a large firm's legislative practice department.

Maureen Shick developed an interest in legislative issues while in high school. "I worked for a state legislative staff before law school. I interned in Springfield, Illinois, for the Illinois House of Representatives and was hired for the house legislative staff after graduation. I had the opportunity to work on myriad issues, including health care." Maureen's work proved to be excellent preparation for law school and for her career in legislative practice.

Chuck Clapton says that he didn't become interested in legislative work until he was in law school. "Originally, I thought I would pursue a career in litigation, but before law school, and as a summer associate in a law firm, I met many attorneys who were dissatisfied in their jobs as litigators. I stumbled into legislative work through a combination of talking to practicing lawyers and taking law school classes that heightened my interest in the topic," Chuck explains.

Chuck nevertheless recommends exploring opportunities in legislative practice by working as an intern while in law school. "Unfortunately, I didn't do a Capitol Hill internship while I was in law school. Such internships are an invaluable means of gaining experience and developing contacts." Asked for his advice to law students, Chuck adds, "It's unrealistic to expect to work for a Congressional Committee immediately upon graduation from law school. I recommend working in the personal office of a Member of the House or a Senator in order to gain familiarity with how Congress works and in order to make contacts. The best way to get in the door is by knowing someone who knows of a position that's available or someone who is looking to hire."

"A good way to prepare for working in legislative affairs at a professional or trade association is by working on a legislative staff," advises Maureen

Shick. "Explore college and law school internships, as well as permanent positions for college graduates. Professional associations are supported by member dues. They have a small number of lawyers, and can't afford to train entry-level attorneys. They often hire attorneys who have worked in law firms and who know something about a particular profession from their law firm experience. When I finished law school, I worked at a large law firm in Chicago for two years, where I handled medical malpractice cases. My law firm experience, combined with my legislative experience in Springfield, gave me a taste of the legislative issues involved in health care," Maureen explains.

What skills are most important to legislative lawyers?

❖ The attorneys we talked to emphasized the importance of **communication skills**. "You must write clearly and speak effectively and with confidence," advises Maureen Shick. "All of your communication must inspire confidence in your clients—in my case, I must inspire confidence in the doctors with whom I work. They must be convinced that I'm familiar with all the legislative issues that impact them. Because they find me credible, they feel comfortable communicating their questions and concerns." Chuck Clapton agrees that communication skills are key. "The ability to research, write, and speak effectively are the most important skills for legislative attorneys," he says. "You can have a great resume, but if you can't communicate with a Member of Congress, if you can't articulate a policy—he or she won't give you even 15 seconds of their time."

❖ **Analytical skills** are also important to attorneys specializing in legislative issues. "You need to be able to see trends and emerging issues that will affect legislation and affect your membership or your client," says Maureen Shick. "You must be able to quickly analyze legislation and its effect," she adds. When legislation is pending, legislative attorneys are often called upon to make immediate recommendations to their clients, which requires apt analysis.

❖ Legislative attorneys must have a **high level of integrity**. "The most important quality for a legislative attorney is integrity," says Janna Day. "Your word must be as good as gold. Legislators and their staff members must be absolutely confident they can rely on you and that you will give them the information they need."

❖ Legislative attorneys must be **sensitive to both internal politics and governmental politics**. "When you work for an association, you become aware of many internal political issues," says Maureen Shick. "Associations are intensely political both in their structure and in their process. You have to be intuitive and sensitive and be careful about stepping on people's toes. And you have to be sensitive to the fact that you are working with volunteers who aren't paid for their work. You must be attuned to personal relationships and committed to creating effective relationships." Governmental politics are front and center as well, according to Chuck Clapton. "When you're dealing with members of Congress, you have to remember that politics is at the heart of things. In the end, this type of job is purely political. You have to be comfortable with the fact that you run the risk of losing your job with every election."

❖ Attorneys who specialize in this field should be **passionate about the legislative process**. "You've got to be able to understand how the government runs. You may have great ideas, but if you don't understand how the process works, you won't accomplish anything," says Chuck. "You've got to be genuinely fascinated by the crafting of legislation and the legislative process. In addition, when I worked for Senator Specter, I learned the importance of sublimating my personal views and beliefs while I worked on behalf of the Senator and his constituents. Sometimes you have to argue for a proposal that you don't personally support or against a proposal that you do support."

❖ **Negotiation skills** can help you become a successful legislative attorney. "Negotiation skills are key," says Chuck Clapton. "They help make your talks with legislators and their staff members productive. Negotiation skills take some time to develop and, though you can begin to develop them in law school, they are largely honed on the job."

What classes and law school experiences do legislative lawyers recommend?

❖ "**Law school classes in legislation** are helpful," says Chuck Clapton. A law school class in negotiation skills is also good preparation for a career in legislative practice. Maureen Shick recalls that her law school offered a negotiations competition that allowed law students to exercise their negotiation skills.

❖ **Law school classes such as moot court and trial advocacy, as well as undergraduate speech classes,** can help you sharpen your public speaking skills. Maureen Shick says that trial advocacy allowed her to develop confidence in her courtroom advocacy skills. That helped her work successfully as a trial attorney and helps her now that she is frequently invited to speak on legislative issues at state and national conferences. "Trial advocacy helped me get over that 'Oh my gosh I'm speaking in public' feeling. It helped me focus on the content of my message, and that has had a tremendous payoff," says Maureen.

❖ **Government internships while in law school or college** provide excellent preparation for a career in legislative practice. Internships also help you develop valuable contacts. While in college, Maureen Shick did an internship with the Library of Congress in Washington, D.C. "I worked for the Congressional Research Service, a non-partisan research arm of Congress. It was a very worthwhile internship. I researched health policy issues, and the internship gave me the experience I needed to move into health care legislative issues later in my career." Though Chuck Clapton didn't do an internship while in college or law school, he highly recommends seeking one. "Internships and informational interviews are the best way to learn about practice in the legislative area. One of the secrets of Capitol Hill is that most offices are dependent on having a pool of dedicated young volunteers to perform many of the day-to-day administrative duties of the office. By getting such a volunteer position, you can exchange your time for experience and contacts."

❖ **Begin to make contacts with attorneys and others in government.** "One way to learn about the legislative field and gain contacts is to volunteer on political campaigns," says Janna Day. Adds Chuck Clapton, "You can build a network of contacts by doing informational interviews with contacts you make through an internship or with alumni of your college or law school who work in legislative affairs. This will give you a better sense of how to get a particular job and tell you more about what different jobs are like."

LEGISLATIVE ATTORNEYS INTERVIEWED FOR THIS SECTION

Charles Clapton
House Committee on Commerce
Washington, D.C.
UNDERGRADUATE: Boston College
LAW SCHOOL: The Catholic University of America, Columbus School of
Law

Janna Day
Fennemore Craig, P.C.
Phoenix, Arizona
UNDERGRADUATE: Brigham Young University
LAW SCHOOL: Brigham Young University, J. Reuben Clark Law School

Maureen Shick
American Academy of Dermatology
Schaumburg, Illinois
UNDERGRADUATE: University of Illinois-Urbana
LAW SCHOOL: University of Illinois College of Law

*Editor's Note: Maureen Shick now works for the American Medical
Association.*

Military Judge Advocates/JAG

What is military practice?

Working simultaneously as military officers and as practicing attorneys, lawyers who are part of the military legal organizations have careers that are inherently filled with adventure. Hollywood has taken note of this exciting career path, highlighting the Judge Advocate General's Corps in a hit television drama aptly named *JAG* and in popular movies such as *A Few Good Men*.

Attorneys who work for the military are called judge advocates and work under the command of a Judge Advocate General (JAG): thus, military practice is often referred to as JAG practice or simply JAG. Each branch of the U.S. armed forces—the Army, Navy, Air Force, and Marines—has its own Judge Advocate General's Corps or Department (the Air Force JAG is a separate department but not actually a Corps). JAG attorneys work in both the civil and military court systems, and their clients are the government and members of the armed forces and their families. Upon accepting a commission to join the JAG, officers are obligated to serve for a period of three years, except in the Air Force, in which JAG officers are obligated to serve four years. Judge advocates are stationed both in the U.S. and around the world.

Upon becoming an officer, JAG attorneys attend a training program which emphasizes courtroom skills and includes classroom instruction on the Uniform Code of Military Justice, which is the military's own criminal code. The training program is designed to help attorneys develop litigation, negotiation, research, and client counseling skills. New JAG officers take on high levels of responsibility shortly after finishing the training program. They may work on a remarkably broad range of legal issues. Usually, they have the opportunity to practice in at least two areas of law during their first three- or four-year tour. Here are just a few of the areas in which they may gain experience:

Criminal Law: Often judge advocates gain litigation experience as prosecutors in military trials by courts-martial. These cases range from misdemeanors to felonies. Judge advocates also work as defense counsel for service members who are tried for violations of the Uniform Code of Military Justice.

Claims and Tort Litigation: The government is sometimes sued by a plaintiff who claims personal injury or property damage as a result of a government employee's negligent act. For example, a plaintiff might file a malpractice claim on the grounds that she was injured by the actions of a military physician or file a property damage claim alleging that his car was damaged in an accident in which the driver of the other car was a military officer. In these types of cases, JAG attorneys represent the government and oversee the resolution of these claims.

Legal Assistance: Judge advocates provide legal advice on a wide range of matters to service members, their families, and military retirees. They may provide personal income tax advice, write wills, assist with adoptions, and help resolve landlord-tenant matters.

Environmental Law: Military bases must comply with federal, state, and local environmental laws. Judge advocates provide advice to military officials on environmental law issues and represent the military before government regulatory agencies.

Civil Law Issues: Judge advocates advise military officials on a host of issues such as ethics, conflicts of interest, constitutional rights, the Freedom of Information Act, and civilian personnel issues.

Labor Law: Judge advocates represent the military in employment discrimination lawsuits and civil service labor disputes, as well as administrative hearings such as Equal Employment Opportunity Commission hearings.

Operational Law: In military actions such as Desert Storm, judge advocates provide legal advice to military leaders on such issues as the lawfulness of targets or the proper treatment of prisoners of war and also provide legal assistance to the service members who have been deployed to the area of conflict.

Contract Law: Army and Air Force JAGs are involved in the multibillion dollar development of new emerging technologies and the procurement of high tech weapons systems which the military needs to accomplish its mission. JAGs are involved in this increasingly complex acquisition cycle—from contract formation to contract award and administration, as well as litigation.

Whatever their area of practice, JAG attorneys tend to be very enthusiastic about their careers and particularly enjoy the abundance of varied practice opportunities and interesting assignment locations offered by the armed forces.

Life as a Judge Advocate

Where do judge advocates work?

JAG attorneys work at Air Force, Army, Marine, and Navy bases in the continental United States as well as in places such as Hawaii, Alaska, Europe, and Asia. Their areas of practice are remarkably varied, as described above.

Who are their clients and what types of cases do they work on?

Major Barbara Zanotti is a judge advocate for the U.S. Air Force. "My first year was in a base legal office," she explains. "I provided advice to commanders on a wide range of criminal matters in that job, and I advised military members, dependents, and their families on a variety of legal assistance issues. My next station was Travis Air Force Base in California, where I worked exclusively as a litigator. There I represented military criminal defendants in major felony cases, including rape, kidnaping, murder, and drug cases. I then moved to a civil litigation position specializing in utilities law. Although I had no previous experience in that discipline, I got excellent training and experience in the Air Force. We tried cases in U.S. District Courts and state utility commissions throughout the country." Barbara was then assigned to teach at the Air Force Judge Advocate General School at Maxwell Air Force Base in Montgomery, Alabama, where she taught trial advocacy, criminal procedure, and evidence. She was then given the opportunity to study for an LL.M. in Litigation and Alternate Dispute Resolution at George Washington University in Washington, D.C. "After completing my LL.M.," says Barbara, "I will head up the Air Force JAG Alternative Dispute Resolution Program." She adds enthusiastically, "My 11-year career has been a wonderful experience!"

Barbara notes that Air Force JAG attorneys begin their careers in a base office. "Each base has a judge advocate who is the senior attorney. Depending on the size of the base, the office may have one to 10 other lawyers on its staff. Those attorneys handle the problems of the base much as a city council would do for a local government. Like local government, they handle matters such as tax issues, labor issues, environmental problems, and so on." Barbara notes that military members and their dependents are authorized to use the base office for legal advice. "Military members turn to the base office for help drafting wills, doing estate planning, and putting together income tax returns. The attorneys also help with landlord-tenant issues and consumer issues such as debt management. The only thing we can't do is represent the military members in court. They would need a private attorney to represent them in something like a divorce. But we can provide advice and counseling."

Captain Mary Card works as a JAG attorney for the U.S. Army. She is stationed at Camp Humphreys, Korea. "I am the Chief of Legal Assistance for Camp Humphreys, Korea," says Mary. "I work in an office with two other attorneys—a prosecutor and the command judge advocate who advises commanders. The area that I serve has approximately 9,000 active duty soldiers, civilians, and retirees. The majority of my clients are active duty soldiers. I also serve civilian employees, spouses of active duty soldiers, and retirees and their spouses. Camp Humphreys is located in Pyongtaek, Korea (two hours south of Seoul). I also serve Suwon Air Force Base in

Suwon, Korea, and Camp Long and Camp Eagle in Wonju, Korea. My clients are individual soldiers, not the United States Army as an institution. Therefore, I develop an attorney-client privilege with the individual soldier."

The range of Mary's duties is staggering. "In addition to being Chief of Legal Assistance, I am the Officer in Charge of the Tax Center, which is open from January to April every year. We prepare and file taxes electronically and maintain income tax forms for all states. I am the installation Victim Witness Liaison. In that capacity I assist victims and witnesses by answering questions about the military justice system, providing referrals to services, and offering support during courts-martial. I am a trial observer under appointment of the U.S. Ambassador. This means that I observe trials of American soldiers in Korean courts to ensure that their rights are protected. I am also a Condolence Payment Officer. In that capacity I make payments on behalf of the Army to surviving family members of civilian employees. I am an alternative representative to the Case Review Committee [CRC]. The CRC reviews all cases of domestic violence and child abuse and makes recommendations to the chain of command on courses of action. Lastly, I am the Hearing Officer for driving license revocations and suspensions. I perform this role for anyone violating traffic laws on Camp Humphreys."

As a Judge Advocate for the U.S. Navy, Lieutenant Commander Robert (Rob) Taishoff handles a wide range of challenging cases. He is currently Chief Prosecutor for the Naval District Legal Services Office in Washington, D.C. "In this job, I've had the opportunity to try some of the Navy's most complex, most 'high-viz' cases. Most of these cases attract both local and national media attention," he comments.

"My caseload is extremely varied," says Rob. "It includes all common law offenses as well as military offenses falling under the punitive articles of the Uniform Code of Military Justice [UCMJ]. Some of our typical military cases involve the distribution and use of drugs, assaults, larceny, and absence offenses [unauthorized absence and/or desertion under the UCMJ]. One drug case I prosecuted involved an accused charged and convicted of possession, distribution, and use of a large quantity of LSD. The investigation involved a reverse sting operation caught on both audio and video tape. The trial lasted five days and was tried before a panel of military members—a military jury."

One of the interesting cases Rob has worked on over the years was tried while he was working as a Navy defense counsel. "My client was a Chief Petty Officer attached to a ship on deployment in the Persian Gulf during Desert Storm. The Chief was accused of attempted rape and aggravated assault upon a British National, an event that allegedly occurred while he was on shore leave in the country of Bahrain. Since the ship and all of the witnesses were located out of the country, the command decided to convene the pre-trial investigation in Bahrain. The prosecutor, investigating officer, my client, and I were flown to the Persian Gulf during the war in order to investigate the charges. The courts-martial was ultimately held in San Diego. As a young judge advocate, I was extremely impressed with the overwhelming obligation on the part of the Navy to see to it that my client got a fair and speedy hearing. I was intrigued by the thrill of flying halfway around the world to perform my duties as a trial attorney."

Rob described for us the many interesting jobs he's had during his career as a judge advocate. "During my first tour in San Diego, I spent 24 months as a trial defense counsel. Most of my time was spent in the courtroom or at my desk in preparation for trial. At any one time I carried and managed a minimum of 25 of my own cases." Rob's next job was as an Assistant Professor at the U.S. Naval Academy. "At only 29 years old, I was already a college professor at one of the nation's premier institutions of higher learning. During my two and a half years at the Academy, I was personally involved in the professional development of nearly 600 Naval Officers. I instructed the midshipmen in the areas of military justice, administrative law, and international law." Next Rob took a temporary one-year assignment at the U.S. Department of State. In this position, he says, "I orchestrated the Navy's defense effort involving a multibillion dollar international claim filed by Iran."

Rob points out that judge advocates have the opportunity to be both prosecutors and defense counsel. "In my role as defense counsel, I represented military clients, both officer and enlisted. These individuals faced criminal charges at courts-martial. As a prosecutor, I was responsible for the provision of prosecutorial legal services and advice to 125 individual commands with 30,000 officers and enlisted personnel all within the greater Washington metropolitan area."

What daily activities are involved in a judge advocate's practice?

The daily activities in which a judge advocate is involved vary significantly depending on the nature of his or her assignment. For a judge advocate who is a civil or criminal litigator, daily activities are similar to those of attorneys engaged in private practice, explains Barbara Zanotti. "The judge advocate's typical day would be like that of any trial lawyer with a particular area of expertise. If they're an environmental litigator or a utilities law litigator, they would be engaged in discovery and gathering of facts, as those areas tend to be very document intensive. If they're working as a prosecutor or defense lawyer, they may be interviewing witnesses and building their case." Military attorneys often have administrative duties, as well. Rob Taishoff says that in addition to the time he spends handling cases, he spends time managing his office. "I supervise an office with three attorneys, two court reporters, and several paralegals," he says.

As Chief of Legal Assistance for Camp Humphreys, Mary Card's top priority is attending to her clients. "I spend most of my time with clients as their individual legal counsel. This includes serving civilians and retirees that are entitled by Army Regulation to legal assistance services. I provide legal advice on military law, consumer law, domestic relations law, landlord-tenant relations, wills, debt issues, efficiency report appeals, and bankruptcy. I conduct legal research, prepare memoranda and legal correspondence, and represent clients in negotiations. I also prepare and present preventative law classes and briefings and maintain and update preventative law hand-outs to give to my clients. In addition, I supervise two civilian employees and two soldiers," she says. "I also visit Camps Long and Eagle, which are in remote locations of Korea, twice a month to provide legal assistance services.

"No two cases have ever been the same!" Mary observes. "The soldiers and civilians that I serve are from all 50 states and some are Korean Nationals. A typical client meeting may be scheduled or may be a walk-in appointment." Mary may meet with the client once or schedule a series of meetings. "When I meet with the client, the client outlines his or her legal problems or questions, and I determine what further information I need from the client; whether there is something I can do for the client immediately, such as make a call or prepare a letter; or if the problem will entail further research. I try to empower my clients as much as I can by giving them directions on things that they can do to help with their cases and things they can do to prevent such problems in the future."

What do judge advocates find rewarding about their practice?

Not surprisingly, the JAG attorneys we talked to enjoyed the immense variety of practice opportunities they are afforded by the military. "I have really enjoyed the variety of challenging jobs the Navy JAG Corps has to offer," says Rob Taishoff. "As evident from my own nine-plus years of active duty, I have done everything from litigation to teaching at the U.S. Naval Academy and working at the State Department. The opportunities are almost boundless. Additionally, as a judge advocate, you have the unique opportunity to pursue a dual career as an attorney and as a Naval Officer with all the professional rewards associated with both."

"One of the rewarding things about working as a judge advocate is that there's always an opportunity to move on to a new position and new challenges. The Air Force does an outstanding job of providing new opportunities," says Barbara Zanotti. "If you're interested in a particular area, even if you don't have training in the area, the Air Force will provide that training. You're encouraged to try new things." When Barbara was assigned to do utility law cases, she had experience as a litigator but not as a utilities lawyer. "The Air Force gave me the training I needed to work effectively in the field," she says. "One of my favorite cases that I've worked on—a case that was especially personally rewarding and satisfying—was a utilities case. It involved a sewer line that was used both by an Air Force base and by a private developer. The stakes were high—the potential exposure for the Air Force was high. The case involved legally complex issues that were just fascinating, including contracts issues and environmental issues."

Barbara adds that judge advocates have tremendous autonomy, even at the earliest stages in their careers. "You get great experience from the very beginning. As you gain seniority, you take on cases of greater significance. When you have a case, the case is yours to handle. There are people there to help you, but you make the decisions. As you become more senior, you have a chance to pass on your expertise to less senior judge advocates. When you're advising other litigators, you have all of the fun and none of the stress!" says Barbara, laughing. But with great seriousness, she adds, "This chance to pass along your experience and insight, to delegate responsibility and authority, to make a difference in someone else's career, is very rewarding." Barbara says that this attitude flows from the top down. "At every level you have tremendous support from your superiors."

Mary Card enjoys the unique opportunity her job gives her to help others. "My sole mission as a legal assistance attorney is to help others, and that is truly rewarding. I am serving in the Republic of Korea in a support capacity and am assisting soldiers as they serve a hardship tour. While all legal problems can be stressful, it is particularly complicated when you are an active duty soldier living in a foreign country serving a hardship tour. It gives me great satisfaction to get results for my clients and to make life a little easier for those serving here.

"One of the things that I really like about JAG," Mary continues, "is the wide variety of practice areas. As an attorney you can work claims, administrative law, international law, legal assistance, operational law. You can prosecute, defend, and everything in between. Whatever your area of interest in law school, you can aspire to work in that area in the JAG Corps."

Her commitment to helping others makes Mary value the diverse roles she plays in her own job. "I find personal fulfillment in my role as a member of the Case Review Committee and as the Victim Witness Liaison. My area of interest in law school was domestic violence, and the Army has given me tremendous opportunities to continue this work. The Army sponsored my attendance at a Joint Service Family Advocacy Course. I was asked to speak at an installation dinner during Domestic Violence Awareness Month and also at a recent Camp Humphreys Women's Health Forum. I really appreciate these opportunities," she says.

Life as a military attorney is not without its humorous moments as well, Mary reports, recalling a particular incident. "Every soldier participates in field exercises where they train with their weapons and equipment," she explains. "One of my duties is to draft and execute wills. One afternoon after drafting a will for a client, I went to the waiting room to ask for three volunteers to serve as witnesses. One soldier who volunteered had just come from his field training and was carrying his M-16 over his shoulder. When it came time for me to ask if my client was executing the will voluntarily and without any duress or coercion, he looked uneasily at the witness with the M-16. We all just had to laugh! This would never happen in civilian practice!"

Barbara Zanotti adds that one of the "fringe benefits" of working as a judge advocate is developing a worldwide network of friends. "I truly have friends around the world," she remarks enthusiastically. When we interviewed Barbara, she had just received an invitation to visit military friends who had recently been assigned to Italy. "They want me to celebrate the New Year with a ski trip to Italy!"

The attorneys we talked to have greatly enjoyed their years as military lawyers. "Working as a judge advocate has been a wonderful experience," says Barbara Zanotti. "It's been 11 years now. I initially thought I would only stay the required four years. But the Air Force has delivered on every promise it has made to me, and it keeps giving me offers I can't refuse."

Mary Card has also enjoyed the JAG way of life. "It's been fabulous so far," she says. "I have had so many opportunities to travel, to do things I never thought I would do—such as fire an M-16, fly in a Blackhawk, and view North Korea from the DMZ [Demilitarized Zone]—and most importantly to be of service to my country."

The Training and Skills Important to Judge Advocates

How do people become judge advocates?

Barbara Zanotti explains that there are several ways to enter JAG. The first is through "direct commission." This means that you go to law school on your own and, while in law school, apply to JAG. The military often recruits new judge advocates through law school on-campus interviewing programs. If JAG doesn't recruit at your campus, you can gather further information at recruiting offices, through the Internet, or through the career services office at your law school. The process, Barbara says, "is highly competitive." She notes that recruits must also meet certain physical standards and attend a JAG training school.

Some judge advocates are already commissioned (have military status) because they are involved in Reserve Officer Training Corps (ROTC) while in college. These prospective law students ask to delay active duty until they can complete law school. Other judge advocates begin as officers on active duty. They then apply to law school, asking the military to pay for their legal education.

Certain JAG attorneys know from the start that they want to be military lawyers. "I began inquiring into a career as a judge advocate during my first year of law school," says Rob Taishoff. "I was first attracted to the career because I desired to serve my country as a Naval Officer. As time went on and I learned more about the JAG Corps, I realized that JAG offered a unique opportunity to move right into the practice of law upon graduation. I had immediate responsibility for a full docket of criminal cases within my first six months of practice. Additionally, the starting pay and benefits are extremely competitive."

Other judge advocates didn't envision themselves as military lawyers when they entered law school. This was the case for Mary Card. "I did not have any prior military experience, I was not in ROTC, and my family did not have a strong military tradition. I think initially it was more curiosity than anything that caused me to sign up for an interview with an Army JAG recruiter during the spring of my second year of law school. I met with a dynamic female JAG attorney who absolutely loved her job and her Army experience. Her enthusiasm was contagious," Mary confides. "I filled out my application that night."

Mary's JAG application story has a storybook ending—or perhaps we should say a storybook beginning. She took a summer job with the Army as a civilian intern in Germany between her second and third years of law school. "I worked for the U.S. Army Claims Service in Mannheim and focused on tort law and adjudicating claims. The work was challenging and the people that I worked with were inspiring. They had traveled all over the world serving their country and warmly welcomed me into their community. I was able to travel extensively on the weekends (eight countries in two months!). The day that I left Germany, a Captain gave me a card that contained a set of Army Captain's Bars [military insignia]. He urged me to 'be all I could be' and as soon as I returned to law school I applied for a direct commission."

What skills are most important to judge advocates?

❖ Strong **writing skills** are important to military attorneys. "No matter what job you're doing in the military, writing is critically important," says Barbara Zanotti. "Communication with the base commander is often done in writing."

❖ Excellent **persuasive speaking skills** are critical to those who are working simultaneously as military officers and as lawyers. "All military officers are trained to speak and to write," explains Barbara Zanotti. "Military officers have been using persuasive techniques and demonstrative techniques in their presentations for ages. You are communicating with a sophisticated audience. You must be able to analyze a problem and present your analysis to a high level military officer in a succinct and persuasive way. Your communications must be short, sweet, and to the point."

❖ Well-developed **advocacy skills**, especially the ability to listen, are key to the success of the JAG attorney. "Every day I work on developing and maintaining my advocacy skills," explains Mary Card. "As a legal assistance attorney, I want to be a patient and understanding listener so that I can fully understand the client's issues and questions. And I want to be a strong advocate so that I can protect the interests of my clients and effectively meet their needs."

❖ JAG attorneys need to be committed to being **team players**. "You need to be able to see and analyze issues and call them the way you see them," notes Barbara Zanotti. "You may see the problem differently than your boss, and you may try to persuade him or her to agree with you. But once the decision is made, you need to respect the decision your superior has made. You owe loyalty to your boss. No senior JAG attorney wants a 'yes' person below, as they want to depend on your independent judgment; but on the other hand, they don't want someone undercutting their experience and authority. In the military the people who help each other are very successful. The military provides an environment in which you can develop while helping others develop. It's a teamwork approach."

❖ Because JAG attorneys are often entrusted with a large range of issues to work on, and because the stakes are high, strong **organizational skills** are helpful, advises Rob Taishoff.

❖ **Resourcefulness** is another skill important to the JAG attorney. "There's more than one way to solve a problem, and it's important to realize that," explains Mary Card. "Resourcefulness is an especially valuable skill here in Korea, where time differences, language barriers, and sometimes less-than-reliable phone and fax capability can be frustrating."

❖ Perhaps most importantly, JAG attorneys must be **committed to their role as military officers**. Barbara Zanotti explains it this way: "You have to be able to be a good military officer, in terms of the way you lead your life, in terms of your core values, in terms of your integrity. We believe in excellence in all we do and service before self. These values may impact your personal life in a variety of ways, and you must be clear about your commitment." Mary Card says emphatically, "To be a successful Army JAG attorney, it's important to realize that you're not only an attorney, but an Officer in the United States Army. Both carry rights and responsibilities. Being a JAG attorney is more than just a job. When you join the JAG Corps, you are adopting a way of life."

What classes and law school experiences do judge advocates recommend?

❖ Because the military involves a lifestyle commitment, being a **well-rounded law student** is important. "If you're at the top of the class and that's all you've done, that may not be enough. Students who have handled job responsibilities, taken care of families, or were involved in civic activities while studying law, for instance, demonstrate an ability to master several things at once, which can make the difference between being selected and not being selected as a JAG," says Barbara Zanotti.

❖ A **wide range of law school classes** is helpful. "Most attorneys starting out in the Army JAG Corps will be legal assistance attorneys, helping people with a variety of problems," says Mary Card. "A strong background in the basics is vital."

❖ **Trial advocacy and moot court classes** can help you develop your litigation skills. "The most important classes by far were trial advocacy and moot court programs," asserts Rob Taishoff.

❖ **Clinical programs**, in which you work with clients on real legal problems, can prepare you for the responsibilities you will take on in the JAG. "Right off the bat you're advising clients," says Barbara Zanotti, "so clinical programs are very helpful." Barbara says that while in law school, she worked as a summer intern in a state's attorney's office, where she handled misdemeanor cases under the supervision of an attorney. "I handled a lot of 'vicious dog' cases that summer," Barbara remembers. "What murder cases are to felonies, dog bite cases are to misdemeanors in terms of the drama and the emotions of the parties involved. It was great experience. I was actually trying cases the summer before my third year of law school." Mary Card also highly recommends clinical experience. "Being a legal assistance attorney is similar to the work I did in the Families and the Law Clinic at Catholic University Law School. Clinical work helps you develop the skills you need." Rob Taishoff also praises clinical experience. "Internships and practical experience such as legal aid clinics go a long way toward preparing an individual for a JAG career. The operative words are *practical experience*, because that is exactly what you get right away as a JAG attorney."

❖ **Public speaking experience** can help you sharpen your communications skills. "While an undergraduate, I participated in a reader's theater group. Practicing your public speaking skills really helps you get over any nervousness you have about making presentations," explains Barbara Zanotti.

❖ **Meet people who work as JAG attorneys.** This is perhaps the best way to determine whether JAG is for you. "Anyone interested in a career as a Navy Judge Advocate should begin developing contacts right away," advises Rob Taishoff. "One way to accomplish this is to volunteer as an intern at a Naval Legal Services Office." You may also want to investigate civilian internships such as the one Mary Card described earlier. Recruiters are always happy to talk with students interested in JAG.

❖ **Learn all you can about the military.** There's a great deal of information available on the Internet. Another way to learn about the military is to review special interest publications. "If you're interested in the Navy, for example, you can subscribe to a Navy publication such as *Proceedings* magazine or the *Navy Times*. The more a lawyer knows and understands the needs and concerns of his or her client, the better the level of representation," advises Rob Taishoff.

MILITARY JUDGE ADVOCATES INTERVIEWED FOR THIS SECTION

Captain Mary Card
U.S. Army, Judge Advocate General's Corps
Camp Humphreys, Korea
UNDERGRADUATE: The Catholic University of America
LAW SCHOOL: The Catholic University of America Columbus School of Law

Lieutenant Commander Robert Taishoff
U.S. Navy, Naval Legal Service Office, National Capital
Washington, D.C.
UNDERGRADUATE: Syracuse University
LAW SCHOOL: Widener University School of Law

Major Barbara Zanotti
U.S. Air Force
Washington, D.C.
UNDERGRADUATE: West Virginia University
LAW SCHOOL: West Virginia University College of Law

Editor's Note: Since we interviewed Rob Taishoff, he has served as Senior Defense Counsel at the Naval Legal Service Office in Washington, D.C., and he is currently serving as Command Judge Advocate and Legal Department Head on board the USS George Washington, a nuclear powered Nimitz class aircraft carrier. Mary Card is now stationed in Germany.

Municipal
Finance Practice

What is Municipal Finance Law?

Though their adventures are unlikely to be portrayed in the latest John Grisham novel, municipal finance lawyers do engage in a special kind of heroics. They are the lawyers who procure funds to build schools, roads, libraries, public transportation systems, parks, and numerous other facilities provided by state and local governments that enhance our daily quality of life.

Instead of using taxes, which may unfairly appropriate current revenues, a municipality will often finance its major infrastructure projects by issuing municipal bonds. The municipal finance attorney may represent various parties involved in the bond offering, such as the municipality, the underwriter, or a financial institution. Municipal finance lawyers see the results of their efforts not in the bonds that are issued but rather in the school or library or bridge that is built.

Municipalities, including states, counties, school districts, special districts such as park districts, and statutory authorities such as the water reclamation authority or state highway commission, issue securities (debt obligations in the form of bonds, notes, or other securities) that are then sold to investors by underwriters. The underwriters, which include investment banks and other financial institutions, generally purchase an entire municipal security issue and then resell the securities to investors. (*See* the Securities Law chapter for further discussion of this process.) The proceeds that the issuer receives from the sale are then used to finance public projects such as airports, streets, and parks. The issuers may also loan the proceeds to non-profit corporations, such as hospitals, for building or renovation projects.

Municipal finance attorneys generally represent either the municipality issuing the securities or the underwriter who purchases and resells the securities to investors. There are many federal and state laws that govern the issuance of securities, as well as local laws that govern when a municipality may or may not seek such financing. Municipal finance attorneys must be familiar with these provisions. They must also be comfortable working with federal and state tax laws, as complex tax issues arise and certain requirements must be fulfilled in order for a municipal bond to acquire tax-exempt status, a key selling point in offering the bonds to the public.

When a municipal finance attorney represents the issuing municipality, he or she drafts the documentation relating to the issuance of the securities, including documents that establish the validity of the securities and verify the federal tax exemption, as well as any applicable state tax exemptions. Municipal finance attorneys who assist the bond issuers may also advise the municipality concerning how to structure the bond issue to meet the municipality's financial and business needs, as well as how to satisfy the referendum or other local requirements authorizing the bond offering.

As with any offer of the sale of securities, those attorneys representing the underwriter usually draft the necessary documents to be submitted to the government, including documents submitted to the Securities and Exchange Commission (SEC), a federal agency that administers securities laws. Another of the attorney's responsibilities is drafting the SEC Rule 10b-5 opinion, an opinion in which the underwriter confirms the accuracy of the information contained in documents that describe the municipal project to prospective investors. In addition, the attorneys for the underwriter often draft the contract between the underwriter and the issuer for the initial sale of the securities.

Life as a Municipal Finance Lawyer

Where do municipal finance lawyers work?

Most municipal finance lawyers work in law firms, often in large firms that have municipal finance departments. Federal government agencies (primarily the SEC) and state government commissions also employ attorneys who work on municipal securities issues. Attorneys who work for banks, financial institutions, and municipalities may also be involved in municipal finance issues.

Who are their clients and what types of issues do they work on?

Patricia (Pat) Curtner is a municipal finance lawyer at the law firm of Chapman and Cutler in Chicago. Pat's clients are government entities of all types and sizes, as well as underwriters and investment bankers. "The government entities are mostly concentrated in Illinois and include cities, towns, library districts, park districts, school districts, and sanitary districts—some of which are very small and some of which are very large," she says. Pat reports that she works on a wide variety of transactions. "They range from very simple and routine transactions to very large and complicated 'hair-raising' transactions. One of the simple transactions could be a $100,000 general obligation bond issue for a school district or park district that doesn't involve complex state or federal tax issues. A complex transaction could be a $300 million multilayer transaction with 15 interested parties and complicated tax and legal questions."

As a municipal finance attorney at Kutak Rock, a large law firm in Omaha, Nebraska, John Petr serves three types of institutional clients: (1) political subdivisions such as cities, counties, states, and their agencies which issue bonds; (2) investment bankers who underwrite or privately place municipal debt offerings; and (3) credit enhancers who guarantee or insure municipal debt obligations. The work he does for each group of clients varies. John explains, "Political subdivision clients generally employ me to serve as 'bond counsel.' In that capacity I am responsible for drafting the principal financing documents, for ensuring compliance with applicable state law and federal law regarding the issuance of federally tax-exempt bonds, and for rendering the central opinions regarding enforceability of the municipal debt obligations and the federal tax-exempt status of such obligations." John adds that his investment banking clients have somewhat different needs. "Investment banking clients generally require advice regarding compliance with applicable federal securities laws, assistance in preparing disclosure materials relative to a contemplated bond offering, and advice as to state and federal laws which impact the structuring of the transaction in question." John says that when he acts as a counsel for a credit enhancer, "It's similar to acting as a lender's counsel in a conventional commercial transaction." His duties include "reviewing the various transaction documents to ensure that the interests of my client in avoiding any unreimbursed credit losses is, to the greatest possible extent, protected."

Charles DeWitt, Jr., works as a municipal finance lawyer at the law firm of Palmer & Dodge LLP in Boston. Charles has a specialized practice within municipal finance—he works on the financing of transportation projects. "My clients are almost always public sector transportation agencies, such as the Puerto Rico Highways and Transportation Authority, the Federal Highway Administration, the Massachusetts Turnpike Authority, and the Albany County Airport Authority. I work with the agencies when they are planning the construction of large transportation projects. Our client base is national; the clients need sophisticated advice on procurement of funds and financial matters. Usually the complications of constructing large projects require innovative plans to construct the project, and they always tax the financial resources of the proponent agency.

"An example of the type of projects we work on would be the construction of the Tren Urbano Project in San Juan, Puerto Rico," explains Charles. "We helped design a first-of-its-kind design/build model for a new transit system that reduced the time of planning, design, and construction for such a project from 15 years to five years. We drafted all of the design/build contract documents. We met regularly with the client to provide advice on environmental review issues, financial plans, right of way acquisition, and other problems that arise in such large projects," he says.

What daily activities are involved in municipal finance practice?

Municipal finance lawyers spend much of their time counseling clients and drafting and reviewing the documents involved in the transactions on which they work. John Petr says, "My typical days assume two different forms, depending on whether I'm in the office or out of the office. When I'm in my office, roughly half of each day is spent on the phone—talking with clients, other professionals involved in the transactions on which I'm currently working, and other attorneys within my firm. The phone time is devoted to discussing ideas for new transactions and trying to resolve problems and negotiate issues in pending deals. The other half of a typical day in my office is spent reviewing and/or drafting documents." John says that about 10% of his days are spent outside the office. "On those days, I'm traveling to or from, or participating in, transaction closings and face to face document negotiations."

John reports that a typical project involves procuring "federally tax-exempt financing for the construction of a new multifamily housing project, a portion of which will be occupied by low-income persons and families." He explains the steps involved in the transaction. "The transaction begins with a conference call or meeting to establish the basic parameters of the transaction, to assign roles to the participating professionals, to establish a timetable, and to outline the structure of the proposed debt issuance," he says. "The deal progresses with an exchange of draft documents, review of such documents by the interested parties, and approval of the documents and other transactions by the relevant political subdivision and the credit rating agency involved. Finally, the principal parties typically gather in a central location to finalize and sign documents and 'close' the transaction." John says that closings can be nerve-racking. "Closings are often tense and unpredictable events, involving small armies of professionals struggling to meet rapidly approaching deadlines, with the fate of substantial projects and large sums of money at stake. As the transaction team struggles to conclude the transaction, interesting, unusual, and unexpected problems can arise and they have to be dealt with quickly."

Pat Curtner reports that she spends a great deal of her time counseling clients. "Client counseling involves hand-holding, problem-solving, and talking the client through the various alternatives that are available for their situation. It's a tremendous investment of time. I believe that it's every bit as important to tell clients what won't work in a particular situation as it is to tell them what will work. Usually there's a wide range of potential solutions or paths to follow to obtain financing, depending on whether the client wants to borrow short range or long range, whether the client wants a bond referendum or not, etc. Each client issue is like a decision tree with lots of branches. My job is to find the most effective way to accomplish the client's goal."

Pat says that drafting and reviewing documents and organizing paper flow is another important part of her job. "I draft the documentation that I am responsible for, and I review the written products of other lawyers. On a simple transaction, I might be working on my own. But on a large transaction, I am working with many different lawyers—typically from outside the firm—who are representing multiple interests." Pat's work also involves legal research. "The research is less about looking at old case law and more about reading statutes and codes and determining how to parse a statute or provision," she says.

Pat also spends time consulting with other lawyers at her firm. Chapman and Cutler has approximately 40 municipal finance lawyers, including Pat, who work exclusively with issues related to municipal bonds, and numerous corporate, securities, banking, public utilities, and bankruptcy lawyers who also participate in municipal transactions. "Consistency and unity of position are important as we work with our clients. I consult with my partners to make sure that another partner in the firm would feel comfortable taking the position that we're taking. There's a fair need to build consensus," explains Pat. Pat also fits public speaking into her already busy schedule. She speaks to bar association groups and trade industry groups. "This is a specialty area that has grown and changed in the 20 years that I've been practicing. I've had the opportunity to do a lot of speaking engagements in which I share my knowledge of the practice."

Like John Petr and Pat Curtner, Charles DeWitt spends much of his time counseling clients. "On a typical day, I spend the majority of my time advising clients about matters involving the intersection of law, policy, and politics. Over half of the advice is rendered in person and the remainder by telephone. Because of the complexity of the problems my clients face, most advice is discussed in meetings of a reasonably long duration with the agency policymakers. When I am not providing advice, most of my time is in consultation with other firm attorneys to develop reasonable alternative solutions for the client."

What do municipal finance lawyers find rewarding about their practice?

The municipal finance lawyers we talked to enjoyed the intellectual challenge of the issues they work on. Explains Charles DeWitt, "The largest reward in my practice is to solve complicated legal, policy, and political issues in a way that leads to the completion of large projects." John Petr says the complex legal issues involved in his work constantly lead to new challenges. "I enjoy the wide range of substantive legal areas relevant to my practice. Every transaction involves issues in contracts, real estate, securities law, municipal corporations, and tax, and the diversity helps keep the work fresh," says John.

Pat Curtner says that another enjoyable aspect of practice in this area is the fact that she works both on her own and in a team setting. "The practice offers an interesting combination of group time and solitary time. When I'm writing a 200-page trust indenture [a written agreement under which bonds are issued], I'm on my own, with time to retreat and reflect on the legal issues, time to reconsider and revise, and time to make sure that my writing reflects exactly what the client wants. This time spent in solitude is tempered with a lot of phone and personal contact with other people working on the deals with you. It's a great combination of activities."

Because much of a municipal finance lawyer's time is spent counseling clients, it's not surprising to hear that client relationships are an aspect of their practice that these lawyers find particularly rewarding. "I really like my client counseling work," says Pat Curtner. "I work hard to help clients find the best solution. It takes time to talk over the advantages and disadvantages of a particular solution. Spending so much time with clients isn't the best way to enhance the bottom line in terms of profitability, but it's satisfying to spend my time doing what I believe lawyers are supposed to do—working as counselors and advocates for their clients." John Petr also finds reward in the relationships he develops with clients and fellow professionals. "What I enjoy most about my practice are the personal and professional relationships I've developed during the course of my career," John says. "My practice is in a niche area, and the professionals involved in particular transactions are often old acquaintances from other, earlier deals. It's relatively easy to forge comfortable personal relationships with the individuals involved."

One of the exciting aspects of municipal finance practice is that lawyers can actually visit the public works projects that were financed and completed thanks to their efforts. Says Charles DeWitt, "It's a great feeling to look at a complete project and say, 'I had something to do with that project.'" Pat Curtner is equally enthusiastic about seeing the results of her efforts. "I like the fact that there are tangible results to my work. My colleagues and I feel that as municipal finance lawyers we actually change the face of Chicago." Pat says that she can't help but feel good about her work as she drives around Chicago and its suburbs. "When I drive around the area, I can actually see the capital development. I see everything from small schools where we developed a way to finance fire safety protection programs to huge new corporate campuses developed for Fortune 100 companies. I know that I actually played a part in making these projects a reality."

Pat finds it satisfying to know that the projects in which she's involved better people's lives. "The schools we finance are among the few safe places that some students have. The teachers we figure out how to pay for have a substantial influence on the lives of young people. The roads, sewers, and other infrastructures we help finance make a real difference in the quality of people's day-to-day lives."

Another thing Pat enjoys about the practice is that the lawyers involved are generally interested in accomplishing a common goal. "The goal is to get the transaction done on time and get it done right. It's collegial that way. Every lawyer involved has a common goal—to get the deal done," says Pat. John Petr makes a similar observation. "The parties are working together toward a common goal—closing the deal. The atmosphere of a typical transaction tends, therefore, to be collegial and non-adversarial."

The Training and Skills Important to Municipal Finance Law

How do people enter the field of municipal finance law?

Some people, like Pat Curtner, enter law practice knowing that they want to pursue municipal finance practice. Pat returned to law school when her two children were two and seven years of age. Pat was highly involved in school politics, and her interest in municipal finance law was piqued through a crisis in the local schools. "When our older child was ready for first grade, the schools didn't open until January 15 due to a teacher's strike. That's when I learned that it wouldn't be litigators who would salvage the school district. I learned firsthand that the white knights were the lawyers who were able to figure out how to get money flowing to the schools." Pat chose to work as a summer associate at Chapman and Cutler because she knew that the firm had a large and well-developed practice in municipal finance. She had a good experience as a summer associate and has been at the firm since she began practicing in 1979.

Charles DeWitt's law practice experience influenced his decision to pursue municipal finance law. He began his career in private practice, "learning traditional lawyering skills" before working as in-house counsel for two transportation agencies. "When I worked for the public agencies, I worked with several people who enjoyed their work on transportation projects. They helped me see the rewards and the excitement involved in this area of practice," he explains. He then returned to private practice at Palmer & Dodge with the expertise necessary to specialize in transportation-related municipal finance law.

John Petr admits that he developed an interest in the area in a more roundabout way. "I stumbled into this field, as, I think, did most of my colleagues in the area. I have yet to meet a bond lawyer who claims to have entered law school with a burning desire to practice as a municipal finance specialist. I joined a firm out of law school with a significant municipal finance practice, was assigned to work in the area after asking *not* to be made a litigator, and, as I grew to enjoy the people I worked with and the work I did, became increasingly comfortable with my practice."

What skills are most important to municipal finance lawyers?

❖ The lawyers we talked to agreed that municipal finance lawyers need to be able to **analyze and solve complex legal problems**. "You must be both analytical and precise, and you must have a good understanding of the public client," says Charles DeWitt. "You must have the ability to identify a client's objectives and find the most efficient means of accomplishing them," adds John Petr. Pat Curtner says, "In this field you're constantly problem-solving. You're talking through—whether with one person or with a finance team—how to raise capital efficiently and cost-effectively and how to minimize risk to all parties concerned."

❖ Lawyers specializing in this field must be comfortable **working with details, while keeping in mind the overall big-picture goals of the client**. "Technical proficiency and attention to detail are extremely important," says John Petr. "The best of the lawyers I deal with, however, and the lawyers my clients most appreciate, are those with the ability to focus on the client's interests in the transaction as a whole—to look beyond individual legal issues and efficiently move the transaction as a whole toward a successful conclusion."

❖ **Organizational skills** are key to success in this field. "Both time management and the ability to organize paper flow are very important in municipal finance practice," says Pat Curtner. "You're both drafting documents and reviewing the written work of others. You have to keep each deal you're working on separate in your mind—you really have to be organized to do this."

❖ Good **legal writing skills** are imperative to municipal finance attorneys. "This area requires strong legal writing skills, particularly with regard to interpreting public statutes and with regard to drafting documents," says Charles DeWitt. Pat Curtner adds emphatically, "Writing long legal documents is a challenge. It's as if you're weaving a precise, seamless web. Your writing must be precise and concise."

❖ Lawyers in this field must be able to **communicate effectively with clients, and listen carefully to their needs**. "You must take the time and expend the effort to know your client and its interests and to make a serious effort to know and understand the interests and motivations of the other parties to and persons interested in a particular transaction," explains John Petr. "You must be able to listen," says Pat Curtner. "It doesn't do any good to draft a beautiful document if the document doesn't reflect what the client wants. You must be an active listener, and your documents must reflect what the client wants done."

❖ Because attorneys in this field are focused on moving deals forward, **diplomacy, tact, and persistence** are important, as are **negotiation skills**. "Getting a deal done is like herding cats," confides Pat Curtner. "It takes a lot of skill to get a deal to move forward. It's not easy. You have to be persistent; you have to know how to negotiate. This isn't a field for the faint of heart."

What classes and law school experiences do municipal finance lawyers recommend?

❖ **Law school classes that help you read, understand, and navigate around legal statutes and codes** are helpful. To sharpen your ability to work with statutes, Pat Curtner recommends taking tax, securities law, and legal drafting. Because negotiations are important in deals, consider taking a negotiations class. "Contracts, real estate, and commercial lending are also helpful," says John Petr. In addition, consider taking a course in municipal law if your school offers one. "Any course that can help you deal with the state and local governments and their interrelation with the federal system is valuable," advises Pat Curtner.

❖ Take **law school classes that help you develop your writing skills.** Legal research and writing courses and seminar courses requiring lengthy research papers can help you become familiar with your strengths and weaknesses as a writer. Participation in law review, other journals, and writing competitions can also help develop your writing skills.

❖ **Gain practical experience in the field** as a summer associate or as an intern. "Find a good firm that practices in the area," says Charles DeWitt. Consider pursuing summer associate positions with firms that have municipal finance departments. Working as a summer associate on municipal finance projects is one of the best ways to determine whether this area of practice is for you. "This is a field in which you need to be trained in an apprenticeship system. Working as a summer associate for a firm that does this type of work is important," says Pat Curtner.

❖ **Participate in law school experiences which require you to work effectively under pressure.** To succeed as a municipal finance attorney, says John Petr, "You must be able to think clearly and carefully about a problem, communicate ideas clearly and persuasively, and you must be able to do this under pressure." Law school exams, which generally test a whole semester's worth of knowledge, give law students a lot of practical experience in performing under pressure. Participating in moot court competition, in which you draft an appellate brief and answer questions about the legal issues in front of a panel of judges, is another way to sharpen your ability to think on your feet and respond under stress.

❖ To learn more about the field, **talk to attorneys who practice municipal finance law.** John Petr recommends that students meet practicing attorneys through bar association activities or professional conferences. Most local, state, and federal bar associations have special membership rates for students, and students are welcome at nearly all of their activities.

MUNICIPAL FINANCE ATTORNEYS INTERVIEWED FOR THIS SECTION

Patricia Curtner
Chapman and Cutler
Chicago, Illinois
UNDERGRADUATE: University of Michigan
LAW SCHOOL: University of Michigan Law School

Charles DeWitt, Jr.
Palmer & Dodge LLP
Boston, Massachusetts
UNDERGRADUATE: Tulane University
LAW SCHOOL: Louisiana State University Paul M. Hebert Law Center

John Petr
Kutak Rock LLP
Omaha, Nebraska
UNDERGRADUATE: Washington University in St. Louis
LAW SCHOOL: University of California at Berkeley, Boalt Hall School of
Law

Public Interest Law

What is Public Interest Law?

A public interest law career gives an attorney an opportunity to make a tangible difference in our society. While many attorneys will become involved in pro bono representation (work without compensation done for the good of the public) at some time during their careers, public interest lawyers choose to devote all of their talents and energy to a particular cause or agenda. Their work benefits individuals and causes that are not generally served by the for-profit bar. What public interest lawyers have in common is their passion for using their legal skills in the spirit of public service. While not everyone agrees with every cause or agenda promoted by public interest lawyers, few people will contend that these dedicated public servants do not provide a necessary voice for causes that would not otherwise be served or supported.

Non-Profit Public Interest Organizations

Public interest lawyers are often identified by the organizations with which they are affiliated and the issues on which they work, whether environmental issues, gay rights issues, or children's issues. Some of these organizations

347

provide representation for individuals (such as battered women or the homeless), while others are committed to advocacy and education designed to bring about social change (such as mental health issues or civil rights issues). Examples of the types of organizations that employ public interest lawyers are:

Legal Services and Legal Aid: Legal Services organizations fill the important role of providing free or low-cost legal representation for low-income individuals on such issues as housing, health, family law, Social Security, and other public benefits and assistance. Legal Services offices are usually incorporated as non-profit organizations but receive funding from the federal Legal Services Corporation. Legal Aid offices do the same type of work but are usually privately funded. Both Legal Services and Legal Aid organizations concentrate primarily on civil issues, rather than criminal cases.

Civil Rights: Civil rights organizations seek to eliminate discrimination against minority groups and individuals in areas such as housing, employment, education, etc. Many of these groups focus on discrimination related to race, ethnicity, national origin, gender, sexual orientation, religion, disability, and age. Examples include the NAACP Legal Defense and Education Fund and the Mexican American Legal Defense and Education Fund.

Children's Rights: These organizations work on issues affecting the welfare of children, from poverty to child care to teen pregnancy to juvenile justice. One example of such an organization is the Children's Defense Fund.

Women's Issues: These organizations work to promote the rights of women. They are concerned with issues such as reproductive rights, women's health, and equal employment law. Examples include the Women's Legal Defense Fund and the National Organization for Women Legal Defense and Education Fund.

Prisoners' Rights: Prisoners' rights groups focus on the social welfare of those who are incarcerated as well as the issues affecting ex-offenders. They work to abolish the death penalty, improve the conditions of confinement, ensure adequate medical care for prisoners, and eliminate employment barriers faced by ex-offenders. An example of such an organization is the American Civil Liberties Union National Prison Project.

Disability and Mental Health Issues: These groups protect the rights and needs of people with physical disabilities, such as quadriplegia, and mental health disabilities, such as schizophrenia. An example is the Bazelon Center for Mental Health Law.

Environmental Protection: There are numerous organizations dedicated to the promotion of environmental issues, from the preservation of waterways to the protection of wildlife. Examples include the Natural Resources Defense Council, the Environmental Defense Fund, and the National Wildlife Federation.

Education Issues: Organizations such as the National Education Association are dedicated to such matters as improving public education, providing special education for the disabled, and ensuring equal access for indigent students.

Gay and Lesbian Issues: These organizations fight discrimination based on sexual orientation and are dedicated to ensuring equal access to employment, housing, medical care, and spousal/partner medical and health benefits. An example is the Lambda Legal Defense and Education Fund.

Elder Rights: These groups focus on the legal needs of senior citizens, such as access to affordable health care, Medicare coverage issues, housing concerns, and age discrimination issues. An example of such an organization is the National Senior Citizens Law Center.

Homelessness and Poverty: While Legal Services and Legal Aid organizations often assist the homeless and the indigent, there are also organizations, such as the National Coalition for the Homeless, dedicated specifically to legal issues related to homelessness and poverty.

Other areas represented by non-profit organizations include, but are not limited to, international human rights (*e.g.*, Amnesty International); reform of the political process (*e.g.*, Common Cause); Native American rights (*e.g.*, Native American Rights Fund); immigration (*e.g.*, National Immigration Rights Law Center); and capital punishment (*e.g.*, National Coalition to Abolish the Death Penalty).

Government Public Interest Practice

Public interest lawyers also work for the government in the federal, state, or local government sectors. Public interest lawyers serve the interests of their constituent citizens and thus include judges, state's attorneys, federal prosecutors, public defenders, agency attorneys, and other government positions.

> **Executive Departments and Agencies**: Executive branches of federal, state, and local governments work on behalf of citizens on issues such as health care, environmental protection, criminal justice, civil rights, and consumer protection. Federal agencies and departments include the Department of Justice (including the U.S. Attorneys' offices), the Equal Employment Opportunity Commission, the National Labor Relations Board, and the Environmental Protection Agency. State agencies include state commerce commissions, pollution control boards, and attorney registration and disciplinary commissions.

> **Legislature**: Lawyers also work for the United States Senate and the House of Representatives and state and local legislative bodies. In the U.S. Congress, for example, lawyers serve on the personal staffs of senators and representatives and on committee and sub-committee staffs.

> **Judiciary**: Attorneys also work for county, state, and federal courts as judges, court clerks, judicial law clerks, and staff attorneys.

> **Public Defenders**: Indigent criminal defendants receive free legal assistance from public defenders at the county, state, and federal level. Depending on the position, the attorneys may work on trials or appeals.

Pro Bono Practice in Private Law Firms

Many private law firms and their lawyers make a generous commitment of time and resources to pro bono legal work. There is a wide range of pro bono clients: indigent individuals represented through a legal clinic or bar association referral service; non-profit groups devoted to civil rights, health care, or environmental concerns; civic and community organizations;

churches and religious associations (as well as anti-religious associations); schools; and organizations pursuing public or civil rights claims.

In many law firms, lawyers are encouraged to handle work on behalf of pro bono clients in the same way that they would handle work for any of the firm's clients. The work may fall within the lawyer's specialty area or it may take the lawyer into another area of law altogether. Numerous criminal appeals and habeas corpus (wrongful imprisonment) petitions, including death penalty review cases, are handled by attorneys at large law firms on a pro bono basis. Young attorneys are often encouraged to develop their brief-writing and appellate advocacy skills by handling these types of cases for incarcerated individuals. Pro bono work therefore offers lawyers a unique opportunity to acquire new areas of expertise while serving the community.

The funds available for legal services are limited, while the need for legal services has risen. Therefore the pro bono efforts of private attorneys and law firms are more important than ever. The American Bar Association (ABA) and state bar associations encourage law firms to make serious commitments to pro bono work. For example, the ABA has challenged the country's 500 largest law firms to commit to a goal of contributing a set number of pro bono hours annually, equal to three to five percent of each firm's total billable hours.

Law firms select pro bono projects in many ways. An individual lawyer within a firm may work with a particular environmental or civil liberties group and thus bring a particular case to his or her firm. Sometimes a firm may commit to a special bar association project such as a legal clinic. In other cases judges appoint private attorneys to handle the interests of an indigent party, whether in a civil or criminal case.

> **Community Legal Services**: Law firms may staff community clinics for low-income clients. The lawyers may handle landlord/tenant issues, government benefit questions, and other such cases. Lawyers may help local non-profit agencies incorporate and, in addition, may serve on their boards of directors and provide business and legal advice.

> **Civil Rights**: Law firms may work on behalf of individuals or groups in civil rights litigation. The attorneys may handle employment discrimination cases (on the basis of race, gender, or age) against public or private employers; protect against unfair treatment of immigrant

groups; work to secure adequate health care or living conditions for prison inmates; or defend First Amendment rights.

Environmental Law: Firms may represent environmental organizations or groups of citizens seeking to protect natural resources, including land, water, air, and wildlife. For example, a firm might represent citizens seeking to protect wilderness lands against commercial exploitation.

International Law: Law firms may be asked to assist public and private human rights organizations. Lawyers in developing countries may ask American lawyers for help in developing models of democratic government, monitoring elections, or drafting environmental laws.

Political Asylum, Deportation, and Immigration Law: Law firm attorneys may represent refugees in political asylum hearings and appeals, work with immigrant groups in securing rights to public benefits and education, or give immigration and tax law advice to religious organizations working with non-citizens.

Real Estate: Law firm attorneys may help non-profit organizations with their real estate transactions or may work with tenant groups to develop low-income housing.

Other areas of pro bono work: Law firms and individual lawyers also work in other areas, including veterans' rights, tax law, labor and employment law, and disability rights. Lawyers often serve on the boards of directors of groups such as community organizations, schools, symphonies, legal services organizations, and other non-profit groups. Lawyers also serve on municipal boards and volunteer their services as arbitrators and mediators. In short, all lawyers in private practice have ample opportunities to perform pro bono work in their own communities.

Public Interest-Oriented Law Firms

A limited number of private, for-profit law firms, usually small in size, are considered public interest firms because of the nature of the cases they handle. They devote a substantial percentage of their practice to areas such as civil rights law, union-side labor law, employment discrimination law, family law, criminal law, immigration law, tenants' rights issues, and workers' compensation cases. They often offer their services on a reduced fee or a contingency fee basis.

Life as a Public Interest Lawyer

Where do public interest lawyers work?

As described above, public interest lawyers work for a broad range of employers, including non-profit public interest organizations; legal services and legal aid organizations; government entities, including government departments and agencies, the legislature, the judiciary, and public defenders' offices; private law firms; and public interest-oriented law firms.

This chapter profiles four public interest attorneys. However, because public interest law is defined broadly and public interest attorneys work in such a wide range of practice areas, you can learn more about public interest careers by reviewing additional chapters in this book.

Here is a list of the public interest attorneys profiled in other chapters of the book:

Admiralty and Maritime Law — Rachel Canty (U.S. Coast Guard); Mark Skolnicki (U.S. Coast Guard)

Appellate Practice — David Blair-Loy (Office of the Appellate Defender); Julie Fenton (U.S. Court of Appeals, Seventh Circuit); Teddi Gaitas (Minnesota State Public Defender); Richard Greenberg (Office of the Appellate Defender)

Criminal Law — Elizabeth Dobson (Champaign County State's Attorney); Timijanel Boyd Odom (Cook County Public Defender's Office); Bill Seki (Los Angeles County District Attorney's Office); Mimi Wright (U.S. Attorney's Office)

Environmental Law — Ignacio Arrazola (U.S. EPA); Keith Harley (Chicago Legal Clinic Environmental Law Program); Vickie Patton (Environmental Defense Fund); Mike Thrift (Office of the General Counsel, U.S. EPA)

Family Law — Sharon Lynn Gibson (Law Offices of Sharon Lynn Gibson); Jeffrey Warchol (Machulak, Hutchinson, Robertson & O'Dess, P.C.)

Government Contracts Practice — Brian Caminer (Chicago Mayor's Office of Workforce Development)

Government Practice — Mary Foster (Illinois Attorney Registration and Disciplinary Commission); Joan Humes (U.S. Attorney's Office); Gail Johnson (Department of Justice, Civil Division); Gretta Tameling (City of Naperville)

Immigration Law — Alberto Benitez (George Washington University Law School Immigration Clinic); Ben Casper (Centro Legal Inc.); Annette Toews (U.S. Immigration and Naturalization Service)

Labor and Employment Law — Maryl Rosen (U.S. Postal Service Law Department)

Legislative Practice: Charles Clapton (House Committee on Commerce)

Military Judge Advocates/JAG — Mary Card (U.S. Army); Robert Taishoff (U.S. Navy); Barbara Zanotti (U.S. Air Force)

Securities Law — John Reed Stark (U.S. Securities and Exchange Commission, Division of Enforcement)

Telecommunications Law — Howard Griboff (Federal Communications Commission Satellite and Radiocommunication Division)

Who are their clients and what types of cases do they work on?

Many public interest lawyers represent indigent individuals. Veronica Hobbs is a Managing Attorney for Legal Services of Northwest Ohio (LSNO), a legal services organization for northwestern Ohio. Veronica's office in Fremont, Ohio is one of four offices and serves a four-county area. "My clients are all low-income individuals who live in the rural areas of northwest Ohio. Most of them are blue-collar workers. Many of them have at most a 12th-grade education. The services I am asked to provide most frequently are in the areas of divorce, custody, child support, government benefits, Social Security, landlord/tenant disputes, domestic violence, consumer law, and unemployment compensation."

Most of Veronica's cases involve domestic violence. "My client is usually a fairly young female, married or has been involved with her mate for several years, has a couple of children, a limited education, and very few job skills. Her husband frequently abuses her, whether it be physically, emotionally, or verbally. He will often have substance abuse and anger management problems, and a history of being abused himself. He will isolate her from her family and friends and discourage her from leaving him by controlling the household finances, threatening more severe harm to her, and/or taking the children. The parties usually have very few assets but many debts. In some cases she's been afraid to report his abuse to the police. In other cases she has reported the abuse, pressed charges, dropped charges, and reconciled with her abuser on more than one occasion. My job is to help my client navigate her way through the emotional, financial, and legal ups-and-downs of a divorce or termination of a relationship."

Patricia (Patty) Hindo, a senior attorney at Life Span Legal Services in Chicago, Illinois, works exclusively with domestic violence victims. "We serve a lot of immigrant women, especially Latina women," Patty explains. "They find out about Life Span's services through shelters, social services agencies, and other legal service providers. When the police go out on a domestic violence call, they share information about Life Span with the woman involved. We also operate a domestic violence hotline. Our clients are in the city of Chicago and throughout Cook County."

All of Patty's cases are family law cases that include divorce, custody, support, and parentage issues. Patty also helps her clients seek orders of protection when their safety is threatened by the abuser. "We also work with undocumented battered immigrant women on their petitions to become legalized. The Violence Against Women Act enacted in 1994 allows undocumented battered immigrant women who are married to U.S. citizens or lawful permanent residents to file their own immigrant petition and acquire residency," she explains. (*See* the Immigration Law Chapter for more information on these types of issues.)

Hunt Brown is the Executive Director of Justice for All, a non-profit legal services organization in Atlanta, Georgia. Hunt's clients are the working poor. "My clients are male, female, black, white, Asian, Hispanic, married, divorced, single, parents, and non-parents. The typical client earns less than 200% of poverty level (not much at all), pays taxes and rent and buys food every week, but cannot afford an attorney. Most clients have been thrust into a legal system they believe they can neither understand nor trust."

Hunt says that his typical case involves family law, "although we have a fair share of landlord/tenant, probate, and misdemeanor cases." He adds, "A lot of cases involve children: child support recovery, custody, modifications of child support and custody. Although one can paint with a broad brush, it belies the truth that each person, each kid, and each case is different. We tell our attorneys that although there are similarities between cases, to the individual clients each matter is the most important event in their lives."

Sherryl (Sherry) Fox is an Assistant Public Guardian for the Cook County Office of the Public Guardian in Chicago. She has worked for both the Juvenile Division of the Public Guardian's office as well as for its Estates Division, which acts as guardian for disabled adults. When the Cook County State's Attorney brings child abuse or neglect charges against one or both of the child's parents (who are usually represented by a public defender), the Public Guardian's office is appointed by the court to represent the child as both the child's attorney and the child's guardian ad litem. "The facts in these cases are truly disheartening," says Sherry. "The children may be tortured or there may be horrible sex abuse. Often the parents inflict the abuse while under the influence of drugs, which can make them do unbelievable things to their children," she says. (*See* the Family Law chapter for more information about guardianships.)

The Public Guardian's office stays involved in the case until the case is closed. The case may be closed when the child reaches the age of majority (age 18), or when the child is adopted, acquires a private guardian, or returns home. This means that the Public Guardian's office follows many children's cases over a number of years. "We have several divisions," Sherry explains. "The juvenile division has at least 125 attorneys. The estates division, which looks after the interests of disabled adults, and in which I currently work, has about eight attorneys. The public guardian's office also has an appeals division and a special litigation unit which litigates class action, civil rights, and other lawsuits on behalf of children and disabled adults."

"My clients are disabled adults," explains Sherry. "They have been adjudicated disabled for some reason, often for Alzheimer's-type dementia or other types of organic brain syndrome. I am the attorney for the Cook County Public Guardian, who has been appointed guardian of their estate and person. Generally, these disabled adults have been abused, neglected, or financially exploited in some way by their children or by lawyers or accountants or strangers able to take advantage of them. Sometimes we become the guardian when there is no family member able or willing to look out for them." Sherry's cases often involve harrowing facts. "There are cases in which these elderly clients have had their 40- or 50-year-old children tie them up and confine them to basements or beat and abuse them. Sometimes our clients are found in abandoned homes filled with little but dirt, trash, and human waste. The facts make a terrifying statement about our society. My job is to make sure that these victims are removed from the abusive situation and to make sure that their health and legal needs are taken care of and their estates protected."

Sherry's work gives her a chance to influence social policy and community standards concerning elder care. "We fight to keep these disabled and generally elderly people in the community where possible. It's generally better for them to live outside an institutional setting. Nursing homes have a huge lobby, and legislators are easily convinced that the best place for the elderly is in nursing homes. Our Cook County Public Guardian brought a lawsuit showing that 50 to 60% of these people can live healthier, more productive lives in the community than they can in nursing homes, and that doing so also saves the state money. We work to get funds to pay for home-based care. We develop innovative programs to help these individuals preserve their dignity and independence and to help them protect their assets."

What daily activities are involved in public interest practice?

The daily activities of public interest attorneys vary with the sector of practice in which they are involved. For the many public interest attorneys who work in legal services organizations, much of their time is spent counseling clients. "There really is no typical day," says Veronica Hobbs. "Legal services in the public interest arena always keeps you on your toes. I do have frequent client contact, whether it is during face-to-face meetings or telephone interviews." Patty Hindo, too, reports that she spends a great deal of time counseling clients. "This includes intake interviews, in which I have an initial consultation with the client, as well as follow-up meetings with the client," says Patty.

Legal services attorneys also go to court and draft petitions and pleadings, explains Veronica Hobbs. "Some days I may be in the office all day doing research, drafting pleadings, judgment entries, or letters. On other days I may be in court all day in one or several of the counties we service. Since I work in a rural area servicing four counties, I have to do a lot of traveling, as many clients have no transportation. At least two days a week I travel to one of our service areas to conduct client interviews."

Patty Hindo reports that she has a similarly hectic schedule. "In addition to my client counseling, I am usually in court an average of three times a week. I participate in hearings and trials, including those on custody and child support issues. I also draft legal documents and have worked on a few appellate briefs. In addition I prepare affidavits for my clients who are seeking orders of protection and who are filing immigration petitions."

When we asked Hunt Brown of Justice for All to tell us about his typical day, he gave us an up close and personal (and drily humorous) view of the daily pleasures and pressures of working as a legal services attorney, including the financial challenges faced by legal services organizations. "My typical day starts with a cup of coffee and a crossword puzzle to jump start my brain. The first order of business is either (a) paying bills or (b) finding money to pay bills, depending upon the circumstances, while making time to either (1) answer member attorney questions (mentor staff members) or (2) recruit new attorneys (interview) followed by governmental paperwork, accounting, correspondence, story pitching to local press regarding how worthwhile, meaningful and unique our services are (which can be a tough sell), and encouraging the local legal community to support our services (which can be an even tougher sell). Most of my time is spent at my desk; too little of it is spent in court." Another small joy of his practice? "Ties are optional, unless I'm going to court," Hunt admits, his good nature shining through.

Sherry Fox says that those attorneys assigned to the Juvenile Division of the Public Guardian's office are in court at least two to three days a week, looking out for the needs of the child. They also have contact with the children's foster parents and stay in contact with workers from different child welfare agencies. "We're constantly checking to make sure that the children are not in situations of neglect or abuse. If the parents have agreed to a drug rehabilitation program, we're following up to see if the parents have indeed complied with the terms of agreement for treatment."

In her work in the Disabled Adults Division of the Public Guardian's office, Sherry notes, her duties are widely varied. "We do so many different things as the guardian of these individuals," she explains. "We protect their assets. We take care of their taxes, we do estate planning, we buy and sell real estate. We are in court all the time, on behalf of our wards, obtaining leave of court to act on their behalf. We are very proactive in litigating to recover moneys or assets that were exploited by relatives, so-called 'friends,' charlatans, and dishonest business people. The elderly are often caught up in scams; they are extremely vulnerable to fraud. For example, we sometimes go after crooked home remodelers who set out to feed on these people and their fears about their homes." Sherry is also involved in medical care decisions. "Because we are the guardian of a disabled person, we must consent to any medical or surgical treatment and make a decision whether to put a DNR [do not resuscitate order] into effect or whether the individual has the capacity to decide that for himself or herself. We work with doctors in determining the capacity of our clients on such issues."

What do public interest lawyers find rewarding about their practice?

Not surprisingly, the public interest attorneys we talked to find reward in the fact that their jobs allow them to make a difference in people's lives. "My clients cannot afford a private attorney," says Veronica Hobbs. "Without organizations such as the one I work for, their legal problems would not be addressed. My reward is the smile on their faces when I have helped them to address these legal problems that no one else would take on. I am a strong believer in fairness and justice *for all*. It is this belief that motivates me every day I come to work. I try to do my part in making fairness and justice for all a reality."

"The most satisfying part of my job is the ability to see people through the legal process," says Patty Hindo. "When I can help an abused woman get an order of relief and help her get away from an abuser, that's especially rewarding," says Patty. "The immigrant women I work with are so vulnerable," she says. "It means a lot to be able to help them get an order of protection and then to help them through the immigration process. When they get a work permit and you see them finally get a job, it's a tremendous feeling to know that you've helped." Patty says that a number of these women continue to stay in touch with her as their lives progress. "They stop by to say hello, and they sent cards when they heard I was pregnant. They are really special people."

"It's an honor and a great privilege to represent both the children and disabled adults," says Sherry Fox. "I really feel fortunate that as a lawyer I can try to make people's lives better. I call it the 'Band-Aids on the Titanic' theory. If you look at the whole problem of abuse and neglect of children or of the elderly, you cannot possibly solve it. But if you look at all the work we do in the Public Guardian's office as isolating and disinfecting a cut and putting a fresh Band-Aid on it, then you can keep moving forward. You have to be surgical in your approach. You have to use your rage at what has happened to these people as a surgeon would use his or her rage against disease—you have to save your energy to treat the wound that's in front of you. You go after the people who are doing wrong, case by case."

Sherry continues, "The work is very heartbreaking and at the same time very challenging. You use all the skills you have—both as an attorney and as a caring human being—to help people who can't help themselves."

When we asked Hunt Brown what he found rewarding about his practice, he said that there are certain moments that are incredibly rewarding. He described these remarkable moments in rather poetic terms. "I helped a 40-year-old retarded man who had been falsely accused of a crime gain an acquittal; his momma cried when she heard the news." He added a few more images to complete the picture: "The moment a client says, 'I understand,' and means it. The day when a young lawyer I helped get started drives up in a new car. The occasional 'thank you' from a client."

Veronica Hobbs told us that another aspect of legal services work she enjoys is the opportunity to handle individual cases from their inception to their conclusion. "I like the fact that I am responsible for my cases from beginning to end. I do the interviews, the research, the footwork, and the court appearances. I get to see the results of my labor," she says. Veronica told us about one particularly rewarding case. "In one of my first cases, I represented a woman with lupus [a joint disease] in a Supplemental Security Income case. Looking at her, she didn't appear to have a problem, but she was in a great deal of physical and emotional pain. We fought for her Social Security benefits for one and a half years. I had been cautioned that lupus cases were very hard to win, but I was determined to win this case. We lost initially, but we appealed. We lost at the appellate level, and she reapplied for relief. The second time around we won. My client received the entire amount of her retroactive benefits check because she did not have to reimburse the Department of Human Services [DHS] for the Disability Assistance she had received during the pendency of the case due to a DHS oversight. I'll never forget the look on her face when I told her we had won and how much money she was going to receive."

The Training and Skills Important to Public Interest Law

How do people enter the field of public interest law?

Public interest attorneys generally enter the field because they have a strong commitment to public service. "I have always been someone who wanted to help those less fortunate than myself," explains Veronica Hobbs. "The career I have chosen affords me the opportunity to do these things and more. I have wanted to be an attorney since I was in junior high school. I turned my focus to public interest law when I was in law school. I took a clinical course in the area of family law, where I represented domestic violence victims at their civil protection hearings. After that I was hooked. I did try working at a law firm, but I found that it wasn't for me. The public interest sector is where I am most comfortable."

"I feel lucky because I have the privilege of helping people who can't help themselves," says Sherry Fox. "I've been able to use my law degree to do something that's made my space and time on this earth worthwhile." Sherry returned to law school when her children were grown. From the beginning of her law school career, she was committed to using her degree in public service. "I worked one year in my law school's criminal defense clinic. I worked for a wonderful clinical professor who really inspired me." Sherry started working for the Juvenile Division of the Public Guardian's office upon graduation from law school and notes that most of their attorneys start straight out of law school. "Generally, in the Public Guardian's office, you start in the Juvenile Division. You're in the trenches; you're in court every day. You do hundreds of hearings."

Sherry was subsequently promoted to the position of courtroom supervisor. In this position she visited with the children involved in the hearings, interviewed them, and made assessments of their needs. She also held permanency planning hearings concerning their future welfare. "In a permanency planning hearing, we set a goal for the child. It may be returning the child to his or her home or it may be long-term foster care or adoption. As a courtroom supervisor, I supervised two or three professional interviewers, several attorneys, and 25 law students working as law clerks. In a year and a half, I helped process thousands of cases."

The Public Guardian then asked Sherry to serve in the Estates Division of the office, where the Public Guardian is the court-appointed guardian of disabled adults. As much as she loved her work with juveniles, Sherry is just as passionate about her work on behalf of disabled adults. "I have the chance to be really innovative in my law practice. We use creative methods to look out for the elderly people for whom we are guardian. We look out for their health, their welfare, their financial well-being. And we try to let them know there are people out there who care. We try to bring dignity to their lives."

Hunt Brown says that while in high school, he made a decision to use his talents to make a difference in people's lives. "In high school I read Arthur Miller's play *Death of a Salesman.* In the second act of the play, Willy Loman [the salesman of the title] is stunned to learn that his neighbor's son is going to argue a case before the Supreme Court. Willy marvels that the neighbor's son didn't even mention the impending challenge, to which the neighbor replies, 'He didn't have to [talk about it]—he's gonna do it.' I realized that I could either go through my life talking about what great things I could do, what great contributions I could make, or I could simply do my very best to achieve them." This personal commitment to making a difference led Hunt to pursue a career as a legal services attorney.

Patty Hindo advises students who are interested in pursuing public interest careers to begin their career planning and networking early in law school. "When public interest organizations hire, they look for a 'demonstrated commitment to public interest law.' To establish proof of your commitment, your involvement needs to start at an early stage in your law school career. Pursue internships and clinical programs. Find out as much about different public interest agencies as you can. Apply for programs and fellowships. Network with other students who are interested in public interest careers. Talk to the professionals in your career services office about public interest opportunities. And consider volunteering in community service programs such as Boys and Girls Clubs or Big Brothers/Big Sisters," advises Patty.

What skills are most important to public interest lawyers?

❖ **A passion for public service** is instrumental to surviving and succeeding as a public interest attorney. As Sherry Fox says, "You *have* to care."

❖ **Strong interpersonal communication skills** are especially important to public interest lawyers. "You must be able to relate to your clients," says Patty Hindo.

❖ Excellent **oral advocacy skills** are also important. "When you are in court, you have to be able to articulate the issues and to specify the relief you want," says Sherry Fox.

❖ Most of the public interest lawyers we talked to mentioned that **patience** is a virtue in the public sector. These lawyers said that patience is an absolute necessity when working with clients for whom the legal system is often frightening and overwhelming.

❖ **Tenacity** is also important. As Veronica Hobbs related in her earlier story about a lengthy Supplemental Security Income case, cases often require repeated efforts to succeed, particularly when bureaucratic processes are involved.

❖ **Foreign language skills** can be a tremendous asset to the legal services attorney. Patty Hindo is fluent in Spanish and advises, "You can take up foreign language skills in college, in law school, or at any point in your career. Spanish, Polish, or Korean—most any foreign language is helpful."

❖ The **ability to cope with crises** is also key to success as a public interest attorney. "You must be able to work under pressure and to work with people who are involved in very emotional life crises," explains Patty Hindo. "You have to care, yet be surgical enough to prevent yourself from burning out," advises Sherry Fox. "You must learn to harness the rage and frustration that you feel when you encounter distressing situations and use that energy in productive ways."

❖ **Organizational skills** are paramount. "You're dealing with a tremendous number of cases, each of which involves numerous issues. You're expected to come up with information about a particular case in short order. You must be able to easily access your files. And being organized helps you deal with the daily emergencies that are inevitable in this type of work," Sherry Fox advises.

❖ Good **time management skills** are also useful to public interest attorneys. Public interest lawyers often put in long days in which they serve a large number of clients with minimal resources. "You have to be disciplined to manage your daily workload and take care to preserve time and energy for the crises that arise," cautions Sherry Fox.

❖ Public interest lawyers must **be resourceful**. "Writing grants and securing funds takes resourcefulness," says Patty Hindo. Adds Sherry Fox, "When you're in the courtroom, you have to use creativity in your arguments to convince the judge to do what you know is right." And if, like Sherry, you have the chance to influence public policy, creativity is also important. "You have to be creative in order to change the law," she says.

❖ Hunt Brown's occasionally facetious comments indicate that a **sense of humor** will go a long way in helping you deal with stressful, and sometimes unusual, situations. He recalls one client who "wanted to sue the Martians for messing with his brain." Hunt jokes, "We had to decline the case, as we had been representing the Martians for years and had a conflict of interest. He appreciated our professionalism."

What classes and law school experiences do public interest lawyers recommend?

❖ Those students interested in legal services positions should take **a wide range of classes,** including family law, immigration law, contracts, civil procedure, real estate, tax law, evidence, bankruptcy, wills and trusts, and criminal law. A wide range of classes helps prepare students to assist a diverse group of clients facing family law issues, landlord/tenant issues, and financial problems. "Seminars related to poverty law can also be helpful," advises Patty Hindo. "The paper you write in such a seminar allows you to explore an area of interest to you and gives you a good topic to talk about in interviews," she adds. "Trial advocacy classes are good preparation for the courtroom," advises Veronica Hobbs.

❖ If you're interested in working for an organization that specializes in a particular field such as environmental law or immigration law, take **courses that focus on the areas relevant to your interest.**

❖ Participate in **public interest internships** while in law school. Many government offices and public interest organizations have summer positions available to law students. In addition, explore your law school's **clinical programs.** Many law schools have clinical programs supervised by law school professors. Law students have the chance to work on cases in which they represent indigent clients. "It's good to know the black letter law that you are taught in class, but the real challenge comes in applying that law to real life experiences," says Veronica Hobbs. "The more comfortable you are doing that, the easier the transition from law school to practicing law."

❖ **Join and take an active role in your law school's public interest organizations.** Many law schools have chapters of the National Association for Public Interest Law (NAPIL), and most law schools have other public interest organizations as well. Some of these organizations sponsor job fairs and events to raise funds for public interest law internships.

❖ **Take a look at the public interest job search guides** in your law school's career services office. There are a number of excellent public interest resources, among them: *Public Interest Profiles*, published by the Congressional Quarterly Foundation for Public Affairs; *The University of Chicago and University of Michigan Public Service Employer Directory* published by Legal Support Systems, Inc.; *Public Interest Job Search Guide: Harvard Law School's Handbook and Directory for Students and Lawyers Seeking Public Service Work*; and *The Harvard Law School and Yale Law School Fellowship Opportunities Guide*.

❖ **Volunteer in community service organizations.** "To learn, do. To develop contacts, volunteer," advises Hunt Brown. Volunteering is a great way to begin to establish a record of demonstrated interest in public interest law that public interest organizations seek when they hire.

❖ **Network, network, network.** "Networking in the public interest community is extremely important," says Patty Hindo. "It's just as important to network in the public interest community as it is in private practice. Meet as many people as you can."

❖ **Become familiar with and come to terms with the salary ranges offered in the public interest sector.** Government salaries may be higher than those paid by public interest organizations, some of which struggle for funding. "I think the thing you have to realize is that you are not going to make a lot of money being a public interest attorney. Your desire to help those less fortunate than yourself has to outweigh the desire to have a big bank account, fancy cars, and designer clothes," comments Veronica Hobbs. Hunt Brown adds that it's helpful when your family and friends support your decision to enter public service. "I have an incredibly supportive spouse. She's supportive both financially and emotionally, and that makes a big difference." He adds, with his usual good humor, "I don't have a BMW, but I do get to make a small difference in the lives of ordinary people. And that's what's important."

PUBLIC INTEREST ATTORNEYS INTERVIEWED FOR THIS SECTION

Hunt Brown
Justice for All
Atlanta, Georgia
UNDERGRADUATE: Washington & Lee University
LAW SCHOOL: Emory University School of Law

Sherryl Fox
Cook County Office of the Public Guardian
Disabled Adult Division
Chicago, Illinois
UNDERGRADUATE: Washington University in St. Louis, DePaul
University
LAW SCHOOL: Chicago-Kent College of Law, Illinois Institute of
Technology

Patricia Hindo
Life Span Center for Legal Services
Chicago, Illinois
UNDERGRADUATE: Fairfield University
LAW SCHOOL: Chicago-Kent College of Law, Illinois Institute of
Technology

Veronica Hobbs
Legal Services of Northwest Ohio
Fremont, Ohio
UNDERGRADUATE: Northeastern University
LAW SCHOOL: University of California at Berkeley, Boalt Hall School of
Law

Real Estate Law

What is Real Estate Law?

Whether it's your first home purchase or your fourth, whether you've found a sleek city condo in move-in condition or an adorable but neglected Victorian with great potential, a real estate attorney is the person you turn to to make sure that the transaction goes through and that you land the home of your dreams. But residential real estate is, in fact, only a small part of the real estate field.

Real estate transactions involve hospitals, schools, hotels and resorts, shopping centers, single family homes, multifamily housing developments, farms, churches, parking lots, and even coal mines. Real estate law concerns every aspect of commercial, industrial, and residential transactions and investments. It involves issues related to the purchase and sale of property, including financing and development; construction contracts; securitized real estate investments; property management and leasing; environmental compliance; and litigation relating to these areas. Real estate lawyers provide their clients with advice concerning all of these matters. They also help their clients navigate through the myriad governmental zoning restrictions and land use regulations necessary in order to move forward with a real estate project.

Real estate lawyers may be called on to represent their clients before state and county commissions, city councils, community organizations, or in state or federal court. While some real estate lawyers specialize in litigation involving contractual or regulatory issues, many specialize in real estate transactions or land use. Those who specialize in real estate transactions advise their clients on tax issues, financing issues, and even environmental issues concerning the transaction in question. Attorneys who specialize in land use often focus on the regulatory aspects of real estate projects. They must be familiar with the federal, state, and local regulations that may affect a particular project. They often use their finely developed negotiation skills to negotiate modifications to the project in exchange for regulatory approval. In some cases regulatory disputes are litigated, in which case the land use attorney may represent either the regulating body or the regulated entity.

Life as a Real Estate Lawyer

Where do real estate lawyers work?

Lawyers who work on commercial real estate transactions often work in the real estate departments of large law firms. These departments may have a number of attorneys, some of whom specialize in real estate transaction and investment issues and others who specialize in land use and zoning issues. These real estate attorneys may work closely with other departments in the law firm, including the environmental department (on issues such as whether a particular piece of property meets environmental compliance regulations) or the litigation department (when a construction contract results in litigation). Other real estate lawyers work for the government, whether for county building and zoning departments or for municipalities including cities and suburbs. Real estate lawyers may also work for corporations, real estate development companies, financial or lending institutions, or title companies. Other lawyers, often in small firms or in general or solo practice, generally handle residential real estate transactions.

Who are their clients and what types of cases do they work on?

Bryan Scott Blade is a real estate transactions lawyer at Frost & Jacobs LLP in Cincinnati, Ohio. He works with a wide range of clients on commercial real estate matters. "My firm's clients range from large national retail chains to individuals," he explains. "The bulk of my work is for regional developers of residential and commercial subdivisions. My clients typically look to me to draft and negotiate contracts and leases and to facilitate the sale and purchase of real estate." Bryan most commonly represents entities that are purchasing property. "In an acquisition I draft and negotiate a purchase contract; assist the client in the completion of due diligence by reviewing title reports, surveys, and environmental reports; prepare closing documents; and close, or complete, the purchase of the property," he says.

Other large firm real estate lawyers, such as Kristine Iida at Sonnenschein Nath & Rosenthal in Chicago, represent lenders and investors in real estate financing deals. "My firm's clients include lenders, developers, and investors in commercial real estate projects. We service clients all across the country. Often the lender is lending to a large company buying real estate properties such as a real estate investment trust, or 'REIT.' REITs buy the properties and then get investors to invest in their portfolio. The investors don't actually own a part of each property; rather, they own stock in the REIT. The investors benefit from investing in a REIT—there are significant tax benefits and the size and diversity of their portfolios help minimize the risk of investing in a single property."

Tina Makoulian of Ballard Spahr Andrews & Ingersoll, LLP in Philadelphia specializes in land use and zoning law. "The majority of the firm's clients are large institutional clients in the Philadelphia area. They include corporations, hospitals, developers, universities, banks, and other lending institutions. They turn to our firm for a variety of services, including lease negotiations and advice concerning loan transactions." Tina explains her role in the typical land use case. "Such a case would involve preparing the application or appeal; meeting with engineers, architects, planners, and traffic experts; preparing for hearings; and representing our clients before municipal planning and zoning boards."

Ira Moltz handles residential real estate matters in Chicago. Ira is a sole practitioner; about one-third of his practice involves real estate transactions (you can read more about Ira's general practice in the Solo, Small Firm, and General Practice chapter of this book). "Most of my clients are private individuals or small businesses," Ira notes. "Often my clients are families selling one home and buying another. I also do some condominium conversions [converting apartments to condominiums]."

What daily activities are involved in real estate practice?

Lawyers who specialize in real estate transactions report that they spend much of their time drafting and reviewing documents, counseling clients, and negotiating terms for the transactions on which they are working. "I spend approximately half of my day drafting contracts, leases, and numerous other real estate documents and the rest of the day on the phone consulting with clients and negotiating documents and transactions," says Bryan Blade. "I regularly attend meetings outside the office in which I discuss projects with clients, and I often visit the project sites."

Tina Makoulian reports that her daily activities are similar to Bryan's. "My typical day is made up of speaking on the telephone with clients, drafting and negotiating financing documents, preparing zoning and land use applications, attending meetings, and representing my clients at hearings." Tina says that because her name appears on publicly posted land use applications, she receives occasional calls from citizens with questions about the projects described in the applications. "I once fielded a flood of phone calls from people who told me they got my name from the local supermarket. They were area residents opposed to a project. It took a moment or two to figure out that they had seen my name on a copy of a land use application posted on the supermarket's bulletin board, and that's how they found me."

Kristine Iida works on real estate investment transactions. About one-fourth of her time is spent on the phone coordinating activities involved in her transactions. "About half my day is spent reviewing, drafting, and revising documents, including purchase agreements, leases, and mortgage documents. Another one-fourth of my day is spent doing due diligence reviews. I'm rarely in court. I do travel periodically, usually out of state on two- or three-day trips. These trips are at the culmination of the deal, when everything comes together."

We asked Kristine to explain what tasks are included in a due diligence review. "My client is usually the lender in a transaction. Because the lender is relying on the value of the properties being acquired with the loan, I review the many legal aspects of the properties on behalf of the lender. The due diligence check means that I am reviewing the title commitments, leases, land surveys, and certificates of occupancy for the properties in question. The certificates of occupancy show whether the property meets local zoning and other legal requirements and disclose things such as building code violations. Environmental law issues also come into play in due diligence checks. Federal regulations are such that, when you purchase property, you could be liable for certain types of environmental cleanup, so you want to make sure there are minimal environmental risks involved in the acquisition of the property. My days are spent thinking about what my client needs to do to protect itself in the purchase or financing of the property in question."

"As a residential real estate lawyer," reports Ira Moltz, "you spend a lot of time on the telephone. You're essentially the coordinator between all the parties involved in the transaction: your party (the buyer or seller), the other party's attorney, the real estate brokers for the buyer and the seller, the buyer's mortgage lender, the buyer's insurance company, and so on. These transactions require a great deal of organization because so many details are involved." Ira says that the typical residential real estate transaction is completed within three months. "In the three months that you are involved, you may make 50 phone calls about the transaction. You're also spending time reviewing documents and talking with your client. Both parties want the deal to go through, but you want to protect your client 100%. The challenge comes in protecting your client without killing the deal. Generally the cases have a happy ending, because everyone has the same goal, which is getting to the closing."

What do real estate lawyers find rewarding about their practice?

The real estate lawyers we talked to greatly enjoy their relationships with their clients. "I particularly enjoy the level of personal contact that I have with my clients," says Bryan Blade. "As a real estate attorney, it is important for me to know and understand my client's business and to work closely with that client throughout the course of a development project."

Tina Makoulian says that her clients are tremendously appreciative of her efforts. "The aspect of the practice that I most enjoy is the contact with and appreciation from clients. Although the large majority of them are institutional clients, it is rewarding to know that my work matters and is appreciated by the individuals managing those institutions."

Kristine Iida says that her clients are tremendously professional and a pleasure to work with. "Our clients, whether lenders, developers, or investors, are very sophisticated in their knowledge of real estate and in their knowledge of the law. They understand the role you play in the transaction, and they make it easy for you to do your very best job." Kristine also likes the fact that transactions work allows her to interact with equally sophisticated legal colleagues, both within and outside of the firm. "In completing the transaction, you work with a team of lawyers. You get a chance to know lawyers in other departments of the firm, and you also meet wonderful lawyers representing the other parties involved in the transaction. The parties have a common goal, which imparts a real team spirit," says Kristine.

"Real estate is my very favorite part of my general practice," confides Ira Moltz. "It's one of the few areas of law practice where legally your clients are in a win-win situation. Early in my legal career, I knew that I enjoyed collaboration more than confrontation. Real estate deals are very positive in nature. The parties are generally willing to cooperate. There are positive end results. I really enjoy being the coordinator of this transaction in which all the parties go home happy."

Real estate lawyers also like the fact that the projects they work on have tangible results. "I take pride in seeing a vacant piece of land transformed into a successful grocery store, drugstore, or residential development," says Bryan Blade. Ira Moltz notes, "There are positive results to residential real estate closings." He comments that he finds reward every time he represents a relieved seller who is moving on to a bigger house or an excited buyer who leaves the closing with a new set of house keys.

"I like the fact that real estate transactions have a beginning and an end," says Kristine Iida. "It's not like litigation that goes on and on and then may be appealed. When you're involved in a transaction, it comes to completion, and then you move on to the next project. You feel a sense of accomplishment." Ira Moltz seconds Kristine's sentiments. "Residential real estate deals aren't five years long—there's a beginning and an end. And the closing itself is rewarding."

The Training and Skills Important to Real Estate Law

How do people enter the field of real estate law?

Some law students know that they're interested in transactional work, and real estate in particular, from the beginning of their law school careers. Bryan Blade knew from the start that he wanted to be a transactional lawyer.

"I always knew I wanted to be a transactional attorney. I never really focused on real estate until my second year of law school, when I was fortunate enough to take two real estate development courses from a practicing real estate attorney. I enjoyed the practical, business aspects of the courses as a refreshing change to the theoretical focus of most law school courses."

Many attorneys learn that they're interested in real estate through working as law clerks or summer associates while in law school. "Before I joined Sonnenschein, I worked as an attorney for a mid-sized firm in Chicago, where I also clerked during law school," says Kristine Iida. "While a law clerk and as an associate, I worked on a number of commercial real estate transactions, as well as corporate law and employment law matters. When I decided to change positions, Sonnenschein was looking for a real estate associate. My experience gave me the skills I needed to land the job at Sonnenschein. As it turns out, I've really enjoyed having a full time real estate practice."

Kristine originally went to law school with the hope of using her foreign language skills. She majored in German in college and is also fluent in Japanese. "I've used both my Japanese and my German skills in my real estate practice," she says. "Because I'm working in commercial real estate, I encounter clients that are based overseas. I worked on one matter involving a large Japanese corporation preparing to open an American office. The company sent over its top management to meet with the firm. I was able to welcome the managers, talk with them, and make them feel comfortable. I've also used my German skills to translate documents." Today's increasingly global economy undoubtedly means that Kristine will have many more opportunities to put her language skills to work. (*See* the International Law chapter for more information on global practice.)

Some people become real estate attorneys purely by chance and yet find that real estate is the right practice area for them. Tina Makoulian is one such person. "I entered this practice area purely through serendipity," she says. "When I graduated from law school, I had no idea what field I wanted to practice in. I received a job offer in this field and decided to give it a try."

What skills are most important to real estate lawyers?

❖ The attorneys we talked to unanimously agreed that successful real estate attorneys are **detail oriented**. "Being thorough, careful, and conscientious are all important," says Tina Makoulian. "The single most important skill for a real estate attorney is the ability to pay attention to details." Kristine Iida explains why details are so critical. "You have to keep the big picture—the deal—in mind, but details are the key to making the deal go through. When you're filing documents related to the transaction, you have to make sure the legal descriptions of the properties are exactly right and that all the numbers are exactly right. You have to carefully calculate transfer taxes and mortgage taxes. Every state has different forms for recording real estate transactions—as a real estate attorney you must be familiar with state and county recording requirements, and you must make sure that your documents conform to those requirements."

❖ Real estate attorneys are trying to move deals to completion, and **strong negotiation skills** ensure that the deals are, in fact, completed. "Negotiation skills are tremendously important," says Kristine Iida. "Negotiation affects so many of the documents you're working with, such as leases and mortgage documents."

❖ **Organizational skills** are also important. Whether in commercial or residential real estate, real estate lawyers handle numerous documents. "Residential real estate files open and close quickly," says Ira Moltz. "There are lots of deadlines along the way. You must be able to handle a great deal of paperwork, and you have to be able to keep it organized."

❖ Because real estate attorneys work closely with their clients and teams of other business professionals, they must have **good interpersonal communication skills**. "You're gaining the trust of your client. You're protecting your client's interests, yet you're urging your client to be reasonable in terms of negotiations," says Ira Moltz. "You have to be good at talking with people and talking them through the transactions," he adds.

What law school classes and experiences do real estate lawyers recommend?

❖ Students interested in this field should consider taking **classes in real estate**. "I found that the real estate transactions and real estate development courses that I took during law school were very helpful," says

Bryan Blade. Classes in zoning and land use and advanced real estate seminars are also useful.

❖ Classes in areas such as **corporations, negotiations, legal drafting, environmental law, and secured transactions** can also be helpful. "As a law student, I would certainly take as many real estate, drafting, and negotiation classes as I could," advises Bryan Blade. "A good basic understanding of corporate assets and how corporations work is important," says Kristine Iida. Adds Tina Makoulian, "If you're interested in real estate finance, I recommend taking a secured transactions course."

❖ Work as a **summer associate or law clerk** in a firm that has an active real estate practice. "You can learn so much from someone who is experienced in the practice," says Ira Moltz. As Kristine Iida explained earlier, working as law clerk helps you develop marketable skills for the employment market. If you're interested in commercial real estate, consider applying at firms with a real estate department. If you're interested in residential real estate, consider working for a general practitioner while you're in law school. "Clerking for an attorney who does this type of work will help you determine whether it's the kind of work for you. It will also help build your confidence," advises Ira.

❖ Consider **working in your law school's legal clinic**. "Legal clinics give you the opportunity to work with real clients. This is a great way to sharpen your client counseling skills," advises Ira Moltz.

❖ If you're interested in zoning and land use law, consider **attending local zoning and planning board meetings**. "I recommend attending such meetings on a regular basis to learn more about the subject," says Tina Makoulian.

❖ **Make yourself part of the community of real estate lawyers** by becoming active in national, state, or local bar associations. "I've enjoyed my involvement in the Young Lawyers Section of the Chicago Bar Association," says Kristine Iida. "I've met other young lawyers who specialize in real estate. The programs the real estate committee has are really interesting and keep you up to date on the latest developments in the field." Bar associations generally allow law students to join for a nominal fee, and students are welcome to attend most of their programs.

REAL ESTATE ATTORNEYS INTERVIEWED FOR THIS SECTION

Bryan Scott Blade
Frost & Jacobs LLP
Cincinnati, Ohio
UNDERGRADUATE: Denison University
LAW SCHOOL: Northwestern University School of Law

Kristine Iida
Sonnenschein Nath & Rosenthal
Chicago, Illinois
UNDERGRADUATE: Ripon College
LAW SCHOOL: Chicago-Kent College of Law, Illinois Institute of
Technology

Tina Makoulian
Ballard Spahr Andrews & Ingersoll, LLP
Philadelphia, Pennsylvania
UNDERGRADUATE: University of Pennsylvania
LAW SCHOOL: Villanova University School of Law

Ira Moltz
Law Offices of Ira Moltz
Chicago, Illinois
UNDERGRADUATE: Northwestern University
LAW SCHOOL: American University Washington College of Law

Securities Law

What is Securities Law?

A security represents an investment in a business. Securities take many forms: shares of stock or partnership units in Microsoft, Amazon.com, or a friend's at-home cleaning business; bonds issued to finance a community building project; a package of loans or mortgages offered for sale by a financial institution; or a financial instrument representing an investment in an electric power generation project in a developing country. An investment in any of these securities has its risks as well as its rewards. Securities lawyers are involved in transactions related to the generation, management, and transfer of these assets or debt instruments. As part of their practice, securities lawyers often become involved in advising their clients concerning the types of instruments and legal structures available for raising capital for businesses.

Both state and federal laws regulate the sale of securities. The Securities Act of 1933 is a federal law which requires that securities sold to the public be registered with the federal government (through the U.S. Securities and Exchange Commission) and that complete information regarding the seller of the stock and the stock offering itself be available to investors. The Securities Act of 1934 governs the operation of stock exchanges and trading. Securities lawyers help their clients through this maze of federal regulations and the equally complex state regulations, which are sometimes referred to as "blue sky" laws. Blue sky laws were given their unusual name in a case in which the court said that the speculative schemes involved had no more basis than so many feet of blue sky. (State v. Cushing, 137 Me. 112, 15 A.2d 740 (1940))

Financing Business Transactions

The term "financing" is a broad term which includes all types of transactions undertaken for the purpose of raising capital, whether a loan from a single bank or the issuance of stock to thousands of investors. A loan from a bank or a group of banks does not usually involve the issuance of securities. However, those loans may be grouped together in a package and then sold as securities to a financial institution or investor group. Almost every other type of financial transaction does require the issuance of securities, and some types of securities must be registered under state and federal securities laws or must be shown to be exempt from those laws. In such cases, lawyers determine whether the transaction should be structured to include securities that must be registered under federal and state laws; consider the tax consequences of the transaction; negotiate the term of the security; negotiate agreements with third parties who are involved in the financing (such as brokers or underwriters); prepare disclosure documents required by state and federal laws; and take whatever steps are necessary to close, or complete, the transaction.

Public and Private Offerings

A public offering involves the offer or sale of securities to the public. Usually a local, regional, or national investment banking house acts as an underwriter, which agrees to purchase the entire security issue for a specified price for resale to the public. A public offering begins with the negotiation of a letter of agreement between the issuer of the stock and the underwriter(s). Public stock offerings also require the filing of a disclosure statement (a detailed registration statement) with the Securities and

Exchange Commission (SEC). Disclosure statements can be extremely complex and involve careful decisions regarding the types of information that must be disclosed about the company. They may involve a description of the stock issuer's business, an assessment of possible liabilities the company may face in litigation, information about its past and present financial condition, and assurances of its future business prospects. In completing such a statement, the lawyer becomes intimately familiar with the company, its staff, and its operations.

Though the SEC sometimes allows registration statements to become effective without review, complex public offerings generally face an SEC review. This involves extensive discussions between the SEC and the lawyer representing the organization making the offering. Once the SEC is satisfied that adequate disclosure has been made, the registration statement becomes effective and the actual sale of securities to the public can begin.

A private placement of securities is the sale of equity or debt securities to a limited group of investors. Private offerings do not require filing a disclosure statement with the SEC, but they do require a statement of disclosure for distribution to potential investors and the same careful evaluation of the types of information necessary for disclosure.

Reporting Requirements

Once a registration statement has become effective, the issuing organization has to comply with federal and state reporting laws. The Securities Act of 1934 requires the issuer to file regular reports in order to keep the public security holders informed about the state of the organization. Securities lawyers counsel their clients concerning the best way to maintain compliance with the 1934 Act. The Act requires the filing of quarterly and annual reports that describe the organization's operational and financial condition. If there is a "voting class" of stock, the 1934 Act requires that the organization prepare and distribute proxy statements that allow the shareholders to vote at the shareholders' annual meeting. The 1934 Act also protects shareholders by requiring that directors, officers, and significant shareholders of the organization's stock file reports detailing their ownership of the securities. If the stock is traded on a stock exchange, the issuing organization must also comply with the rules of that exchange.

Life as a Securities Lawyer

Where do securities lawyers work?

Most lawyers who specialize in securities law work in law firms or for the government, whether for the SEC or for state commissions that regulate the securities industry. Many large and mid-size law firms with a business-oriented practice have lawyers who specialize in securities law. Other attorneys practice on their own or associate with a small number of other attorneys.

Who are their clients and what types of cases do they work on?

Securities lawyers who work for law firms represent a broad range of clients—including investors, brokerage houses, financial institutions, and corporations. Sarah Beshar, a partner at Davis Polk & Wardwell in New York, says that she represents a mix of financial institutions and corporate clients. She explains that she handles matters for a number of large, well-known financial institutions as well as for all kinds of corporations, from Fortune 100 companies to start-up companies. "My specialty is in the retail area; a number of my clients are retail organizations. I get involved when they want to go public [make a public stock offering to raise capital]. I help them reorganize so that they're in a position to go public. We stay with these clients as general corporate and securities lawyers, assisting them with securities compliance. When the companies grow and expand, we guide them through the issues related to expansion and their ongoing capital requirements." About half of Sarah's clients are based in New York City; the rest are scattered throughout the U.S.

Mark Longenecker, Jr., a securities and mergers and acquisitions lawyer at Frost & Jacobs LLP in Cincinnati, is the chair of his firm's Business/Corporate department. Mark reports that his clients are generally corporations in Cincinnati and outlying areas of the city. "My clients typically need a wide variety of services, some of which they get from me and some of which are provided by other lawyers in the firm under my direction." Mark's practice involves all types of securities and corporate representation of public and private corporations, including public and private offerings, initial public offerings (IPOs), and the organization and financing of start-up ventures. Mark also provides advice to his clients concerning the duties of officers and directors of the corporation, as well as guidance concerning acquisitions and corporate restructurings.

Jerome (Jerry) Tatar has his own practice in Oak Brook, Illinois, a suburb outside of Chicago. Jerry's clients include public and private corporations, brokerage houses, and small businesses trying to raise capital. Jerry also represents individual investors who allege that their investment was mishandled or that they were misled during the investment process. Securities litigation is about 20% of his practice. "An individual investor may believe that a broker didn't follow a proper plan or was looking out for his or her own interest as opposed to the investor's interest," he explains.

Much of Jerry's practice involves client counseling. "I often work with companies that are just starting up or that are entering a new phase of expansion. These organizations are looking for additional funds to help them grow through an offer of securities. My role is putting together the disclosure documents so that people are fully informed before they invest their money. I assist the client in meeting state and federal regulations. I explain what they have to do with regard to preparing and filing documents, I tell them what they can and can't say in their disclosure materials, and I explain how they can go about selling the securities."

"As a government lawyer, you have only one client—the people of the United States," explains John Reed Stark of the Division of Enforcement, U.S. Securities and Exchange Commission, in Washington, D.C. "Every minute of your day is spent working to make things better for U.S. citizens—in this instance, to protect and preserve the integrity of the U.S. securities markets." The proper maintenance of capital markets requires the free flow of information and strict adherence to guidelines governing the markets. As the Chief of the Office of Internet Enforcement, John investigates and prosecutes civil securities violations that involve the Internet. The cases he handles generally involve stock market manipulation, financial fraud, and phony securities offerings. John says, "There's no typical case. Each investigation has a unique dynamic that makes it fascinating—an anonymous informant, an emerging area of fraud, a high profile issuer of securities, etc." As an example, John recalls a case he worked on in which he and his boss were on their sixth conference call with two anonymous informants. "My boss and I called them #1 and #2. Just before the four of us hung up, #1 said to the other informant, 'Hey, Joe, call me back!' and #2 said 'Okay, no problem, Wayne.' When we hung up, they had confirmed their identities by their own words—I had company records and was able to figure out who they were."

What daily activities are involved in securities law practice?

Because they spend so much time counseling clients, lawyers practicing securities law spend a great deal of time in telephone conferences and in meetings with their clients. "A lot of work is done over the phone. But if I'm involved in a deal, we still tend to have on-site meetings," explains Sarah Beshar. "We go to the corporation and we see the company, the site, the corporate offices, and the stores. We fly out early in the morning and home in the evening. It makes for a long, but productive, day." Sarah's transactional work also involves teams of lawyers from her firm. "Sometimes we'll have a meeting with three or four general corporate lawyers, two tax lawyers, one environmental lawyer, an employee benefits lawyer, one or two other specialists, and one or two paralegals." Each of these specialists may have input into the disclosure made in the securities offering.

Mark Longenecker conducts most of his securities practice from his office. He reports that, like Sarah, he spends a good deal of time in telephone conferences and at meetings. "A securities transaction requires some substantial planning meetings with the client, the drafting of documents, and participation in due diligence meetings to ascertain that the information used in drafting is correct." As an attorney with over 20 years of experience, Mark spends a significant amount of time supervising young attorneys in implementing client plans and drafting documents.

Jerry Tatar's time is spent handling litigation matters as well as putting together information for public offerings. His securities litigation work is typical of other types of litigation work—drafting documents, conducting discovery (depositions and interrogatories), conducting legal research, preparing materials for hearings. (*See* the Civil Litigation chapter for further information on these activities.) Much of his litigation is handled in arbitration (an out-of-court hearing handled by an impartial mediator). Brokerage accounts often require that disputes be handled in arbitration, rather than through the court system. The complaint is filed with the National Association of Securities Dealers and is tried in a hearing in front of a single arbitrator or a team of arbitrators. "Arbitration is less expensive and more efficient than traditional litigation. Whether in litigation or arbitration, most cases settle," explains Jerry.

Jerry's work helping companies put together public offerings requires a great deal of data gathering. "I gather information about the company, its officers and directors, its history, its marketing issues, and its competition. I put the information together in a form that is a disclosure document but is also a marketing piece. There are often negatives about a company—and they need to be stated. For example, a company with an operating history of losses needs to show how its leadership has turned things around for the future. You must set out the true information—the positives and the negatives. As a result, people who invest are truly committed and informed."

John Stark of the SEC says that most of his time is spent at his desk or in meetings. He explains, "The investigation of securities violations requires spending a lot of time reviewing documents, testimony, and market data."

What do securities lawyers find rewarding about their practice?

The securities lawyers we talked to are truly fascinated by the business world. "I really enjoy the business aspect of the practice," says Sarah Beshar. "I like learning how my clients' businesses work and learning why the businesses do what they do." Adds Jerry Tatar, "I enjoy seeing my clients' success. I value my role in helping them make their businesses succeed."

Securities lawyers were also enthusiastic about the wide range of people with whom they work. "My job involves lots of people contact," says Sarah Beshar. "I meet a huge range of wonderful characters all across corporate America. It's fascinating to meet these people and learn about what they make, whether it's designer apparel, razors, or high tech instruments." Mark Longenecker explains that his greatest reward comes from working with his colleagues at Frost & Jacobs. "The most personally rewarding aspect of my job is seeing a substantial document in its final form that we have written together as a team."

Jerry Tatar finds reward in working with individual investors who are victims of securities fraud. "I've worked with people who decided to retire based on the predictions of a broker using fraudulent practices. It feels good when a wrong has been righted." He adds, "Brokers can be wronged, too. Some investors use litigation to guard against losses. I feel good about protecting brokers who are wrongfully accused, as well."

Lawyers who work for the government have a unique opportunity to provide a valued public service. When we asked John Stark about the rewards of his practice as an SEC lawyer, he responded, simply and emphatically, "Public service and doing justice."

The Training and Skills Important to Securities Law

How do people enter the field of securities law?

Some attorneys become securities lawyers because of their interest in business. Explains Mark Longenecker, "My current practice is an outgrowth of my early interest in business. My interest in this area was fostered by a number of attorneys at my prior firm and my current firm who showed me that this practice area can be very rewarding and very exciting." Sarah Beshar joined the corporate department of Davis Polk after law school. She rotated through the various business practice areas of the firm, including mergers and acquisitions, lending, and securities. "I chose to do securities law. I've always been interested in business. I enjoy learning about the intricacies of our clients' businesses." Sarah adds that although it's not necessary to have a financial background, it can be "wonderfully helpful." She says that a familiarity with business or accounting is a "huge advantage, but not necessary."

Sarah believes that large firms offer the best training for a career in securities law. "A large firm gives you the opportunity to try different areas of corporate practice. It's important to become a well-rounded corporate lawyer first. This makes you a better securities lawyer—you have more depth, more knowledge," she explains.

Some attorneys enter the field of securities law by chance. For John Stark of the SEC, "It was chance, more than anything else. I saw an ad, thought it was interesting, had an interview, and accepted the job, mostly because I was bored by my firm. I hadn't even taken securities courses in law school. But I had always known I wanted to be some type of prosecutor, and working for the SEC has given me that opportunity." As John's career continued, he took advantage of opportunities at the Division of Enforcement. After starting as a staff attorney, John moved up to Senior Counsel, then to

Special Assistant United States Attorney. He then became Special Counsel for Internet Projects, and finally moved into his present position as Chief of the newly created Office of Internet Enforcement. "Unlike firm life, where the goal remains primarily to make partner, the government offers a variety of tracks for advancement, but also the opportunity to make your own opportunities," explains John.

Jerry Tatar's undergraduate degree was in political science. He then pursued a graduate degree in social work and became a social services administrator before entering law school. His first job as a law student was working for an attorney specializing in securities law. Upon graduation, he began his career in a small firm and eventually developed his own practice. "It's helpful if you can find a mentor in this area. Often law graduates start at large firms that have securities law departments and develop an expertise in the area."

What skills are most important to securities lawyers?

* **Well-developed legal skills, including legal writing skills,** play a critical role in the success of a securities lawyer. Mark Longenecker says simply, "The most important skills for a lawyer's success in this area are a very broad knowledge of the law and a good legal drafting style."

* The lawyers we talked to agreed that securities lawyers need **good analytical skills**. John Stark and Sarah Beshar stress the importance of analytical skills. "You need to be able to spot problems, solve them with good judgment, and move on," Sarah says.

* **Creativity** is important in this area of law practice. "Things aren't always black and white," explains Jerry Tatar. "This type of work requires creative problem-solving. You need to be creative in order to find good solutions. You need to think outside the box."

* Because they do so much client counseling, **communication skills** are especially important to the securities lawyer. "The ability to articulate is important. Presentation skills are key. Enthusiasm and energy are tremendous assets," explains Sarah Beshar.

* Securities law requires **leadership and team-building skills**. Sarah Beshar speaks passionately about the importance of teamwork. "You need to move your own team, your client, and a large transaction

forward. This involves leading a large team of people. You have to motivate the team members and help them work through their differences. Securities law is not as confrontational as other areas of practice. Everyone wants to get to the same place—they want to move the project forward." Sarah notes that Davis Polk offers team-building classes to assist attorneys in developing these skills.

❖ The practice of securities law demands close **attention to detail**. Says Jerry Tatar, "The practice is extremely detail-oriented. You have to be willing to take the time to fight through a lot of documents. You have to like gathering and organizing information."

What classes and law school experiences do securities lawyers recommend?

❖ Take a **securities law class** in law school. Says Mark Longenecker, "Courses to prepare one for this field are extremely important and include securities law and all kinds of business planning courses. Without that background in law school, it can be difficult to pick up all of the lingo and the complicated aspects of the practice through on-the-job training."

❖ Consider taking other **business-related courses** in law school. Jerry Tatar recommends courses such as tax and corporations and partnerships. Sarah Beshar warns students not to overdo business-related courses, however. "Be sure to take courses you enjoy so that you maintain your enthusiasm for the study of law. It's important to be a well-rounded lawyer."

❖ If you plan to do securities litigation, take a **trial practice class**, advises Jerry Tatar. "Even if you don't do litigation," he says, "the classes are excellent preparation for thinking on your feet and dealing with high pressure situations."

❖ **Gain practical experience by working as a law clerk or a summer associate** for a firm that handles securities-related issues or as a government intern. "Clerking for a law firm is a great experience. It opens lots of doors," says Jerry Tatar. John Stark advises law students to consider internship programs that allow them to work for the government offices in which they are interested. "Law schools have internship programs that can place students in offices that will never open up until after years of practice. Internships also allow students to network and build connections that can last a lifetime."

❖ **Work as a judicial extern during law school or as a judicial law clerk upon graduation.** A judicial clerkship or externship will help you develop strong writing skills. Clerkships also offer the unique opportunity to form a relationship with a judge and his or her clerks. These mentoring relationships are an outstanding way to build your legal network. John Stark says, "Law clerks always seem to have a leg up under all the circumstances."

❖ Become involved in your **law school's clinical programs**. Clinical programs allow you to practice your analytical skills, problem-solving skills, and client counseling skills. Even if the clinics aren't related to business law, they offer an excellent way to build the skills valued by securities lawyers. Says John Stark, "I think that clinics, no matter what one sees as a future career, are always the best classes to take."

❖ Jerry Tatar recommends finding a **summer or part-time job in a brokerage house or as a runner on the floor of a stock exchange**. He comments, "No matter how lowly the job, it's a great way to find out what happens in a brokerage house or in an exchange. You learn what happens on a daily basis; you learn how the stock market works. These are truly valuable experiences."

SECURITIES ATTORNEYS INTERVIEWED FOR THIS SECTION

Sarah Beshar
Davis Polk & Wardwell
New York, New York
UNDERGRADUATE: University of Western Australia
LAW SCHOOL: University of Oxford (U.K.)

Mark H. Longenecker, Jr.
Frost & Jacobs LLP
Cincinnati, Ohio
UNDERGRADUATE: Williams College; Denison University
LAW SCHOOL: Harvard Law School

John Reed Stark
U.S. Securities and Exchange Commission, Division of Enforcement
Washington, D.C.
UNDERGRADUATE: Union College
LAW SCHOOL: Duke University School of Law

Jerome A. Tatar
Jerome A. Tatar, Attorney at Law
Oak Brook, Illinois
UNDERGRADUATE: Knox College
LAW SCHOOL: Loyola University Chicago School of Law

Solo, Small Firm, and General Practice

What is Solo, Small Firm, and General Practice?

The term "general practitioner" brings to mind a lawyer in the mold of Abraham Lincoln—a pillar of the community who represented shopkeepers, farmers, businesses, and accused criminal defendants while also finding time to be involved in politics and local government. Today's small firm and solo practitioners, whether in rural or metropolitan areas, handle a myriad of legal problems, may serve as part-time prosecutors or government employees, and are active in bar associations and other community activities.

While large firms often generate the most coverage in legal publications and the popular press, and large firms have a high profile at many law schools because of their participation in on-campus interviewing programs, solo and small firm practitioners make up the bulk of legal practice. A 1994 report published by the American Bar Foundation (a 1994 Supplement to the *Lawyer Statistical Report* published by the American Bar Foundation and the American Bar Association State Ranking Report) reported an estimated 946,000 lawyers in the United States; of that number 44% were in solo practice or in very small firms of five or fewer lawyers. Of the approximately 690,000 lawyers in private practice, solo practitioners accounted for 45% and small firm lawyers represented an additional 15%. Thus nearly two-thirds of the lawyers in private practice were in solo practice or in small firms.

Many solo practitioners and lawyers in small firms have general practices in which they service members of their community by handling a variety of legal matters, just as Abraham Lincoln did. They may assist individuals and small and mid-size businesses or may provide special counsel to a large business. They may assist individuals by drafting wills; setting up estate plans; handling tax matters; dealing with divorces, child custody issues, adoptions, and other family law issues; conducting real estate closings; and providing representation in personal injury or employment law matters. They may assist businesses with their incorporation needs as well as with contracts, tax, employment law, and collections issues. Other solo and small firm practitioners specialize in representing individuals or businesses in particular legal areas, such as family law, estate planning, personal injury, or employment law.

Whether they are general practitioners or whether they specialize in a particular practice area, solo and small firm practitioners face a unique set of challenges and find an abundant array of rewards in their practices. Solo and small firm practitioners are highly involved in both the representation of their clients and in the entrepreneurial challenges of establishing and maintaining a law practice, as well as the administration of a law firm. They must think about issues such as how to develop and keep clients; how to finance their practices; how to hire, train, and effectively manage a legal staff, including support personnel, paralegals, and law clerks; how to bill their clients and collect their billings; and how to plan and budget for the future.

The rewards are rich and diverse. Solo and small firm practitioners have the satisfaction of being completely responsible for their own business, from determining their office decor and the associated overhead to determining their work style and pace and the associated lifestyle benefits.

Solo and small firm practitioners can often build flexible schedules that allow them to participate in community leadership, whether with the park district or the school board or the community caucus, and yet have time to spend with their families. Another reward of solo and small firm practice is that the practitioners have the opportunity to work closely with their clients on a daily basis. Like Abraham Lincoln, who signed his letters to clients, "Your obedient servant, A. Lincoln," solo and small firm practitioners have a genuine opportunity to use their talents to guide fellow members of their communities through our legal system.

Life as a Solo, Small Firm, or General Practitioner

Where do solo, small firm, and general practitioners work?

Solo, small firm, and general practitioners have offices in large cities, suburbs, towns of all sizes, and rural areas. Many solo practitioners share office space with another lawyer or a group of lawyers to keep overhead costs at a reasonable level. Space-sharing arrangements are also helpful to new solo practitioners who may receive client referrals from the attorneys with whom they share office space. Some solo practitioners work part-time for the government and spend the balance of their time handling cases for individuals and businesses. In some small firms, each practitioner may handle a different practice area—one attorney may handle family law issues while another handles estate planning. In other small (or "boutique") firms, all the members of the firm specialize in a particular area of the law, such as plaintiffs' personal injury law or estate planning. In yet other small firms, all the attorneys are general practitioners and each handles a wide variety of cases.

In addition to the attorneys profiled in this chapter, a number of solo and small firm practitioners are profiled in other chapters of this book, including:

Family Law — Sharon L. Gibson (Law Offices of Sharon Lynn Gibson); Kathleen Hogan Morrison (Law Offices of Kathleen Hogan Morrison); Beverly A. Pekala (The Law Offices of Beverly A. Pekala); Harry Schaffner (Schaffner & Van Der Snick, P.C.); Jeffrey Warchol (Machulak, Hutchinson, Robertson & O'Dess, S.C.)

Labor and Employment Law — Mary Mikva (Abrahamson Vorachek & Mikva)

Securities Law — Jerome A. Tatar (Attorney at Law)

Trusts & Estates Law — Mary Baker Edwards (Blue & Edwards, P.A.); William Sheridan (Finger Hochman & Delott, P.C.)

Who are their clients and what types of cases do they work on?

Solo and small firm practitioners may represent individuals or businesses or both, depending upon the nature of their practice. Emil Caliendo is a general solo practitioner in Chicago. Most of his clients are individuals. "My clients are typically working class people in and around the Chicago area who require a variety of legal services. Some of the more common services I perform for my clients relate to real estate and small business conveyances, corporations issues, domestic relations, personal injury, worker's compensation, misdemeanor criminal defense, traffic court defense, probate, and wills." Emil also works for the State of Illinois. "I am also a Legal Advisor for the Illinois Secretary of State. In this role I advise state employees and officials on the administration of state laws relating mainly to traffic regulation, the automobile sales and parts business, and the commercial driving school industry."

David Feldkamp is a solo practitioner in Louisville, Kentucky. About 30% of David's clients are businesses. "The businesses are small and include contractors, subcontractors, body shops, construction companies, and a number of small landlords." For the landlords, David writes their leases and handles evictions. For the other small businesses, David handles contract disputes, incorporations to limit liability, the purchase and sale of businesses, and some collections work (collecting past due bills). David estimates that 70% of his clients are individuals, for whom he works on matters including bankruptcies, plaintiffs' personal injury cases, estate planning, and probate work. "Every solo practitioner has to decide for himself or herself what cases he or she can best handle. I tried to identify the areas of high client frustration and avoid those. So two areas that I try to avoid are family law and collections. I do some limited collections work for businesses, but generally, once an individual reviews the risks and rewards of collecting past due funds, they decide they don't want to chase bad money with good money."

David also works part-time for the government—he spends half of his time as a prosecutor for the Jefferson County, Kentucky, District Attorney. This means that he cannot handle criminal matters as a private attorney, as that would create a conflict of interest. "My role as a prosecutor is mainly in dependency court, where I look out for children who are victims of abuse and neglect. The work has given me an excellent chance to develop my skills as a trial attorney, as I have to prove in court that the child in question is at risk," he says.

Ira Moltz is a general practitioner with two offices: one in downtown Chicago and the other in northwest suburban Arlington Heights, Illinois. "I have a one-person practice, and that one person is me," says Ira, with his characteristic good humor. "The majority of my clients aren't Fortune 500 companies but are rather small business people or private individuals. There's a lot of overlap between my business clients and the individuals I serve, as the small business people may come to me to handle a divorce or house closing, and the individuals may have business issues they bring to me." Real estate matters comprise about 30% of Ira's practice. "The fees that one can charge for residential real estate closings are really quite modest. At the low end, the fee may be $300 and at the high end, the fee may be $600. As a solo practitioner, you need to do a number of real estate closings to make them worthwhile. Most general practitioners do them not because they are great money makers, but because you meet people in the community who may come to you for other legal matters and who can provide referrals within the community."

Nevertheless, Ira says, "Real estate is my favorite area of law. It's not confrontational; it's one of the few areas of law in which there's a win-win situation for everyone involved." (You can read more about Ira's real estate practice in the Real Estate Law chapter of this book.) Ira provides his business clients with advice on incorporation and contract disputes, and he represents them in any litigation in which they may become involved. For private individuals Ira handles family law issues and criminal defense matters and prepares wills and trusts. Like many general practitioners, there are some matters that Ira doesn't handle; for example, he refers bankruptcies or personal injury cases to other attorneys who specialize in those areas.

Laura Todd Johnson, of Johnson & Slate, a two-person firm in Tucson, Arizona, specializes in employment discrimination work. Her law partner specializes in criminal defense work. "Before we opened our own practice, we worked as city prosecutors together," explains Laura. "My clients are primarily women who have been discriminated against in the workplace. They are hurt and upset, and, understandably, they are disgruntled employees. Some cases involve racial discrimination or discrimination due to disability but, by far, most are sexual harassment cases."

After eight years in a mid-size litigation firm, Yvonne Owens opened her own practice, Owens & Associates, in Chicago in January of 1997. Yvonne specializes in employment law. She has no associates yet, but she has two law clerks and a paralegal. "My clients range from individuals to small firms to mid-size corporations with as many as 600 employees. I currently have three or four corporate clients that I work for on a consistent basis." Yvonne explains that she seeks to offer a wide variety of services to her corporate clients. "My firm does more than just handle employment discrimination. I also do corporate training and counseling. I do corporate seminars on issues such as preventing sexual harassment claims, making the best hire, etc. My corporate clients are in the commodities industry, which is an industry with a history of sexual harassment. I work on the defense side of cases for my corporate clients. But I also handle plaintiff's work for individuals. My clients include college professors and administrators and other professionals, and the defendants include such large organizations as the Chicago Transit Authority and the City of Chicago."

What daily activities are involved in solo, small firm, and general practice?

"Because as a generalist I handle so many different legal matters, my activities vary significantly from day to day," says Emil Caliendo. "Whether it's reviewing a real estate contract in my office with an anxious young couple purchasing their first home or going to court to address a jury on the first day of a trial against a high-powered insurance company, each day brings a new and different challenge." Emil told us a story that illustrates that, when working with individuals, no legal matter is ever routine. "The most memorable experience I had as a practitioner occurred early in my legal career. A client asked me to prepare her will. During the initial consultation, we discussed the important aspects of estate planning. I took copious notes and gathered all the necessary information concerning her estate and her intended beneficiaries. I prepared the will in accordance with her wishes and it was executed at my office at our second meeting. 'A job well done,' I thought to myself. About two weeks later I was informed that the woman had passed away and that she had been suffering from a terminal disease for some time prior to her initial meeting with me. Upon hearing this sad news, I realized how utterly insensitive I had been to what the woman was going through during her initial consultation with me. I also realized for the very first time that, as a young lawyer, I needed to develop a greater sensibility and keener insight into the real-life problems my clients experience." Since he started practicing in 1980, Emil has built a base of loyal clients who come back to him because they know he handles their issues with the sensitivity they deserve.

David Feldkamp told us that as a general practitioner, he handles a wide range of matters on a daily basis. "I'm usually in court, in front of a judge, once or twice a week. Most every day I'm at court to file pleadings. Most every day I'm meeting with clients. I also do legal drafting, drafting complaints, wills, trusts, motions, and other legal documents. Legal research can be expensive for my clients, so I usually hire law clerks to do it at an hourly rate. On an average day, I have a couple of client meetings, draft five or six letters, and have several hours worth of phone calls. Whenever I'm out of the office, I come back to a stack of phone messages. Returning calls is a top priority. The chief complaint clients across America have of their lawyers is that they don't return phone calls. Sometimes it's a chore to return calls, as you may be delivering bad news or dealing with difficult personalities, but every day those calls have to be returned. It's the right thing to do," explains David.

David says that as a solo practitioner, he spends some time each week on firm administration issues. David shares office space with a group of attorneys in Louisville. "As part of my space-sharing arrangement, the other attorneys and I hired a really good office manager. She keeps track of expenses and makes sure the bills are paid each month. She also makes sure that the clients pay their bills. She's a tremendous help. If I didn't have her services, I would have to spend as many as 20 hours a week on administrative matters, which simply doesn't make economic sense. During the business week, I need to be practicing."

Ira Moltz reports that his general practice guarantees that each day is different than the last. "What I do varies tremendously from day to day. I like the variety. I'm in different places on different days." On any given day, Ira may be at one of his offices, at a house closing, arguing a motion in court, conducting a deposition, or preparing for trial. Most days he has meetings with clients and spends time talking with clients and other attorneys on the phone. Ira says that he may handle as many as 50 telephone calls a day. "Sometimes I feel like I need to be in three places at once, and that can be stressful. Sometimes it's hard to fit everything I need to do into the course of a day, but that's what makes general practice so interesting—it's never humdrum, it's never boring."

Employment lawyer Laura Todd Johnson spends a good part of her time counseling clients and preparing cases for trial. "The sensitive nature of the cases means that most of the cases ultimately settle, but they may settle on the eve of trial," she reports. This means that Laura, like any litigation attorney, is involved in drafting and responding to motions, undertaking discovery, and interviewing witnesses (*see* the Civil Litigation chapter for more information on these activities). "I spend a significant amount of time each day either on the phone answering clients' questions or meeting with prospective clients in my office," says Laura. "I may do as many as three or four telephone consultations per day, in which people want to know what their legal rights are in a particular employment situation." Laura says that though she spends the bulk of her time on her case work, being part of a two-person firm means that she spends a significant amount of time handling the business aspects of the practice. "Law firm management involves everything from choosing a telephone system to making sure the photocopier is running," she says. "When you have your own practice, you have to be humble enough to fill the stapler and change the toner cartridge in the photocopier. This can be hard to get used to at first when you're accustomed to working in government or large firm practice."

Yvonne Owens' employment law caseload includes 20 cases that are currently in litigation, including 12 in federal district court, four in state courts, and the balance before the Illinois Human Rights Commission. In addition, she has a number of cases pending before the Equal Employment Opportunity Commission, the Illinois Department of Human Rights, and the Chicago Commission on Human Relations. The day before we interviewed Yvonne, she had taken and defended a total of five depositions. On other days, she says, she may conduct a training class at a corporation in the morning and handle a deposition in the afternoon. "I organize my practice so that each day that I'm in the office, I do one client consultation, meeting either with a current client or a new client. I also draft and argue motions, handle pre-trial conferences, engage in discovery, and interview witnesses. Right now I am working on my first appeal to the Seventh Circuit."

Yvonne also conducts informational seminars and training sessions for her corporate clients. "I provide clients with the information they need about employment issues, from hiring to promotion to termination. I teach corporate employees how to document employee performance problems and how to prepare for and conduct employment reviews. I show managers how and what to document with regard to employee performance problems. I also conduct seminars on management skills. People skills are tremendously important to managers. Relating to your employees is an acquired skill. I teach managers how to train and nurture and supervise their employees so that they are working with the best employee possible."

Management of her firm also occupies Yvonne's time. "I'm taking care of billing as well as managing my own staff. I'm often out of the office, so it's especially important for me to set up work assignments for my staff members to give them an idea of what I expect them to accomplish on a daily and weekly basis." Yvonne's entrepreneurial duties don't end there. "I also think very consciously about marketing. I have a marketing plan, and I'm pretty systematic about following it because it's the bottom line for the firm—getting business and keeping it is key." Yvonne notes that being an entrepreneur means taking care of the mundane things as well as the exciting things. "From getting and taking care of the clients to ordering the supplies I need to collecting the money and paying the bills—I get to do it all. Everything!" she says with satisfaction.

What do solo, small firm, and general practitioners find rewarding about their practice?

"My image of a lawyer is that of a professional whom people can count on for legal advice and assistance, no matter how big or small the problem might be," says Emil Caliendo. That's exactly the kind of lawyer that Emil's general practice allows him to be. "The greatest satisfaction I derive from my practice comes from my clients. My clients come to me for legal advice and assistance in their time of need. They place their confidence and trust in me. There is no greater reward for a lawyer than the knowledge that the people to whom he provides services have complete confidence in his integrity, ability, and character."

David Feldkamp agrees that helping people with a wide variety of legal problems makes general practice particularly rewarding. "I really enjoy meeting with my clients," David says. "They come to your office, and they see your degree framed on the wall. You may be the only attorney they know. It's a position of trust. It's an incredibly rewarding thing to have people put their trust in you and to have them expect you to do a good job. I really try to put myself in their shoes and to be frank and forthright with them. It's refreshing to meet each new client because of the trust and confidence they have in you."

David is enthusiastic about the challenges a general solo practice offers. "Every now and then you really feel the power of the law when you, alone, take something to trial and win for your client. Winning is both exciting and rewarding. When you get a judgment against someone or you win a case, you really feel the power of the law and how it affects people. The law is really a life-changing force." David also likes the fact that he sees the results of his work. "I have a friend who works for a big firm on large cases. Once he hangs up his jacket in the morning, he doesn't move beyond the confines of his office, and because the cases last for years, he seldom sees the results of his work. I, on the other hand, need to see the results of my work. And I get to see them on a daily basis. My job as a general practitioner is very task-oriented. A client comes in with a problem and the question is, how are we going to solve it? I get immediate feedback from the client, work on resolving the problem, and move on to the next thing. I'm constantly getting feedback from clients."

David confides that he enjoys the intellectual rigor of his practice. "I like the daily testing I encounter when I go to court. You're always learning, and you're always challenging yourself to do your best, because you're up against some of the finest people in the profession every day. When a trial or hearing goes well, you can say to yourself, 'I'm glad I'm a lawyer. This is fun!' And that's why you practice law, so that you can have those moments. There are lots of hard times, but there are those special moments that make it all worthwhile. Such a moment might occur when you ask just the right question on cross-examination, and you know you asked just the right question, and you know that the judge and the opposing attorney know that you did quality legal work, and that's really enjoyable."

Ira Moltz enjoys the variety of cases he works on as a general practitioner. "My favorite issues involve real estate, because real estate deals generally have happy endings. But I have to admit that I really like the variety of my general practice. Things are never routine. And one of the best parts of being a general practitioner is that you develop marketable skills in a number of legal areas, which means that you're not at the mercy of the marketplace. You're constantly developing a new expertise and staying ahead of market trends."

"I enjoy getting up in the morning," says Laura Todd Johnson about the joys of having her own employment law practice. "I'm following through on my dream of making a difference in people's lives. I care so much about these people, and it means so much to me to make a difference in their lives. I just love the relationships I develop with my clients. When my clients leave my office, they look visibly relieved because they've found someone to help them. Many clients say to me, 'You are the first person who actually listened to my story and understands what I'm talking about.'"

Employment lawyer Yvonne Owens extols the joys of opening your own firm. "The pursuit of the dream of having your own firm can be one of life's most rewarding experiences. Following your dream means you get the opportunity to make as much money as you want to make, to service the clients you want to service, and to contribute to the legal community and the community at large," Yvonne says. "But," she cautions, "no one can fulfill this dream but you. Starting your own firm is something you have to do for yourself. In essence it's a gift you give yourself. And you're entrusted with using that gift in the appropriate manner. You have it all—credentials and skills and the opportunity to use them to benefit your clients and the community."

Recently, Yvonne won her law school's young alumni achievement award. When she received the award, she told the law school audience, "I came to the law school to learn and now I go to serve. A successful legal career is all about service." Yvonne says that before she had her own firm, service was a remote idea, even though she was active in bar association activities. "Everything seems so different now that I'm working one-on-one with plaintiffs in employment discrimination cases," she says. "I walk in their shoes through their workplace and imagine what they've suffered. That's made me a better lawyer, from both the plaintiff's perspective and the corporate perspective."

Yvonne says that having her own firm allows her to exercise greater creativity and control in her work with clients. "I can use my creative ideas in ways that never would have been encouraged in a more conservative firm." Yvonne offers an example of a client who received a death threat at work. "The threat involved a slang phrase, and the employer took it as a joke," she explains. Working closely with her client, Yvonne developed a video for a pre-trial conference. "I went out on the street and interviewed people, asked them what this slang phrase meant, and filmed people's responses. The people on the street unanimously believed that my client had, indeed, received a death threat. In addition, I reviewed about 20 popular movies in which this slang phrase was used as a death threat and incorporated those video clips in my video presentation. The result was a 10-minute video I presented at a settlement conference. The video made quite an impression. Everyone's eyes were glued to the monitor." Yvonne's presentation made a strong case for her client. "The majority of judges are conservative white males," she says. "There's little likelihood that they would have familiarity with this street terminology. The video allowed me to put the language of the threat in context as it was perceived by the plaintiff. Moreover, the project was an exciting way to use my creativity on behalf of my client."

The lawyers we talked to said that having their own practices allowed them to create their own schedules. Laura Todd Johnson notes that small firm practice has allowed her to invest more time in her family. "I have three boys. My husband is the stay-at-home parent. Going out on my own has allowed me the flexibility I need to spend time with my family." Says Yvonne Owens, "I work long days, but each month I schedule a day for rest and relaxation. That's a day to relax and read a novel or go to a day spa. I didn't have such flexibility before," she says. "My days are beyond 'nine to five,'" reports David Feldkamp. "Usually I'm here until 6:30 p.m. just to get all my phone calls returned." David generally works about 55 hours per week—"But I always make sure to schedule my vacations," he says. When we talked to David, he was preparing to leave for a much anticipated week-long fishing trip to Canada.

The Training and Skills Important to Solo, Small Firm, and General Practice

How do people enter solo, small firm, and general practice?

Most attorneys who open their own firms first gain experience working for other lawyers, whether in a large, mid-size, or small firm or for another solo practitioner. Yvonne Owens asserts that experience in an established law firm is critical. "Go and work for someone else first. Learn the tools of the trade. It's easier to go from being a lawyer to being an owner and a lawyer than it is to learn to be a lawyer and a business owner at the same time." Yvonne worked as a paralegal, then as a law clerk, and then practiced for eight years at a mid-size firm before opening her own shop. "Working in a firm teaches you an incredible number of things, such as how a docketing system should be set up and how to organize case files. It's best to learn all these things by working in a firm first."

Yvonne assures prospective entrepreneurs that they'll know when the time is right to set out on their own. "How much time you spend in another firm isn't as important as the amount of experience you get while you're there. You want to feel both proficient and competent, and you want to feel ready to supervise others doing legal work before you start your own firm. At some point you'll just know that it's time to go out on your own. You'll get what I call the 'entrepreneurial itch.'" Yvonne chose to confine her practice to employment law, the area of law in which she had practiced previously. "It's important for solo practitioners to be careful about the cases they take. I focus on the area of practice in which I'm confident. I venture a bit beyond it and do housing discrimination and some basic breach of contract cases, but for the most part I stick to the area of law in which I feel most experienced and confident."

Office-sharing arrangements allow attorneys who are setting up their own practices to work with experienced practitioners while sharing overhead costs. While David Feldkamp was in law school, he worked as a law clerk for one of the attorneys with whom he now shares office space. Though he's just been out of law school since 1996, David's experience as a prosecutor and his contacts in his space-sharing arrangement have provided him with an excellent foundation for establishing his own general practice. "Contacts are so important," he says. "It's not realistic to say 'I'm going to hang out a shingle and start practicing' on the day after you pass the bar. That could be financially risky and dangerous from a malpractice standpoint. You need to surround yourself with experienced practitioners who will hand you cases and give you guidance on what you're doing. If you're thinking about a solo practice, try to meet someone who will invite you into their practice and mentor you. I was fortunate to meet that person while I was working as a law clerk during law school."

Ira Moltz also advises lawyers who are interested in opening a general practice to pair up with an experienced practitioner. "Get a job working for someone else for a while, to keep yourself out of trouble and to build your confidence. It's easy to get in over your head. You need to learn what cases to take on and what cases to refuse. New solo practitioners usually take on their worst cases out of enthusiasm and ignorance. Start with an employment situation and then move on to a mentoring situation, such as a space-sharing arrangement. No matter how smart you are and how highly motivated you are, there's so much you don't know when you first start out. Having a mentor there to help makes all the difference."

Ira worked for two years as an appellate defender for the State of Illinois doing criminal appeals work (*see* the Appellate Practice and the Criminal Law chapters of this book for more information on criminal appeals) before moving on to work for two and a half years for one solo practitioner and three years for another. He then started his own practice. He, too, shares office space with a group of attorneys. "There's a lot of camaraderie among those of us who share office space. We enjoy each other's company. Sharing a suite also allows us to pool our resources so that we can afford attractive office space. Impressive office space is important for solo practitioners, as it gives clients confidence that you're well established and successful."

David Feldkamp says that working as a prosecutor also provides great training to those considering a solo practice. "Working as a prosecutor is the best experience you can get, because you get to try a lot of cases, you have a tremendous amount of responsibility, and you're highly visible. You sharpen your legal skills and your oral advocacy skills on a daily basis. As a prosecutor you also meet a lot of attorneys within the jurisdiction, and you win their respect. That helps when it comes to client referrals down the road."

Laura Todd Johnson also advises those attorneys thinking of starting their own firm to begin by working first for the government or for a law firm. "As much as I love my practice, I don't recommend doing this right out of law school. You need experience first. There are only so many times you can call your friends when you don't know the answer," she cautions. Laura first gained significant trial experience as a prosecutor (*see* the Criminal Law chapter). "There are so many positives about working as a prosecutor. Within a year I had done 100 trials. I recommend that anyone interested in pursuing a career as a trial attorney consider working as a prosecutor." Laura left the prosecutor's office to pursue a position at the Equal Employment Opportunity Commission (EEOC). She worked at the EEOC for six years before pursuing her dream of opening her own employment law practice. (*See* the Labor and Employment Law chapter for a detailed description of employment law practice.)

Laura further explains, "Most people who open their own employment law practice first develop their expertise in the area as attorneys for the EEOC or other agencies, such as the Arizona Civil Rights Division of the Attorney General's Office. Employment law is a highly specialized area and it's a field in which you really need specialized training. Starting out at an agency such as the EEOC allows you to become immersed in employment law issues and helps you understand all the facets of discrimination. I wouldn't have been able to start my practice without that experience."

David Feldkamp says that his law clerking experience was pivotal in his decision to become a solo practitioner with a general practice. "During law school I spent one summer as a summer associate for a firm in Tennessee. The other summer I worked for the solo practitioner I now share space with. Experiencing the contrast between the two environments convinced me that solo and small firm practice was for me. My advice is this— when you're at your summer associate or law clerking job, work hard, do exceptional work, but also take time to watch what's going on around you. Keep your eyes open and think about these things: What kind of lives do the attorneys live? How late do they work? What is their lifestyle like? Can they take vacations? Really pay close attention. You'll intuitively know the right direction for you."

What skills are most important to solo, small firm, and general practitioners?

❖ Because solo and small firm practitioners work closely with their clients, it's important to **like people**. "You must like people to be a successful general practitioner. I truly enjoy working with my clients; it's great fun," says David Feldkamp. Laura Todd Johnson seconds David's feelings. "I love the connection I have with my clients," she says.

❖ Solo and small firm practitioners must **be passionate in their advocacy for their clients**. Says employment lawyer Yvonne Owens, "You have to believe not only in yourself but also in your client's cause. My practice is more than just a business; it's a cause. The purpose of my practice is to eradicate employment discrimination using the means available to both employers and employees." Explains Laura Todd Johnson, "As a plaintiff's employment lawyer, I work on a contingency fee, which means I am paid (beyond court costs) a percentage of the settlement, if any. You're not doing this type of work to make large sums of money. You must have real compassion for your clients and believe the opportunity to help them is reward in itself."

❖ **Good listening skills** make for satisfied clients who spread the word about your services and help your business grow. "When clients come in, you need to remember that you're their employee," says David Feldkamp, "and you need to know what their problem is and listen to what they want to do about their problem. I ask every client, 'What are your goals? What are your expectations?' I make sure that the client articulates their goals, and then I work with the client to help determine strategy. Lawyers love to gab, and it can be a challenge to force yourself to listen, but it's critically important." Employment lawyer Yvonne Owens agrees that listening skills are paramount. "Next to family matters, employment issues are closest to people's hearts. Self-esteem is tied to employment. People constantly assess their lives by asking, 'Are things going well at home? Are things going well at work?' When clients feel that they've been wrongfully terminated, their anger is palpable. Working as a plaintiff's attorney in this field has helped me sharpen my listening skills, an area that wasn't as well developed for me when I had only corporate clients."

❖ Solo and small firm practitioners must **be comfortable asking for advice**. David Feldkamp says that as a solo general practitioner, he's not afraid to reach out and ask questions of more experienced attorneys. "People love to get called and asked for advice," he says. "It's flattering for more experienced attorneys to be asked to share their expertise. As a solo practitioner, you have to realize that it can be catastrophic *not* to ask for advice. In my network I have a number of people I can count on, including a highly experienced family law practitioner, a high level personal injury attorney, and a person with a tremendous amount of litigation experience. It's important to surround yourself with experienced practitioners, and it's comforting to know that they're there."

❖ Those attorneys who develop their own practice need a **high level of energy**. "To be successful as a general practitioner, you need both the interest and the drive to take on a variety of legal matters and issues. Each case is different and poses a new set of challenges. The level of success you experience in general practice will be measured by the degree of dedication you have to each case," advises Emil Caliendo.

❖ Solo and small firm practitioners need outstanding **organizational skills**. "When you have your own practice, everything falls on your shoulders. You have to be disciplined," says Laura Todd Johnson. "I'm fortunate because I've been blessed with good organizational skills. I'm one of those people who has all the clothes in my closets organized by color. But if organizational skills don't come naturally to you, you must find systems that work in order to keep your practice running smoothly." Yvonne Owens is more blunt when it comes to the importance of organizational skills. "Strong organizational skills are imperative. If you're not organized, your practice will end up in chaos."

❖ **Good business skills** are critical to those who open their own practices. "Set up a business plan," advises Yvonne Owens. "I find that even if the plan isn't extensive, a written business plan has more impact than letting your business ideas float around in your head. Commit your plan to paper—'This is what I plan to do in this particular time period.' Be realistic, but set goals for yourself." Adds Laura Todd Johnson, "It helps to know something about accounting and marketing. Learn as much as you can before you start your practice." David Feldkamp advises, "You have to remember the importance of doing everything a good business would do, including keeping expenses low, revenue high, and constantly monitoring personnel issues."

❖ **Marketing skills** are key to success as a solo or small firm practitioner, whether you're a general practitioner or specialize in a particular area of law. "I like marketing," confides Yvonne Owens. "I enjoy meeting people and I enjoy socializing, so marketing comes naturally. I do it under the auspices of having fun. For me marketing isn't a hard sell, but simply meeting people and telling them about my practice." Yvonne says that though marketing comes easily for her, she developed a written marketing plan. "I have a methodical approach to marketing. I identify the corporate clients I want to target for prospective business. I'm also part of several bar association referral lists."

❖ Solo and small firm practitioners must be **comfortable with the personal and financial realities of operating your own practice**. "You have to have capital when you start out in order to get your practice going," says David Feldkamp. "You may have to finance equipment or other things. If you have contingency fee cases, lawyers are expected to pay the costs for expert witnesses and court costs up front. This means that you won't be reimbursed for these costs or paid for your time until the case is resolved, and then you will receive a percentage of any of the plaintiff's recovery." David says that he's careful to talk openly with clients about fees. "When I first started my own practice, it was tempting to give every client a break. I once talked with an experienced general practitioner about some clients that I had, telling him that they were such fine people and so financially pressed that I planned to cut my fee for them. The attorney said to me, 'Did you tell them how much you would charge for your services? Did they understand your fee? Did you earn your fee? If you cut those clients a break, they'll remember you as the nicest guy who ever practiced law, with the emphasis on *remember*, since that's all you'll be—a memory. You won't be in practice any more." David thought carefully about the seasoned practitioner's message. "I came to terms with the fact that my time was valuable, and that

I had to make sure my clients paid for my services. The fiscal realities of practice are inescapable."

Ira Moltz, too, cautions that the first few years of solo practice can be challenging. "It's an emotional roller coaster," he says. "Emotionally and financially, it's up and down and up and down. You need financial support as well as emotional support. And it's important to know that no matter how skilled you are and how personable you are and how wonderful a lawyer you are, you'll still be subject to market factors over which you have no control."

Yvonne Owens says that the financial stresses of solo practice ease over time and are outweighed by the excitement of watching your practice grow and thrive. "Each step of the way, you see your progress," says Yvonne. "I started my practice with a desk, a borrowed chair, and five orange crates—two crates for my guests, two for files, and a spare! Now my office is packed to capacity. I just had a large set of file cabinets delivered, and I even own my own chair—I gave back the borrowed one," she notes with good humor and undeniable pride.

❖ "A **positive attitude** will be your greatest asset" as a solo practitioner, says Yvonne. "You need a positive attitude because you will hit bumps along the road, whether it's a hostile opposing counsel or a difficult client. You have to be able to truly believe and know in your heart that tomorrow will be a better day."

What classes and law school experiences do solo, small firm, and general practitioners recommend?

❖ "If you plan to be a general practitioner, the **general law school curriculum** is important," says Ira Moltz. A wide variety of classes such as civil procedure, property, contracts, criminal law, torts, family law, bankruptcy, commercial paper, negotiations, legal drafting, and labor and employment law can be helpful.

❖ General practitioner Emil Caliendo recommends a **wide variety of undergraduate classes** as well, including government, political science, sociology, writing, and communications classes.

❖ **Basic business courses** can be helpful in establishing your own practice, whether you take accounting for lawyers as a law student or an accounting class as an undergraduate student. And if you plan to specialize in a particular area of law, such as employment law, patent law, or estate planning, take **classes designed to strengthen your knowledge in the relevant areas**. For example, Laura Todd Johnson recommends that aspiring employment lawyers take classes in employment law, tax, and business.

❖ **Trial advocacy, moot court, and other litigation-related classes** can help you develop the oral advocacy skills you'll need as a solo practitioner or small firm attorney. "Any trial advocacy classes are helpful, as they train you to think on your feet," advises Laura Todd Johnson. If you plan to be in the courtroom, "Evidence is the number one most important class you can take," says David Feldkamp. "With any other subject, you can go back to the office and look up the answer to your question. But when you're in the courtroom, you have just one second to make an objection, and you better make the right decision."

❖ **Clinical programs** can help you prepare for a solo or small firm practice, as they give you the chance to work with real clients on real-life issues. Many law schools offer clinical programs in which you sharpen your client counseling skills and courtroom skills under the supervision of a clinical professor. You'll also learn a great deal about developing relationships with clients. "There's no substitute for working with real clients," says Ira Moltz.

❖ **Work as a law clerk for a solo or small firm practitioner**. Whether you work during the summer or over the school year, you'll learn whether a small firm or solo practice is for you. As David Feldkamp described earlier, his experience as a law clerk for a solo practitioner convinced him that solo practice offered the intellectual challenge and the lifestyle that was right for him. Yvonne Owens suggests that if you work as a summer associate at a large or mid-size law firm, "Choose a program that gives you challenging legal work and a glimpse of life as it is for practicing attorneys. Don't be tempted by the range of social events offered—instead look hard at the type of experience you'll acquire over the summer."

❖ **Meet and talk to practitioners and become involved in bar association activities**. "It's never too early to start making contacts," counsels Yvonne Owens. "Bar association activities are a great place to start. All of the bar groups—from the American Bar Association to the city bar associations to women's and minority bar associations—have been tremendously helpful to me. The relationships you develop through the years will truly make a difference when you decide to go out on your own. And you need to start developing those relationships years before you do go out on your own."

SOLO, SMALL FIRM, AND GENERAL PRACTICE
ATTORNEYS INTERVIEWED FOR THIS SECTION

Emil Caliendo
Law Offices of Emil Caliendo
Chicago, Illinois
UNDERGRADUATE: Rosary College
LAW SCHOOL: Northern Illinois University College of Law

David Feldkamp
Law Offices of David Feldkamp
Louisville, Kentucky
UNDERGRADUATE: Vanderbilt University
LAW SCHOOL: University of Kentucky College of Law

Laura Todd Johnson
Johnson & Slate
Tucson, Arizona
UNDERGRADUATE: University of Arizona
LAW SCHOOL: University of Arizona James E. Rogers College of Law

Ira Moltz
Law Offices of Ira Moltz
Chicago, Illinois
UNDERGRADUATE: Northwestern University
LAW SCHOOL: American University Washington College of Law

Yvonne Owens
Owens & Associates
Chicago, Illinois
UNDERGRADUATE: Loyola University Chicago
LAW SCHOOL: Chicago-Kent College of Law, Illinois Institute of Technology

Tax Law

What is Tax Law?

It's often said that only two things in life are certain: death and taxes. Tax attorneys spend their time trying to ease the financial burdens associated with both. For individuals, tax attorneys use trusts, gifts, and various tax planning structures to reduce the burdens of income taxes and estate taxes, and they assist in devising investment strategies. For small businesses and corporations, tax attorneys also use various structures to ease the burdens of taxes, typically in the context of planning organization structure (*e.g.*, partnership or corporation) and determining the tax consequences of financial decisions and transactions. Each financial decision made by a corporation, from financing of debt to depreciation of assets, must involve a consideration of the impacts of the tax code.

The basic idea of taxation is simple: imposing a financial obligation upon individuals and companies to finance the many services provided by government, including building schools and roads, securing national defense, and providing social services. But the variety of taxes we have—at the federal, state, and municipal levels—and the wide range of activities that are taxed (as well as the wide range of activities that are exempt from taxation) make for a remarkably complex area of law. Tax lawyers help their clients navigate the highly technical statutes which make up our tax laws. Tax lawyers work in a wide variety of fields, several of which are described below.

Tax Planning for Businesses and Tax-Exempt Organizations

Business entities, such as corporations and partnerships, are subject to specific treatment under the tax code based on their structures and their actions. When such organizations are formed, tax planners work to analyze the implications of incorporating or forming a partnership. Tax attorneys also work to structure business transactions to meet the client's financial objectives while minimizing the tax consequences.

Tax attorneys interact with securities and banking attorneys in devising the appropriate structure for a securities offering, bond offering, or other form of capitalization. The tax lawyers help choose the type of financing to be used and the structure of the specific financial transaction. Issuance and sale of securities (*see* the Securities Law chapter) have different tax implications than debt offerings such as bonds or commercial loans. Repayment of loan obligations and sales of assets to finance acquisitions all may implicate complex rules of the tax code.

Tax attorneys will also be intimately involved in an acquisition or divestiture in order to devise the most advantageous structure of the transaction and the resulting structure of the corporate entity. In addition, tax attorneys assist businesses with issues involving the distribution of profits, treatment of capital gains and losses, write-offs of non-performing assets, and establishment of retirement and other benefit plans. If the organization contemplates a merger or reorganization, tax attorneys advise on the consequences of each alternative.

Non-profit organizations, such as charities and private foundations, also have special tax planning concerns. The Internal Revenue Service (IRS) and state tax authorities have complex requirements for establishing and maintaining tax-exempt status. Tax attorneys guide these organizations through the procedures necessary to gain and preserve tax-exempt status.

Tax Litigation

Some attorneys specialize in tax-related controversies. Individuals or businesses may be subject to investigation or an audit by the IRS or by state or municipal tax authorities, or they may have an attempt to shelter or exempt money from tax collection disallowed. Attorneys may represent their clients at audits or litigate issues in the U.S. Tax Court and the U.S. District Court. Tax controversies may involve negotiations with the IRS, and tax treatment issues may be heard in the U.S. District Court.

Employee Benefits

Tax attorneys play an important role in designing and administering employee benefit plans. This includes pension, profit-sharing, employee stock ownership, and 401(k) plans. Attorneys counsel organizations concerning the selection and design of such plans as well as the long range financial implications represented by such plans. Attorneys also provide advice concerning the reporting and disclosure requirements of the Employment Retirement Income Security Act (ERISA), a federal act that governs the funding and administration of pension plans.

Personal Estate Planning and Tax Planning

Tax attorneys also work in the field of estate planning, which involves helping individuals plan the distribution of their estate either prior to or upon their death. There are numerous tax consequences that stem from the use of gifts and trusts to ease the burden of taxes upon the transfer of the estate. Attorneys working in this area help individuals plan for the distribution of their assets to beneficiaries and to charitable organizations. They may also advise clients concerning trusts, in cases such as providing for minor children or grown children with disabilities. (*See* the Trusts and Estates Law chapter for more information on these activities.)

Individuals also call upon tax attorneys to help them manage their income and investments in ways that minimize their tax liabilities. Regardless of income level, the use of a will to avoid probate or the use of life insurance, with its tax free cash value accumulation and tax free distribution status, constitute tax planning at its most fundamental level.

Life as a Tax Lawyer

Where do tax lawyers work?

Attorneys specializing in tax law may work in law firms, corporations, and government agencies. Large law firms may have departments that specialize in tax issues, estate planning, and employee benefits. Small and mid-size firms may have several attorneys that specialize in tax practice. Some tax attorneys specializing in estate planning may be engaged in solo practice.

Other tax practitioners work for corporations; a large number of tax attorneys are employed by large accounting firms such as Arthur Andersen or Deloitte & Touche. Still other tax attorneys work for the Internal Revenue Service and for state and local tax authorities.

Who are their clients and what types of cases do they work on?

Many tax attorneys work with corporate clients. Patricia Sweeney is a tax controversy specialist at the law firm of Miller & Chevalier in Washington, D.C. Her clients are primarily large multinational corporations. "They have very sophisticated in-house tax staffs who come to us for assistance with their most complicated matters," she explains. "We work together as a team to efficiently staff and solve the problem at hand." Patricia says that a typical case arises from an adjustment (a determination that an additional tax payment is required) proposed by an IRS agent. "These adjustments usually involve at least $10 million and frequently in excess of $100 million. We strive to resolve the issue to the client's satisfaction at the earliest point in the process. If the issues cannot be resolved administratively within the IRS, we will litigate the issues either in the Tax Court or the Court of Federal Claims."

Joe Goldman is a tax attorney at the Washington, D.C. office of Jones, Day, Reavis & Pogue, a very large law firm with over 20 offices in the United States and abroad. "I practice in the area of general corporate tax planning," Joe explains. "Over the last few years, much of my work has been for large multinational companies and for banks. Companies often seek our advice as to how to structure a merger, acquisition, divestiture, or restructuring in the most tax-efficient manner while achieving stated business goals. And banks ask us to examine and help develop cross-border tax-advantaged financial products and financing techniques, something which is commonly referred to as structured finance."

Though Joe's work is primarily transactional, he has also represented clients in IRS tax audits and appeals matters (so-called tax controversy work). "The hearings are administrative proceedings in a relatively informal setting at which compromise plays a large role and final settlement is often reached. If we can't agree, we get our litigators involved."

"I work with a tremendously diverse range of clients," says Jeff Fritz, a tax attorney at the Minneapolis office of the accounting firm Deloitte & Touche. "Here in Minnesota you can work with companies as large as Honeywell or General Mills, and yet you still have the opportunity to work with small start-up companies. One of the things I really like about working at Deloitte & Touche is getting the chance to work with clients that range from the largest Fortune 500 companies to start-up ventures to everything in between." Jeff especially enjoys his work with small businesses. "The start-up companies rely on us for tax advice and business advice. They may have a CFO, but he or she may not have tax experience. I have the chance to provide them with a broad range of business advice on tax issues as well as human resources, compensation, and general business issues." In addition to his work in corporate tax consulting, Jeff does individual tax consulting, including year-end tax planning.

What daily activities are involved in tax law?

Tax attorneys spend time evaluating how changes in tax laws affect existing organizational structures and advising their clients about the effects of those changes on their business plans. "Know your client and know the law," emphasizes Joe Goldman. "Every morning over breakfast (after reading the sports section), I check the *Washington Post* and *New York Times* for general business developments and for any news reported on the matters on which I'm involved. Clients expect me to know what's going on, and I have to be prepared to field their calls. When I get into work, after putting out any fires, I do a quick search on the Internet to pick up any client news I might have missed. I also have to keep up with the tax law, which changes every day. So I browse the *Daily Tax Reporters* for major developments in federal and international tax law and flag articles to review when there's a spare moment. Although it might take less than an hour a day, I regard these as essential capital building activities."

Joe says the heart of a day's activities varies with the matters on which he is working. "Structured finance, for example, requires heavy duty research and analysis, as well as a good deal of creativity and a lot of writing, including memos to fellow Jones Day attorneys, to clients, and for the file. But I'm not sitting in a back office doing this with my door closed. The entire process is interactive and collaborative—with the client, with other tax lawyers at Jones Day, with our corporate lawyers, and with tax lawyers on the other side of the transaction. This translates into lots of time on the phone and in meetings."

Tax controversy specialist Patricia Sweeney reports that in her practice, there's really no typical day. "It very much depends on the stage of the case I am working on and how many matters are on the front burner," she says. "A day can be spent on the phone with several clients regarding factual development or strategy. A day can be spent interviewing witnesses. A day can be spent in meetings with the client or colleagues developing strategy. A day can be spent in court or in negotiations with an IRS agent or an IRS appeals officer. A day can be spent researching and writing a brief. Or a day can be spent doing a combination of all these things." She adds that her days often include intriguing activities that you don't necessarily think of when you think of the activities of a tax attorney. "A case that we litigated in the Court of Federal Claims involved a casualty loss to timber resulting from the volcanic eruption of Mount St. Helens [in Washington state]. Courtroom testimony and photographs would not have given the judge a full appreciation of the magnitude of the destruction or an understanding of the taxpayer's timber management practices. We took the witness, the judge, his clerk, opposing counsel, and the court reporter up in a helicopter to view the volcanic destruction. The witness testified on the record in the air and at selected ground sites." Patricia adds, "It certainly wasn't your typical day in court!"

Jeff Fritz is a senior manager at Deloitte & Touche. "At my level, I'm on the phone a lot, talking with clients. I also spend time meeting with clients. We're assigned to the clients in teams. A team consists of at least three or four attorneys at different levels of seniority. Our teams have internal meetings in which we develop the ideas and strategies we want to bring out to our clients. We then go out to meet with owners and/or chief financial officers and directors. The meetings are often informal but, if the team is meeting with a large organization such as Honeywell, we may put together a more formal PowerPoint presentation," says Jeff.

"The consulting side of tax has expanded exponentially in the last five years," Jeff adds. "Our firm is putting a much greater emphasis on people skills. You're constantly advising and working with clients." He explains that the attorneys in his accounting firm begin as staff associates, then work through progressive levels of responsibility to become managers, senior managers, and finally directors or partners. "There are more opportunities than ever for staff-level attorneys to get out in front with clients," he says. "Every team assigned to a client has at least one associate or senior associate. When I go out to talk with clients, I always bring one or two people with me. This is a great opportunity for less senior attorneys."

What do tax lawyers find rewarding about their practice?

The tax attorneys we talked to enjoyed the intellectual challenge of their work. "I am never bored," Patricia Sweeney comments. "There is a continuous intellectual challenge inherent in tax work. Not only is the field complex, it is constantly changing." Joe Goldman agrees. "You have to be comfortable working with a complex system of constantly changing rules. I like knowing that each day I am expanding my expertise. There's rarely a day that I look back on that I didn't learn something new," he says.

Tax attorneys have the opportunity to help their clients solve complex legal and financial problems. "It's rewarding to provide value for your clients," says Jeff Fritz. "You're helping your client save tax dollars. In tax consulting you're welcomed with open arms. Clients realize that you can save them money and offer them value for the time you spend advising them." Joe Goldman finds it gratifying to work with clients who sincerely value his efforts. "We add a great deal of value to our clients and I find that they appreciate our efforts."

Tax attorneys use the word "teamwork" with pride. They enjoy working with other professionals to solve problems. "I am working with sophisticated clients who appreciate working as a team," says Patricia Sweeney. "It's tremendously satisfying when we resolve an issue." Jeff Fritz values his co-workers, the very people who are invaluable to his teams. "The relationships I have with the people I work with are very rewarding. I work with simply outstanding people. These people have lots of integrity. They're incredibly talented. And they're fun to work with!" Joe Goldman has the highest regard for his colleagues. "Finding job satisfaction depends not just on where you work but with whom you work. I work side by side with really smart people whom I respect. They are people who are sincerely interested in my personal life as well as my professional development. I'm lucky to work with people I like and admire," Joe adds with a sense of gratitude.

Jeff Fritz also enjoys the close relationships he develops with his clients. "I enjoy developing strong relationships with my clients. A number of my clients consider me not just their 'tax person' but their friend. A lot of the small businesses I work with are family owned. It's rewarding to get to know the first and second generations of the family and to help the family develop a business succession plan."

The Training and Skills Important to Tax Law

How do people enter the field of tax law?

Many lawyers who enter the field of tax law have a background in accounting or business. Jeff Fritz of Deloitte & Touche earned an accounting degree before entering law school and was hired by the firm through an on-campus interview as a third year student. Large accounting firms such as Deloitte & Touche often interview at law schools through on-campus interview programs. They generally interview third year students, but occasionally hire interns to work during the summer between the second and third year of law school.

Jeff explains that it's not necessary to have an accounting degree to be hired as a tax attorney at an accounting firm. "An accounting degree or some accounting classes are preferred but not required," he says. "We've hired some attorneys without accounting degrees or accounting experience. In this case, the firm generally pays for the new hire to take three or four university-level accounting courses."

Though Joe Goldman majored in accounting as an undergraduate, he didn't think about law school until a business professor with a legal background suggested it. While in law school, Joe first considered a career in litigation. After his first year, he spent a summer at a law firm where he worked on a number of litigation projects. "That's when I decided I didn't want to be a litigator. Litigation is concentrated in fact—and I wanted to spend more time learning and creatively interpreting the law than arguing specific facts. That summer, I worked on one tax project, and I decided to take some tax law classes my second year of law school."

After his second year of law school, Joe worked as a summer associate at a large Chicago law firm. "I spent half of the summer working in tax law and half of the summer working in corporate law. Although the tax work was interesting, I was attracted to the pace of the corporate practice and decided to join the corporate group." Joe worked for three years as a corporate law associate at the New York City office of the same firm. "But I found that I was consistently most interested in, and drawn to, the tax issues," he comments. "So I switched to the tax department and pursued an LL.M. in tax while working full-time. This was an excellent opportunity—during my night classes, I was 'spoon-fed' complicated legal concepts, and during the daytime I was applying those legal concepts on the job."

When he moved to Washington, D.C., Joe took his current position as a tax associate at Jones Day. He couldn't be happier with his decision to pursue tax practice or his career path. "It has proven to be a great career move. My corporate background gives me a 'bigger picture' perspective, which the corporate lawyers appreciate, and I am now bilingual, speaking both corporate-speak and tax-speak."

Law firms hiring tax attorneys generally agree that an accounting degree is helpful but not necessary. "Many people are afraid to go into tax if they don't have an accounting background," notes Patricia Sweeney. "I am proof that this is not a prerequisite. I came into the field with a background in political science and had never taken an accounting class." Patricia discovered her penchant for tax law while a law student. "In law school I focused on tax because I had a professor who made the field sound fascinating. After law school I began working on projects involving tax controversy work. I enjoyed the people I worked with and found the work even more interesting than I expected."

"In hindsight, some business courses would have been helpful," says Patricia. "But you can pick up what you need as you go along." Patricia explains that the most important qualification for the field is "a serious commitment to learn the tax law and the clients' businesses. There are various ways to tackle this. I chose to take a year off after I had practiced for a short time to pursue my LL.M. in taxation."

What skills are most important to tax lawyers?

* Tax attorneys need **creative problem-solving skills**. Clients come to you because they expect you to have creative but practical solutions. As Joe Goldman mentioned earlier, clients seek creative solutions to complex problems.

* **Strong analytical skills** are important to the tax attorney, as he or she must be able to spot the issues, analyze the tax code, and formulate strategies. "You have to have strong analytical skills in order to provide value for your client," says Jeff Fritz. Adds Joe Goldman, "It also helps to be able to explain complicated concepts in simple terms. You have to speak to your clients and other lawyers in words they understand."

* Good tax attorneys need **excellent writing skills**. "This field requires a great deal of writing," says Patricia Sweeney. "If you don't like to write and rewrite, you need to choose another field," she advises. "You need to be able to 'tell the story' as to why your position is right."

* Because tax lawyers focus on developing innovative solutions to complex problems, **both legal and factual research skills** are critically important. "You need to be a good legal researcher," advises Patricia Sweeney, "and you should enjoy learning and relearning the tax law, as it constantly changes. In addition, you need to be good at factual development. You have to learn how to ask the right questions and to assess what you are being told. To be good in this area, you have to keep digging both factually and legally until you are comfortable that you are putting together the best argument that can be crafted."

* Tax lawyers work closely with their clients on a daily basis. This means that they must have **excellent interpersonal skills**. "When we hire, we're putting more and more emphasis on communication skills," says Jeff Fritz. "We look for 'executive presence'—your ability to form

relationships, inspire a client's confidence in you, and work in a team with other professionals." Adds Joe Goldman, "Tax law isn't done in the back room. It's interactive and team oriented. Personality is important. In other words, you must 'play well with others.'"

❖ To work effectively with clients, tax attorneys must have **a sincere interest in business and in their clients' businesses**. "With each client, I try to learn as much about their business as I can, both from the client and from business publications," says Patricia Sweeney.

❖ Tax lawyers must **earn the confidence of fellow attorneys and clients**. "I participate in interviewing attorney candidates at my firm," says Joe Goldman. "Really well prepared candidates ask intelligent questions during the interview and interesting follow-up questions. We look for candidates who are not just engaging, but who inspire confidence." Joe adds that confidence and pride are an important part of making the grade as an associate. "Have pride in your work product and try to really 'own' your assignments and take charge of your work," he advises. "Your dedication will become apparent to those you work with."

What classes and law school experiences do tax lawyers recommend?

❖ Jeff Fritz recommends taking two to four **basic tax classes** in law school. "This will help you determine whether you really want to work as a tax attorney," he says. "Take as many tax classes as you can," says Joe Goldman, adding, "Once you start practicing, consider pursuing an LL.M. in taxation. It will help expand your breadth."

❖ Take an **accounting class while in undergraduate school or an accounting for lawyers class while in law school**, advises Joe Goldman.

❖ **Meet tax practitioners**. "While I was in college, I worked in a law firm. The experience gave me the chance to talk to lawyers who practiced in different areas. I picked their brains, asking them what they liked about their work," says Joe Goldman. "Talking informally with lawyers allows you to assess if you'll be happy as a lawyer and whether you'll enjoy practicing in a particular field," Joe adds. "If you're interested in tax controversy work, talk to someone who is practicing in the field," recommends

Patricia Sweeney. "The best place to start is by meeting the tax professors at your law school. Also visit the alumni office of your law school. The alumni office can put you in touch with alumni who are doing what you want to do."

❖ **Gain practical experience by participating in your school's clinical program**. Law school clinical programs offer the opportunity to work with real clients on real issues—excellent training for the client-intensive field of tax law. Some schools offer tax clinics, which provide exceptional training. If your school doesn't have a tax clinic, consider volunteering your services to a community based **income tax assistance program**. "Such programs aren't difficult to find," says Jeff Fritz, "and they provide excellent experience."

❖ Another way to gain practical experience is by **working as a law clerk or as a summer associate** in a law firm with a tax practice. Large firms generally hire summer associates to work during the summer between the second and third year of law school, and small firms often hire students to work during the summer or throughout the school year. "The advantage of being a summer associate is that you actually do the type of work you'll be doing as a lawyer," says Joe Goldman. "You do the research, attend the meetings, talk to the clients. Summer associateships actually give you the experience of 'being' a junior associate."

❖ **Participate in bar association activities**. Bar association activities provide an excellent forum for meeting people who do the type of tax work you want to do. The American Bar Association and state and local bar associations have sections or committees related to tax law. Students can generally join bar associations for very low fees.

TAX ATTORNEYS INTERVIEWED FOR THIS SECTION

Jeff Fritz
Deloitte & Touche
Minneapolis, Minnesota
UNDERGRADUATE: University of Notre Dame
LAW SCHOOL: University of Minnesota Law School

Joe Goldman
Jones, Day, Reavis & Pogue
Washington, D.C.
UNDERGRADUATE: Yeshiva University
LAW SCHOOL: Columbia University Law School

Patricia Sweeney
Miller & Chevalier, Chartered
Washington, D.C.
UNDERGRADUATE: University of Michigan
LAW SCHOOL: Boston University School of Law

Telecommunications Law

What is Telecommunications Law?

Telecommunications suffuse our daily lives. People around the world rely on radio and television for their news and entertainment. Telephones have become almost indispensable, and cellular phones are no longer the exclusive domain of high-power executives. Brightly colored pagers have become status symbols for American teens. The signals for these devices are carried on the electromagnetic spectrum, and behind all of these conveniences lies the web of telecommunications law.

Telecommunications law arises out of the statutes contained in Title 47 of the United States Code, the regulations set forth in Title 47 of the Code of Federal Regulations, and related statutory or regulatory authority. Two federal agencies are directly responsible for regulating the use of the electromagnetic spectrum to provide telecommunications services. The National Telecommunications Information Administration (NTIA), a part of the Department of Commerce, regulates spectrum allocated to the federal government for use of governmental interests such as defense, national security, and space exploration. The Federal Communications Commission (FCC), which is an independent agency, regulates all non-government portions of the electromagnetic spectrum, pursuant to the Communications Act of 1934, as amended ("Communications Act"), which makes up most of Title 47 of the U.S. Code. An overview of the Communications Act reveals the industries regulated by the FCC. For example, Title II of the Communications Act addresses landline telephone service; Title III deals with wireless communications, including cellular, personal communications services (PCS), broadcasting, paging, and satellite transmissions; and Title VI governs cable television.

For many years telecommunications law primarily concerned regulation of monopolies. Most significantly the Bell System, which included the 22 local Bell operating companies owned by AT&T, sold local and long distance telephone service (including international calling), as well as customer premises hardware (such as telephones, lines, and switchboards) and the telephone directories. In the late 1970s, upstart companies such as MCI and Sprint attempted to sell their own long distance services, but they needed AT&T connections to reach the phones of residential and commercial customers (commonly known as "the last mile" connection, as it connects the service over the last figurative mile from the central wiring into private homes and businesses).

In 1984, by terms of the settlement in the antitrust litigation between the U.S. Department of Justice and AT&T (*see* the Antitrust Law chapter for more information on this type of litigation), ownership of the 22 local phone companies was transferred from AT&T to seven Regional Bell Operating Companies (RBOCs). The original RBOCs were NYNEX, Bell Atlantic, BellSouth, Ameritech, U S WEST, Southwestern Bell, and Pacific Bell. The RBOCs retained local and toll calling services and the ability to publish white and yellow page telephone directories, but they could not sell long distance services or equipment. At that point AT&T became a long distance carrier, subject to intense competition from companies such as MCI and Sprint.

In 1988, the RBOCs were permitted to offer certain enhanced services, such as voice mail. But the most dramatic change in the industry occurred when Congress passed the Telecommunications Act of 1996 ("1996 Act"), amending large sections of the Communications Act of 1934. The 1996 Act opened the RBOC territory to competition in local calling. The RBOCs would be permitted to sell long distance services after completing a 14-point checklist demonstrating how they were allowing connection to local calling for long distance companies, such as AT&T and MCI. With the passage of the 1996 Act, the world of telecommunications law changed forever. As individual RBOCs applied to the FCC for approval to provide long distance in specific geographic locations, litigation ensued on the grounds that the RBOCs had not satisfied the 14-point list set forth in the 1996 Act. Telecommunications lawyers for the RBOCs countered with an attack on the authority of the FCC to set rules for how carriers would interconnect with each other in local areas.

Several of the RBOCs subsequently merged in an effort to attain economies of scale in their markets. AT&T then merged with TCI (at the time, the country's largest cable television provider), and announced its intention to offer local calling and Internet access through cable networks— bypassing the RBOCs' connections for the last mile. Microsoft Corporation joined the fray with an effort to provide a system for Internet access through the television (WebTV), while America Online (AOL) responded with litigation seeking "open access" to the cable lines of AT&T/TCI.

Phone companies are providing video services . . . cable companies are providing telephone services . . . and everyone is trying to provide Internet services. As these examples show, today's telecommunications law is undergoing radical change as industries converge. Telecommunications law involves oversight of competition in local and long distance telephone services, as well as wireless communications (*i.e.*, PCS competing with cellular), video programming distribution (*i.e.*, direct broadcast satellite competing with cable), and the yet-uncharted domain of the Internet. Merger and acquisition activity continues in this area as service providers attempt to secure access to traditional telephone wire connections, cable television lines, wireless services, and the Internet. The challenge for the telecommunications lawyer in the new millennium will be sorting out the various rights and obligations of service providers as well as the myriad of state and federal government regulations.

Whereas telecommunications was once described as a "regulated industry," it is now more accurately described as a "deregulated industry." The result of deregulation is increased competition, which, in theory, lowers prices and increases the level of service provided to consumers. Telecommunications law thus comprises the varied transactional work, government policymaking, and constitutional analysis involved in the ever-changing world of telecommunications. Clients seek advice concerning statutory provisions and regulatory matters by which they must abide. Telecommunications lawyers also lobby, negotiate mergers and acquisitions, and provide advice on business matters (*see* the Corporate Law and Legislative Practice chapters for more information on these activities).

In this field, lawyers work with a diverse range of clients. They range from international multimedia corporations diversifying from one segment of the communications industry into others to one-station radio broadcasters, single-system cable operators, and small rural telephone cooperatives. They also include program producers, computer manufacturers, computer service providers, and entrepreneurs who have invented new communications technologies.

Federal and State Telecommunications Regulations

Federal regulators have exclusive jurisdiction over interstate telecommunications service (*i.e.*, long distance telephone service between states). The federal government also has sole regulatory authority over broadcasting (*i.e.*, television and radio), communications by satellite, and many forms of wireless communication such as public safety and private data transmission services.

Federal regulators share regulatory power with the states with respect to intrastate telephone service (*i.e.*, service within a state), including traditional local telephone services by wire and wireless common carrier services such as those provided by cellular telephone companies (although not all states have chosen to regulate wireless services). Federal authorities also share jurisdictional duties with local authorities (generally municipalities) over cable television regulation. For example, municipalities grant franchises to cable service providers so they can access the physical rights of way to deliver service. A telecommunications lawyer's clients may therefore include:

> **Telephone companies**: Traditionally called "common carriers" because they are authorized to provide service upon request on a non-discriminatory basis to all customers. This service can be offered through land-based wires or, as with cellular providers, via the airwaves.

> **Broadcasters**: Broadcasters include radio and television stations. There are complex regulations limiting the number of broadcast stations any one entity may own, both on a national and local basis, resulting in many transactions concerning the buying and selling of stations. There are also limited restrictions on what can be broadcast.

> **Cable companies**: Cable systems have traditionally faced regulation at both the local and national level but are rapidly moving toward deregulation. The Cable Consumer Protection and Competition Act of 1992 created a substantial array of rate regulation and other

restrictions, with oversight responsibility divided between federal and local officials, but the Telecommunications Act of 1996 eliminated many of these regulations.

Local governments: These include entities seeking to assert local jurisdiction over telecommunications services, such as municipalities, franchising authorities, and public utility councils.

Other telecommunications organizations: These organizations provide services such as wireless cable, satellite communications, and private wireless transmission networks; they also include trade associations representing regulated telecommunications industries.

Life as a Telecommunications Lawyer

Where do telecommunications lawyers work?

Telecommunications lawyers work for large and mid-size law firms that have telecommunications departments, as well as for specialized small to mid-size "boutique" practices in which all attorneys specialize in telecommunications law. Though a limited number of firms practicing telecommunications law are located throughout the country, most telecommunications lawyers practice in the Washington, D.C. area. This reflects the important role the federal government continues to play in the regulation of communication. The government, in fact, employs a number of telecommunications attorneys in federal and state regulatory agencies.

Telecommunications lawyers also work for corporations, including common carriers such as Bell Atlantic and MCI; cable companies such as Comcast; multimedia corporations such as NBC and The Tribune Company; radio and television broadcasters such as CBS; and Internet service providers such as America Online.

Who are their clients and what types of cases do they work on?

Rosemary Harold is a telecommunications attorney at Wiley, Rein & Fielding, a large law firm in Washington, D.C. "My firm's clients run a wide gamut of players in the communications field, including broadcasters, cable programmers, large 'local exchange' telephone companies, cellular telephone and other wireless communications service providers, international satellite service providers, equipment manufacturers, and even small entrepreneurs who have come up with a new proposal for using the spectrum [frequencies through which communication signals travel] for some communications purpose," Rosemary says. "I personally work most often with mass media clients, the largest of which are sophisticated New York or Los Angeles-based entities and the smallest of which include the owners of a single radio station located in a sparsely populated area."

Rosemary's clients have a wide range of needs. "The clients depend upon my skills in and knowledge of the telecommunications field. They draw upon certain skills and knowledge frequently, whether it involves knowing the right staff person to call at the FCC to facilitate a broadcast station acquisition, being able to recite the latest developments (published or rumored) in a pending rulemaking or legislative matter, or knowing how to structure a complex FCC 'pleading' (which is a substantive advocacy document, resembling a brief, written on the client's behalf) to put the best face on the client's desired outcome of the matter in question," she explains.

Lee Petro is a telecommunications attorney in the Washington, D.C. firm of Gardner, Carton & Douglas, a national law firm with over 250 attorneys. Previously Lee was an associate at a boutique telecommunications firm also located in Washington. "I specialize in broadcast communications law," Lee explains. "The clients that I work for are primarily radio and television stations, equipment manufacturers, and telecommunications services companies. The range of clients changes day to day and week to week, from long distance carriers to small enterprises breaking into the telecommunications industry. The radio and TV stations I work with are located in small, medium, and large-size markets, owning anywhere from a single station to an entire group of stations. These stations need to prepare the regulatory filings that are required of them by the FCC," he says.

The Telecommunications Act of 1996 has had a major effect on Lee's clients. "The 1996 Act eliminated restrictions on how many radio stations an entity could own. Before the 1996 Act, an entity could own 12 AM stations and 12 FM stations. Now that there are no such restrictions, broadcast groups have become much larger. For example, Clear Channel and AMFM now each own more than 400 radio stations," Lee says. Lee has represented clients before the Department of Justice and the FCC who were "concerned that the large group-owners were earning a disproportionate share of the local radio market's revenues and, as a result, violating federal antitrust laws." Lee's practice thus requires that he have a keen understanding of the intricacies of antitrust law.

"Most of our work is representing broadcasters or communications companies before the Federal Communications Commission," Lee continues. "There are many Commission requirements that our clients must meet. For example, if you want your station to increase its coverage in a market, that action must be authorized by the FCC. Or if you want your telecommunications firm to offer its services internationally, that must be approved by the FCC. I help the clients prepare their documentation and then present it to the FCC." Lee explains that his work involves offensive and defensive strategies. "In this field you must help your clients look at what their competitors are doing, all the while examining whether your client can take advantage of market conditions to improve their service. If your client owns five stations and someone wants to start a new station in that market, you want to confirm that the new station won't cause interference with the five stations your client already has. Part of that involves looking at contour maps showing audience coverage and reviewing them to make sure the new station won't interfere with the client's overall service or market share."

Maria Arias-Chapleau is a telecommunications lawyer for AT&T in Denver, Colorado. "As an in-house attorney, my clients are the divisions of AT&T—whether the consumer division, the business division, or the international division. I'm Chief Regulatory Counsel for AT&T's Western Region, which includes the 14 states that make up the RBOC called U S WEST. I work on regulatory issues involving these 14 western states, from Washington to Minnesota," Maria explains. "I handle anything regulatory that's related to these states, whether it's a consumer issue, a business issue, an international issue, or a merger issue. If a regulatory matter is appealed to federal or state court, my office handles the appeal. We assist AT&T with its regulatory needs, whether they are state or federal proceedings."

Maria's job takes her beyond traditional law practice. "My job is more than just practicing law. I work with state advocates, who work in front of state commissions funded by the state legislature, on heated public policy issues. Often I'm working on matters impacted by the political viewpoints of appointed or elected officials—there's a legislative interplay between my work and the political scene. Part of my job is training in-house and external experts on law and public policy," Maria explains (*see* the Legislative Practice chapter for a discussion of these kinds of activities). Maria's job requires that she work with a wide range of people, including other attorneys, state managers, political advocates, docket managers, and subject matter experts in regulatory proceedings.

"In my position at AT&T, I'm participating every single day in making new law," Maria comments. "Because the Telecommunications Act of 1996 updated the Communications Act of 1934, no law goes with it other than what has been developed since 1996. Every six months or so, it's as if telecommunications law has completely changed. I'm managing a lot of different proceedings in a constantly changing area of law." Even the concept of what a long distance company comprises has changed, Maria explains. "With the acquisition of TCI and Media One [cable companies], the company has broadened its scope. Now we need franchise approvals, we have cable right of way issues, and we're becoming involved in new areas of the law and a new sector of government regulation." Maria's work also involves negotiating and arbitrating with the independent telephone companies and the RBOCs; working on satisfying the requirements for providing universal services for rural areas; dealing with tariff issues (negotiations for rates paid to access certain equipment); making sure that other carriers are abiding by the law and not violating state regulatory or antitrust laws; giving legislative presentations; conducting local workshops on matters such as new services and new regulatory policies; and filing merger applications.

Howard Griboff is an attorney-adviser at the FCC in Washington, D.C. Howard works for the Satellite and Radiocommunication Division of the International Bureau of the FCC. "Lawyers, economists, market analysts, and engineers are among the 1,800 employees at the FCC," Howard explains. "The Communications Act requires us to perform our duties for the public interest, convenience, and necessity. Essentially our clients are the American people. In the past decade, the focus of the FCC has changed from one of regulating monopolies to one of deregulating competitive markets. Thus, to an extent, we also serve the regulated industries themselves, which want their activities approved so they can compete in the marketplace, provide service to the public, and, hopefully, profit financially. Commissions such as the FCC and FERC [the Federal Energy Regulatory Commission] are independent agencies, created by Congress to oversee a particular area of the law because the industries have highly specialized needs. It's really as if such Commissions form a fourth branch of federal government. As an independent agency, the FCC conducts notice and comment rulemaking proceedings in order to promulgate regulations, but we also adjudicate disputes just like judges do."

Howard goes on to explain that the International Bureau of the FCC was formed in 1994. "This occurred when nations started coming together in the World Trade Organization [WTO]. The WTO recognized that artificial geographic boundaries between countries were being stretched by the telecommunications industry. There needed to be some sort of cooperation between countries with regard to telecommunications services. Also, satellite technology has become more predominant—and when it comes to satellite technology there are no geographic boundaries at all. International Bureau staff came together from different bureaus of the FCC with the purpose of working on these new international issues. We attend WTO meetings, negotiate spectrum rights and positions for satellite orbits, and work with members of the industry to determine how we can help them with their international concerns."

What daily activities are involved in telecommunications law practice?

"As a senior associate in a large communications law practice," says Rosemary Harold, "my daily activities are wildly varied—which I enjoy, but it can get frantic. I spend most of my time in the office, either on the phone with clients or drafting a variety of documents, including FCC pleadings and applications related to broadcast licenses, appellate briefs, articles for trade publications, and speeches to be delivered by partners." Partners in the practice, notes Rosemary, have somewhat different responsibilities. "Partners spend more time on the telephone and less time writing than I do, although that can vary depending on a particular lawyer's skills and the client's needs. Agency hearings or court appearances are rare but not unknown. Partners often will spend time on informal lobbying visits to the FCC staff on behalf of a client and may become involved in lobbying efforts on Capitol Hill. I've had the opportunity to draft many documents used in such lobbying efforts and have begun to accompany partners on some lobbying visits." (*See* the Legislative Practice chapter for more information on lobbying activities.)

Rosemary has many tales to recount concerning the matters she's handled as an associate. "I've done some interesting content regulation work in connection with the Children's Television Act of 1990. My favorite story centers on the stunned surprise of my then-fiancé (and now husband), a former litigator who has almost twice as many years of law practice experience as me. He couldn't believe it when I told him I had to get up on Saturday morning to watch cartoons in order to review them for their educational value—and he really couldn't believe that I was not only going to stay glued to the TV set for the morning, but that I could bill the time to clients!"

As an attorney at Gardner, Carton & Douglas, Lee Petro says that most of his day is spent interacting with clients and responding to their questions and concerns. "Responding efficiently to clients day to day is the most important aspect of the work," he says. "A radio station may call first thing in the morning with a question such as how much to charge a mayoral candidate for advertising on the station. That mayoral candidate may be standing in the radio station owner's office waiting for an answer. Or a station owner may need to know whether he can donate advertising air time to a local hospital. You have to be able to answer such questions right away." Lee reports that he works with a variety of clients, from large group-owners to local broadcasters located in rural communities. "All of these clients generate different questions. I'm dealing with legal questions that range from the intriguing to the rudimentary. Sometimes there's no clear-cut answer to the client's question—you have to review FCC decisions, ponder the client's question, and provide the best advice possible. Clients also need assistance applying for broadcasting licenses, preparing their annual reports for the FCC, understanding the legal implications of upgrading their broadcast facilities, etc."

Lee reports that he also spends a great deal of time doing legal research and writing. Not surprisingly, he says that the focus of his days is communication. "I'm constantly communicating with clients or the FCC through phone calls or in writing. Not every issue is going to change the world, but many questions can be resolved with a simple phone call. I seldom go to court unless I'm involved in an appeal of an FCC ruling."

Maria Arias-Chapleau says that the Denver AT&T office has both regulatory and commercial lawyers; six of the attorneys in her office are regulatory lawyers. As the chief regulatory lawyer for AT&T's western region, Maria is involved in a wide range of activities. Maria represents AT&T at numerous regulatory hearings. "I also work on pleadings, prepare testimony for hearings, meet with subject matter experts, and work on building coalitions within the industry." Maria's job requires that she attend numerous meetings, "99% of which are substantive. Because telecommunications is changing so quickly, it's important for our regulatory lawyers to talk about the hottest, latest, greatest telecommunications cases. We also meet with the commercial lawyers to share information," Maria explains. "In addition, I meet with political officials, and I attend roundtables involving lawyers, activists, and residents in the region. I also oversee administrative staff meetings." (*See* the Corporate Law and the Legislative Practice chapters for more information on these activities.)

Maria says that her job involves a great deal of writing. "I do an incredible amount of policy-related writing that must be grounded in facts. For that reason, I also do research. I do about 50-60% of the amount of research that I did in private practice, so I do more writing than research. I also draft pleadings and motions." Maria's job also involves a significant amount of travel. "I travel to hearings, workshops, and settlement negotiations." Because Maria's office handles issues in a 14-state area in the western United States, much of her travel is within that geographic area.

Howard Griboff's job at the FCC involves policymaking. "I meet with colleagues and we decide FCC policy," he says. "Should we deregulate this industry? Why or why not? Can we license multiple applicants in a spectrum block without causing interference to each other or incumbent occupants of that spectrum? We may include telecommunications industry players in the meetings and ask them to help us arrive at solutions."

Howard reports that his FCC job offers ample opportunity to exercise his writing skills. "I spend lots of time writing," he says. He also spends a good deal of time fielding questions from the public. "Every day I receive calls from the public. For example, my name recently appeared on a public notice about the merger involving PrimeStar, a satellite TV company. And sure enough, I received calls from concerned citizens. I explain the facts and answer any questions they have."

What do telecommunications lawyers find rewarding about their practice?

The lawyers we talked to obviously enjoy working in a field of constant and continuous change. Rosemary Harold enthusiastically describes the industry. "The media/communications field is incredibly dynamic. In one syllable words, that makes it a lot of fun! And it's exciting to be in the know about things that often make big headlines in the press!" Howard Griboff is equally effusive, and encourages young lawyers to explore the field.

"Telecommunications is as hot an industry as you can get into as a lawyer. The law is new and constantly evolving. It's a very exciting place for new lawyers because it's not an area of the law in which you need a lot of apprenticeship time. Whether you're working at a firm, for the government, or for the industry, your learning curve rapidly catches up to that of seasoned attorneys."

These lawyers also enjoy the people with whom they work, both clients and colleagues. "My firm represents individual broadcast owners as well as large group-owners. Thus I serve a variety of client needs each day," says Lee Petro. "I enjoy hearing their words of thanks, the tone of satisfaction in their voices. Once their questions are answered, they feel they can go on the air, and I feel I can go on to serve more clients and help them out with their problems. My work provides a way for me to help other people resolve their problems. It's rewarding to do something that I care so much about," Lee confides.

Howard Griboff says that his favorite part of his job is interacting with the public. "I appreciate knowing that after talking with me, someone in America tells their friends, 'The government isn't so bad. I talked to someone at the FCC today who was really helpful. He made me feel really comfortable talking to him and now I know what I need to do next.' The government gets such a bad rap, and I enjoy providing people with a positive image of government service." He adds, "I get to work with wonderful visionaries at the FCC, and they're not only intelligent, they're genuinely nice people."

Maria Arias-Chapleau has high praise for her colleagues at AT&T. "The most rewarding part of my job is teamwork," she says. "I always look forward to cross-team meetings. My colleagues and I worked so hard to build our region, to be the best lawyers we can, and to provide the best training for new lawyers. We genuinely like each other, and we work very closely together. We have so many responsibilities and so much to do that there's not a lot of time to have fun. So we try to really enjoy working with each other. We encourage each other to take the time to enjoy our families and pursue our outside interests. The most wonderful part of my job, the thing that makes all the hard work worth it, is this sense of teamwork and the exceptional people that I work with."

The lawyers we talked to value the opportunity they have to make an impact on public policy. "I enjoy the policymaking part of my work," says Maria Arias-Chapleau. "It's rewarding to have an argument you make in a brief appear in an order that ultimately becomes the law for a particular state," she explains. Howard Griboff also finds the policymaking aspect of his work rewarding. "Being a government lawyer has the benefit of making decisions based on what is best for society," Howard adds, with obvious pride in his work.

"What I like about my job is that I work with both technology and public policy," explains Lee Petro. "This field offers the opportunity to work with both government and technology." Lee, a political science major in college, has a long-standing interest in public policy. "I've always been interested in the social impact of government decisions. And the technology side of the practice means that there's always something new going on in the field that keeps it interesting."

These lawyers are also inspired by the intellectual rigors of telecommunications practice. "There's tremendous opportunity for intellectual challenge," says Rosemary Harold. Maria Arias-Chapleau agrees, commenting, "So many of the issues we are working on are new. Every year technology is different. This is a great field for someone who really likes to be an advocate and a litigator, but who also enjoys working on issues beyond the courtroom, such as workshops, legislative forums, and industry presentations." She adds, "The best way to describe my job is that it involves incredibly intense litigation work; it's a really tough litigation job. You have the chance to gain exceptional experience by doing 9 to 12 hearings per year. All direct testimony is pre-filed. At the hearings we do just cross-examination. So we spend weeks and months preparing written testimony. It's very exciting, but it's very challenging."

The Training and Skills Important to Telecommunications Law

How do people enter the field of telecommunications law?

Some students enter law school knowing that they want to specialize in telecommunications law, having been inspired by their undergraduate or graduate studies. "I knew from my undergraduate work that I wanted to work in public policy, and I knew that Washington, D.C. would be the place to be," says Lee Petro. "After working as a paralegal in a communications law firm for one year," he says, "I sought out a law school that had a special institute for communications law, and chose to go to Catholic University in Washington, D.C." Lee continued as a part-time law clerk for the firm while in law school and contacts from that employer led to his current position at Gardner, Carton & Douglas.

Rosemary Harold entered law school after working for several years as a newspaper reporter and editor covering courts and law-related issues. "I first became interested in media law when I was in graduate school pursuing a master's degree in journalism. After I worked as a journalist, I decided to act on my desire to try to get into law school and eventually work for media clients. I found myself gravitating towards communications law because it offered me the opportunity to do a considerable amount of First Amendment-related policy work and appellate work, as well as many chances to develop ongoing relationships with clients who vary tremendously in their size, their needs, and their sophistication in understanding the law."

Howard Griboff also entered law school after working in the communications field. "I had a long-standing interest in radio and TV and the effect they have on people. I created my own undergraduate major, a combination of communications, business, and psychology." After college Howard worked as a market researcher for a "rep firm," a company that sold local advertising time to national advertisers on behalf of television stations around the country. He then bought a radio station ("with other people's money," he admits) and managed the station for four years. "My experiences owning and managing the radio station influenced my decision to go to law school. I often felt that my not having a legal education hindered my success as an entrepreneur," he says. After law school Howard worked for three years in a Washington, D.C. boutique firm specializing in telecommunications law before joining the FCC.

Maria Arias-Chapleau began her career as a commercial litigator. "I was a junior partner at a large firm in Chicago. I received a call from a law school classmate who was working for a search firm. She told me about a fantastic opportunity working for AT&T in commercial litigation, which was my specialty. While I was at the law firm, I did mostly discovery work, and I was eager to expand my experience. I was also interested in AT&T because I was interested in international law. I'm Hispanic and I speak Spanish fluently, and I hoped to have the chance to use my language skills." Maria began her career at AT&T as a commercial litigator in the Chicago office. "It was a great experience. I managed outside counsel, I did labor and employment work, and I did some bankruptcy work. I then had a chance to help AT&T with its regulatory work." It was the chance of a lifetime, according to Maria. "The regulatory work offered me the chance to do my own hearings, to have my own experts. Over 90% of our regulatory hearings are handled in-house. I was responsible for everything, including hearings, motions, briefs, and testimony.

"My work as a regulatory attorney in Chicago was excellent preparation for my current position of Chief Regulatory Counsel for the AT&T Western Region," Maria continues. "Now I manage the regulatory attorneys in our office. I also head a team of people who help us on our cases, including paralegals, subject matter experts, legislative experts, and outside counsel. Our office is the command control center for the U S WEST states. I have the opportunity to act as a strategist. I make sure that we, as a company, take the right positions on novel issues."

Most law graduates who enter telecommunications law begin their careers in a law firm setting. "It's very rare to get a job at the FCC straight out of law school," says Howard Griboff. "Generally, you need at least two to three years of experience in a law firm." Similarly, corporations hire attorneys with several years of law practice experience. "Traditionally, you need four to five years of law firm experience before entering a corporation," says Maria Arias-Chapleau. Maria explains that corporate legal departments generally have lean staffs. "You need to come in with some training, because you have to hit the ground running," she says. "When we hire regulatory attorneys at AT&T, we look for attorneys who have worked at large firms, who have attended good law schools, who have good academic credentials, and who have strong litigation experience. When hiring commercial litigation attorneys, we may be somewhat less restrictive in terms of the required length of experience."

What skills are most important to telecommunications lawyers?

❖   Telecommunications lawyers must have **strong communications skills**. "It's very important to have good communications skills," says Maria Arias-Chapleau. "The only way for us to accomplish all of our work, which involves political, legislative, and regulatory issues, is for us to communicate effectively."

❖ **Writing skills** are very important. "Most cases boil down to highly specific and technical matters that you must word so that your client can understand them," notes Lee Petro. "The client is interested in running his or her station; the legal side of things is just one of many issues he or she has to attend to. You have to understand the issues and then be able to explain them to your client—who is busy running their radio station—in a two-page letter rather than in a 15-page brief."

❖ Lawyers specializing in this highly technical area must be **attentive to detail**. "In telecommunications, you're dealing with nuances in both technology and the law. A single word in a regulation or an application for a license can make or break your case. Making sure your applications comply with the rules is of utmost importance—if they don't, you're not providing the service your client deserves," says Lee Petro. FCC attorney Howard Griboff reiterates that details are critically important. "Having your client's transaction denied because you didn't take enough time to properly complete a form, or because you filed a form without proofreading it, ruins your credibility with your client and at the agency. Attention to detail is equally crucial inside the FCC as well. It's embarrassing for you—and the agency—to have your rules overturned in court due to an obvious procedural error."

❖ Telecommunications lawyers must have good **interpersonal skills**. "When you work with administrative agencies, it's especially important to have good 'people' skills," says Rosemary Harold. "Unlike the stereotypical 'attack dog' role assigned to litigators, communications attorneys need to be able to switch nimbly back and forth among a variety of roles, including acting as a 'cajoler' for agency staff; a counselor and resource for clients; a lobbyist for the agency, the White House, and Congress; and an all-around advocate as the situation calls for it. The ability to play these different roles, and to recognize when a particular guise is appropriate, is essential," Rosemary explains.

❖ **Negotiation skills** are helpful to lawyers who work in industries subject to government regulation. Maria Arias-Chapleau explains, "Negotiation is key. When you're working with the regulatory staff on a hearing, and you know that your position is not going to fly, you have to be able to negotiate effectively with the commission and its staff. I'm constantly negotiating with opponents, in informal proceedings as well as formal proceedings." Maria notes that negotiation skills are helpful in other areas of her work, as well. "Even within our office, we're negotiating with each other for resources, such as securing the use of an in-house expert."

❖ **Teamwork skills** are important to lawyers who work in the telecommunications field. According to Maria Arias-Chapleau, "When you're in an in-house position, you generally have a large volume of work and a limited number of resources. It's critically important to be a true team. You have to communicate constantly with each other and be supportive of your colleagues. This enhances our odds of success," she says. Rosemary Harold also emphasizes the importance of teamwork. "This is definitely not a practice area conducive to solo practice, because, among other things, you have to be able to do the requisite 'information gathering' for clients concerning developments at the FCC or on Capitol Hill. This works best if you're comfortable interacting with your colleagues and working in a group environment," Rosemary explains.

❖ Telecommunications law is a field in which practitioners tend to know each other. Howard Griboff believes that the **ability to network** is key to telecommunications lawyers. "Telecommunications is a field in which you *have to* make yourself known in the field. This is an industry of recognition, in which people meet and remember each other." Howard advises that such networking skills are helpful when it comes to planning your career. "The better your networking skills, the greater the extent to which you can guide your career."

What classes and law school experiences do telecommunications lawyers recommend?

❖ Take advantage of your law school's **telecommunications law classes**, and get to know the professors who teach those classes. Some schools may offer specialized curricula in the field; other schools may offer basic courses and a limited number of advanced level seminars. Lee Petro explains, "The specialized telecommunications program I pursued at Catholic University Law School required me to take nine telecommunications law courses in addition to my regular law school course work. It made me a big believer in specialty programs." Pursuing classes in the appropriate field can show a prospective employer that you are sincerely interested in the practice, advises Rosemary Harold. "Firms generally are looking for some demonstrated interest among applicants seeking communications law positions, even if that interest is limited among law students to classes taken in school or hands-on experience with college media," says Rosemary.

❖ If you're considering a telecommunications law career, be sure to take **administrative law** and also consider a **negotiations** class. "Administrative law is absolutely key for any type of telecommunications practice," says Howard Griboff. **Business-related courses** such as tax and accounting for lawyers are also helpful, according to Lee Petro. "Communications is a business-related field. Because you're likely to work with both established and start-up companies, it's important to be comfortable with accounting and tax principles that affect all businesses," Lee explains.

❖ Take law school classes that will help you **sharpen your writing skills.** Many law schools offer advanced courses that allow you to write papers on subjects in which you are interested. Participation in law review, which allows you to gain sophisticated legal writing and editing experience, can also be helpful. "Law journals give you a chance to process the law from an intellectual standpoint, which is something that you'll be doing every day in practice," says Lee Petro. "The experience you get on a law journal requires you to edit your own legal writing as well as that of others. This experience is excellent preparation for law practice." In addition, investigate writing contests sponsored by your school or an outside organization.

❖ Take law school classes that help **sharpen your oral advocacy skills.** Howard Griboff recommends participating in moot court. "Moot court experience helps you be more confident as a public speaker, especially if you have the slightest fear of public speaking. You can even find moot court competitions focused on your area of interest. For example, the Federal Communications Bar Association sponsors an annual National Telecommunications Moot Court Competition." Lee Petro emphasizes that moot court allows you to practice thinking on your feet, a skill important to telecommunications lawyers. "The main part of your job as a telecommunications lawyer is responding to client questions. You're put on the spot and expected to provide an answer. Moot court can help you practice fielding tough questions. Once you're working, your moot court experience will help you come off more smoothly when you're working with clients," Lee advises.

❖ **If you want to do regulatory litigation work** in the telecommunications area, **take courses to prepare you for a litigation career**, such as moot court, trial advocacy, evidence, and administrative law. "Part of being a good litigator is being a good public speaker," says Maria Arias-Chapleau. "You can't be persuasive in front of a court or commission if you're not a good public speaker. Moot court can help you prepare for litigation practice; it's a good way to exercise your public speaking skills and your ability to think on your feet."

❖ **Gain practical experience** by taking a summer associate position or law clerking position with a law firm that has a telecommunications law practice or with a government agency or corporation that has an internship program. "Whether you're a summer associate, a law clerk, or an intern, any practical experience you can get is time well spent," advises Lee Petro. "Even if you work only four hours a week as a clerk or an intern, you'll be exposed to the practice area as well as to people who can be networking contacts," he adds. Lee believes that attending a law school with a specialized program in telecommunications law helped him open doors. "By the time I graduated from law school, I had completed several internships, which made me more valuable in the job market," he explains.

❖ **Network, network, network.** Make yourself part of the telecommunications law community by becoming active in bar association activities of the American Bar Association or the Federal Communications Bar Association. Most bar associations have memberships available for students, for which they charge a nominal fee. Maria Arias-Chapleau recommends becoming active in your local community. Maria, who was born in Mexico and has lived in the United States since she was four, is involved in the Denver Hispanic Chamber of Commerce and Denver's Latin American Education Fund; she has found her involvement a way to make contacts as well as to serve the greater community.

TELECOMMUNICATIONS ATTORNEYS
INTERVIEWED FOR THIS SECTION

Maria Arias-Chapleau
AT&T
Denver, Colorado
UNDERGRADUATE: DePaul University
LAW SCHOOL: Northwestern University School of Law

Howard Griboff
Federal Communications Commission—International Bureau
Satellite and Radiocommunication Division
Washington, D.C.
UNDERGRADUATE: University of Pennsylvania
LAW SCHOOL: UCLA School of Law

Rosemary Harold
Wiley, Rein & Fielding
Washington, D.C.
UNDERGRADUATE: The College of William & Mary
LAW SCHOOL: Georgetown University Law Center

Lee Petro
Gardner, Carton & Douglas
Washington, D.C.
UNDERGRADUATE: Michigan State University
LAW SCHOOL: Institute of Communications Law Studies, The Catholic
University of America Columbus School of Law

*Editor's Note: Since our interview with Rosemary Harold, she has become
a partner at Wiley, Rein & Fielding.*

Tort Law: Personal Injury and Insurance Defense Litigation

What is Tort Law?

In the civil litigation arena, the term "trial lawyer" typically causes us to think of the plaintiffs' and defense personal injury bar. Personal injury lawyers provide access to the civil court system for those without financial means by handling cases on a contingency fee basis, which means that the attorney is only paid a percentage (usually one-third) of any recovery. Yet these are the same lawyers who bring the numerous cases against the tobacco and firearms industries and the manufacturers of potentially dangerous products such as vehicles with side-mounted fuel tanks, asbestos, breast implants, and diet pills, and who seek recoveries in mass disasters such as an airline crash or a structural building collapse. The litigation of these high-profile cases—as well as the more typical cases involving injuries suffered in automobile accidents, incidents of medical malpractice, and other cases of negligence—composes the practice known as personal injury and insurance defense.

In law schools and in legal vernacular, this area of practice is known as tort law. A tort is a civil (non-criminal) injury, other than a breach of contract, that results in damages. A person (or an organization) has committed a tort by acting or failing to act in circumstances in which he had some obligation or responsibility toward another and is therefore liable for the resulting injury. The obligation can be one of a toy manufacturer to provide a child-safe product, or a doctor to act in accordance with accepted medical procedures, or a store owner to keep an area clear of debris or water.

When a person's physical health, mental health, or property is damaged through tortious conduct, the injured party (the plaintiff) often brings a claim for money damages, including medical expenses and lost wages due to the injury. The plaintiff may also seek recovery of punitive damages, which are intended to punish the wrongdoer and deter similar conduct on the part of others. Large awards of punitive damages by juries in tort cases have been severely criticized by manufacturers as imposing an unjustified cost on consumers. In response, the plaintiffs' bar contends that large damage awards have the effect of prompting companies to make safer products.

If the defendants, whether individuals or organizations, have liability insurance and the tortious act falls within the scope of the insurance contract, the defendants are represented by insurance defense attorneys, who specialize in tort litigation. The insurance defense attorneys, though hired by the insurance companies, represent the insured party. The law firms bill the insurance company for the hours they spend defending the insured. Costs for defending such cases are significant and are ultimately paid through insurance premiums.

Negligence

The doctrine of negligence is based on the idea that persons or companies in certain situations have obligations in their conduct toward others from which injury could result. Negligence results when someone fails to use such care as a "reasonably prudent" and careful person would use under similar circumstances. Negligence might include a motorist's failure to yield the right of way or reduce speed under adverse conditions such as snow or sleet. Negligence can include acts such as failure to properly install a gas furnace or pour a foundation for a house, the discharge of harmful chemicals into the atmosphere or water by a company, or the improper design or construction of the roof of a large stadium. Some obligations or responsibilities are so important that companies are subject to strict (absolute) liability negligence standards. For example, it is not sufficient that an airplane wing be reasonably sound; rather, the wing must properly function under any and all conditions or the manufacturer is absolutely liable for resulting injuries.

Many negligence cases arise from auto accidents. Depending on the nature of the injuries and the parties involved, these cases can be surprisingly complex and often involve third parties. An injured person may sue the driver of another vehicle but may also sue other parties alleging they were negligent. For example, in an accident involving a taxi driver, the taxicab company would likely be included as a defendant in the suit as being responsible for any negligence on the part of its employees. Defendants in these suits may allege that the plaintiff contributed to his own injury, resulting in a counterclaim for negligence against the plaintiff.

Other negligence cases arise from premises liability issues. For example, a guest who is injured on a homeowner's property may sue the homeowner for negligence for an injury sustained while using the homeowner's pool or for leg injuries sustained when bitten by the homeowner's dog. Premises liability claims are often made against businesses, as well. A grocery store patron may slip and fall on a bunch of grapes in the produce aisle or a guest at a department store may be injured on an escalator or in a revolving door.

Professional Malpractice

Claims against professionals such as doctors, lawyers, and accountants are known as malpractice cases. These cases arise when a plaintiff claims that a doctor, lawyer, accountant, or other professional failed to exercise the ordinary skill and capacity that a prudent and reputable member of that profession would exercise under the circumstances. A plaintiff may allege that she incurred injury as a result of the doctor's negligence in a face-lift procedure, resulting in severe and constant head pain and inability to work due to the pain. A plaintiff may argue that his lawyer failed to file his case within the statute of limitations, thereby compromising his legal rights, or that his lawyer drafted a faulty will that left the family farm to the wrong person. Professional malpractice cases are incredibly complex and are often handled by defense attorneys who specialize in the area.

Wrongful Death

When a tort results in a person's death, the decedent's beneficiaries (spouse, parents, or children) have a statutory right to bring a wrongful death action. Wrongful death actions can arise out of auto accidents, accidents on the insured's property, or as a result of medical malpractice. These cases are among the most complicated cases in tort litigation practice and are generally handled by attorneys with expertise in such litigation.

Product Liability

People who are injured by defective products can bring a strict liability claim as well as a negligence claim against the manufacturer and those involved in the distribution of the product. Plaintiffs may allege that the defendants designed or manufactured a defective product or failed to adequately warn of foreseeable dangers. The concept of strict liability means that the seller is liable for any and all defective or hazardous products that unreasonably threaten a consumer's personal safety. The premise of strict liability is based on the idea that when a manufacturer, such as a drug company or an auto company, presents its goods to the public for sale, the manufacturer represents that they are suitable for their intended use. In order to establish strict liability, the plaintiff must prove that the product was defective when placed in the stream of commerce.

Such cases may involve drugs, such as the Thalidomide cases, in which a drug prescribed for morning sickness resulted in birth defects, or the controversial Fen-phen, a diet pill alleged to cause heart malfunctions. They may involve medical devices, such as breast implants, which were alleged to have caused immune disorders. They may also involve mechanical products such as automobile locks that prevent passengers from escaping in the event of an accident or children's portable cribs that are susceptible to collapse. When people contract salmonella from tainted milk purchased at a grocery store or *E. coli* from hamburger patties, food products become the basis of product liability lawsuits. Many product liability actions against large manufacturers are brought as class actions and may involve millions of dollars in recoveries.

Life as a Tort Litigator

Where do personal injury and insurance defense lawyers work?

Most plaintiffs' personal injury attorneys work in small firms or on their own. Insurance defense attorneys may be part of small, mid-size, or large firms that specialize in insurance defense work, or they may work in-house for corporations or insurance companies. Sometimes they work in the insurance defense litigation departments of large general practice firms.

Corporations and insurance companies also employ attorneys who supervise tort litigation handled by outside attorneys.

Who are their clients and what types of cases do they work on?

Plaintiffs' personal injury lawyers typically represent injured individuals. Michael Muldoon, a plaintiffs' attorney at Corboy & Demetrio, P.C., in Chicago, explains, "My clients are people who are injured due to the negligence of others or due to defective products. My clients include those who are injured by defective products, auto collisions, construction accidents, and unsafe premises. Our firm also handles airline disaster cases and medical malpractice cases." Michael's clients may seek damages (financial compensation) for lost income, pain and suffering, disability and loss of normal life (something that clients could do before the accident occurred but can no longer do as well), disfigurement, and loss of consortium (loss of society and sexual relations). His firm also handles wrongful death cases for the beneficiaries of those who have been killed due to negligence or defective products.

Richard (Rick) Foster is a defense attorney and partner at the 20-person firm of Donohue Brown Mathewson & Smyth in Chicago. Donohue Brown specializes in the defense of tort litigation. Rick handles a variety of cases, including medical malpractice, products liability, and legal malpractice cases, as well as class actions. "Most of my cases involve medical malpractice and products liability defense," says Rick. "My clients are nurses, doctors of every stripe, lawyers, auto manufacturers, a press manufacturer, corporations, and insurance companies. I handle the cases from cradle to grave— from the time they are filed through settlement or trial and appeal. I enjoy the academic and procedural challenges my cases pose throughout different stages of litigation," he adds.

Kevin Burke and Thomas Browne are partners in the large insurance defense and corporate practice firm of Hinshaw & Culbertson in Chicago. Kevin specializes in medical malpractice defense work. He explains, "My practice is primarily related to the defense of physicians and hospitals, which include HMOs, nurses, and residents. Each case involves self-education in the underlying medicine at issue. As professional service providers, my clients demand a level of commitment that exceeds that of other tort defendant clients. My typical case involves a severely brain-damaged baby in an action asserting negligence in labor and delivery management. I have also developed a subspecialty in neurosurgical negligence cases involving spinal or central nervous system injury. These are labor intensive and have a verdict range in the area of $2 million to $10 million. While the large cases are time consuming, I have a number of smaller ophthalmology cases, orthopedic cases, and primary care cases."

Thomas Browne specializes in the defense of legal malpractice cases. "My clients are lawyers who come directly to me with legal problems or whose professional liability insurance carriers name me to defend their interests. The insurance carriers are located across the country; the lawyer/clients are usually located within a 50-mile radius of my office." Thomas explains that the typical legal malpractice case is highly complex. "Most cases involve multiple plaintiffs and defendants and multiple theories of recovery. Most often these theories of recovery include one or more of the following: negligence, breach of contract, breach of fiduciary duty, intentional wrongdoing, and/or statutory violation." Legal malpractice work requires a thorough knowledge of the law beyond tort law. "Legal malpractice cases always involve a case within a case," says Thomas. "That is, the lawyer's conduct is involved, but so are the merits of the matter for which the lawyer was retained. As a consequence, my practice involves virtually every area of procedural and substantive law."

"Product liability work is somewhat unpredictable and rarely boring," says Margaret Costello of Dykema Gossett PLLC, a large firm in Detroit, Michigan. Margaret is part of Dykema Gossett's litigation group, one of the firm's largest practice groups. "Typical product liability cases that I have handled—if there are such things—are generally of two types. The first involves allegedly defective industrial equipment, such as a press, forklift, or sawhorse that injures a worker. The second type of case involves automobile product liability and crashworthiness issues, in which a person in an auto accident alleges injury due to some design defect in the car. I usually represent corporations and insurance companies."

C. Patrick (Pat) McLarney is a senior product liability attorney at Shook, Hardy & Bacon L.L.P., a large firm based in Kansas City, Missouri. Shook Hardy has a sizable product liability department with over 150 attorneys; the firm's attorneys have led the defense of the tobacco industry. Pat explains, "Most of my clients are institutions—mostly corporations or insurance companies in the Fortune 500. A typical case would involve the sale of a product which is alleged to have caused some injury. Generally there are a large number of cases filed against my client all over the country on this product." Pat was one of the lead attorneys for the class action arising out of the Hyatt Hotel skywalk collapse in Kansas City, Missouri. He was also hired as lead trial counsel by the Missouri Board of Architects, Engineers and Land Surveyors to revoke the licenses of the engineers who designed the Hyatt Hotel.

What daily activities are involved in tort litigation practice?

Tort litigation attorneys are engaged in the wide variety of activities handled by all litigation attorneys—drafting pleadings, writing and arguing motions, gathering facts through discovery, and representing their clients in pre-trial hearings, settlement negotiations, trials, and appeals (*see* the Civil Litigation chapter for more information about these activities). Says plaintiffs' attorney Michael Muldoon, "My days often involve motion practice (responding to motions and arguing them in court) and discovery (the finding of facts through written requests such as interrogatories and requests to produce and through sworn testimony of the parties and witnesses in depositions). I have a lot of contact with my clients. The initial contact with a client is in person, but we communicate closely by phone throughout the case. I'm frequently in meetings, whether they're with lawyers, clients, or insurance adjusters." Michael says that most cases eventually settle before the trial begins. "I usually end up trying at least one or two cases a year," he says. "Some attorneys in our firm will handle as many as four or five trials per year."

Insurance defense attorney Rick Foster reports that he, too, has about one or two cases per year that actually go to trial and result in a verdict. Rick's activities vary from day to day. "I spend time drafting pleadings and letters and a good deal of time on the phone talking with clients, insurance companies, and opposing attorneys. I usually take two to three depositions [sworn statements of witnesses] per week." Rick's work requires periodic travel to take witness depositions and to observe product testing. Rick says that the fact-finding involved in his work often takes him in interesting directions. He may attend automobile crash tests or even autopsies. "One of my most memorable days in practice involved attending autopsies of the four people killed in an accident, allegedly by a vehicle fire. The autopsies were conducted in a tent at the cemetery where the parties were buried;

they had died over three years before. The issue was whether or not there was a fuel system defect that caused the fire, resulting in the death of the occupants, or whether the crash killed the vehicle occupants before the fire began. The autopsies determined that the decedents did not inhale soot, proving that they were killed by the crash and before the fire started. Because I was able to observe firsthand the condition of the victims' lungs, I was better able to cross-examine the plaintiff's expert at trial."

Kevin Burke explains how he spends his days as a medical malpractice defense attorney. "A typical day begins by going through mail which is generated on each lawsuit file. This mail includes pleadings, motions, and client requests for information. Phone calls arc then returned from the previous day. On a daily basis, my appearance in court may be required for motions or status hearings on pending cases. Depositions usually take place in the afternoon and, therefore, preparation is required during the morning and often the night before." When we talked with Kevin, he was preparing to meet with an exhibit maker to prepare demonstrative evidence for a breast cancer malpractice trial.

The lawyers we talked to emphasized that a great deal of their time is spent in the discovery, or fact-finding, process. "The vast majority of my time is spent on discovery," says Margaret Costello. "Discovery includes conducting and attending depositions of witnesses and parties, reviewing documents, drafting and responding to discovery requests, attending inspections of accident sites/equipment, and interviewing and preparing expert witnesses." Legal malpractice attorney Thomas Browne says, "My work often involves the review and analysis of rather voluminous documents. I often take depositions for all or part of the day." Pat McLarney says that "no day is typical," but explains that in an average week, he spends "a half day in court, one to two days in meetings or depositions outside of the office, one day in meetings in the office, and the balance of the week at my desk."

What do tort litigators find rewarding about their practice?

Michael Muldoon finds great personal reward in his work as a plaintiffs' attorney. "At the end of the case I feel I've actually been able to make a difference in this injured person's life. The client has received enough money to have peace of mind. Perhaps the client can afford to purchase a home that he can adapt to accommodate his wheelchair. The compensation the client receives helps restore her peace of mind and dignity. When people are injured, when they have disfigurement and severe disability, they feel lessened. The compensation they receive in a personal injury case reaffirms that they are getting 'justice.' They feel that part of them is being made whole, that their dignity is restored." Michael also enjoys the close personal relationships he develops with his clients. "I had a wonderful client in her 80s who was run over by a city bus when she was crossing a street in the Loop [downtown Chicago]. She had severe injuries—her internal organs were crushed. She's made a great recovery and has been able to travel around the world twice since her recovery. My secretary told me that she would secretly love to adopt this client as her grandmother, and I can see why," he confides. "These client relationships make my practice as a plaintiffs' attorney incredibly rewarding."

The defense attorneys we interviewed mentioned how much they enjoy the relationships they develop with fellow professionals. "I often have the distinct pleasure of working with some of the finest lawyers in the city," says Thomas Browne. "I like working with my expert witnesses," says Kevin Burke, "because of my respect and admiration for their accomplishments." Pat McLarney, who has over 30 years of experience as a product liability lawyer and has served as managing partner of his firm, says that he's enjoyed mentoring younger, less experienced attorneys at his firm. "The most personally satisfying thing for me has been to provide interesting, rewarding work for others in the law firm and to watch them develop their careers," he reports.

The lawyers we talked to also enjoyed the intellectual challenge of their work. "Each case requires that I learn about something new," says Rick Foster. Whether he's learning about a disease or a medical procedure, Rick says, "I love 'becoming' a doctor—learning that medical issue from the doctor's point of view." Rick also enjoys the challenge of developing a sophisticated familiarity with that medical issue in order to discuss the issue at the scientific level of his medical experts. Margaret Costello, too, enjoys the constant learning that defense attorneys are required to do. "I especially like learning things I know nothing about, such as engineering and technical processes." She adds, "As a female and someone with no engineering or technical background, male opposing counsel and experts often underestimate my knowledge and ability. It's interesting and amusing to watch their behavior change when they realize the expertise I've developed," she says.

Attorneys specializing in tort litigation find that their days unfold in unpredictable ways, and they enjoy the variety of activities their practice requires. Says Thomas Browne, "There's tremendous variety in my daily work." Margaret Costello adds, "I like the variety. I like that things are often unpredictable and that I'm exposed to a variety of people, places, and situations." Margaret notes that things can be more unpredictable than one might expect. She says that field inspections—where attorneys visit the site of the accident or view the equipment involved in an accident or product liability case—are often great adventures. Margaret tells us that during field inspections, she's driven a garbage truck, climbed to the top of ski-lift towers—she even conducted one inspection among a field of cows.

Tort litigators also report that they enjoy the excitement inherent in the adversarial process. "I enjoy setting up and preparing a case well, so as to back the other side into a corner," says Margaret Costello, "and, personally, I enjoy the competitive aspect of litigation—at least most of the time!" Kevin Burke says that the most rewarding part of his practice involves trial work, particularly cross-examining opponent's experts and delivering closing arguments. "Successfully cross-examining an opponent's expert while on trial is particularly rewarding, as experts often underestimate lawyers. And then at the closing argument, the lawyer finally gets a chance to argue the case—you, as the lawyer, have total control." Rick Foster, too, enjoys cross-examinations. "There's a great deal of challenge in questioning people who have information that they don't want you to know and meeting the challenge by getting them to disclose that information." Rick adds that he truly enjoys being on trial. "Being on trial can be disruptive to your personal life—it can be difficult to see your family, hard to eat, and impossible to sleep. But when you're on trial you have the luxury of concentrating on one thing. You have a single, intense focus on your client's interest and the issues in the case. There's nothing like it," he says.

The Training and Skills Important to Tort Litigators

How do people enter the field of tort litigation?

Many people enter the field of tort litigation directly out of law school. The wide variety of tort cases—some involving less serious injuries and a demand for lesser damages—allows attorneys who have recently graduated to gain experience drafting motions and responding to discovery requests, taking depositions, arguing motions in court, and attending pre-trial conferences. Depending on the complexity of the cases, some attorneys may try cases in their first year out of law school and may even have their own case load in their first years of practice. Whether on the plaintiffs' side or on the defense side, this area of law provides excellent opportunities for law school graduates who want to be in the courtroom.

Some law students know early on that this is the area they want to pursue, based on earlier experiences. "When I was a junior in high school I did not know any lawyers," says Pat McLarney. "I attended a program put on by the American Legion called 'Boys State,' which was like a summer camp. One of the activities you could participate in was a mock jury trial." The Boys State experience, as well as high school speech team experience, heightened Pat's interest in a career as a trial lawyer. Product liability law was a natural fit. "I grew up on a farm and learned about agriculture. This and my college courses in the sciences have helped me in my work as a trial lawyer in a technical field."

"I always wanted to be a lawyer, and I decided in law school that I wanted to do medical work," says Kevin Burke. "I researched to find the top medical malpractice trial firms, applied, and got lucky," he says. Rick Foster took a year off between college and law school to work as a legal assistant in a large firm, where he was involved in commercial litigation. "I saw even the best and the brightest new commercial litigators wouldn't be in the courtroom for years. It was clear that wasn't what I wanted. I wanted to be on the front lines. I wanted to get in the courtroom right away. While I was in law school, I interviewed at a large firm that did insurance defense cases, and I learned that new associates went to court right away and did depositions right away. I was sure I wanted to litigate, and I knew I wanted to be in the courtroom as soon as possible. The firm was a very good match for me."

Michael Muldoon started clerking at his plaintiffs' personal injury firm in his second year of law school. "I knew from the beginning that this is what I wanted to do. Clerking gave me the opportunity to help prepare for trials and to observe the trials in cases on which I had worked. As a law clerk, I had the chance to go into the judge's chambers to see the attorneys argue motions in limine (motions to keep particular evidence from the jury) and learn how judges rule on such motions. I got to sit in on depositions. I fell under the spell of the drama of the courtroom," says Michael. Michael told us that his father is a general practitioner and that his brother is a lawyer. He says he saw his dad "make a good living helping people." Michael, too, has followed that path. As a plaintiffs' attorney, he says he is able to make a good living doing what is most important to him—helping injured victims seek justice.

There are also those who pursue a career in tort litigation as a second career. "A number of nurses and medical professionals go on to pursue their law degrees," notes Rick Foster. "They often work in insurance defense firms, where they use their expertise to defend medical professionals accused of negligence." Margaret Costello pursued law as a second career. She was 35 when she graduated from law school. She had worked as a psychologist and has masters' degrees in both clinical psychology and rehabilitation administration. "I actively chose a career in law as a second career," she says, "but litigation, including product liability, primarily was something I was thrust into by being in a particular place at a particular time."

Other attorneys gain litigation experience in another field before pursuing tort litigation. "My career started in the area of commercial litigation," says Thomas Browne. "Another lawyer in the firm who had been handling legal malpractice actions found that there was more work than he could cover. My background was perfect for this type of work, so I began to concentrate on defending legal malpractice cases which involved an underlying commercial matter." Michael Muldoon notes that a number of attorneys with experience as state criminal prosecutors ultimately pursue personal injury work. "They have a great deal of trial experience and they are used to having the burden of proof. As the plaintiff in a personal injury case, you have to prove up your case just as a criminal prosecutor does."

What skills are most important to personal injury and insurance defense lawyers?

❖ All of the tort litigators we interviewed agreed that **oral and written communication skills** are critically important to success in this practice area. Says Michael Muldoon, "No matter how much you know, it doesn't count unless you can clearly communicate that information. You need to communicate with clients, judges, other attorneys, law clerks—and, ultimately, with the jury." Adds Pat McLarney, "Speaking and writing are of primary importance. Gain as much public speaking experience as you can—whether at church, through mock trial programs, or talking to civic groups. Practice writing short, succinct articles for newspapers or other publications."

❖ **Analytical skills** are key to success in this area of law. Explains Thomas Browne, "A legal malpractice defense lawyer must have sharp analytical skills. He or she must be able to sort through piles of documents, court papers, and other written materials and identify the real issues." Margaret Costello agrees. "A defense lawyer needs to formulate the best defenses and strategy to set the case up as favorably as possible," she comments. Adds Kevin Burke, "A trial lawyer must think objectively and recognize the other side's strengths. I continue to develop these skills with each year of practice."

❖ The lawyers we talked to stressed the importance of **interpersonal communication skills**. "People skills are so important," says Margaret Costello. "You have to make the court like you and make the jury like you. You have to make the most of every deposition, and to get what you need in a deposition, you have to develop a rapport with the witness being deposed. I think my background in clinical psychology helps me with this," she adds. Michael Muldoon stresses the importance of building strong relationships with fellow attorneys. "I really rely on my colleagues. I strategize with other attorneys in the firm. Especially when I'm about to go to trial, it's helpful to me to talk over my case with my colleagues, and it's absolutely thrilling to talk about strategy with great attorneys such as Phil Corboy [the firm's senior partner]. Having the confidence of my colleagues means a lot." Kevin Burke singles out one of the most important interpersonal communication skills. "Above all, be a good listener," he says.

❖ Attorneys specializing in tort litigation need **strong organizational and time management skills**. The cases often involve complex issues—thus there are many witnesses, numerous documents, and a great deal of evidence to sort through. "You have to have the ability to manage your cases," says Michael Muldoon. "You're often working on several cases at the same time. You have to know the varying facts and issues and the applicable law. You need to be both thorough and efficient in researching the facts and the law." Kevin Burke notes that managing time is a

skill important to those in this field. "Time management is most challenging, particularly when preparing for a trial," he says.

❖ The attorneys we talked to emphasized the importance of a **sincere
interest in tort law and a commitment to becoming an outstanding
litigator**. "This is a profession, not a job," says Rick Foster. "Be
devoted. When you go home in the evening, take the advance sheets
[recent published opinions] with you. When our firm is hiring, I look
for new lawyers who have a good attitude. I look for lawyers who want
to learn and master this area of law and who show a real love for this
area of law."

What classes and law school experiences do tort litigators recommend?

❖ The attorneys we talked to recommended a **wide range of law school
classes, including torts, evidence, civil procedure, complex litigation, special and equitable remedies, and negotiations**. "Evidence
and civil procedure are very important for the trial lawyer," says Kevin
Burke. Rick Foster asserts, "Negotiations is one of the most important
classes a law student can take. In the class, you work in teams, negotiating to reach agreement. Your grade may depend on being able to reach
an agreement." Thomas Browne urges students to take a well-rounded
course load. "Because legal malpractice cases can involve any area of
law, a comprehensive background in major areas of practice is also helpful—for example, real estate, domestic relations, intellectual property,
contracts, and U.C.C. [the Uniform Commercial Code]."

❖ Take **trial advocacy classes** and **participate in moot court competitions**. Trial advocacy classes give students the opportunity to try a case
before a mock jury. They provide excellent preparation for students planning a trial law career. "Take as many trial advocacy classes as you can,"
says Rick Foster. "Moot court teaches brief writing and oral advocacy
skills and provides excellent training for practicing in this field," he adds.

❖ Whether in high school, college, or graduate school, **speech classes and
writing classes** can help you prepare for a career as a tort litigator. Says
Pat McLarney, "Writing and speech classes are especially valuable. I participated in speech contests in high school and even after graduating

from law school. All of those experiences have been helpful." Adds Michael Muldoon, "Any speech classes are helpful. And liberal arts classes that require writing and creative research, such as sociology and history, are helpful as well."

❖ **Gain practical experience by working as a law clerk or summer associate** for a firm that practices tort litigation. "The best way to prepare for practicing in this area is by working with people who are doing the work," advises Margaret Costello. "If you're considering personal injury work, get clerking experience at a firm," says Michael Muldoon. "This helps you become familiar with the motion practice involved in this field and gives you excellent research and legal drafting experience." Adds Thomas Browne, "If you want to pursue a career in legal malpractice, my best advice is to hire on with a firm that handles a significant volume of legal malpractice cases. Good training is essential, and the best training comes from those individuals with the most experience in the field."

❖ **Keep up with the latest developments in the field of tort law.** "I would advise students to read about the practice area in verdict reporters [newspapers that report jury verdicts] and local daily law periodicals in the jurisdiction," says Kevin Burke. Margaret Costello agrees, recommending that students "keep abreast of recent law practice developments."

❖ **Become part of the community of tort litigators** through involvement in professional associations. Prospective employers are likely to view a student's involvement in professional associations as a sign that the student is comfortable in professional circles as well as proof that you have the skills necessary to client development. Students can generally become members of state, local, and national bar and professional associations for a small fee. "Students and young lawyers should join and become active in relevant practice sections and committees or organizations like the American Bar Association (ABA), American Trial Lawyers Association (ATLA), or the Defense Research Institute (DRI), as well as state and local bar associations. Read the publications of these groups," advises Margaret Costello. Kevin Burke also encourages students to become involved in professional associations. "Contact professional societies and attend their seminars to meet people. After a speaking event, introduce yourself to speakers and tell them of your interest in this area of law. Be aggressive, and don't get discouraged."

TORT LAW: PERSONAL INJURY AND INSURANCE DEFENSE
LITIGATION ATTORNEYS INTERVIEWED FOR THIS SECTION

Thomas Browne
Hinshaw & Culbertson
Chicago, Illinois
UNDERGRADUATE: Northwestern University
LAW SCHOOL: The John Marshall Law School

Kevin Burke
Hinshaw & Culbertson
Chicago, Illinois
UNDERGRADUATE: Boston College
LAW SCHOOL: New England School of Law

Margaret Costello
Dykema Gossett PLLC
Detroit, Michigan
UNDERGRADUATE: Pennsylvania State University
LAW SCHOOL: Detroit College of Law

Richard B. Foster III
Donohue Brown Mathewson & Smyth
Chicago, Illinois
UNDERGRADUATE: Northwestern University
LAW SCHOOL: University of Illinois College of Law

C. Patrick McLarney
Shook, Hardy & Bacon L.L.P.
Kansas City, Missouri
UNDERGRADUATE: St. Benedict's College
LAW SCHOOL: University of Missouri School of Law

Michael K. Muldoon
Corboy & Demetrio, P.C.
Chicago, Illinois
UNDERGRADUATE: University of Notre Dame
LAW SCHOOL: Chicago-Kent College of Law, Illinois Institute of
Technology

Trusts and Estates Law

What is Trusts and Estates Law?

No matter how big your investment portfolio, how notable your modern art collection, or how rare your collection of antique silver, when the time comes for you to leave this world, you can't take your assets with you. The estate lawyer's role is to help a client arrange his or her financial affairs so that, upon the client's death, the client's assets are distributed exactly as he or she wishes and the tax consequences of distributing that property are minimized.

What a person acquires during his or her lifetime—both real estate and personal property—makes up that person's estate. Someone's estate may include real property, such as homes, condominiums, farms, and summer cottages; vehicles, including cars, pickup trucks, fishing boats, yachts, and Lear jets; furniture, such as antique dressers, family pianos, Persian rugs, Crate and Barrel sofas, and futons passed down from a college roommate or older sibling; household items, such as Baccarat crystal, heirloom china, and pots and pans from Target; personal items, including jewelry—whether sapphires from Tiffany's or costume jewelry from Wal-Mart—and art work—whether kindergarten scribblings or Van Gogh originals; family documents, such as diaries, photo albums, or the family Bible; and money, including stocks, bonds, and personal savings accounts.

The law of estates and trusts governs the use of certain types of instruments, such as wills, living trusts, or charitable trusts, to provide for an orderly distribution of the assets and payment of any debts or liabilities of the estate. Developing an effective estate plan can be very challenging, as each client has a unique set of assets and unique family, business, and financial concerns. A client who owns a family business will want to ensure that there is a smooth transition in ownership of the business assets. A client who has a disabled child will want to plan for that child's future well-being. Grandparents may want to look out for the educational needs of their grandchildren and great-grandchildren. An art collector may want to make sure that her collection is distributed to a particular museum or sold to benefit a particular charitable organization.

A client with even a modest estate may seek to use his or her will as an instrument for rewarding some family members—the "good" daughter— and punishing others—the "black sheep" son. Some clients may even express disapproval for family members by rewarding someone outside the family—the kind waitress or the helpful neighbor. And many clients, even those with the most modest estates, choose to provide some financial benefits to charitable organizations, educational institutions, or churches and synagogues, as well as to family members.

Lawyers who work in estate planning work closely with their clients, often over a period of many years, and tend to become close to their clients. They know a great deal about their clients' financial matters and family relationships. When a client considers how to dispose of his estate upon his death, he is making decisions that reflect and are intertwined with personal values. Often the estate planning attorney must become involved in decisions regarding the care of an elderly dependent of the client or the means that will be used to care for the client and a spouse through their later years. The estate lawyer often becomes a true family counselor, helping the client work through both financial and personal issues.

Estate Planning

Estate planning attorneys interview their clients concerning their wishes, conduct a thorough analysis of their clients' personal assets, and then provide recommendations. After reviewing the recommendations with the client, the estate planning attorney drafts estate planning documents which may include one or more of the following:

A will—a document specifying how property is to be distributed upon the client's death;

A trust—an arrangement where property is held by one party (the trustee, which is often a bank) for the benefit of another (the beneficiary or beneficiaries), either during or after the life of the grantor;

Power of attorney—an instrument authorizing someone else to act as one's agent or attorney;

A living will—a document that states that, if a medical situation arises where the client cannot reasonably expect to recover, he or she be allowed to die and not be kept alive by artificial means or heroic measures.

These documents may be modified often during the client's lifetime as a result of changes in the client's economic, marital, or family situation.

Estate Administration

Most people die intestate, or without a will. State law then determines how their estate is distributed. The administration of the estate—the process of identifying, appraising, collecting, and distributing the property—may be especially complex when someone with a large estate dies without a will, and those family members inheriting such an estate may find themselves with large tax bills. In cases where there has been careful estate planning and a will has made specific provisions for distribution, tax consequences may be minimized.

When someone dies with a will, or testate, the attorney represents the executor, a person appointed by the decedent to carry out, or execute, the provisions of the will. The executor, with the help of an attorney, is responsible for determining the decedent's tax liabilities and providing for payment of the taxes out of the estate; for paying the decedent's creditors; and for paying to defend the estate against any lawsuits. The attorney also helps the executor with the disposition of the decedent's assets. Sometimes guardianship issues arise with regard to young children or disabled adult children who are incapable of managing financial matters without assistance. Sometimes estates become the subject of family disputes. It's not uncommon for those who feel they've been unfairly treated in a will to contest the will, and the resulting lawsuits are called estate litigation. The attorney's role in helping the beneficiaries of an estate often leads the attorney to work with a new generation of family members on estate planning issues.

Formation of Trusts

The law allows great flexibility in arranging trusts for a broad range of purposes. A trust, as explained earlier, is an arrangement in which the client's money or property is held by one party—often a bank or financial institution—for the benefit of another, who is called the beneficiary. There are many types of trusts. Often they are set up to minimize the tax consequences of financial distribution. For example, to ensure that grandchildren receive the maximum benefit of a financial gift and to protect the assets from estate taxes, grandparents may set up generation-skipping trusts to provide assets to their grandchildren. An older person can set up a trust through which he or she receives payments until death and can arrange for the trust to then make payments to the heirs, to a university, or to a charitable organization. Parents with adult children who are disabled by mental illness may set up a trust that allows the disabled person a degree of financial independence but allows the trustee to guide the disabled person's financial decisions. Trust law is extremely complex, requiring those practitioners specializing in this area to keep abreast of the latest developments in both trust law and tax law.

Life as a Trusts and Estates Lawyer

Where do trusts and estates lawyers work?

Many lawyers specializing in this area work in law firms. They may work in small firms that specialize in estate planning or in estate planning departments of mid-size and large law firms. As part of their practice, general practitioners may draft wills and advise clients concerning estate planning issues. Some lawyers specializing in trusts work in the trust departments of financial institutions.

Who are their clients and what types of issues do they handle?

Mary Baker Edwards is an attorney who specializes in trusts and estates at Blue & Edwards, P.A. in Towson, Maryland. Mary has a wide range of clients. "I always represent individuals," she explains. "They range in age from their early 20s to their late 90s. They come from all walks of life and they have estates of all sizes, from small to very large. Most of my clients live in the city of Baltimore or in Baltimore County." Mary's work with her clients involves guiding them through the estate planning process. "When I meet with them, I discuss ways to structure their estate planning documents so as to minimize death taxes and accomplish their goals. I draft the documents and, once they meet with the client's approval, I supervise the execution of the documents."

"My clients are individuals with relatively high net worth, generally ranging from $2 million to $20 million," says William (Bill) Sheridan, of Finger, Hochman & Delott, P.C. in Chicago. "My clients tend to be doctors, lawyers, dentists, and owners of closely held businesses. I help my clients with estate planning issues from A to Z, including the creation of trusts to save tax dollars and protect against creditors, setting up trusts for minors and disabled people, making arrangements for financial gifts that minimize tax consequences, drafting wills, assisting with insurance issues, and assisting in post-death planning and administration."

Jennifer Johnson Rahn, Vice President and Trust Officer at Bank One in Springfield, Illinois, explains, "My caseload within the trust department determines who my clients are. I currently work with testamentary trusts. The person who created the trust is deceased. Some of the trusts were created as long ago as the 1920s or the 1940s. My clients are the beneficiaries of the trusts—the children, grandchildren, or spouse of the individual who created the trust. My role is to help my clients solve issues involving the assets." Sometimes family members may be uncomfortable managing the assets of the trust; Jennifer provides financial guidance. She assists the individuals with tax planning and coordinates investment management. "I administer the accounts in conjunction with the investment arm of the bank. My job is to be familiar with the trust document and its provisions and to disburse the funds in accordance with the agreements." Jennifer also develops new trust relationships with clients. "Trusts are incredibly flexible," she says, so part of her job involves showing new trust clients how they can protect and manage their assets through trusts.

What daily activities are involved in trusts and estates practice?

The estate planning lawyers we talked to explained that their daily activities involve the drafting and review of legal documents. "I draft and review documents, I write letters and memos, and I also spend time reviewing files," says Bill Sheridan. Mary Edwards agrees, commenting, "I spend a lot of time drafting estate planning documents and conferring with clients, either on the phone or in face to face meetings."

As Mary's comment suggests, this is a very people-oriented area of law practice. Lawyers in this field spend a great deal of time talking with clients and other business advisers. "Most of the day," explains Bill Sheridan, "I'm on the phone or in meetings, talking to either my clients or people who advise my clients, such as stockbrokers, business advisers, and insurance agents."

As a bank trust officer, Jennifer Rahn spends her day talking with trust beneficiaries and other professionals. "I often meet with my trust beneficiaries," she says, "but I also interact with many types of professional people. These include beneficiaries' accountants and lawyers as well as people in other divisions of the bank." Jennifer works with trust beneficiaries on a remarkably broad range of issues. "I may help the beneficiaries get financing for a mortgage. Because farms are often held in trust, I may help the beneficiaries weigh the merits of selling assets connected to the family farm." Jennifer notes that much of her job involves counseling—on both complex financial strategies and basic financial issues. "Sometimes I help people create budgets so they can live within their means. Occasionally I meet someone who has never written a check before and who has no concept of cash flow. We try to do everything we can to help our clients with their financial issues."

Because lawyers in this field work so closely with individuals, they often become highly involved with their clients. "There's a different personal dynamic with every client," confides Jennifer. "It depends on the needs of the individual. Sometimes you become a close counselor of the family. I've been at several of my clients' bedsides when they've died, and I've planned a number of funerals. Client relationships can be wonderful—it's as if you become an adjunct member of people's families." Though her job involves minimal travel, once a year, Jennifer's bank sends her across the country to meet personally with out-of-state beneficiaries. Such trips help build and maintain client relationships.

Mary Edwards tells us that these close relationships with clients can result in unusual client requests. "One of my clients lives with her mentally disabled 45-year-old son. The client herself has had a series of strokes that have resulted in diminished capacity. One day she called and asked me to come to her home to remove 'the box on the wall that's making noise.' After several minutes of questioning her to determine what this box was (questions such as, 'Is it bigger than your stove?'), I determined that the mysterious box was a burglar alarm system. The client had purchased the system from a door to door salesperson and didn't know what it was, much less how to use it." What did Mary do to help her frightened and confused client? "I tracked down the company who sold it to her and convinced them to remove it from her house at no charge." Not exactly part of Mary's job description, but not an unusual effort on the part of an estate attorney highly devoted to her clients.

"When you're an estate planning lawyer, you're dealing with people as opposed to businesses," says Bill Sheridan. "Your clients tell you things they wouldn't tell anyone else. Every family is unique," he explains. "One thing I know for sure is that there aren't any Ozzie and Harriet families out there. *Every* family has its problems, whether they're medical problems or emotional problems or relationship problems." He continues, "As an estate planning lawyer, you are truly the family's lawyer. Over the years your clients grow closer, they feel more at ease with you, and they confide in you. You truly know everything about them."

What do trusts and estates lawyers find rewarding about their practice?

The trusts and estates lawyers we talked to reported that they enjoy being able to make a difference in people's lives. Explains Mary Edwards, "I feel that I'm really helping people, whether I'm helping them save tax dollars when I do estate planning or helping them get through a rough time after the death of a family member, when I'm doing estate administration." Jennifer Rahn adds, "This is a field in which you can make a difference. You can truly have an impact on people's lives. You can take a very difficult situation, smooth it out, and find a solution that's satisfying to the family."

Bill Sheridan explains that he enjoys helping people solve complex problems through estate planning. "Estate planning does more than just solve tax problems. It can help resolve personal and family conflicts and can improve family relationships," he says. "I tell my clients that there is no problem that can't be solved. I explain that there may be a cost involved in solving the problem, but that there *is* a solution." Bill notes that people are often highly emotional about the family issues they talk to him about. "One of my clients was a doctor with a number of children, including a daughter who is severely retarded. When my client came to see me he was very upset and highly emotionally charged. He cared deeply about all his children and wanted to provide for all of them. He was concerned that providing for his special needs child would make him unable to provide for his other children. I told him that there was a solution, a way in which he could provide for all of his children, but, as with most solutions, it wasn't without costs. I helped him set up a special needs trust for his daughter and an estate plan leaving assets to his other children. The next time I met with the client, he was much calmer. It was clear that he felt very relieved that we had found a way to look out for the well being of his entire family."

The challenge of handling a wide variety of tasks is something Jennifer Rahn finds particularly rewarding. "There's something different going on all the time. I always come in every morning with a plan for my day, but within a half hour the day begins to unfold with a life of its own," she says. Even the amazing range of client personalities adds spice to Jennifer's days. "Different clients expect different behaviors. Some people need you to be reassuring, other people need you to be tough." Jennifer also says she enjoys the fact that her job affords her the chance to be involved in and give back to the city's professional community. "I do public speaking for the bank's trust department. I speak to civic organizations and do programs for the Illinois Institute of Continuing Legal Education," she says. "I also serve on the boards of several not-for-profit organizations," she says. "I enjoy the chance to meet new people and to share my expertise with other professionals."

The Training and Skills Important to Trusts and Estates Lawyers

How do people enter the field of trusts and estates law?

Some law students plan a career in trusts and estates. Mary Edwards reports that she worked as a paralegal in the field for five years before going to law school. "I decided to work a few years before going to law school. I attended the Institute for Paralegal Training in Philadelphia to learn how to be a paralegal. In the paralegal program, I chose to specialize in estates and trusts because my grandfather was an estates and trusts attorney."

Bill Sheridan's father was a lawyer specializing in estate administration, and he must have been especially inspiring, as four of his seven children are lawyers. After Bill graduated from law school, he worked as a business professor at a state university. His father came to observe one of his classes; after the class, Bill and his father had a heart-to-heart talk. Knowing how much he had enjoyed his own career as an estates lawyer, Bill's dad urged him to use his talents as an estate planning lawyer rather than as a business professor. Bill followed his father's advice, working in the trust department at Harris Bank in Chicago for three years and then as an estate planning attorney at a large Chicago law firm. Eight years ago he and several of his partners left to form a small firm, where Bill specializes in estate work.

Other attorneys end up in the field serendipitously. "I fell into this line of work," says Jennifer Rahn. Upon graduation from law school, Jennifer moved to Springfield, Illinois. One of the first things she did was attend a bar association luncheon for young lawyers. "At the luncheon someone mentioned that one of the banks in town was looking for an attorney to work in the trusts department," she says. "I got the job and I've been in the field ever since." She notes, "You don't have to have a law degree to be a trust officer, but it's very helpful. Banks now actively recruit lawyers for their trust departments."

What skills are most important to trusts and estates lawyers?

❖ Trusts and estates lawyers need outstanding **interpersonal communication skills** and must **truly like working with people**. "In this field," says Bill Sheridan, "technical proficiency alone isn't enough. You need to be able to develop relationships. Developing rapport with clients is key." Explains Mary Edwards, "You really need to be a 'people person' to be an estates and trusts lawyer, because you interact so closely with clients. If you are too shy or too abrasive, clients won't feel comfortable with you. It's essential that clients feel comfortable with you, because when you're talking with them you're dealing with two highly charged issues: financial assets and death." Whether in a bank setting or a law firm setting, attorneys may be expected to develop new business. "You have to really be comfortable with all kinds of people to be comfortable doing business development," says Jennifer Rahn.

❖ Good **counseling skills** are critically important to the trusts and estates lawyer. "You have to be comfortable in a counseling role," says Bill Sheridan. "In order to provide your clients with the best advice, you need to get them to open up and communicate with you. You have to know what to ask them to get them to open up." Bill suggests that one of the best ways students can prepare for their roles as counselors is to go through counseling themselves. "Being part of the therapy or counseling process helps you understand counseling from the client's point of view. Clients seeking your advice are discussing issues they find highly emotional. Understanding your own emotions helps you understand, identify, and cope with your client's emotions," advises Bill. Jennifer Rahn says that she enjoys the counseling role that's inherent in her work, but adds that it can be stressful. "Sometimes when you're counseling a client, the discussion can veer from financial issues to personal issues. For example, one client I worked with confided that she was a victim of domestic violence. I helped her seek refuge in a shelter for battered women."

❖ Lawyers in this field must have **technical proficiency**; they must have a firm grasp of the complex provisions covering wills, trusts, and estate planning documents, as well as a mastery of tax law. "One of the best things you can do early on in your career is to develop your technical proficiency," says Bill Sheridan.

❖ Trusts and estates lawyers need strong writing skills—**both legal writing skills and business writing skills.** "Drafting and reviewing legal documents is a critical part of the practice," says Bill Sheridan. "I do a lot of written correspondence," says Jennifer Rahn. "When you're writing to clients, you want to make sure that your writing is free of technical jargon. It's incredible how often I'll talk to clients who receive letters from their personal lawyers and don't understand what their lawyer is saying because the lawyer has used legalese. When I write to my clients, I try to be an interpreter for the legal community. I want my clients to clearly understand the information I'm communicating. That's an important part of my job."

❖ **Organizational skills** are also important to lawyers in this field. "I'm constantly juggling tasks—reviewing files, returning calls, and talking to my clients' professional advisers," says Bill Sheridan, advising that students entering this field be well organized and attentive to detail. "You have to be fairly well organized to do this type of work," says trust officer Jennifer Rahn. "I deal with 130 accounts and some of those accounts have multiple beneficiaries. I'm keeping track of a lot of people and a lot of information. Being well organized helps."

What classes and law school experiences do trusts and estates lawyers recommend?

❖ The lawyers we talked to highly recommend **estates and trusts classes,** including advanced seminars in estate planning, and tax law classes, including personal income tax and estate and gift tax. They also advise taking a negotiations class. "You do quite a bit of negotiating in this field," says Jennifer Rahn. Mary Edwards also suggests that students take basic courses in real estate law and corporate law so that they're prepared to work with all kinds of assets.

❖ **A wide variety of undergraduate classes** can be helpful as well. "An understanding of the financial and investment world is helpful. Consider undergraduate business classes such as finance, investments, assets, and securities," says Jennifer Rahn. Undergraduate course work in business writing, speech, counseling, and psychology can also help you develop the skills you need for this communications-oriented field of law.

❖ Work to **develop strong oral and written communication skills.** Writing articles—whether for a legal journal, a school newspaper, or a bar association publication—can provide excellent writing experience. An added bonus is that you'll have a polished writing sample available when you're ready to interview for attorney jobs.

❖ **Develop your counseling skills.** Working in your school's clinical program, where you're actually advising clients, can help. In addition, volunteer counseling opportunities abound. Consider volunteering to be a peer counselor in your school's career services office. Ask your career services director whether you can help first year students learn to use the career services office's research materials. Volunteer to be an alumni adviser—talking about your own law school or college experiences—to students at your college or high school. Participate in your law school's pro bono programs, through which you have a chance to help people who can't afford legal representation. Finally, consider learning first-hand about counseling from the client's point of view. Talking with a therapist or counselor or even a career counselor—where you're the client—can help you learn a great deal about what makes clients feel comfortable.

❖ **Gain practical experience in the estates and trusts field** by working as a law clerk or summer associate. "Students interested in this area can explore a number of options," suggests Bill Sheridan. "They might consider working for a firm with an estates and trusts department, in a bank, or working on estate matters for the county guardian's office [*see* the Public Interest Law chapter]." Working in the field allows you to make contacts that can be invaluable in your search for an attorney position when you finish law school.

TRUSTS AND ESTATES ATTORNEYS INTERVIEWED FOR THIS SECTION

Mary Baker Edwards
Blue & Edwards, P.A.
Towson, Maryland
UNDERGRADUATE: University of Richmond
LAW SCHOOL: University of Maryland School of Law

Jennifer Johnson Rahn
Bank One
Springfield, Illinois
UNDERGRADUATE: Coe College
LAW SCHOOL: University of Illinois College of Law

William J. Sheridan
Finger, Hochman & Delott, P.C.
(now Hochman, Dolgin, Delott, Galarnyk & Prohov, P.C.)
Chicago, Illinois
UNDERGRADUATE: Fairfield University
LAW SCHOOL: University of Illinois College of Law

About the Author
Lisa L. Abrams, J.D.

Lisa L. Abrams graduated from the University of Illinois College of Law in 1985. She worked as an insurance defense attorney at a large law firm in Chicago before joining Chicago-Kent College of Law where she was the Assistant Dean and Director of Career Services. Lisa developed in-house job search programs for students, outreach programs to legal recruiters and hiring partners, and a job search support group for law graduates in conjunction with the Chicago Bar Association. She has also published numerous articles on career planning and development for the National Association for Law Placement.

Currently, Lisa works as a consultant, providing career planning advice to law students and career transition advice to lawyers. She also provides consulting services to businesses on leadership, team building, change management, and communication strategies. In addition, Lisa develops and teaches courses in career development, leadership, and adult learning strategies for the Masters in Training and Development Program at Roosevelt University in Chicago. Lisa, her husband (a patent attorney), and their two Polish lowland sheepdogs live in Winnetka, Illinois.

Other Titles Available

What Law School Doesn't Teach You... But You Really Need To Know

Expert Advice for Making Your Legal Career a HUGE Success

"Be yourself." "Avoid gossip." "There's no such thing as a stupid question." If you believe statements like these, you could jeopardize your job. Why? Because the new lawyers who stand out follow a much more subtle set of rules. Rules that you can use to transform your job, whether you work for a law firm, government entity, public interest organization, or any other legal employer!

In this book, you'll learn the trade secrets that make top lawyers say, "I wish I'd known that when I started out!" You'll discover hundreds of tips and strategies, including:

Author: Kimm Alayne Walton, J.D.
ISBN: 0-15-900453-5
Price: $19.95

- How to turn down work when you're swamped without saying the dreaded "no"
- How to negotiate for more money
- How to use gossip to your advantage
- How to make an outstanding first impression
- How to take criticism and make yourself shine

Author Kimm Alayne Walton talked to lawyers and law school administrators all over the country, asking them for their best advice for new lawyers. Whether you're going for a summer clerkship, your first permanent job, or you've already started your career you'll find a wealth of invaluable insider tips you can use right now. With *What Law School Doesn't Teach You . . . But You Really Need To Know*, you'll feel as though you have hundreds of top-notch mentors at your fingertips!

America's Greatest Places To Work With A Law Degree
And How To Make The Most Of Any Job, No Matter Where It Is!

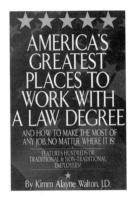

With *America's Greatest Places to Work With A Law Degree* you'll find out what it's really like to work at hundreds of terrific traditional and non-traditional employers — from fantastic law firms, to the Department of Justice, to great public interest employers, to corporate in-house counsel's offices, to dozens of others. You'll learn lots of sure-fire strategies for breaking into all kinds of desirable fields — like Sports, Entertainment, the Internet, and many, many more. You'll discover the non-traditional fields where new law school graduates pull down six figures — and love what they do! And you'll get hundreds of insider tips for making the most of your job, no matter WHERE you decide to work.

Author: Kimm Alayne Walton, J.D.
ISBN: 0-15-900180-3
Price: $24.95
(776 Pages, 6" x 9")

The bottom line is, no matter what you like, there's a dream job just waiting for you. Discover it in *America's Greatest Places To Work With A Law Degree.*

Guerrilla Tactics For Getting The Legal Job Of Your Dreams
Regardless of Your Grades, Your School, or Your Work Experience!

Whether you're looking for a summer clerkship or your first permanent job after law school, this national best-seller is the key to getting the legal job of your dreams.

Guerrilla Tactics for Getting the Legal Job of Your Dreams leads you step-by-step through everything you need to do to nail down that perfect job! You'll learn hundreds of simple-to-use strategies that will get you exactly where you want to go.

Guerrilla Tactics features the best strategies from some of the country's most innovative career advisors. The strategies in *Guerrilla Tactics* are so powerful that it even comes with a guarantee: Follow the advice in the book, and within one year of graduation you'll have the job of your dreams . . . or your money back!

Author: Kimm Alayne Walton, J.D.
ISBN: 0-15-900317-2
Price: $24.95
(572 Pages, 6" x 9")

Pick up a copy of *Guerrilla Tactics* today . . . and you'll be on your way to the job of your dreams!

The Best Of The Job Goddess
Phenomenal Job Search Advice From America's Most
Popular Job Search Columnist

"Should I wear my wedding ring to Interviews? How can
I get a job in another city? I was a Hooters girl before law
school — should I put it on my resume?" In her popular
Dear Job Goddess column, legal job search expert Kimm
Alayne Walton provides answers to these, plus scores of
other, job search dilemmas facing law students and law
school graduates. Her columns are syndicated in more
than 100 publications nationwide.

The Best Of The Job Goddess is a collection of the Job God-
desses favorite columns — wise and witty columns that
solve every kind of legal job search question! If you're
contemplating law school, you're a law student now, or
you're a lawyer considering a career change — you'll
enjoy turning to the Job Goddess for divine guidance!

Author: Kimm Alayne
Walton, J.D.
ISBN: 0-15-900393-8
Price: $14.95
(208 Pages, 4-1/4" x 9")

Proceed With Caution
A Diary Of The First Year At
One Of America's Largest, Most Prestigious Law Firms

Prestige. Famous clients. High-profile cases. Not to mention a starting salary exceeding six figures.

It's not hard to figure out why so many law students
dream of getting jobs at huge law firms. But when you
strip away the glamour, what is it like to live that
"dream"?

In *Proceed With Caution*, the author takes you behind the
scenes, to show you what it's really like to be a junior
associate at a huge law firm. After graduating from an Ivy
League law school, he took a job as an associate with one
of New York's blue-chip law firms.

He also did something not many people do. He kept a
diary, where he spelled out his day-to-day life at the firm
in graphic detail.

Proceed With Caution excerpts the diary, from his first day
at the firm to the day he quit.

Author: William F. Keates
ISBN: 0-15-900181-1
Price: $17.95
(166 Pages, 6" x 9",
hardcover)

The National Directory Of Legal Employers
38,000 Great Job Openings
For Law Students And Law School Graduates

The National Directory Of Legal Employers includes a universe of vital information about one thousand of the nation's top legal employers — in one convenient volume!

The National Directory Of Legal Employers includes the name of the hiring partner. The starting salary. How many people the firm intends to hire over the next year, and the criteria they'll use to choose successful candidates. The *Directory* also includes the specialties each firm practices, how the firms view their working environments, their achievements, their major clients, and their plans for the future.

Author: The National
Association for Law
Placement (NALP)
ISBN: 0-15-900454-3
Price: $39.95
(1,573 Pages, 8-1/2" x 11")

Beyond L.A. Law:
Stories Of People Who've Done Fascinating Things With A Law Degree

Anyone who watches television knows that being a lawyer means working your way up through a law firm — right?

Wrong!

Beyond L.A. Law gives you a fascinating glimpse into the lives of people who've broken the "lawyer" mold. They come from a variety of backgrounds — some had prior careers, others went straight through college and law school, and yet others have overcome poverty and physical handicaps. They got their degrees from all different kinds of law schools, all over the country. But they have one thing in common: they've all pursued their own, unique vision.

As you read their stories, you'll see how they beat the odds to succeed. You'll learn career tips and strategies that work, from people who've put them to the test!

Author: The National
Association for Law
Placement (NALP)
ISBN: 0-15-900182-X
Price: $17.95
(192 Pages, 6" x 9")